James Drummond

The Epistles of Paul the Apostle to the Thessalonians, Corinthians, Galatians, Romans and Philippians

James Drummond

The Epistles of Paul the Apostle to the Thessalonians, Corinthians, Galatians, Romans and Philippians

ISBN/EAN: 9783337020781

Printed in Europe, USA, Canada, Australia, Japan

Cover: Foto ©Lupo / pixelio.de

More available books at **www.hansebooks.com**

INTERNATIONAL HANDBOOKS TO THE NEW TESTAMENT.

Edited by ORELLO CONE, D.D. To be completed in four volumes.

I. **The Synoptic Gospels.** By GEORGE L. CARY.
   In press.

II. **The Epistle of Paul the Apostle to the Thessalonians,** etc. By JAMES DRUMMOND.

III. **Hebrews, Colossians, Ephesians,** etc. By ORELLO CONE. *In preparation.*

IV. **The Fourth Gospel, Acts,** etc. By HENRY P. FORBES. *In preparation.*

INTERNATIONAL HANDBOOKS
TO THE
NEW TESTAMENT

By ORELLO CONE, D.D., Editor, GEORGE L. CARY, L.H.D.
JAMES DRUMMOND, LL.D., and HENRY P. FORBES, D.D.

THE EPISTLES

OF

PAUL THE APOSTLE

TO THE

THESSALONIANS, CORINTHIANS, GALATIANS, ROMANS

AND

PHILIPPIANS

BY

JAMES DRUMMOND, M.A., LL.D., LITT.D.

Principal of Manchester College, Oxford
Author of "The Jewish Messiah," "Philo Judæus"
"Via, Veritas, Vita" (Hibbert Lectures), etc.

G. P. PUTNAM'S SONS
NEW YORK AND LONDON
The Knickerbocker Press
1899

COPYRIGHT, 1899
BY
JAMES DRUMMOND
Entered at Stationers' Hall, London

The Knickerbocker Press, New York

GENERAL PREFACE TO THE SERIES.

THESE Handbooks constitute an exegetical series covering the entire New Testament and constructed on a plan which admits of greater freedom of treatment than is usual in commentaries proper. The space generally devoted in commentaries to a minute examination of the grammatical construction of passages of minor importance is occupied with the discussion of those of a special interest from a doctrinal and practical point of view. Questions of the authorship and date of the several books are treated in carefully-prepared Introductions, and numerous Dissertations are inserted elucidating matters of graver moment.

The books of the New Testament are treated as a literature which in order to be understood must be explained, like all other ancient literatures, in accordance with the accepted principles of the grammatical and historical interpretation. The aim of the writers has been to ascertain and clearly set forth the meaning of the authors of these books by the application of this method in freedom from dogmatic prepossessions.

The purpose has been constantly kept in view to furnish a series of Handbooks to the New Testament which should meet the wants of the general reader, and at the same time present the results of the latest scholarship and of the most thorough critical investigation.

Accordingly, more prominence has been given to the statement of the results of the critical processes than to the presentation of the details of these processes by means of extended discussions of questions of Greek grammar, philology, and exegesis. Hence, while the advanced student will find much to interest him in these volumes, it is believed that ministers who have not the time to occupy themselves with the refinements of minute hermeneutics, superintendents and teachers of Sunday-schools, and Bible-students in general will find them suited to their needs. The text used is that of the Revised Version, although for the purpose of saving space the text has not been printed, and the passages explained have been indicated in part by references only and in part by references together with a few initial words.

THE EDITOR.

PREFACE.

OF the inadequacy of the present little commentary no one can be more painfully aware than the author. It has been my endeavour to follow the plan laid down for this series of Hand-books, and present an exposition adapted to the needs of those who have sufficient interest in theology to wish for a fuller understanding of the Epistles of Paul, and yet not enough technical scholarship to draw them to the larger commentaries on the Greek text. The limits necessarily imposed upon the work have obliged me to pass over many topics which arise in connection with the Epistles, but are not absolutely necessary for the elucidation of their meaning, and to make only a brief reference to several discussions which would have required ample space for their satisfactory treatment.

For the illustration of particular points I have freely availed myself of Weber's *Jüdische Theologie*. The conservatism of rabbinical teaching may render it probable that views which are found only in the later literature represent correctly the opinions of an earlier time; but they ought to be used with caution, and they are quoted only as expressive of the Jewish tone of mind, and illustrative of the Apostle's thought, not as necessarily indicative of the source from which that thought was derived, or from which it was an intentional deviation.

By the kind permission of the Universities of Oxford and Cambridge, the commentary is based on the text of the English Revised Version, which the reader is supposed to have open before him, and the accuracy of that translation is assumed wherever it has not appeared to be sufficiently in error to call for remark. The use of Greek has been for the most part avoided; but it has been found necessary to use it in the discussion of some of the more difficult and controverted passages. These more technical discussions have been printed in small type, and may be passed over by any reader who would find them too exacting. The bulk of the material contained in them, however, may be understood even by those who are unacquainted with Greek. I have also occasionally introduced into foot-notes parallels in Greek which have struck me in the course of my reading.

It ought to be needless to add that this commentary has not been written in the interest of any sect or any particular school of thought; and however widely I may dissent here and there from current interpretations, it has been my simple endeavour to find out, by faithful study, the real meaning of the Apostle. But that a mind so transcendent meant many things which have not yet been discovered, or that some others may have penetrated farther into his thought than has been permitted to me to do, I can readily believe. Such as it is, I send forth this volume in the earnest hope that it may contribute something to the furtherance of Christian truth, and the quickening of spiritual life in the readers.

JAMES DRUMMOND.

OXFORD, December, 1898.

CONTENTS.

                                                                        PAGE

THE EPISTLES TO THE THESSALONIANS.

INTRODUCTION.	The First Epistle	1
	The Second Epistle	6
FIRST THESSALONIANS.	Analysis	15
	Commentary	17
SECOND THESSALONIANS.	Analysis	33
	Commentary	35

THE EPISTLES TO THE CORINTHIANS.

INTRODUCTION.	The First Epistle	43
	The Second Epistle	48
FIRST CORINTHIANS.	Analysis	55
	Commentary	59
SECOND CORINTHIANS.	Analysis	133
	Commentary	135

THE EPISTLE TO THE GALATIANS.

INTRODUCTION		189
GALATIANS.	Analysis	193
	Commentary	195

THE EPISTLE TO THE ROMANS.

INTRODUCTION		243
ROMANS.	Analysis	247
	Commentary	251

EPISTLE TO THE PHILIPPIANS.

INTRODUCTION		355
PHILIPPIANS.	Analysis	361
	Commentary	363

THE EPISTLES TO THE THESSALONIANS[1].

INTRODUCTION.

THE FIRST EPISTLE.

ACCORDING to the most probable opinion, Paul's correspondence began at Corinth during his second missionary journey. He and Silas had been driven out of Thessalonica by the violence of the Jews, who, unable to find them, had dragged Jason and some of the brethren before the magistrates on a charge of treason. This persecution, apparently successful in its primary object, would naturally be continued, and the Jews would do their best to stamp out the incipient church. Allusion is made to these circumstances in 1 Thessalonians i., 6, and ii., 14, and iii., 3 and 4. The First Epistle was written to defend the Christian preachers against calumnious attacks, probably emanating from unbelieving Jews; to comfort the brethren under their afflictions; to reassure them about those who "had fallen asleep" before the coming of the Lord; to correct certain abuses (such as an inclination to heathen licentiousness, and to a fussy idleness, springing perhaps from an expectation of the immediate coming of Christ); and,

[1] For an account of Thessalonica and the founding of the church there see the Commentary on Acts, or any of the standard Lives of Paul.

finally, to exhort believers to live in a manner worthy of their faith, showing a becoming conduct towards those without, and following that which was good both towards one another and towards all men. It is evident that a considerable period, at least several months, must have elapsed since Paul's visit; for the Thessalonian disciples had become an example to all the believers in Macedonia and Achaia,[1] and had shown their brotherly love towards "all the brethren in the whole of Macedonia."[2] Such expressions need not be too closely pressed; but there must have been several little churches in the latter country, and some in Achaia, before any writer could think of using them. A similar indication, though less decisive, is afforded by ii., 18, where Paul speaks of his repeated, though ineffectual, desire to visit the Thessalonians, and by iv., 13, where he alludes to those who had died since the formation of the church. It is therefore probable that the Epistle was written after Paul had been for some time in Corinth. Other allusions forbid us to place it later. According to Acts,[3] Paul expected Silas and Timothy to join him at Athens, but the author only relates that they came to him in Corinth.[4] Now the Epistle[5] informs us that Paul was so anxious for news that he decided to be left alone at Athens, and sent Timothy to confirm the believers in their faith; and when Timothy returned bringing a good report, he was greatly comforted. Here Silas is not mentioned, and it is evident that he was not with Paul at Athens; but as the Epistle is from "Paul and Silvanus and Timothy" it is apparent that he must have rejoined his party afterwards. These facts admit of easy reconciliation if we suppose that Timothy, according to Paul's direction, hastened to him at Athens, while Silas for some reason remained behind at Berœa; that Paul then despatched Timothy to Thessalonica; and that finally the latter, on his way back, picked up Silas, and with

[1] i., 7.   [2] iv., 9, 10.   [3] xvii., 15.   [4] xviii., 5.   [5] iii., 1 *sq.*

him followed Paul to Corinth. The letter was probably written soon afterwards. If these considerations be valid, the Epistle must be dated about the year 53 according to the usual chronology, or perhaps a few years earlier.[1]

The genuineness of this Epistle was not, so far as I know, called in question till modern times, when it was attacked by Baur. It was accepted by Marcion as well as by the Catholic Church; and though the testimonies to it are not very early, still it was in general circulation at a time when the old men at Thessalonica must have known pretty well whether it was genuine or not. In this respect a letter addressed to a particular church is in a very different position from one written either to a private individual or to an indefinite group of churches. It must have been publicly known whether an epistle had come down among the cherished possessions of a congregation or was newly foisted in from some unknown quarter. This consideration seems to me to lend great additional strength to the external evidence of the genuineness of most of the Pauline Epistles. We must, however, briefly notice the principal objections which are urged in the present instance.

In energy of style and power of thought the Epistle is undoubtedly inferior to Romans, Corinthians, and Galatians. But then a writer is not always at his highest level. When the great Epistles were written, not only was Paul's mind more mature, and his experience among churches and parties greatly enlarged, but he was roused to the vigorous exercise of his finest gifts by controversy, and by deep pondering on the various problems which were forcing themselves on the attention of Christendom. At an earlier period he wrote out of an affectionate solicitude, and was not concerned with any

[1] It is impossible to discuss in this brief commentary the chronology of Paul's life. Able scholars have recently thrown back the accepted dates a few years. This change makes no difference in the significance of the Epistles, and therefore does not greatly concern the interpreter

question which severely taxed his thought. The style corresponds with this more equable frame of mind; but we can observe the same warm heart, confident faith, elevated spirituality, and balanced judgment as in the greater Epistles.

The expectation of the second coming[1] is expressed in greater detail, and I think I must frankly add with greater crudity, here than elsewhere. But though this expectation may have been modified, and lost some of its Jewish features, in the course of time, it is distinctly present in other Epistles. Even in the grand chapter on the resurrection in 1 Corinthians we are told that we shall not all sleep, but we shall all be changed, showing that the Apostle still included himself among the possible survivors at the second advent, and reference is even made to the "last trumpet," which shall summon the dead to rise.[2] Therefore, although we may wish that our Apostle had been infallible, and had not been so possessed with an idea which to us must appear groundless, and indicative of a certain degree of blind enthusiasm, we cannot regard the enunciation of this belief as any argument against the genuineness of the writing in which it occurs. We must learn to accept the revelations of God upon His own conditions. *We* say we must have something infallible, or we will recognise nothing Divine about it; *He* gives us truth hemmed in by human limitation, and leaves something to our own experience and spiritual wisdom. Paul himself said that we have our treasure in earthen vessels, and that knowledge must pass away; but that is a truth which men are always unwilling to accept. Before leaving the subject of the second coming we must observe that the description of it contains an expression which has very properly been urged as an evidence of genuineness. No forger in the post-apostolic time would have ascribed to Paul a belief that he would survive to witness the grand consummation.[3]

---

[1] iv., 13 *sqq.* [2] xv., 51, 52. [3] iv., 15-17.

A more particular objection is founded on the statement made in reference to the Jews, "The wrath came upon them to the uttermost."[1] This, it is said, must refer to the destruction of Jerusalem. There is another reading, "has come." If we could regard the latter as correct, it would relieve the difficulty, for at the time when the Epistle was written, society was becoming demoralised in Palestine; the fanatical champions of revolt were gaining complete ascendency; and it was growing more and more evident that Rome would have to assert its power, and crush the rising anarchy with a strong hand. But the perfect tense has such scanty support that we are obliged to accept the other reading,[2] and this properly points to some definite event. It is suggested that it is used in a prophetic sense, the past denoting the certainty of fulfilment, or pointing to the determination of the Divine purpose. I confess this does not appear to me very satisfactory, and I would suggest that possibly one of the miserable riots under the procuratorship of Cumanus made a deep impression on Paul's mind, and is referred to by him in the present passage.[3] If these explanations be thought unsatisfactory, and reference to the destruction of Jerusalem seem more probable, then we may regard the statement as an editorial comment, rather than allow that it proves the spuriousness of the whole Epistle.[4] It is generally admitted, even by followers of the Tübingen school, that the adverse criticism has broken down, and that the Epistle must be accepted as Paul's.

[1] ii., 16.
[2] Weiss, however, retains the perfect tense, and supposes that the "wrath" was shown in the judicial hardening of the people (*The American Journal of Theology*, i., p. 333, and *Die paulinischen Briefe*, p. 481 *sq.*).
[3] See Josephus, *Ant.*, xx., v., 3–vi., 3. Cumanus was procurator A.D. 48–52.
[4] In this case might it possibly be borrowed from The Testaments of the Twelve Patriarchs, Levi, 6, ἔφθασε δὲ ἡ ὀργὴ κυρίου ἐπ' αὐτοὺς εἰς τέλος, instead of the latter being dependent on Paul?

THE SECOND EPISTLE.

The Second Epistle to the Thessalonians bears, like the First, the names of Paul and Silvanus and Timothy. This fact at once leads us to suppose that it was written not long after the First, while the three men were still together at Corinth. The remaining contents of the Epistle are quite consistent with this hypothesis.[1] Its general structure and the tenor of its teaching are similar to those of the First Epistle; but some points are dwelt upon at greater length, or more strongly emphasised. Certain persons were disturbing the minds of the community by saying that the day of the Lord was already present. They apparently professed to know this through some spiritual revelation or through an epistle of Paul's[2]; and probably in consequence of such teaching the inclination to neglect one's work, and live without regard to the regular order of society, had increased, and required detailed admonition.[3] It seems at first sight very strange that anyone could maintain this position, but we may connect it with an equally curious assertion, referred to in 2 Timothy,[4] that the resurrection had already taken place. Such statements could be maintained only by giving them a spiritual, or rather a metaphorical interpretation. We can easily imagine some enthusiasts declaring that the Christian Church was itself the kingdom of the Lord, and that therefore the day of the Lord had come with its establishment, that the old order of society was thereby dissolved, and Christians were under no obligation to observe its rules. On its more spiritual side we can sympathise with this position, and think it nearer to the real facts of life than Paul's apocalyptic views. Nevertheless, its apparent spirituality was counterfeit, and led to immoral results; and we see the superiority of Paul in the fact that while he accepted so

---

[1] The allusion in iii., 2, to a persecution against Paul himself may be explained by a reference to Acts xviii., 12 *sqq*.

[2] ii., 2.   [3] iii., 6 *sqq*.   [4] ii., 18.

much of the visionary belief of Judaism, he never allowed it to disturb his sense of present moral relations, but used it to quicken and elevate the life of men in this common, working-day world. Thus we learn that it is possible to be nearer to material fact, and yet farther from spiritual truth; to have more knowledge and less wisdom. In saying this I am assuming that Paul's eschatology was mistaken, a survival from his rabbinical days—filled indeed with Christian meaning, but destined to pass away under the teachings of history. Alford, I suppose, gives expression to a common view when he says: "*Have we, in any sense, God speaking in the Bible, or have we not?* If we have,—then of all passages, it is in these which treat so confidently of futurity, that we must recognize His voice: if we have it not in these passages, then where are we to listen for it at all?"[1] The answer, however little it is seen through the veil which lies upon the heart of Christendom, is almost too obvious,—in 1 Corinthians xiii., in Romans xii., in the Beatitudes, in the parable of the Prodigal Son, and numerous other passages which find an answer in the conscience and the heart. It is assumed that the inspiration of Apostles can have no analogy in us, and that, therefore, we must seek it most in those things which to us are impenetrable mystery, while the oracles of the Holy Spirit in consecrated souls are to be set aside as common things, which bear no witness to the operation of God. Thus the grandest and clearest truths of the Gospel are neglected as within the range of uninspired humanity, and men have sought for God where least He is to be found, amid fantastic interpretations and apocalyptic dreams.

The genuineness of Second Thessalonians has been more extensively questioned than that of the First Epistle. Baur, believing that "the man of sin" must refer to Nero, who was expected to return and play the part of Anti-Christ, and that the "one that restraineth" was Vespasian, places it

[1] Greek Test., 2nd edition, iii., p. 64.

soon after the death of Galba, probably in the year 70. It was thus, according to him, written before the First Epistle, which, in his view, refers to the destruction of Jerusalem. The objections of Baur have been frequently answered; but even so judicious a critic as Weizsäcker rejects the Epistle, mainly on the ground that it is too obviously an imitation of the First.[1] Those who look at the problems of early Christianity from my own point of view could not be sorry to relieve Paul of an Epistle which has no permanent spiritual value, and presents so strongly a very questionable apocalypse. Nevertheless the weight of argument seems to me to incline in favour of its genuineness. The external attestation, though not of the earliest or strongest kind, is nevertheless, as we have seen, not to be lightly set aside. Are Weizsäcker's reasons sufficient to establish a charge of forgery? He points out the fact that both in its general structure and in passage after passage the Second Epistle presents striking parallels to the First. With this is combined the further alleged fact that much of the language and style is unpauline. Such appearances always admit of two explanations, and it seems impossible to lay down any rule of judgment to which criticism is bound to conform, and by which it must correct the aberrations of individual impression. You may say that the imitator betrays himself at once by his success and his failure, or you may say that the author naturally repeats the same sentiments in similar circumstances, but varies the expression. Now, if the Epistle be genuine, it would appear to have been written in order to correct certain errors in regard to the second coming. This being the case, it would be quite natural for Paul, writing perhaps only a few weeks later, to follow the same vein of thought as in the First Epistle, only enlarging on certain points which required particular attention. Thus, in the First Epistle, he exhorts his readers to be quiet, and to do

[1] *The Apostolic Age*, i., p. 295 *sqq.* (trans.).

their own work, as he had desired them.¹ This is explained by the fuller statement of the Second Epistle. He had heard that certain persons were neglecting their work, and living in a disorderly way; and he enjoins on such persons to do their work quietly and eat their own bread, reminding them how he had laid down the rule when he was with them, that if a man would not work he should not eat.² In connection with this there is another allusion which seems to me unlike the work of a forger. In the First Epistle, in quite a different connection, Paul reminds his readers of his life among them, and, along with other things, mentions how he worked day and night that he might not be burdensome to any of them.³ There is no very apparent reason for his dwelling on this fact. If the Second Epistle be his, it is evident that he was giving his readers a gentle and kindly hint, which he expected them to understand; for he there repeats the statement almost in the same words,⁴ but brings it into immediate connection with the idle busybodies. He then adds a reason which Weizsäcker says is quite different from any that Paul gives elsewhere: he and his companions did this that they might make themselves an example for the imitation of the disciples. Weizsäcker has not pointed out that this is only an added reason; the other, that they should not be burdensome to anyone, is given first. But how exactly in place is the added reason here. Paul's leading purpose, no doubt, in working for his own livelihood, was to maintain his independence, and spare the resources of his disciples; but it may very well have been a secondary consideration that in so doing he was setting a good example to those who might be tempted to trade upon the Gospel, or to give themselves up to an idle excitement, for we know that Paul considered his own conduct to be worthy of imitation.⁵

¹ iv., 11. ² iii., 10 *sqq*. ³ ii., 9. ⁴ iii., 8.
⁵ See 1 Thess. i., 6; 1 Cor. iv., 16, xi., 1; Phil. iii., 17.

Much will depend on the interpretation which we give to the passage about the man of sin. It is alleged that the views here expressed contradict those of the First Epistle, in putting off the coming of the Lord to an indefinite future. But this allegation depends on a misunderstanding of a word in ii., 2, which is translated in the Authorised Version by the phrase "is at hand," but is corrected by the Revised Version into "is now present." In this Epistle, as in the First, Paul clearly believes that the second coming is not far off. His mind is so full of it that it is made a special ground of exhortation; and it is still "we" who are to be gathered together to Christ.[1] This, I think, is against the idea of forgery. A writer in the post-apostolic age would have represented Paul as putting off the appearance of Christ till after his own time, and would not have said that the mystery of lawlessness was already working, and was only delayed by some individual who restrained until he was taken out of the way. According to the Epistle, Paul had spoken of these things while he was at Thessalonica. The same details are not given in the First Epistle; but there is nothing to contradict them, and it appears incidentally that Paul had included the second coming in his oral teaching, for he says that the readers know that the day of the Lord comes as a thief in the night.[2] This is quite an incidental agreement. As to the substance of his doctrine, we may observe that the two Epistles are in harmony in postponing the advent to an indefinite, though not distant future, and that the "sudden destruction" of the First[3] answers to the "eternal destruction," and the "slay" and "bring to nought," of the Second.[4]

If, however, it could be shown that the man of sin was Nero, and that there was an allusion here to his supposed return from the East to play the part of Anti-Christ, the

[1] ii., 1.   [2] v., 2.   [3] v., 3.   [4] i., 9; ii., 8.

late origin of the Epistle would be proved. But in fact the idea of an Anti-Christ, who should lead the forces of iniquity in their last assault, was Jewish, and there is not a single feature in the man of sin, as here portrayed, to identify him with Nero. The passage is of course exceedingly obscure, and one of its difficulties is the absence of any clear motive for Paul's declining to write down what he appears to have taught plainly by word of mouth. Still it is susceptible of a hypothetical explanation which suits the supposed time and circumstances of the Epistle. In 1 Thessalonians ii., 14-16, the Apostle uses very strong language in regard to the opposition and wickedness of the Jews. It is therefore probable that the man of sin is the apocalyptic leader of Jewish apostasy. He is to sit in the Temple of God, which must probably mean the Temple in Jerusalem, and is to take upon himself the authority of God. Paul had already had bitter experience of the mystery of Jewish defection, and it seemed to him that the zeal of his countrymen for the letter of the Law was only sinking them deeper into lawlessness. The delay in the final outbreak of their fanaticism was due to some restraining power, "that which restraineth,"[1] and this power was represented by a person, "one that restraineth."[2] This may be the Roman sway wielded by the Emperor. Judæa and Rome were now in fierce antagonism, and the violence of zealots was held in check only by the heavy hand of military force. Paul may have thought, in these enthusiastic moments, that heathenism must shortly crumble to pieces, and then the stage would be clear for the final conflict between good and evil. To write plainly of the removal of an Emperor might be easily construed into a charge of treason, and he therefore expressed himself in language which was clear only to those who were in possession of the key. I do not say that this view is undoubtedly

---

[1] ii., 6.   [2] ii., 7.

correct, or in all respects satisfactory; but it is at least as good as those which suggest a later time.

The only other objection which we need notice is founded on the words in iii., 17, "The salutation of me Paul with mine own hand, which is the token in every epistle: so I write." Here two points are dwelt upon: it is said that in the second epistle which he ever wrote, Paul could not have referred to the token in "every" epistle; and that he could have had no occasion to warn his readers against forgeries by calling attention to his autograph. But we cannot be sure that Paul had not already written several letters which have not been preserved. Such communications may have been short and of minor importance, and therefore allowed to perish; and even if they were very few they would have established the practice of correspondence, and justified the Apostle in referring to "every epistle." In regard to a suggestion of possible forgery, we must observe that this subject is touched upon in another part of the Epistle.[1] According to the most obvious interpretation, it would seem that the erroneous views about the second coming were supported by an appeal to some epistle wrongly ascribed to Paul. Whether there really was such a letter is not very clear. It is contended with some force that Paul would have expressed himself with indignation against an actual forgery, and accordingly some think that he refers only to a misunderstanding of the First Epistle. But perhaps the difficulty is sufficiently explained by the suggestion that there was a vague rumour that a letter had come from Paul containing the incriminated doctrine. This assumption may have arisen out of a misunderstanding of the First Epistle, and then have created an impression that another one had been received. Thus without the improbable supposition of an actual forgery there would be adequate reason for Paul's slight and passing allusions, which seem to point

[1] ii., 2.

more to a possibility than a fact. On the other hand, such vague allusions, which are quite independent of one another, and yet mutually explanatory, are not like the work of a forger. Still less can we believe that a forger would have committed himself to the statement in iii., 17. He would naturally have noticed what Paul's real usage was, and have conformed his statement to the apparent facts. Now the words, "The salutation of me Paul with mine own hand," occur in 1 Corinthians xvi., 21, and Colossians iv., 18, and in no other Epistle. In Galatians Paul speaks of having written with his own hand; but the remaining Epistles give no indication of the kind. It therefore seems altogether unlikely that a forger would have sought to authenticate his work by a statement which was so obviously not borne out by the facts. But if Paul wrote the words, they express his intention; and this intention was satisfactorily fulfilled if he always added the benediction in his own handwriting.

On the whole, then, it appears to me that the subject and its treatment suit best the time and circumstances of Pauline authorship, and the very passages which are relied upon as an evidence of forgery are more surprising from a forger than from Paul. The argument from language and style is not such as to require special notice in this summary statement; for it may be applied in either direction according to the bias of the critic. When the forces are pretty evenly balanced, tradition, that is to say, the general opinion of people living nearest to the time of composition, assumes its natural authority; and I must therefore accept the Epistle, at least provisionally, as genuine.

FIRST THESSALONIANS.

ANALYSIS.

ADDRESS AND GREETING, i., 1.

I. THANKFUL AND DEFENSIVE ALLUSIONS TO THE PREACHING AMONG THE THESSALONIANS, AND THEIR RECEPTION OF THE GOSPEL, i., 2–iii., 13.
   1. Thanksgiving for the faith and love of the Thessalonians, and their manner of receiving the Gospel, i., 2–10.
   2. Defensive statement of the way in which Paul and his companions preached and lived among them, ii., 1–12.
   3. Thanksgiving for their reception of the Gospel in spite of persecutions, ii., 13–16.
   4. Paul's wish to visit them, which was frustrated, ii., 17–20.
   5. Account of the mission of Timothy, and its results, iii., 1–10.
   6. A prayer for their continuance in holiness, iii., 11–13.

II. EXHORTATIONS AND DOCTRINES, iv., 1–v., 22.
   1. Exhortations, iv., 1–12 : a. To purity, 1–8 ; b. To mutual love, and to becoming conduct towards the outside world, 9–12.
   2. Doctrine of the last things, iv., 13–v., 11 : a. The dead in Christ shall rise at his coming, and description of his coming, iv., 13–18 ; b. The uncertainty of the time, and the need of constant vigilance and sobriety, v., 1–11.
   3. Various exhortations, v., 12–22.

CONCLUSION. Prayer for their sanctification ; pray for us ; salute the brethren ; see that the Epistle be read ; closing benediction, v., 23–28.

FIRST THESSALONIANS.

COMMENTARY.

THE Epistle opens with an address and greeting, which is here given in its shortest and simplest form (i., 1). Paul does not describe himself as an Apostle, probably on account of the informal and affectionate character of the letter. The same peculiarity is observed in the Second Epistle, in Philippians and Philemon. The union with himself of Silvanus and Timothy does not affect the Pauline authorship, which is made sufficiently manifest in ii., 18. Similarly he joins other persons with himself in the Epistles to the Corinthians, Galatians, Colossians, Philippians, and Philemon. Silvanus is the same as Silas, mentioned in Acts as Paul's companion on his second missionary journey. On the way they were joined by Timothy, probably a much younger man, and the three laboured together in founding the church at Thessalonica. Their experiences must have been similar; and as Paul generally uses the first person plural, there is no reason why we should not suppose that, for the most part, he is speaking in the name of his companions as well as his own.

In God the Father and the Lord Jesus Christ (i., 1). —As the Christian congregations in Judæa are distinguished from the Jewish synagogues by being "in Christ" (Gal. i., 22), so "the assembly" (for this is the meaning of the word translated "church") of Christians in a Gentile city were in God and Christ. To believe in God as their Father was a new faith to these converts, and they had come to it through the acknowledgment of Jesus as their Lord. These were the central and controlling ideas of Paul's preaching, and they suitably make their appearance in one form or another in the opening of every Epistle.

Grace to you, and peace (i., 1).—For the meaning of this greeting, see Gal. i., 3, where its deeper sense is more closely connected with the topics discussed in the Epistle.

Paul opens the subject by giving thanks for the spiritual excellence of the Thessalonians, and their manner of receiving the Gospel (i., 2-10).

Your work of faith (i., 3); that is, the work which belongs to faith. The singular denotes the collective activity. Compare Gal. v., 6.

Patience of hope (i., 3).—The Greek is stronger than our "patience," and refers to the manly endurance which characterised their lofty expectations. Observe the union of faith, love, and hope, the three abiding principles of 1 Cor. xiii., 13.

Hope in our Lord Jesus Christ (i., 3).—In the Greek the genitive is used, and it seems best to regard Jesus as the object hoped for, the reference being to the second coming, of which, in this Epistle, the Apostle's mind is so full.

Your election (i., 4).—The word indicates that the disciples were not only called, but chosen. Paul's doctrine of election must be considered elsewhere. Here it must be sufficient to remark that the reception of the Gospel by some, and its non-reception by others, was hardly a matter of human will, and that the progress of great religious movements depends upon forces which are not ours.

How that (i., 5).—The meaning of the Greek is doubtful. With this translation the following words define the manner of the election; with the translation "because" they give the reasons for Paul's knowledge that the disciples were elect, namely, the power with which he was inspired to preach the Gospel, and the admirable way in which they received it.

In the Holy Ghost (i., 5).—There is no article in the Greek; but if "Holy Spirit" be regarded as a proper name, this is not necessary. As the expression, however, stands between "power" and "assurance," with which it seems strictly parallel, it is very harsh to give it a personal meaning. The words indicate three kinds of Divine influence, the powerful speech, the holy exaltation, the fervid conviction, which thrilled and subdued the hearts of the listeners.

Ye became imitators of us, and of the Lord (i., 6).—The manner of imitation is defined by the reference to "affliction." In the cheerful endurance of persecution they followed Paul and his companions, nay, the Lord himself, who is the great example of righteous suffering for the word of God. The persecution is again referred to in ii., 14, and its beginning is described in Acts xvii., 5 *sqq.*

Joy of the Holy Ghost (i., 6); that is, joy inspired by the indwelling of the Spirit of God, the joy that attends the consciousness of acting in obedience to the Divine will.

Ye became an ensample (i., 7).—This must refer to a time subsequent to Paul's visit, for the church at Thessalonica was itself the second that was founded in Europe. Its fidelity furnished a model for all others. Macedonia and Achaia are the names of the two Roman provinces into which Greece was divided.

The word of the Lord (i., 8).—I think "the Lord" here means Christ, as in *v.* 6, and usually in Paul. Thessalonica, being a busy commercial town, served as a good starting-point from which the sound of the Gospel spread over Greece. This sound was connected with the faith of the converts, which the Apostle accordingly mentions, thereby changing the construction of the sentence, which would naturally close with the words "in every place." Observe that the faith spoken of is that directed towards God. This was fundamental in the conversion of the Gentiles; and that the church was composed of Gentiles appears from the following verse, where it is said that the disciples had turned unto God from idols.

They themselves (i., 9); that is, the people in Macedonia and Achaia. Wherever Paul went, the news of his work at Thessalonica, and of its success, had preceded him, so that he had not to tell the story.

To serve a living and true God, and to wait for his Son from heaven (i., 9, 10).—These verses probably contain in a condensed form the substance of Paul's doctrinal teaching at this time. The resurrection of Jesus is ascribed to the agency of God, and is probably referred to here both as proving the Divine sonship of Jesus (see Romans i., 4) and as presupposed in his expected return. "The wrath" is used not only of the anger which God feels against sin, but of the manifestation of His retributive justice, which Paul expected soon to break upon the world. The Greek does not suggest that this wrath was "to come" in some indefinite future, but that it was "coming," as though it were actually on the way. From the dread crisis Jesus was continually delivering men by gathering them, through the preaching of the Gospel, into the kingdom of God.

Paul now takes up, and treats at greater length, the subject of i., 9; first, describing his manner of preaching and living among the Thessalonians (ii., 1–12), and, secondly, referring to their reception of the Gospel in spite of persecutions (ii., 13–16).

The Apostle seems to be here defending himself against actual or possible charges. There is, however, no reason for supposing that these were made by Jewish Christians within the church. They are rather advanced by opponents of the whole Christian movement, who sought to discredit it by accusing its leaders of sordid and selfish motives. Paul, fear-ing that some of the brethren might be influenced by such attacks, endeavours to strengthen them by appealing to their own better knowledge. He had borne persecution no less than they; he had worked for his own bread; and he had treated them with all gentleness and love.

Found vain (ii., 1).—The Greek is "empty"; that is, it was not empty of power and influence, as that of pretenders would have been.

Of error (ii., 3); literally "out of error"; that is, it does not spring from error. The reference is general, to his preaching at all times and places.

Nor of uncleanness (ii., 3).—The meaning is a little uncertain, but the word is probably used of impurity of motive, and base desire of gain.

A cloak of covetousness (ii., 5); a specious pretext which served to conceal a real covetousness.

Been burdensome, or, as the margin has it, *claimed honour*[1] (ii., 6).—The Greek is literally "to be in weight." This may refer to the burden of maintenance, as is clearly the case in *v.* 9, where the construction is different, but a word from the same root is used. See also 2 Thess. iii., 8; 2 Cor. xi., 9, xii., 16. This meaning suits very well the reference to covetousness, and is strongly supported by the parallel passages. The other sense comes from the application of the word in a figurative way, like our own "weight," as when we speak of a man of weight and dignity. This is favoured here by the allusion to seeking glory from men, and by the contrast of "gentleness" which follows. The two meanings, however, need not be widely separated in the present passage; for it would be as men of weight and distinction that they would claim the right of maintenance.

Apostles (ii., 6).—The word is here used in its wide sense, and includes Paul's companions. They naturally followed the same rules when working together.

---

[1] So in the English Version. The American edition is different.

Gentle (ii., 7).—The margin tells us that "most of the ancient authorities read *babes*." The words have no resemblance in English, but in Greek they differ only by a single letter; and as this letter happens to come at the end of the previous word, it was easy for a transcriber to make a mistake, for in the ancient manuscripts the words were not divided by a space from one another. The context requires "gentle," which also has ample authority.

For this cause (ii., 13), refers to the whole of the previous statement: we were so earnest in our work that we also (as well as you who received the benefit) are most thankful for your acceptance of our message.

The word of God (ii., 13).—"Word" denotes the substance of the message, the rational thought contained in it, not the particular phraseology in which it was expressed; so that if a claim to inspiration is found here, it relates to the truths themselves, not to the manner of their presentation. It is the kind of claim which all men make on behalf of a truth which has come to and commands them. Such truths work energetically, and prove their Divine power, in the lives of those who believe them.

For (ii., 14), introduces a proof that the word of God was operative in them: they bore persecution as bravely as the Judæan churches, which had been the first to receive Christianity.

Your own countrymen (ii., 14).—It is harder to bear persecution when it comes from those who ought to befriend us. According to Acts xvii., 5, the Jews were at the bottom of the mischief, but they acted through the rabble of the city, and inflamed them by political misrepresentations.

Who both killed the Lord Jesus, etc. (ii., 15).—This vehement attack on the Jews is probably suggested not only by the persecutions in Palestine, but by the bitter opposition which they offered to Paul in Macedonia. It is well to bear in mind this aspect of the facts, for it appears sometimes to be forgotten. The judicial murder of Jesus placed an insuperable barrier between Jews and Christians, and, in the eyes of the latter, marked the culminating sin of the nation. Christianity was cradled in persecution. It began by offering a great victim to the religious blindness and hardness of the Jews, and wherever the Christian preachers went they were dogged by Jewish calumny and violence.

Forbidding us to speak to the Gentiles (ii., 16).—These words explain in what way the Jews were "contrary to all men." By thus acting they were continuing the sin of the crucifixion, and filling up whatever may have been lacking there. Compare Matt. xxiii., 32. For the final clause of this verse see the Introduction.

Paul's earnest affection for the Thessalonians had made him wish to visit them more than once (ii., 17-20).

For a short season (ii., 17).—These words show that no very long time can have elapsed since his visit. Having been driven away prematurely, he was anxious about the results of his work, and wanted to see the brethren face to face that he might complete what he had begun.

Satan hindered us (ii., 18.)—He was prevented by adverse circumstances, of what nature we are not told. The Apostle, following the belief of his time, ascribes them to Satan. If any are unable to follow Paul in this view, they do not deny his inspiration except on that particular point. It is a subject on which he never dwells, though he occasionally accepts the current language. The coming of Christ was very near to his heart, and filled him with expectation; yet there he was under a mistake, which history has corrected. We must learn that inspiration is limited, without denying its reality.

As Paul could not visit the Thessalonians himself, he sent Timothy to confirm them, and was comforted by the good report which he received of their faith (iii., 1-10).

For an explanation of the circumstances see the Introduction.

We thought it good (iii., 1).—Though Paul retains the plural form, he seems now to be referring exclusively to himself, having distinctly intimated in ii., 18, that such was his meaning.

We are to suffer affliction (iii., 4).—We must notice once more how largely the thought of persecution enters into Paul's writing. It was not mere sporadic violence, but was constant in its assaults. It was what all religious reformers, and not least the first Christian disciples, had to expect. But it had its compensations, the joy and thankfulness which were awakened by the triumph of a holy cause, and by the steadfastness of believers who had many a temptation to desert.

The first part of the Epistle concludes with a prayer for the readers' increase in love and holiness (iii., 11-13).

In the expression of this devout wish it is clear that the Lord Jesus is regarded as personally active in directing the affairs of the Church, of which, under God, he was the head and leader. God and the Father are here, as elsewhere, identified, and, if we are to understand language in the usual way, the Lord Jesus is plainly distinguished from God. The word "direct" (*v.* 11), however, is in the singular. The same phenomenon is observed in 2 Thess. ii., 17, whence it has been supposed to follow that, though the Father and Jesus are two persons, they are one substance. But in fact it is a regular Greek construction, in such a case, to allow the verb to agree with "the nearest or the predominating subject."[1] This construction suggests itself most readily when the verb occupies the first place, for then successive nominatives are added as a kind of afterthought. The New Testament affords many examples (for instance, Acts xxvi., 30). When the verb follows, it is habitually in the plural in the New Testament, but this is not necessitated

---

[1] See Donaldson's *Greek Grammar*, third ed., p. 400.

by classical usage, and the present passage may be an exception on quite other than the theological ground which has been suggested. The activity is regarded as one, Christ acting in accordance with the will of the Father.

The Lord (iii., 12).—This is the reading accepted by recent critics as having most authority. It is, however, not absolutely certain, some few authorities reading "God," and others omitting the subject altogether. If the reading be retained I think the reference is to Christ, not only on account of Pauline usage generally, but on account of the application of the word in the immediate context.

Coming (iii., 13), literally "presence." It is a technical word and more expressive than "coming." It implies that, however Christ may have been spiritually present with his Church, he was, comparatively speaking, absent (compare 2 Cor. v., 6). The word occurs six times in the two Epistles to the Thessalonians; elsewhere only once in Paul (1 Cor. xv., 23).

The second part of the Epistle is devoted to exhortations, and doctrinal statements respecting the future life and the second coming of Christ (iv., 1–v., 22).

The first subject dealt with is the need of personal purity, on which Gentiles had very lax notions, and which Paul evidently had great difficulty in enforcing (iv., 1–8).

In the Lord Jesus (iv., 1); that is, as living in and influenced by him. The exhortation was not Pauline, but Christian. A similar idea is expressed by the words *through the Lord Jesus* (iv., 2); the commands were given under his direction, and in his name. This is dwelt upon to add weight and solemnity to the exhortation. The references here and in v. 6 to Paul's oral teaching are interesting as showing how earnestly he insisted on holiness of life as part of his commission in founding churches.

His own vessel (iv., 4).—There are two principal interpretations of this expression. Some understand it of the body.

But this is not suitable to the emphatic "own," or to the idea conveyed by "possess himself of"; and moreover the sentence would thus become simply an enlarged repetition of the command to abstain from fornication. It is therefore more generally understood in the sense of a wife; and this meaning is sufficiently justified by examples, and is favoured by the similar teaching of 1 Cor. vii., 2. It is sometimes said that Paul takes a low view of marriage. He undoubtedly looks upon it as a proper remedy for heathen vice. But is it not part of his greatness that, in spite of his own somewhat ascetic temperament, he was not blind to social and physiological facts? He sought not to destroy, but to hallow; and the "sanctification and honour," of which he here speaks, disclose his high ideal of the relation of the sexes, and his faith that Christian marriage could transform a physical instinct into holy love and mutual reverence.

Wrong his brother in the matter (**iv., 6**).—As there is no apparent change of subject, the reference must be to adultery, or anything whereby the marriage relation is imperilled.

Who giveth his Holy Spirit unto you (**iv., 8**).—This phrase suggests, not distinct personality, but spiritual influence, the inworking of the Divine holiness in the heart. God gives this transforming and sanctifying power; but man may reject it, and so in yielding to impurity he is rejecting God Himself by violating the Spirit which is His.

This subject is succeeded by a delicate admonition to increase of brotherly love, and, with more emphasis, to a quiet and dignified behaviour towards outsiders (iv., 9-12).

Taught of God (**iv., 9**).—This is expressed in Greek by one word, "God-taught." The word deserves notice as illustrating Paul's comprehensive view of inspiration.

That ye study to be quiet (**iv., 11**).—The connection between this advice and that to brotherly love is not immediately apparent, but we may suppose that there was a tendency to fussiness and neglect of their proper business, on the part of some members of the church, in fulfilling the offices of kindness, and this may have excited the animadversion of heathen neighbours.

Honestly (**iv., 12**).—The word does not refer to honesty in its modern sense, but to a becoming and dignified deportment.

Nothing (**iv., 12**).—The Greek may be masculine, "no man." Whichever may be preferred, the warning is against becoming dependent through neglect of their proper work.

The restless spirit which has just been alluded to was partly due to mistaken notions connected with the second coming of Christ; and we find here a line of transition to the following passage, which sets forth the doctrine of the last things (technically known as eschatology) (iv., 13-v., 11).

Paul had probably learnt that some of the disciples were troubled with uncertainty about the fate of those who died before the coming of Christ, and he begins by reassuring them on this point (iv., 13 18).

It seems clear that the Apostle expected that he himself and some of his readers would survive to witness the return of Christ (iv., 15, 17), and that he conceived of this return in a manner which depends on a view of the universe which has forever passed away. Alford says: "Either these details must be received by us as matter of practical expectation, or we must set aside the Apostle as one divinely empowered to teach the Church." One who lays down such an alternative is no real friend of Christianity. Alford himself admits that Paul was mistaken as to the time of the coming; but then, he says, this was not revealed, and, in support of this statement, appeals to Mark xiii., 32. It seems clear, however, that Paul believed that the nearness of the second advent was revealed, though not its precise time. And this is exactly what is laid down in Mark: the coming of the Son of Man, with all its glorious accompaniments, was to be witnessed by the existing generation; this is asserted with the most solemn asseveration, and only "the day and the hour" are unknown. Yet these things did not come to pass, and the first generation of Christians was mistaken. It is not for us to dictate to the Almighty how He shall reveal Himself, but to learn humbly from experience; and what we are really taught by this passage is to distinguish between "the deep things of God," which are in truth disclosed to spiritual insight, and apocalyptic visions of future events, which do not properly belong to the matter of revelation. Where Paul appears as the inspired teacher is in the sober spiritual use that he makes of a view which has sometimes given rise to the wildest fanaticism. The view itself belongs to the age, and perhaps at that time it was not yet possible to believe in the Messiahship of Jesus without it.

By the word of the Lord (**iv., 15**).—Paul distinctly appeals to the authority of Christ. Some suppose that he refers to a private revelation; but I think it is more likely that he has in mind some accepted teaching. Long eschatological discourses are ascribed to Christ in the Gospels, and, though the exact statement here made is not found, it is implied in the promise that the Son of Man will gather together his elect (Matt. xxiv., 31; Mark xiii., 27). What Paul meant literally we may understand in the spirit, not in the letter; and the abiding lesson of the passage is this, that those who die in the Lord shall not be separated from him, but God has in store for them greater things than the heart of man conceives.

But though the coming of Christ was not distant, its precise time was quite uncertain, and therefore there was need of constant vigilance and sobriety (v., 1-11).

This view exactly corresponds to the representations in the Gospels; and it is this union of confident expectation of a near event with uncertainty as to the definite moment of its arrival that keeps our vigilance on the strain. The most tremendous occurrence that may be thousands of years off excites only a languid interest.

Cometh as a thief in the night (**v., 2**); that is to say, quite unexpectedly. This was evidently a familiar figure in Christian teaching: see Matt. xxiv., 43; Luke xii., 39; 2 Pet. iii., 10; Rev. iii., 3, xvi., 15.

As travail (**v., 3**).—The figure is founded on the uncertainty of the time. There may possibly be some allusion to the "birth-pains of the Messiah": see Matt. xxiv., 8.

Sons of light (**v., 5**), a Hebrew form of expression, denoting an intimate connection with, and possession of, the attribute of light.

They that sleep sleep in the night (**v., 7**), a literal statement, to be applied metaphorically.

The breast-plate of faith and love, and for a helmet the hope of salvation (**v., 8**).—Appropriately to the context only defensive armour is here alluded to. Compare the fuller working out of the metaphor in Eph. vi., 11-17; and see also Rom. xiii., 12, and 2 Cor. x., 4.

For God appointed us (**v., 9**).—The sense of a Divine purpose of love towards us ought to strengthen every holy resolution; but it seems clearly implied that it may be otherwise.

Whether we wake or sleep (**v., 10**).—The metaphor here seems to be changed, and to refer to life and death. This was the object for which Christ died in our behalf, that, whether in this waking world or in the sleep of death, we should live with him, sharing in the same exalted life of righteousness. The precise idea is not very clear, for sleeping suggests unconsciousness, which is not compatible with the life that is spoken of. But I think there is a recurrence to the thought of iv., 14: fulness of life with Christ awaits us, whatever may be our condition at his coming; therefore let us who look for that coming act in a manner worthy of our lofty hopes.

Several miscellaneous exhortations are now introduced, describing with beautiful simplicity some of the finest features of the Christian life (v., 12-22).

Know them that labour among you (**v., 12**).—It is evident from this verse that the church had received some organisation, and had presidents, who, along with other work, had the duty of admonishing, differing probably from regular teaching, and implying some amount of authoritative discipline. This may explain the subjoined advice to "be at peace among yourselves"; for a quarrelsome and disorderly spirit is connected with want of submission to proper authority. The word "know" is used in a Hebrew sense, implying regard and friendship. Compare Gal. iv., 9.

Rejoice alway (**v., 16**).—A joyous temper is one on which Paul sets great store. It is closely connected with thankfulness, which not only flows forth for every obvious blessing, but in everything finds traces of the love of God; and it is nurtured by prayer, the inward communion which consecrates every word and deed.

Prophesyings (**v., 20**).—This does not refer to predictions, but answers rather to our "preaching." It is the inspired enunciation of truth, and an appeal to the hearers.

The exhortations are succeeded by a prayer for the readers' sanctification, and an assurance of its accomplishment (v., 23, 24).

Spirit and soul and body (**v., 23**).—In this division the spirit refers to that higher portion of our nature which can enter into conscious communion with God; soul, to the animal principle of life, including intelligence in its lower ranges. Hence the psychical ("natural") man is one in whom the spiritual element is dormant; the spiritual man, one in whom it has wakened to its true life, and become recipient of the Spirit of God.

Calleth (**v., 24**): present tense, as in ii., 12. He who calls cannot change; He will accomplish His own work.

The Epistle closes with a request for the prayers of the church; a direction to salute the brethren, and to see that the letter is publicly read; and the usual benediction (v., 25–28).

A holy kiss (**v., 26**).—The customary kiss of greeting was to be more than conventional among the Christians; it was to be given in the full consciousness of the holiness of brotherhood.

I adjure you (**v., 27**).—The reason for such a strong mode of request is not apparent. Perhaps we may find some explanation in the word "all." It might be read at a public meeting, and this might be thought sufficient; yet many might be absent. Paul was anxious that all who needed such strength and comfort as it could impart, should have the benefit of hearing it.

SECOND THESSALONIANS.

ANALYSIS.

ADDRESS AND GREETING, i., 1, 2.

I. INTRODUCTORY THANKS, ENCOURAGEMENT, AND PRAYER, i., 3-12.
   1. Thanksgiving for the Thessalonians' increase in faith and love, in spite of persecutions, i., 3, 4.
   2. Promise of recompense and of the destruction of persecutors, at the coming of Christ, i., 5-10.
   3. Prayer that the disciples may be worthy, i., 11, 12.
II. DOCTRINAL STATEMENT ABOUT THE EVENTS BEFORE THE SECOND ADVENT, ii., 1-12.
III. EXHORTATIONS, MINGLED WITH THANKSGIVING AND PRAYERS, ii., 13-iii., 15.
   1. Exhortation to stand fast in the doctrine which they had received, ii., 13-17.
   2. Request for their prayers that Paul and his companions may be delivered from wicked men, iii., 1, 2.
   3. Assurance that they will be confirmed, and do what is enjoined, iii., 3-5.
   4. Exhortation to withdraw from the disorderly, and work quietly for their own bread, as Paul himself had done, iii., 6-15.

CONCLUSION: Benediction suited to the exhortations. Authentication of the Epistle. Closing benediction, iii., 16-18.

SECOND THESSALONIANS.

COMMENTARY.

The Epistle begins, as usual, with an address and greeting (i., 1, 2).

Paul unites Silvanus and Timothy with himself, as in the First Epistle. See the Introduction.

The first part may be treated as introductory to the main subject (i., 3–12).

It begins with a thanksgiving for the growing faith and love of the Thessalonians (i., 3, 4).

As it is meet (i., 3).—These words are a mere tautology unless we connect them closely with the following clause,—as is meet on account of your growing faith.

We ourselves (i., 4), as well as others (see 1 Thess. i., 8, 9), to whom we might be expected to leave the commendation of the results of our own work.

The allusion to persecutions from which disciples suffered leads the Apostle to speak of the rest which they would enjoy, and the destruction which would come upon their enemies, when Christ was revealed (i., 5–10).

Token (or *proof*, i., 5).—The sufferings of the good, the triumph of evil, in the present are an evidence of future judgment, if we believe that God is just.

To the end that (i., 5).—This probably expresses the end contemplated in the judgment, that you who have suffered for the kingdom of God should be pronounced worthy of it. The "kingdom of God" is here regarded not only as established in the hearts of individuals, but as triumphant in the world through the return of Christ, and therefore becomes coincident with the Messianic kingdom.

For which ye also suffer (i., 5).—Observe the form of expression, which is identical with that which is used in connection with the sufferings of Christ.

If so be that (i., 6).—This form of supposition, so far from indicating doubt, is rather applied to that which cannot be reasonably doubted: there must be a change from the present oppression, so surely as God is just.

Rest with us (i., 7).—These words naturally suggest a judgment near at hand, for there is no intimation that Paul and his readers were to die before it took place. This is important in comparing the doctrine of the Second Epistle with that of the First.

To them that know not God, and to them that obey not the Gospel (i., 8).—Two classes of men are thus distinguished, which answer roughly to heathens and Jews, though of course Gentiles who had deliberately rejected the Gospel might be included in the latter class. It seems clear from this and other passages that the first Christians believed that a great crisis was coming upon the world as decisive and sweeping as in the days of the deluge. The world was lying in wickedness, and must be cleansed by a purifying judgment, a manifestation of Divine "wrath" against sin. This judgment was to be executed through the agency of Christ; and out of the general ruin those who accepted the Gospel would be saved. At a later time Paul presents his views in a loftier strain, and seems to have looked for a longer development and a richer harvest of salvation.

Eternal destruction from the face of the Lord (i., 9).—Though the word translated "eternal" does not necessarily denote everlasting duration, the destruction is clearly regarded as final. I think, however, that it is doubtful whether duration, long or short, entered into the conception. The view was bounded by the coming of Christ, and the establishment of his glorious kingdom, and beyond that no inquiry was raised. All that belonged to it was in the future "age," and as such was reckoned part of the eternal world as distinct from the present order of things. Once, however, in a later Epistle, Paul strains his glance into a more distant future, and sees the time when the Messianic reign will be over, when every enemy will be subdued, and "God will be all in all" (1 Cor. xv., 24-28). These last words express a far-reaching and all-inclusive faith. In the present passage "destruction" naturally suggests extinction of conscious being, or may refer to the ruin of the higher nature brought about by guilt.¹ In any case there is no allusion to physical torture, and the subject is treated with a reverent reserve which less inspired theologians would have done well to imitate. Separation from the presence of the Lord is inevitable; for sin cannot see holiness.

This picture of future judgment is followed by a prayer that the Thessalonians may be counted worthy (i., 11, 12).

Worthy of your calling (i., 11): not, worthy of being called at the last day; but, worthy of your Christian calling which ye have already received.

The Apostle now proceeds to the subject for the sake of which the Epistle was written. He corrects an error which had arisen in regard to the second coming of Christ, and makes a doctrinal statement about "the apostasy" and "the man of sin" (ii., 1-12).

For the general meaning of this passage I must be content with referring to the Introduction. It would be impossible in this brief commentary to discuss the various opinions which have been held in regard to an apocalypse where

---

¹ Lysias uses the phrase ἀπώλεσεν αὐτήν of moral ruin. *Pro cæde Eratosth.*, § 2.

imagination can so easily run wild, and where the man of sin may be so conveniently found in some religious or political foe. The only plausible conjectures as to the true explanation must, I think, be founded on the beliefs and circumstances of the time.

Spirit (ii., 2).—This must refer to some supposed revelation, communicated in the spirit, when the reflective powers were suspended, and the thoughts were carried away upon a tide of emotion.

Or by word, or by epistle as from us (ii., 2).—This certainly seems to imply that there was some letter in circulation which was said to be from the Apostle and his companions, and also misleading reports about things that they had said. Whether this letter was an actual forgery, or whether it was some document which, in mistaken reports, was attributed to Paul, or whether, perhaps, it existed only in rumour, it is impossible to decide. If Paul knew that there was deliberate forgery, we should expect him to administer a severe rebuke. The words do not admit of the explanation that the reference is only to a misunderstanding of the First Epistle.

The falling away (or *apostasy*, ii., 3).—The article points to a well-known apostasy, of which the Apostle had doubtless spoken at Thessalonica. The Jews expected a great outburst and concentration of wickedness before the advent of the Messiah. "The apostasy" need not necessarily refer to Christian faithlessness. To the Apostle the Jewish opposition to the Gospel was already a sort of apostasy, and he may have expected this to reach a climax, and become an overt revolt against God Himself, before Christ returned. In this case he would naturally expect the Antichrist to spring from the same race as the Christ. This whole representation, whether the man of sin be Jewish or heathen, is hard to reconcile with Rom. xi.; but in the next few years Paul was compelled by circumstances to work out the logical results of his own spiritual principles, and he may have shaken off more and more the clinging shreds of his rabbinical thought.

The temple of God (ii., 4) can hardly mean anything but the Temple in Jerusalem, though some would understand it of the Christian Church, which is described in these words by Paul himself (1 Cor. iii., 16). Here, however, there is nothing to suggest a figurative meaning. The present tenses describe the character of Antichrist without reference to time.

I told you these things (ii., 5).—We have here another glimpse into the subjects of Paul's oral teaching. The Thessalonians had a key to the meaning of this passage which we no longer possess.

He may be revealed in his own season (ii., 6).—This expression (with that in *v.* 3) suggests that the Antichrist was already in existence, though not yet manifested.

The mystery of lawlessness (ii., 7) was already working, pursuing its hidden way in the corruption of mankind; but the time was to come when every restraint would be removed, and the man of sin be revealed with his false signs and wonders. Then Jesus would return, and destroy him with a breath (*v.* 8).

They received not the love of the truth (ii., 10).—The men who were to fall under the power of Antichrist, then, were first to be guilty of a rejection. They might have loved the truth, but they chose rather to cling to their own opinions. In the minds of too many, love of truth means love of some popular dogma: it really means love of that which is true, and a deep desire to find it and submit oneself to it. The Divine punishment for an egotistic attachment to prejudice is *a working of error* (ii., 11): only the simplicity of aim from which self is wholly banished can impart a just judgment. And here we must distinguish between truth of moral and spiritual intuition, which belongs to purity of heart, and truth of intellectual view, which depends also on the extent of knowledge and the powers of thought. The former truth seems to be that which is here contemplated, for it is contrasted with "unrighteousness" (ii., 12). It is not the involuntary error, which may attend the sincerest love of truth, but the blinding "pleasure in unrighteousness," that renders men liable to judgment.

From his doctrinal statement the Apostle, as usual, turns to exhortation, which is here mingled with thanksgiving and prayer (ii., 13–iii., 15).

Chose you from the beginning (ii., 13).—This can hardly mean "from the beginning of the Gospel," as there is nothing to suggest this, but must be understood quite indefinitely, "from the beginning of things," signifying that their election was part of the providential plan of the world. The reading in the margin, "as first-fruits," differs in the Greek by only a single letter from that which is adopted in the text. Paul uses the expression "first-fruits" elsewhere, but not "from the beginning"; hence the former may have been a conjectural emendation. There would be no propriety in calling the Thessalonians first-fruits, for they were not the earliest believers even in Macedonia.

Sanctification of the Spirit (ii., 13).—This may mean sanctification produced by the Holy Spirit; but as there is no article in the Greek, it may mean simply sanctification of spirit, referring to the human spirit. For the latter use of "spirit" compare 2 Cor. vii., 1.

Stand fast (ii., 15).—This exhortation shows that Paul did not forget the existence of human conditions. It was through no will of their own that the Thessalonians were selected to hear the Divine call through the Christian preachers; but it did depend on their own will whether they would be true to their higher privileges and responsibilities. Paul, with his profound sense of having been called to be an Apostle, nevertheless felt that he must fight, and buffet his body, lest, having preached to others, he himself should be rejected (1 Cor. ix., 27).

The traditions (ii., **15**).—This translation, though no better can be offered, is a little misleading; for the word, with us, implies something which is handed down orally through successive generations. The Greek may include this, but does not necessarily denote more than that which is handed on from one to another. Here it refers to the teaching which Paul had received, and then delivered to the converts at Thessalonica. Compare 1 Cor. xi., 23, and xv., 3, where the corresponding verb is used.

The evil one (iii., **3**).—The Greek adjective may be either masculine or neuter, and there is nothing in the context to justify us in giving a confident decision. "One" is not expressed in the Greek.

The succeeding exhortation (iii., **6-15**) is evidently directed against some disorders which were known to exist in the church, and which were probably connected with the mistaken views about the coming of Christ. A contempt for the common and necessary pursuits of the world might spring either from a false spirituality or from a belief that the old order of society was already in the pangs of dissolution.

Withdraw yourselves (iii., **6**).—Paul does not advise any harsh treatment, but only that the disciples should not associate themselves with an erring brother in his erroneous conduct. We may contrast this with the formal excommunication which he requires in the case of the offender at Corinth. In both instances the offence is not doctrinal, but moral; and here it is foolish and mistaken rather than wicked. If, however, any man, after this warning, refused to submit to the Apostle's authority, the rest were to have no company with him; but even then he was not to be expelled from the society, but admonished as a brother (iii., 14, 15).

If any will not work, neither let him eat (iii., **10**).—This was a recognised principle among the rabbis.

The exhortation is followed by an appropriate benediction (iii., 16).

Peace is the opposite of an agitated mind and disorderly conduct. Whenever the Lord might come, he was the Lord of peace, and the peace of a trustful and dutiful heart was the best evidence of his blessing. Paul expressly includes "all," embracing the disorderly who most needed it, in his benediction.

The Apostle now authenticates his letter by his autograph (iii., 17. See the Introduction), and closes the Epistle with a benediction (iii., 18), once more mentioning "all," to show that the faults which he found it necessary to reprove did not exclude any brother from his Christian blessing.

THE EPISTLES TO THE CORINTHIANS.

INTRODUCTION.

THE FIRST EPISTLE.

THE date and place of composition of First Corinthians can be satisfactorily determined. It was written from Ephesus[1]; and it is clear that it was so during the Apostle's second visit, for Apollos is referred to as having been at Corinth, and watered what Paul had planted,[2] and at the time of writing he was again at Ephesus.[3] As Paul expresses his intention of remaining at Ephesus till Pentecost,[4] we may conclude that the letter was despatched not very long before the termination of his visit, certainly within its closing year, and it is perhaps a fair inference from the allusion to the Passover and the Feast of Unleavened Bread that it was composed when that festival was approaching.[5] The reason alleged for his remaining, that "a great door" was opened to him, certainly shows that he was looking forward to a period of effective activity; but a couple of months might satisfy this expectation. That the period was not very long is proved by his intention of proceeding to Corinth "*shortly*."[6]

The occasion of the letter is equally clear. Paul had already written to Corinth, probably in consequence of reports

---

[1] xvi., 8; see also 5 and 19. [2] i., 12; iii., 4–6.
[3] xvi., 12.   [4] xvi., 8.   [5] v., 6–8.   [6] iv., 19.

which had reached him, warning the brethren to give no encouragement to that impurity which was such a disgrace to Grecian morals, and not least in Corinth.[1] From the earnestness with which the Apostle pleads, and from his repeated references to the subject, it is plain that he found it difficult to convince the converts of the sinfulness of unlawful indulgence. This letter has been lost, perhaps owing to its brevity and the limited range of its topics. It seems to have raised various connected questions at Corinth, and the disciples wrote to Paul for further instructions in regard to marriage and divorce and mixed marriages.[2] Their epistle was apparently sent by the hands of Stephanas, Fortunatus, and Achaicus,[3] and the opportunity was embraced of consulting the Apostle about several other difficulties which had arisen in the church, such as the use of meat offered to idols,[4] the exercise of spiritual gifts,[5] the denial of the resurrection of the dead,[6] the "collection for the saints" in Jerusalem.[7] We cannot be sure that all these subjects were included in the lost letter from the church; for Paul had other sources of information. He had been told by the people of Chloe that the church was divided into factions, according to the preference which was felt for one or another teacher.[8] Whether Chloe was a resident in Corinth or Ephesus we cannot determine. A report had reached the Apostle of an act of incest, such as was not named even among the Gentiles,[9] and of shocking divisions and disorders in the celebration of the love-feasts and of the Lord's Supper[10]; and mutual alienation had reached such an extreme that brother went to law with brother before heathen magistrates.[11] In the public services, too, the women, taking advantage of the gift of prayer and prophecy, and of the

---

[1] v., 9.   [2] vii., 1.
[3] xvi., 17. Weizsäcker takes a different view; but the question does not affect the interpretation of the Epistle, and need not be discussed.   [4] viii., 1.   [5] xii., 1.   [6] xv., 1, 12.   [7] xvi., 1, 3.
[8] i., 11.   [9] v., 1.   [10] xi., 18 *sqq*.   [11] vi., 1 *sqq*.

Christian equality of all before God, made themselves unduly prominent, and gave offence by departing needlessly from established custom.[1] These various subjects are generally treated with penetrating insight and breadth of wisdom, and from the highest ethical and spiritual position; and the treatment is accompanied by profound reflections, and gives occasion for a grand outburst of eloquence in celebration of love as the greatest of the virtues and the enduring essence of the Christian life; but occasionally, and especially in the last-mentioned topic, the arguments must appear to us strange and inadequate, and the whole mode of presentation falls below what we should expect from one who declared that in Christ there was neither male nor female. We may explain this in part from the disorders existing in the church. It may be that certain women had made themselves offensively prominent, and had afforded to society outside an opportunity for charging the Christians with encouraging forwardness and immodesty in women. Paul's teaching was destined in time to work a mighty change; but it was a change which he was not led by his temperament to anticipate and press forward, and we have here one more evidence that he shrunk from giving needless offence, and did not insist on carrying out his principles when it seemed inexpedient, and no duty required him, to do so.

A few words must be said about the party divisions at Corinth, a subject on which the quantity of conjectural writing is in the inverse ratio of our certain information. The passage from which we must start is i., 12, "Each one of you saith, I am of Paul, and I of Apollos, and I of Cephas, and I of Christ." We must notice first the different interpretations of the verse itself. The existence of a Christ-party has been got rid of in various ways. The simplest and most probable is that which attributes the words, "I of Christ," to those who declined to assume a party name, and

[1] xi., 3 *sqq.*; xiv., 34 *sq.*

adhered to the broad ground of Christian faith. A less plausible explanation refers the statement to Paul himself; and one still more forced makes it the common cry of the three previously mentioned parties, each arrogating to itself the name of Christ, and denying it to the other two. The last two interpretations must, I think, be rejected as contrary to the plain meaning of the words, the last clause, "and I of Christ," being completely co-ordinate with those that precede. This objection applies also, though with less force, to the first explanation; and when we turn to 2 Corinthians x., 7,—"If any man trusteth in himself that he is Christ's, let him consider this again with himself, that, even as he is Christ's, so also are we,"—it becomes evident that there was a party which not only ranged itself under the name of Christ, but denied the right of others to do so. We are compelled therefore to recognise the existence of four parties, or at least of four names employed in the promotion of party interests. Baur discovered in these divisions the fundamental antithesis of primitive Christianity, and accordingly ranged them into two groups, Pauline and Petrine. Paul and Apollos agreed in maintaining the cause of Gentile freedom. Their Jewish-Christian opponents formed a single party, which looked up to Peter as their chief, and on dogmatic grounds sought to appropriate the name of Christ. This view, accepted in the main by a great number of writers, has been variously modified by suggestions of some distinction, more or less clearly marked, between the parties of Peter and of Christ. There is probably some truth at the bottom of this hypothesis; but it seems very improbable that the controversy between Jewish and Gentile Christianity had reached an acute phase at Corinth, for Paul makes no allusion to it, and adduces not a single argument against the observance of the Law. He treats the divisions purely as the result of a factious preference for one teacher rather than another. Instead of arguing against the claims of Peter he argues against his own,—"Was Paul crucified for you, or were you baptised in the name of Paul?"—and when he adds another to himself he chooses Apollos, who (unlike Peter) had been at Corinth, and watered where Paul had planted. Of himself and his brother teacher he declares, "He that plants and he that waters are one"; and the whole basis of his contention is that there were no differences of principle to justify a separation. The divisions sprang out of a carnal assumption of superior wisdom, and were to be overcome by humble submission to the highest wisdom of the Spirit of God, and a consequent refusal to glory in men. All this points to Greeks, with their love of disputation and faction, rather than to Judaisers who, in the opinion of Paul, were imperilling the very existence of the Gospel. In the Second Epistle [1] it becomes evident that a violent personal attack had been made on Paul, and apparently by the Christ-party, but, so far as we can gather, the attack was on the man Paul, and not on the Gospel which he preached. He was accused of walking according to the flesh, seemingly in the sense of seeking his own interest,[2] and the attack still proceeded from Greeks, if we are to judge from the sneer at his bodily feebleness and his contemptible speech,[3] and from Paul's fear that the result of all this strife and jealousy would be the impenitence of men who had given way to licentiousness.[4] Still they seem to have rested their pretensions on the expectation of someone who was coming to preach another Jesus, and give them a different Gospel,[5] and they may have been influenced by men already present who boasted that they were Hebrews, Israelites, the seed of Abraham, ministers of Christ, and who may have been actually personal disciples of Jesus, and claimed superiority on that ground.[6] From all this I should infer that, though Jewish opponents of Paul were at work in Corinth, the danger of

[1] x.–xii. [2] x., 2; xi., 7; xii., 16.
[3] x., 10; xi., 6. [4] xii., 21. [5] xi., 4. [6] xi., 22 sq.

Judaising had not seriously arisen, and the mass of Paul's enemies were Greeks, who were moved, not by questions of principle, but by factious and personal motives.

THE SECOND EPISTLE.

Owing to the want of direct information there is some uncertainty as to the movements which called forth the Second Epistle; but from scattered statements and allusions they may be inferred with sufficient probability. When Paul despatched the First Epistle he intended to remain at Ephesus till Pentecost, and then to journey through Macedonia, and go on to Corinth. It was his purpose, on his arrival, to send approved men, with letters, to Jerusalem, to convey the contribution of the Corinthian brethren; or if it should be thought better for him to go himself, he would require them to accompany him (presumably that no suspicion should be thrown upon his good faith). It was his desire, however, to remain for a considerable time, and perhaps to spend the winter in Greece, so as to be able to go whithersoever circumstances might call him. This he thought better than paying at once a passing visit.[1] His intention of going to the Corinthians is alluded to elsewhere. He had sent Timothy to them to remind them of his doctrine and practice,[2] and begs that the latter may be kindly received, and sent on his way in peace.[3] In consequence of this mission some were puffed up, thinking that Paul himself would not come; but he assures them that he will come, and acquaint himself, not with their word, but their power.[4] In another passage he says that he will give further instructions about the Lord's Supper when he comes.[5] Neither in these statements nor anywhere else in the First Epistle is there a word to imply that Paul had yet paid more than one visit to

---

[1] 1 Cor. xvi., 1-8.   [2] iv., 17.
[3] xvi., 10, 11.   [4] iv., 18, 19.   [5] xi., 34.

Corinth, that, namely, in which he founded the Church, and planted the seeds which Apollos watered.[1] But when he wrote the Second Epistle, it is clear, if we follow a natural interpretation, that he had paid two visits. He was ready to come a third time.[2] This third time he was coming, and he writes in his absence what he had said to them when he was present the second time.[3] He alludes, moreover, to a visit which he had paid in grief,[4] and this cannot have been the first visit, with its joyous founding of the church. It has therefore been conjectured, with considerable probability, that Timothy brought such distressing news of the factious and immoral tone of the community that Paul, oppressed with grief and indignation, hurried off across the Ægean, in order to assert his authority in person. This visit was not satisfactory, and was necessarily brief; and I think it was probably on this occasion that Paul formed the purpose described in 2 Corinthians,[5] from which he afterwards departed, thereby exposing himself to a charge of levity. It may seem an objection to this view that his purpose was formed in the confident persuasion that he and the Corinthians gloried in one another, and this is hardly consistent with a painful and unsuccessful visit. But this mutual glorying is referred to "the day of our Lord Jesus," and he may well have felt assured that, in spite of a temporary antagonism, their permanent relation to one another in Christ would reassert itself, and they would soon be ready to welcome him once more. Mangold thinks that he formed his plan in Ephesus, and carried out the first part of it by his journey to Corinth, and then, owing to the

---

[1] Schmiedel, however, (in the *Hand-Commentar*,) thinks the second visit took place before the writing of the First Epistle. Weiss takes the same view, and thinks the visit is referred to in 1 Cor. xvi., 7. (*The American Journal of Theology*, vol. i., p. 357.) On the other side see Dr. J. H. Kennedy, in *The Expositor*, Fifth Series, vol. vi., p. 302. [2] xii., 14 [3] xiii., 1, 2. [4] ii., 1. [5] i., 15-16.

4

opposition, altered his course, and returned to Ephesus. But he might just as well have retreated into Macedonia, and there was no reason why the Corinthians should know anything about the ulterior intentions with which he started. If he was suddenly called away from Ephesus, he probably meant to return, and carry out his purpose of remaining till Pentecost. The visit to Corinth would therefore be made as short as possible ; and he may have told his friends that instead of putting off his next visit till he had gone through Macedonia, as he had said he would do in the First Epistle, he would call upon them on the way, and afterwards return again from Macedonia, to pay the longer visit which he originally contemplated, before proceeding to Judæa.

This order of events explains the writing of another lost letter. On his return to Ephesus Paul may have felt that his visit had failed of its desired effect, and that it would be better for him, before visiting Corinth again, to endeavour, through one of his weighty and powerful letters, to reestablish friendly relations. This letter, as we shall see, succeeded in its object ; and it may have been the contrast between the ill success of his visit and the effectiveness of his letter which gave rise to the scoff about the feebleness of his personal presence. The reality of this supposed letter seems to be established by allusions in 2 Corinthians. In vii., 8, Paul speaks of having grieved his readers by the Epistle. This in itself might possibly refer to the First Epistle, which contains some strong and plain advice, and is not free from censure. Nevertheless grief can hardly have been the predominant feeling which such an Epistle excited, and there is no suggestion in it that it might cause alienation between the writer and the readers. But about the reception of the letter here alluded to Paul was in the utmost anxiety,[1] and he gives the warmest expression to the relief and joy which he experienced when he learnt that it had not

---

[1] ii., 13, vii., 5 *sqq.*

only caused grief, but had led to repentance, and called forth the old feelings of affection towards himself. Another point is this, that Titus is referred to as though he had been the bearer of the letter, certainly as one who had been at Corinth to observe its effect, and to bring back a report of the impression which it had made.[1] But in 1 Corinthians it is Timothy who is referred to as having been sent to Corinth,[2] and there is no mention of Titus. The inference seems inevitable that the allusion in 2 Corinthians must be to an intermediate and lost epistle. This conclusion is confirmed by Paul's description of the state of mind in which he wrote. It was out of much affliction and many tears,[3] a state of restless anxiety of which there is no evidence in the First Epistle. It is also very doubtful whether the person who had caused grief, and whom Paul so readily forgives, without the slightest allusion to his having committed a heinous sin, can be the incestuous man of the First Epistle; it is much more likely that he was someone who had been insolent to the Apostle during his short and unexpected visit, and had been rebuked by the good sense of the majority.[4] For an offence of this kind the words are adequate and worthy; for a loathsome sin, such as was not named even among the Gentiles, the language of forgiveness would have been far more serious, and the reference far more distinct.

These combinations may not be conclusive; but they at least clear up certain difficulties, and give an intelligible account of the course of events. We must now return to more certain ground. On leaving Ephesus Paul proceeded to Troas, where he hoped to meet Titus; but, failing to do so, he went on into Macedonia.[5] There also he was full of anxiety,—" Without were battles, within were fears,"—till at last Titus arrived, bringing joyful news of the improve-

---

[1] ii., 13, vii., 6, 13, 14. Titus is further referred to in viii., 6, 16, 23, xii, 18.
[2] iv., 17, xvi., 10.   [3] ii., 4.   [4] ii., 5-11.   [5] 2 Cor. ii., 12 sq.

ment in the state of things at Corinth, so that he was filled with consolation and joy.¹ It was then that he wrote the Second Epistle; for it is evident from further allusions that he was still in Macedonia at the time of its composition.²

The contents of the Epistle were suggested by the course of events. In its composition Paul at the beginning associates Timothy with himself. It falls into three main divisions: i.–vii., viii.–ix., x.–xiii.

The first begins with personal references and explanations, and passes on insensibly into some of Paul's grandest thoughts, the contrast between the old covenant of the letter and the new covenant of the spirit; the revelation of God in the heart and in the face of Christ; the eternity of things unseen; the immortality that awaits us; our responsibility for the things done in the body; the power of the love of Christ, which leads the way through death into life, and makes a new creation for all who are in him; the universal love of God, who in Christ is reconciling the world to Himself, allowing him who knew no sin to go down into the sorrow and sin of humanity that men might rise in him into the righteousness of God. These more general reflections are succeeded by an exhortation not to be yoked with unbelievers, but to be perfectly pure in flesh and spirit³; and then the Apostle recurs to his personal history, and his relations to the Corinthians.

The second division deals with the collection for the poor Christians in Jerusalem.

The third division, which begins with "Now I Paul myself," is a vigorous defence of his apostolic authority against his adversaries, and contains some interesting particulars of his life. The tone of these concluding chapters, x., 1–xiii., 10, is quite unexpected, and is indeed so markedly different from that of the previous part of the Epistle, that many able critics are unable to regard them as belong-

---

¹ *Ib.*, vii., 5 *sqq.*   ² viii. 1, ix., 2, 4.   ³ vi., 14–vii., 1.

ing to the same composition. The most plausible conjecture is that they are a part of the lost letter, which was written in sorrow. The tone and the subject appear suitable; and it has been pointed out that certain expressions in the earlier chapters receive a fitting explanation when regarded as references to what is here said. Thus iii., 1, and v., 12, may allude to the self-commendation in xi. and xii.; and v., 13, may refer to the "visions and revelations" of xii., 1–7. An objection to this hypothesis is found in the want of any definite instruction about the offender; but this part might have been omitted as of temporary interest. A more formidable objection is the difficulty of supposing that any editor would stupidly patch together letters which existed apart, and in doing so would place the earlier and condemnatory one last. Moreover, if we have correctly traced the order of events, this portion of the Epistle must be subsequent to the lost letter; for it refers to the gibe about the feebleness of Paul's personal appearance, compared with the force of his writing, which the powerful effect of this letter suggested. Undoubtedly the chapters take us by surprise; but it may be that, if we knew all the circumstances, the change of tone would be explained. It is pretty evident that Paul's feelings, as is so often the case with men of ardent temperament, were subject to rather violent alternations; and it is possible that some new and agitating reports reached him before he wrote these chapters. Or, without any fresh circumstances, Paul may have been aware that, although the church, as a whole, had been restored to a better frame of mind, still there was peril from the persistent efforts of a small faction, who strove to undermine his influence by appealing to the authority of Christ, being led by Jewish-Christian intruders, who represented themselves as alone qualified to speak in the Master's name. It may have been one object of the Epistle to break forever the power of this aggressive and unspiritual faction; and Paul may have thought it best to deliver the attack after he had secured the favourable attention of the church, and drawn forth principles which lay at the root of the division. The supposition that these chapters are a subsequent letter, written under new conditions, offers no advantage if the foregoing suggestion be tenable, or if we suppose, as we may fairly do, that some short interval elapsed between the completion of chapter ix. and the composition of x.[1]

The Epistle has a unique conclusion. To the usual words, "The grace of the Lord Jesus Christ," Paul adds, out of the fulness of his heart, "and the love of God, and the communion of the Holy Spirit, be with you all." Thus this great Christian benediction had its origin, not in any doctrinal or intellectual interest, but in the sorrow which the divisions and the impurity of the Corinthian disciples excited in the mind of Paul. "The grace of Christ" might indeed include all else; but on this occasion he could not but add the love of God, which would bind them together into a true fraternity, and the communion of the Holy Spirit, which, dwelling in their hearts, would save them from all unclean living, and join them to one another and to God in the fellowship of a common sanctity. Great Christian thoughts are born of high emotion, and they lose their identity when they stiffen into formulæ from which the Divine fire has departed.

[1] A good summary of the arguments in favour of the hypothesis that these chapters belong to the intermediate letter may be seen in Professor McGiffert's *History of Christianity in the Apostolic Age*, pp. 311 *sqq.*, and arguments on the other side in Jülicher's *Einleitung in das N. T.*, pp. 63 *sqq.* Also see the connection of thought carefully explained by Weizsäcker, *The Apostolic Age of the Christian Church*, i., pp. 359 *sqq.* (trans.). There is a very able discussion in support of the hypothesis, by Dr. J. H. Kennedy, in two articles in *The Expositor*, Fifth Series, vol. vi., and a reply, which seems to me hardly adequate, by the Rev. N. J. D. White, in the next volume.

FIRST CORINTHIANS.

ANALYSIS.

OPENING OF THE EPISTLE, i., 1-9. a. ADDRESS AND GREETING, 1-3. b. THANKSGIVING FOR THE GRACE THAT WAS GIVEN TO THEM, AND ASSURANCE THAT GOD WILL CONFIRM THEM TO THE END, 4-9.

I. THE DIVISION INTO PARTIES, i., 10-iv., 21.
  1. Introduction to the subject, i., 10-16.
  2. Warning against the wisdom of the world in contrast with the spiritual power of the Gospel, i., 17-ii., 5: a. The preaching of the cross does not appeal to human wisdom, i., 17-25; b. This is shown by the actual Christian facts, i., 26-31; c. Paul's own preaching was not of the sophistical type, ii., 1-5.
  3. The method in which the Divine wisdom is revealed, ii., 6-16.
  4. Paul could give only elementary teaching to the Corinthians, owing to their want of spirituality, a want which still continued, iii., 1-4.
  5. The various teachers are simply ministers of God, on whom everything depends, iii., 5-iv., 5: a. They are simply ministers, engaged in one work, iii., 5-9; b. They are responsible for what they build on the one foundation, iii., 10-15; c. No one should set up his own wisdom, and no one should limit himself to special teachers, iii., 16-23; d. Nor should hasty estimates be formed of the ministers of Christ, iv., 1-5.
  6. The instances of himself and Apollos were used in order to withdraw the Corinthians from all party conceit, iv., 6-13.

7. Final admonition, and reference to his intended coming, iv., 14-21.

II. REMONSTRANCES AGAINST VARIOUS SINS, v., 1-vi., 20.
  1. The case of incest, v., 1-8.
  2. Correction of a misunderstanding of a previous letter, v., 9-13.
  3. They ought not to prosecute their brethren before heathen courts; fraud and other sins rebuked, vi., 1-11.
  4. Argument against fornication, vi., 12-20.

III. ANSWERS TO QUESTIONS ABOUT MARRIAGE, vii., 1-40.
  1. Directions for married people, vii., 1-7.
  2. Various directions about unmarried and married people, and about mixed marriages, passing into advice not to change one's social condition owing to the acceptance of Christianity, vii., 8-24.
  3. Directions about virgins, and about remarriage, vii., 25-40.

IV. ANSWERS TO QUESTIONS ARISING OUT OF THE EXISTENCE OF IDOLATRY, viii., 1-xi., 1.
  1. Rule in regard to eating sacrificial meat, viii., 1-13.
  2. Relinquishment of one's own rights for the sake of others illustrated by the example of the Apostle, ix., 1-27.
  3. Warning from the example of the Israelites in the wilderness, x., 1-13.
  4. The special Christian feast and idolatrous feasts are quite incompatible, x., 14-22.
  5. Rules of practice, and final exhortation, x., 23-xi., 1.

V. DISORDERS IN THE MEETINGS OF THE CHURCH, xi., 2-34.
  1. Directions about the conduct of women, xi., 2-16.
  2. Directions about the Lord's Supper, xi., 17-34.

VI. SPIRITUAL GIFTS, xii.-xiv.
  1. Statement of the general principle, xii., 1-3.
  2. There is a variety of gifts under the direction of the same Spirit, xii., 4-30.
  3. The praises of love, xii., 31-xiii., 13 : a. Transition from the preceding, xii., 31 ; b. All gifts worthless without love, xiii., 1-3 ; c. The characteristics of love, xiii., 4-7 ; d. The eternity of love, xiii., 8-13.
  4. The inferior value of the gift of tongues, xiv., 1-25 : a. It did not conduce to the edification of the Church, xiv., 2-19; b. It was not profitable to unbelievers, xiv., 20-25.

       5. Rules to be observed in speaking with tongues and prophesying, xiv., 26–33.
       6. Rules about women, xiv., 34–36.
       7. Conclusion, xiv., 37–40.
VII. THE RESURRECTION, xv.
       1. Paul had preached the fact of Christ's resurrection, xv., 1–11.
       2. If there is no resurrection, Christ was not raised, and the Christian's faith is vain, xv., 12–19.
       3. Assertion of the fact, and outlook into the future, xv., 20–28.
       4. Further arguments, chiefly from the demoralising effect of unbelief, xv., 29–34.
       5. The manner of the resurrection, and the nature of the future body, xv., 35–49.
       6. All must be changed, and put on incorruption, xv., 50–58.
VIII. THE COLLECTION FOR JERUSALEM, xvi., 1–4.
     CONCLUSION: Personal references and salutations, xvi., 5–24.

FIRST CORINTHIANS.

COMMENTARY.

The Epistle opens with an address and greeting (i., 1-3), expanded with some weighty phrases, owing, we may suppose, to the gravity of the subjects with which the Apostle's mind is full.

Called to be an Apostle (i., 1), an Apostle by virtue of a Divine call (see Rom. i., 1), with a possible allusion to the attacks on his apostolic authority.

Sosthenes (i., 1), otherwise quite unknown. The description of him as "the brother" simply marks him as a Christian. He probably had some connection with Corinth.

The Church of God (i., 2).—This grand name is frequently applied to the Christian communities. It reminds us of the time when the Jews and Christians were distinguished from all others as the worshippers of one God. Christianity was a great theistic movement, a Divine call to worship the Father in spirit and in truth.

With all that call upon the name of our Lord Jesus Christ (i., 2).—In this great Epistle, though it is specially addressed to Corinth, Paul would speak to all who bear the Christian name. He thus reminds the Corinthians that they are part of a widely extended brotherhood, to which they owe allegiance. The expression "call upon the name" is borrowed from the Old Testament, where the Israelites are distinguished as those who call upon the name of Yahveh, and it is sometimes said that it therefore implies the worship of

Christ as God. It does not, however, in itself convey the idea of worship, but indicates the distinctive name to which appeal was made, and by which the Christians were separated not only from the heathen, but from the Jews.

The word translated "call upon" is used technically of appealing to a higher tribunal, Acts xxv., 11, 12, 21, 25; xxvi., 32; xxviii., 19; and this sense is applicable to 1 Peter i., 17, and 2 Cor. i., 23. This sense, with a slightly figurative turn, is often applicable in the Old Testament. An appeal to God generally implies prayer; but the word is used also of calling upon wisdom (Prov. ii., 3),[1] upon death (Prov. xviii., 6), upon wretchedness (Jer. iv., 20; xx., 8), and of appealing to Egypt (Hos. vii., 11), also of deep calling upon deep (Ps. xli., 8). To appeal to the name, or call on the name (in the Hebrew, "to call in the name"), is not the same as to worship the person bearing that name, but to make use of the name itself, properly to invoke it upon oneself, and hence to bear it as a distinctive mark. This latter use is illustrated by the occurrence of the passive form, as in 3 Kings viii., 43, "Thy name has been called upon this house," equivalent to "This house has been called by thy name": see also Deut. xxviii., 10; 2 Par. vii., 14; Jer. vii., 10, 11, 14, 30; xiv., 9; xv. 16; Dan. ix., 18, 19; Amos ix., 12. See also Ps. xlviii., 12, "they invoked their names upon their lands"; that is, "they called their lands after their own names." In the New Testament we have an instructive example in James ii., 7, "the honourable name which was called upon you," that is "by which ye are called"; and in Acts ix., 21, we have the expression "called on this name," the person being understood, showing that the name itself is the important thing. I think, then, the reference here is to the name to which Christians appealed, and which they invoked upon themselves as that which set them apart from the surrounding world.

The Apostle's goodwill towards his readers is expressed by a thanksgiving for the grace with which they were enriched (i., 4-9).

The passage is remarkable for the constant repetition of the name of Jesus Christ, probably to mark him emphatically as the head of the Church, in opposition to all inferior

---

[1] My references to the Old Testament are to the LXX, as I am discussing a Greek verb.

leaders. The commendation shows that the Corinthian church as a whole was regarded by Paul with satisfaction; but it is noticeable that he selects for particular approval the more intellectual qualifications, utterance and knowledge, and the "gifts" which were not always exercised in the most spiritual manner, as we learn from xii.–xiv. The Corinthians, like the Thessalonians, were waiting for the second coming of Christ, which was believed not to be far off.

My God (i., 4), expressing a deep sense of personal relationship. He was the ultimate source of all the grace that came to the world in Christ.

The testimony of Christ (i., 6), that is, the testimony borne to Christ by the Christian preachers.

The fellowship of his Son (i., 9) expresses fellowship with Christ through participation in his spirit, and, through him, membership in the large communion of all who are his. The word fellowship is the same as that which is translated "communion" in the last verse of the Second Epistle, where substantially the same idea is conveyed by "the communion of the Holy Spirit."

After this general introduction we proceed at once, with words of exhortation, to the first of the several subjects treated of in the Epistle, the division of the church into parties (i., 10–iv., 21).

For a brief notice of opinions about these parties see the Introduction. It is impossible here to discuss the question at length, and happily the spiritual lesson remains, whatever may be our view.

The first paragraph introduces the subject, and mentions the source of Paul's information, the members of Chloe's household (i., 10-17).

We do not know who Chloe was; but she must have been known and respected by the church at Corinth. On some points Paul had been consulted by letter; on others he had more private information.

Through the name of our Lord (i., 10).—He gives a solemn

emphasis to his exhortation by appealing to the one name which all disciples took upon their lips.

Divisions (i., 10).—It is clear that these "schisms" (to use the Greek word) were parties within the same body, and did not amount to a separation into rival churches. Indeed the exhortation seems only to imply that such divisions might arise. *Contentions* (i., 11) actually existed; and these in time begot enmity, and enmity divisions.

Each one of you saith (i., 12).—This shows how far spreading the evil was. As soon as favourite teachers were compared everyone joined in the fray. Some clung to Paul, the founder of the church. Others were captivated by the eloquence of Apollos, who visited Corinth soon after Paul had left it, and who no doubt taught substantially the same doctrine as his predecessor. Then, apparently, some Judaising Christians must have gained influence, and brought the name of Cephas into prominence. It would seem that they must have attacked Paul, who was obliged to make an elaborate defence of his apostolic authority. It does not follow, however, that they truly represented Peter, who may have disapproved, as strongly as Paul, of the use of his name for party purposes. Lastly, some used the name of Christ himself in a factious way, perhaps claiming to be his followers in a more complete sense than the others.

Is Christ divided? (i., 13).—Divisions are due to partial apprehension: is Christ divided, so that each faction may have, as it were, a piece of him instead of receiving him in his fulness?

Was Paul crucified for you? (i., 13).—As he is attacking, not a party, but the existence of parties, Paul properly chooses his own name rather than that of Apollos or Peter. As we shall see, he could defend himself when necessary, but it was a profound grief to him that his name should be used where only that of his beloved Master ought to stand. He is therefore glad that he baptised so few, as the administration of the rite by him might have caused misunderstanding. For Crispus (i., 14) see Acts xviii., 8 ; for Gaius, Rom. xvi., 23 ; for Stephanas (i., 16), 1 Cor. xvi., 15, 17.

The last words of the paragraph bring in, rather abruptly, a reference to the manner and subject of Paul's preaching. To this he returns farther on; and meanwhile this brief allusion serves to introduce a warning against the wisdom of the world in contrast with the spiritual power of the Gospel (i., 17–ii., 5).

First, the Apostle shows that the preaching of the cross does not appeal to human wisdom (i., 17-25).

The contrast is between a spiritual religion, to be apprehended only by spiritual faculties, and, on the one hand, an external religion, proud of its sagacity in demanding signs (miracles and prodigies) before it will believe, and, on the other hand, a rational opinion, reached by the difficult path of philosophical speculation. The cross, to those who could see it, revealed a depth of self-sacrificing love for sinful man to which all that was spiritual in them bowed down, and which became thenceforward a Divine power in their lives, drawing them into communion with that eternal love of which the cross was the supreme earthly manifestation. But this could not be unveiled except to the spiritual eye. To the ordinary Jew, a Christ on a cross instead of on a throne of glory, the greatest life given as a ransom for many, was an offensive absurdity. To the Greek with his love of fine talk and subtle discussion, the direct appeal to the heart, the revelation of God to the higher spiritual affections, was foolishness. But those who had been gifted with a purer insight found in the crucified teacher a power and a wisdom with which they meant to conquer the world.

Perishing (i., 18).—This is probably used in reference to the coming judgment; but the proposition is true of all in whom the spiritual faculties are in a state of decay.

It is written (i., 19).—The quotation is from Isaiah xxix., 14. The words referred to the formalism and faithlessness of Israel. Here they receive a wider application. The process was actually going on before the eyes of the Christian preachers: Christianity was regenerating men, while philosophy was impotent.

Where is the wise? (i., 20).—This may be the general term, of which the Jewish scribe and the Greek disputer are the species.

In the wisdom of God (i., 21).—According to grammatical usage this must mean, not "through the wisdom," but "in the midst of the wisdom of God." Though encompassed by His wisdom, of which the tokens are on every side, yet by the path of wisdom the world had not found Him. Divine knowledge enters the human heart by a different method.

The truth of the foregoing representation is established by an appeal to the actual facts (i., 26-31).

The description here given of the social position of the Christians was probably true wherever they were found; but it may have been particularly so at Corinth, where the population of the restored city was largely recruited from the class of freedmen and their families.

Wise after the flesh (i., 26), wise merely on the intellectual and worldly side, but without the wisdom that comes from moral and spiritual soundness. Not many whom the world would describe as wise were called; and there were few men of influence and rank among the disciples.

Chose (i., 27, 28).—Observe the repetition of this word, emphasising the fact that the initiative in spiritual things is with God, who chooses His own instruments to accomplish His purposes, and makes His divine power more manifest through the feebleness of His visible agents. It might be better to translate "elected," so as to preserve the verbal connection with the substantive "election."

Of him are ye in Christ Jesus (i., 30).—These words may

be understood in two ways: either, by virtue of being in Christ ye are sprung from God, and are His children; or, from Him as a source, by virtue of His election, ye are in Christ ("of" being in the Greek "out of" or "from"). The latter meaning suits the context best.

Who was made unto us wisdom (i., 30).—Wisdom here stands in opposition to the lower wisdom of the world, and the other characteristics are added to complete the picture. This form of expression is far more significant than a statement that Christ imparted to us wisdom and righteousness. These things are not detachable, like a doctrine or a ceremony, but are modes of living personality; and it is not by receiving certain instructions from Christ, but by the communion of his spirit with our own that we become wise and righteous. The new religion implied a soul transformed and enkindled by the Son of God.

It is written (i., 31).—The quotation is abridged from Jeremiah ix., 24, which, with the previous verse, ought to be read; for here, as in other instances, Paul seems to have had the context in his mind, though he quotes only what is necessary for his immediate purpose. The connection of thought shows that "the Lord" is God, as in the original passage.

In accordance with the view which he has just presented of the Gospel Paul reminds his readers that his own preaching had not been of the rhetorical and sophistical kind (ii., 1-5).

Mystery (ii., 1).—The reading "testimony," mentioned in the margin, is so well attested that it is preferred by some competent scholars. The two words bear a considerable resemblance to one another in the Greek, and "mystery" may be borrowed from verse 7. By this verse we must explain it, if it be genuine. If we read "testimony," the reference must be to the testimony borne to God in the Gospel.

Jesus Christ, and him crucified (ii., 2).—See notes on i., 17-25, and 30. This was fundamental; for from him who had no perception of the Divine love and the spiritual grandeur manifested on the cross the Gospel was hidden. The Apostle, of course, does not mean that he taught nothing, for he alludes farther on to several things that he had taught, but rather that he had allowed the story of Christ and him crucified to bear its own message to the heart, and that he had not accompanied it with intellectual theories and reasonings. Yet the rich contents of this admitted of further unfolding and various applications, so that in the next chapter Paul describes this teaching as elementary, fitted for babes in Christ. But because it was elementary, it was necessary that it should be perfectly mastered before any edifice of disputable teaching could be safely reared upon it.

I was with you in weakness (ii., 3).—From the connection I think the Apostle must refer not to conscious weakness and apprehension in relation to the greatness of his mission, but to something in his mode of address that was observable by others. Great orators, like Cicero, are often conscious of fear and trembling; nevertheless they command the passions of their audience. But it was remarked of Paul that his bodily presence was weak, and his speech of no account (2 Cor. x., 10). Probably he seemed timid and nervous in manner, and could not attract unsympathetic listeners by his fluent speech and sounding platitudes. But if the heart was responsive, the poor speaker was forgotten in the mighty play of new emotion.

Demonstration of the Spirit and of power (ii., 4).—Paul contrasts " demonstration " with the mere plausibility of the sophist; and this demonstration proceeded from the Spirit and power of God.

That your faith should not stand in the wisdom of men (ii., 5).—This points out the Divine object in the course which has been described. The Gospel came through what appeared to worldly men to be weakness and folly, in order that the believers' faith should not be based on the passing arguments of a favourite leader. The proof of God is the felt power of God in the soul; and those who have felt His living presence will bow together before Him, and not dispute about the respective merits of Paul and Apollos. Though the treatment is only allusive, the main theme is never forgotten; but the whole of this exalted exposition tends to lift the readers into that supreme reverence where the petty factions of partiality and self-will disappear.

Having spoken of the simplicity and apparent folly of the Gospel, Paul subjoins a supplementary paragraph, showing that there was a higher wisdom than that of the world, and describing the manner in which it was revealed (ii., 6-16).

The passage is one of the most profound in the Epistles, and, though the general sense is clear, is not without exegetical difficulties.

Speak wisdom among the perfect (or *them that are full-grown* (ii., 6).—Whichever translation we adopt, the reference must be to mature Christians, those who were no longer "babes in Christ." As this wisdom was reserved for the more advanced, it must represent something different from that of which the Apostle has hitherto spoken, and cannot mean that the foolishness of the Gospel was really wisdom in the eyes of men competent to judge. Christianity, resting on a different basis from that of philosophy, nevertheless had its intellectual side, and its implicit contents might be unfolded into a system of wisdom. This statement, then, anticipates the view of the Alexandrian theologians, who maintain the legitimacy of a Gnosis, an intellectual presentation of the contents of faith. If we ask for examples of the "wisdom" of which Paul speaks, we must refer to his Epistles generally, in all of which he deals with a variety of subjects that are not obviously included in "Jesus Christ and him crucified."

Not of this world (ii., 6), rather "this age," referring to the present, in contrast with the future age after the return of

Christ. Christian wisdom followed altogether different lines.

Rulers . . . which are coming to nought (ii., 6).—Some understand this of demonic powers; but the context is against this meaning. Paul has expressed the view that the great things of the world are to come to nought, in i., 28, and he here repeats the thought. We need not, however, limit the word to "rulers" in the strict sense: the statement is general; those who governed the present order of things were already losing their hold, and the new kingdom of righteousness was making its way against them.

God's wisdom (ii., 7).—Paul felt that the truths which he unfolded were more than human speculation. As, in the field of science, Kepler exclaimed, "O God, I think Thy thoughts after Thee," so in the field of morals and religion the Apostle was visited with thoughts which came to him with the authority of eternal truth. And this confidence of his is not proved to be a vain thing because he had the treasure in an earthen vessel, and to some extent the wisdom of the passing moment succeeded in impressing its shape upon his visions.

In a mystery (ii., 7), that is, in the form or manner of a mystery, something hidden from the mass of men, and revealed only to the initiated. There is no reason for assuming a reference to esoteric doctrine, reserved for a particular class of Christians. The allusion is rather to the newness of Christian truth, which was taught to all disciples so far as they were able to receive it. In relation to the outside world it was a mystery, and up to the present time had been hidden.

Which God foreordained (ii., 7).—Strictly speaking the wisdom itself cannot be foreordained, but only its manifestation in the world. It is one of Paul's favourite thoughts that the world's history was controlled by a Divine purpose, of which the ultimate issue was the spiritual glory of the Kingdom of God.

They would not have crucified the Lord of glory (ii., 8).—Jesus is here described as one to whom that spiritual glory especially belonged. He was the Master and Leader of the new community of God's children. Observe, Paul ascribes the crucifixion, not to hatred of goodness, but to spiritual blindness. Such blindness, however, may imply various degrees of guilt.

As it is written (ii., 9).—The passage quoted, evidently as Scriptural authority, is not found in the Old Testament; but it is perhaps a reminiscence of Isaiah lxiv., 4. Some have supposed it to be derived from an apocryphal book.[1] In regard to the meaning of the words two points must be noted: first, that the things in question are what God prepared for them that love Him, all the spiritual enrichment that comes from the communion of Divine love; secondly, that the discernment of these things does not come through the ordinary channels of knowledge, the senses and the intellect, which deal with more extraneous and material subjects. "The heart" is regarded as the organ of the understanding.

Unto us (ii., 10).—The immediate reference is to Paul and other Christian teachers, as we see from verse 13; but we miss the deepest lesson of the passage if we limit the truth here enunciated, and make it refer only to a miraculous communication of knowledge to the Apostles. Paul tells his readers that the Spirit of God dwells in them (iii., 16). He is unfolding a spiritual law, and what he says of himself is true of others in their several degrees.

Revealed them through the Spirit (ii., 10).—Paul nowhere defines his doctrine of the Spirit, and any explanation must

---

[1] There is a striking parallel to the first part in the poem of Empedocles, Περὶ φύσεως:—τὸ δ' οὖλον ἐπεύχεται εὑρεῖν
Αὕτως· οὔτ' ἐπιδερκτὰ τάδ' ἀνδράσιν οὔτ' ἐπάκουστα
Οὔτε νόῳ περιληπτά.
Quoted by Sellar, *The Roman Poets of the Republic*, p. 295.

be to a certain degree tentative. Whatever else it may embrace, I think it expresses the essential character of the Divine personality, breathed forth upon the souls of men, and so passing into human consciousness. It is through this indwelling in the conscious life that it becomes the revealing organ of Divine knowledge; and it can reveal, because, being a Divine essence, it explores the deep places of God. According to this explanation it includes the self-consciousness of God; but it also denotes that whereby God enters into immediate communion with man. I do not think, however, that it is used here of the third person of the Trinity in the sense of the later theology. For, first, it is clearly regarded as analogous to the spirit in man; and even if we adopt here the Pauline trichotomy into spirit, soul, and body, we cannot assign distinct personality to the spirit. This division of human nature, instead of furnishing an analogy, presents a marked contrast; for, according to it, man consists of three substances in one person, not of three persons in one substance. Secondly, it is said that none but the Spirit of God knoweth the things of God. But Paul would surely never have ascribed this knowledge only to the third person, to the exclusion of the other two. The meaning of this statement we must proceed to examine in the following verse.

The spirit of the man (ii., 11).—We must observe in this verse the want of logical coherence. We should expect, not "who among men," but "what in man?" or, instead of "save the spirit," "save through the spirit." This shows that we must not always insist very strictly upon the form of expression. Next we must inquire what is meant by the spirit of man. Does it mean the concrete third element in each man, the spirit as distinct from the lower soul? I think not: for, first, it would have been more natural to write simply "his spirit" instead of the longer phrase before us; and, secondly, though Paul would have denied that any but the spiritual could have a perfect knowledge of man, he would hardly have committed himself to a proposition which would seem to deny all knowledge of human things to men in whom only the lower mind was awake. He is evidently making a statement which he expects to be recognised as true as soon as it is presented. I think, therefore, it is better to take "spirit" in a general sense, the nature or essence of humanity, "the spirit of man" (as the Greek may be translated), in opposition to any spirit that is lower than human. The proposition, then, is equivalent to this: it is only by possessing the spirit of humanity that we can know humanity. It may be objected to this that the spirit is said to know, and therefore it must be the individual mind. But we have seen that, from the point of view of a grammarian, the structure is faulty; and, moreover, the personification is a very natural one. No one would be puzzled if we said that malice could not know love, that stinginess could not understand generosity. Interpreting the sentence thus we find that every word is needful, and we are led on by a necessary inference to a profound truth: as nothing beneath man can know man, so only the Spirit of God can know God; and man can know God only so far as this Spirit reveals itself to human consciousness. Justice, holiness, love, dwell eternal in the heart of God; and these depths of His being cannot make themselves known through the path of intellectual teaching, but only by unveiling their faces to the inward eye.

"*The spirit of the world*" (ii., 12), the spirit or character which we still describe as worldly, intent on transient things, and, in its small wisdom, blind to the glory of God. This application of the word "spirit" confirms our previous interpretation.

"*The spirit which is of God*" (ii., 12), literally "out of God," breathed forth, as it were, from the depths of His own being.

"*Comparing spiritual things with spiritual*" (ii., 13).—The meaning is uncertain; but perhaps the translation "combining" (which the Greek admits) best suits the context,—combining spiritual truths with spiritual words.

"*The natural man*" (ii., 14), that is, the man whose governing principle is the soul (in Paul's trichotomy), all the intellectual and emotional life which is beneath the spiritual. Why such a man cannot know spiritual things is sufficiently apparent from the remarks already made.

"*Judgeth all things*" (ii., 15): better, "judgeth of all things." In opposition to the "natural man," the spiritual not only sees things which are hidden from the former, but is raised altogether to a higher plane of judgment. The extent of "all things" must of course be limited, though not very precisely, by the context. While the spiritual man is thus able to judge, he is himself judged of by none; men of a lower type cannot interpret him correctly. It is not very evident why this latter statement is inserted; but I think it refers to the divisions at Corinth, and prepares the way for the rebuke of the next chapter. The unspiritual Corinthians were unable to judge of the very men whom they were extolling as leaders. Those who were claiming a pre-eminence for Paul only proved that they were incapable of understanding him. Compare iv., 3.

"*For who hath known the mind of the Lord, that he should instruct him?*" (ii., 16).—This is quoted from Isaiah xl., 13. We should expect here "the spirit" instead of "the mind"; and the word is actually "spirit" in the Hebrew, but the LXX have translated it by "mind," and Paul follows them. "Mind" differs in meaning from "spirit," and denotes rather the reason and thought of God, but it must be here used as substantially equivalent. It is generally assumed that this verse is intended to prove the statement immediately preceding: no one knows the mind of the Lord, and therefore, as we have that mind, no one can judge of us. I cannot help thinking, however, that the statement is far too subordinate to call for this scriptural proof, and that Paul would have shrunk from implying that he himself was as inscrutable as the mind of God. I suppose, then, that the proof refers to the whole of the preceding passage, the purport of which it briefly sums up: not even the wise and powerful of this world could know the wisdom and mind of God; but *we* have the mind of Christ, which was filled with the Spirit of God, and therefore we are able with him to look into the deep things of God.

Having laid down general principles, Paul now comes more directly to the question of divisions, and secures an easy transition by reminding his readers of their immature condition when he was among them. Their jealousy and strife proved that this immaturity had not yet passed away (iii., 1-4).

"*Carnal*" (iii., 1, 3).—This is a harsher word than its Greek equivalent, for we apply it only to an excessive dominance of the bodily appetites. In Paul it seems to refer to the whole tendency of life and thought, as governed by lower impulses and worldly motives rather than by the spirit. Thus in the present passage "jealousy and strife" prove the existence of a carnal temper, for these subserve no higher than earthly ends, and are impossible to genuine spirituality.

"*Are ye not men?*" (iii., 4); that is, just like others, in no way raised above the common crowd. The use of the word in this sense is very significant, for it implies that the spiritual man is, in a manner, more than man; he is a temple of the Holy Spirit. Later theologians, though still in the centuries when Christianity was young, expressed a similar thought by the bold assertion that God had become man in order that man might become God.

In order to see the folly and impropriety of the divisions it was necessary to take a just view of the function of the Christian preachers: they were simply ministers of Christ, and were labouring for far other than their own ends; each had his own gift, and contributed accordingly to the building up of the Church (iii., 5-iv.,5).

"*Apollos . . . Paul*" (iii., 5).—He selects these two as having both laboured in person at Corinth. Peter was known to the Corinthians only by repute.

"*The Lord*" (iii., 5).—It is generally thought that "the Lord" here means God, and not Christ, as in the context only God is referred to. This meaning might be supported by an appeal to Romans xii., 3. But Paul so habitually reserves the title Lord for Christ when he is not influenced by an Old Testament passage that I am inclined to think the reference here is to Christ. The specially Christian gifts were bestowed and took form through him, so that he might be spoken of as the giver. Compare Eph. iv., 11.

One (iii., 8).—He who plants and he who waters are one in their work and their aim, each labouring for the harvest which God alone can give. The only distinction is in the individual toil, which will receive its proportionate reward.

We are God's fellow-workers (iii., 9).—Notice the emphatic repetition of "God" to whom every thing is to be ultimately referred. The Church did not belong to this man or to that, but to God. We fall below this truth whenever as leaders we strive for our own ends or as disciples disputatiously exalt one leader above another.

The notion of a building suggests the comparison which follows (iii., 10-15). There is only one foundation; but various kinds of structure may be reared upon it, some of finest quality, some of worthless rubbish. The day of judgment, which will dawn upon the world in fire, will test each man's work. That which is sound and good will remain unharmed; the bad will perish in the fire, but the unskilful builder himself will be saved, like one escaping through the flames. We must observe that as the building is figurative, the fire too must be figurative. The general effect of this paragraph is to point out the responsibility of teachers; but to fit it into the argument I think we must suppose a latent reference to the real leaders of the parties, who were resident in Corinth, and who are clearly referred to in vs. 18. The error to which Paul alludes may be moral and spiritual rather than doctrinal, though I see no reason for excluding the latter. We must observe that Jesus Christ himself is the foundation; theories about him are superstructure.

From the teachers Paul passes to the community, and in doing so reverts to the concluding figure of vs. 9, "Ye are God's building" (iii., 16-23). Not only were they reared by God, and not by man, but they were God's temple, and were holy through the presence of His Spirit; so that if anyone destroyed that temple by splitting it up into incoherent parts, God would destroy him. The warning is deeply impressive, though the nature of the destruction is not specified. May we not say that the man will lose the sense of the Divine presence, and be given over to his own vain wisdom?

Let no man deceive himself (iii., 18).—These words may be applied to what has just been said,—let no man imagine that he can evade his responsibility; but probably the reference intended is wholly to what follows. The conceit of wisdom, as wisdom was estimated in "the present age," was a piece of pure self-deception; and the only way to become really wise was to cast off this conceit, and become what the world would call a fool, yielding himself in humility to the leading of the Spirit. In the judgment of God the judgment of men is reversed, and what is called wisdom is really folly.

It is written (iii., 19).—The first quotation is from Job v., 13. Commentators quote from Plato, "all knowledge, separated from righteousness and other excellence, appears to be craftiness, not wisdom." The quotation in the next verse is from Psalm xciv., 11. Paul changes "man" into "wise," showing here as elsewhere that he is not particular about the letter of Scripture, if he gives the general sense, and the passage serves to illustrate his thought.

Let no one glory in men (iii., 21).—This is an inference from what has just been said: if the Divine estimate of men is such, there is nothing to glory in. But another reason is added. This glorying in particular men was only cutting oneself off from the vast treasure that in truth belongs to us. We may learn from every teacher, yea, from the universe itself, and all its solemn incidents. This grand utterance admits of wide application, and reaches its highest truth when in utter self-surrender the child can say to the heavenly Father, "All mine are Thine, and Thine are mine." But men lose this infinite wealth in the petty claims of self.

Ye are Christ's (iii., 23).—The thought seems to be,—teachers belong to you, not you to the teachers; but you belong to Christ, and not to those who are only his messengers. I think there must also be a delicate allusion to the Christ-party. If it could be said generally, "Ye are Christ's," no one had a right to say, "*I* am Christ's" in distinction from others who were no less so.

Christ is God's (iii., 23).—Thus the thoughts are carried up to Him on whom all alike depend, and in whose presence all earthly distinctions vanish. As usual in Paul, Christ is markedly distinguished from God. To say that God means only the first person of the Trinity, or that Christ is spoken of only in his human nature, or that, though as the Son he belongs to the Father, he is nevertheless co-eternal and co-equal, appears to me (though I am sure no irreverence is intended) to be irreverent supplements to the great Apostle's teaching.

As no one was to glory in men, Paul shows, by way of contrast, the view which ought to be taken of the Christian preachers: they were simply stewards who had to administer what was entrusted to them, and no one was competent to judge of them except the Master who employed them (iv., 1-5).

Ministers (iv., 1).— The word so translated appears

only here in Paul's Epistles, but does not differ much in meaning from other words which have the same translation.

The mysteries of God (**iv., 1**); that is, the truths which had been hidden, but were now revealed. The application of the word to the sacraments is of later date.

That a man be found faithful (**iv., 2**).—This is the one thing necessary in a steward. He is not to adopt measures of his own, but simply to discharge with fidelity the duties entrusted to him. It is implied that only his master can judge how faithful he has been; for he only knows what he has committed to his trust.

Judged of you (**iv., 3**); better "judged of by you." The word here used does not in the least imply adverse judgment, but an examination or judgment, to see how the thing really is. Examples of its use may be seen in Acts xxiv., 8, xxviii., 18; 1 Cor. ii., 14, 15, x., 25, 27, and ix., 3 (where the context gives it a depreciating sense). It is used by Paul only in this Epistle. Here the following verses seem to show that it refers to favourable judgment: it gives me little pleasure that you should boast about me, for you cannot know how faithful I have been; nay, I do not know myself.

Man's judgment (**iv., 3**); literally "a human day," the word "day" being apparently used technically, as in iii., 13. for a day that comes with the revealing light of judgment.

Yet am I not hereby justified (**iv., 4**).—The fact that even my own conscience does not accuse me of unfaithfulness is not sufficient; for I may be mistaken. To one who looks for a Divine judgment, all human judgments become insignificant, and he knows that faults may come to light which he himself has failed to see.

The Lord (**iv., 4, 5**); clearly Christ, through whom, according to Rom. ii., 16, God will judge the secrets of men.

Paul has spoken of himself and Apollos, but he has transferred his remarks to them simply as examples: he has referred to the leaders and indeed the members of parties generally; and he now

attacks the conceit and factiousness of the Corinthians with the keenest irony (iv., 6-13).

Not to go beyond the things which are written (**iv., 6**); literally, "you might learn this, ' do not go beyond, etc.,'" which gives the impression that the words were a current saying. "Which are written" must, by usage, refer to the Old Testament; and, in the present connection, Paul may allude to such passages as he has quoted in i., 19, 31, iii., 19, 20.

For the one against the other (**iv., 6**).—The meaning probably is that no one should be puffed up on behalf of any particular teacher, against his neighbour who prefers some other teacher. "The other" is rendered "his neighbour" in vi., 1, correctly.

Who maketh thee to differ? (**iv., 7**). — Evidently men prided themselves on following certain leaders, and looked down on those who were not of the party. But supposing a man has some wisdom, it is no ground for vanity, for a man has nothing precious that he has not received from God. This is the basis for humility in all things.

Already are ye filled (**iv., 8**).—"You imagine you have all the glory of the Messianic kingdom;—I wish you had, and we Apostles should be in a very different position."

The Apostles last of all (**iv., 9**); that is, as the last and lowest of men. The details of the following description are sufficiently clear. "Fools" and "wise," "weak" and "strong" must be understood from the contrast already drawn between the weakness and folly of the Gospel in the eyes of men, and the wisdom and power of the world.

Paul could not retain his irony and indignation long; so now he changes his tone, and ends this portion of his letter with a kindly admonition, not, however, unaccompanied by a threat that he would use his authority if he found it necessary (iv., 14-21).

Tutors (**iv., 15**), a word properly applied, not to teachers, but to slaves who had the charge of children, and conducted them to school; but here we may give it rather a wider meaning, as it clearly refers to all who taught the Corinthians subsequently to their conversion by Paul, who, as their founder, stood to them in the relation of father.

Be ye imitators of me (**iv., 16**); that is, in the matter of which he is treating. Let them equally abjure self-importance and worldly wisdom.

For this cause (**iv., 17**); to enable you to imitate me. Timothy had probably been despatched after the news of the divisions had been received from the people of Chloe. See Introduction.

My ways which be in Christ, even as I teach everywhere (**iv., 17**).—We must still interpret by reference to the main subject. Paul sought no personal pre-eminence in his manner of teaching; he sunk himself in his message; he wanted no Pauline party; and if he was sometimes obliged to assert his authority, it was only when vital interests seemed to be at stake, and the Gospel to which his life was given was attacked in his person.

If the Lord will (**iv., 19**).—Here, as elsewhere, it seems doubtful whether God or Christ is meant. I think, when there is no clear reason to the contrary, "the Lord," stands for Christ. Paul, I think, believed that the movements of the Apostles were still, in some way, under the direction of Christ, and he could not feel sure that he might not be summoned elsewhere.

Not the word . . . but the power (**iv., 19**).—"Power" can hardly be used here of miraculous gifts, but has a general sense, spiritual force of character, in opposition to mere talk. It was the powerful spell which all men feel in a godly life, and not fine speeches, that proved the reign of God within the soul.

With a rod (**iv., 21**); literally, "in a rod," illustrating the use of the preposition "in." See also v., 8, where again "in" is translated by "with."

In love and a spirit of meekness (**iv., 21**).—The combination of the "spirit of meekness" with "love" shows that it denotes a moral quality, and that "spirit" is used, just as we use it, to express the tone and character of mind, as when we say a man acted in a bad spirit, or showed a kindly spirit. "Spirit" is properly the breath or effluence that goes forth from anything, and is thus an expression of its essential principle. This verse properly forms the close of the section dealing with parties, and shows what a serious evil Paul considered them to be; but nevertheless the grave doubt which it suggests may have been partly induced by the next subject, to which, at all events, it forms a suitable transition.

The second section of the Epistle is devoted to remonstrances against various sins (v., 1-vi., 20).

The first case dealt with is one of incest, in which the Apostle's moral indignation is roused to the highest pitch (v., 1-8).

Among you (**v., 1**).—These words would, I think, be more properly connected with "reported." The sin was a matter of common talk in the church, and not something hidden in secret which might, on that account, have been overlooked. How constantly has this been repeated in the history of the Church. The foulest sins have been tolerated, while men have been puffed up with their orthodoxy.

Hath his father's wife (**v., 1**).—Of course the man's step-mother must be meant. Many commentators think that an actual marriage is intended; but this must be left doubtful. The woman, we must suppose, was not a Christian, as her case is not considered. If we judge from this passage alone, it would seem that the father was dead; for no notice is taken of the wrong inflicted upon him, and he, if living, would probably have roused the church to some action in the matter. The supposed references to this case in the Second Epistle must be considered in their proper place, and at present I will only express my agreement with those who think that in these passages some other interpretation must be sought.

Present in spirit (v., 3).—This illustrates the use of the word "spirit," which cannot here denote the actual substance of the mind; for that could be no more present than the body. The words must mean, present in thought and purpose, and influencing all who respected his authority.

To deliver such a one unto Satan (v., 5).—It is impossible to decide with certainty what is meant by these words. The only other place where the phrase occurs is 1 Tim. i., 20, where the object is that those so delivered may be taught not to blaspheme. One would suppose that Satan would rather teach men to blaspheme, and take away their hope of salvation. He seems to be regarded in these passages as the spirit of adversity, according to the representation of him in the Book of Job, so that moral good might result from a temporary subjection to him. Compare 2 Cor. xii., 7, where Paul calls his thorn in the flesh a "messenger of Satan," and this was given to him in order to keep him humble. See also 1 Thess. ii., 18, where, instead of Satan, we should probably say in modern times "adverse circumstances hindered us." It is clear that in the present passage something more is intended than excommunication, for this would have no tendency to destroy the flesh. Though we cannot reach the exact details, we should notice the great solemnity of the judgment here passed, and contrast the deep grief and indignation which Paul expresses towards immorality with the gentle and reasonable way in which he treats mere doctrinal error, as in regard to the resurrection. We should observe also that the punitive sentence was to be the impressive act of the assembled church, not of a particular order, and that they were to pronounce it under a deep sense of their connection with Christ and the requirements of that "name" which they bore.

A little leaven (v., 6).—This may refer to the moral

laxity, which allowed the Corinthians to glory, and, if it went on, would corrupt their moral life. If it refers to the sin itself, "a little" applies, not to its intrinsic character, but to its extent relatively to the number of believers.

Our Passover (v., 7).—This is the only place where Paul uses this comparison. The figure which runs through *vv.* 6-8 may have been suggested by the approach of the feast of the Passover, which was observed in the Christian churches as well as among the Jews.

Paul is led by the subject to correct a misunderstanding of a previous letter, which has not been preserved (v., 9-13).

He had directed the brethren to keep no company with immoral men, but intended this to be a regulation within the brotherhood itself. Neither he nor they could judge outsiders; but they should not even eat with a bad man as a member of the brotherhood. We must once more observe that it is for purely moral offences that excommunication is urged. If Paul was acquainted with the parable of the tares, he cannot have understood it as some of its later interpreters. It is astonishing that such men as are specified were found within the Christian community at that time; but many may have been attracted to the Church through bad motives, hoping to prey on the charity of the brethren, or even through a superstitious dread of the approaching judgment, from which they fancied the Gospel would magically save them.

Put away the wicked man from among yourselves (v., 13).— The words are so close to those of Deut. xxiv., 7, that we must take them as a quotation.

A very different subject is now introduced, suggested perhaps by the reference to judging in the last two verses; and the disposition to bring charges against a brother before heathen courts is rebuked (vi., 1-11).

Unrighteous . . . saints (vi., 1).—The former word describes unbelievers, unrighteousness being, from the Jewish and Christian point of view, the prevailing characteristic of the heathen world. The word may retain here its stricter sense of "unjust," so that it marks the absurdity of the course which is censured. Similarly "saints," though a common designation of Christians, is peculiarly appropriate here, for those who are holy are most likely to give a true judgment. The Jews, likewise, were forbidden to bring their disputes before heathen tribunals.[1]

The saints shall judge the world (**vi., 2**).—This is assumed as a well-known fact, and was most likely to have been learned from Daniel vii., 22, "Judgment was given to the saints of the Most High." Paul expected Christ to be the judge at his coming, and therefore commentators say that the saints are to be his assessors; but the passage here does not call them assessors, and it may be that Paul had in mind the Messianic period, when the saints would continue to act as judges. It is also possible that he had no very clearly defined idea, beyond the expectation that in some way the saints would ultimately judge the world, instead of being judged by it.

We shall judge angels (**vi., 3**).—This also the Corinthians were expected to know. In rabbinical teaching the righteous occupied a dwelling in heaven nearer to the throne of God than angels.[2] Such speculations belong to the knowledge that passes away. But understood in the spirit they have a grand lesson. Those whose judgment, guided by the spirit of Christ, may rise to the highest things, and discern the right and wrong even of angels' deeds, are adequate to deal justly with the petty affairs of life; and if we have a difference with a brother, we should rather seek for their decision than resort to the arbitrament of law. The Christians, we should observe, were in a different position from the Jews. The latter had their legally recognised courts in connection with the synagogues; the former had no legal juris-

---

[1] Weber, *Jüdische Theologie*, 1897, p. 78 *sq.*
[2] See Weber, *Jüdische Theologie*, p. 404.

diction, and among themselves could only submit their disputes to a friendly arbitration.

Who are of no account in the church (**vi., 4**).—As the translation stands, this must mean the heathen. The difficulty in this interpretation is that the Christians could not "set" or appoint heathen judges. The sentence may, however, be translated as in the margin; and then the meaning is, if we must have these petty tribunals, appoint those who are of no account among you, and do not waste the time of sensible men. The irony is then explained by what follows: "I say this to move you to shame." Notwithstanding the slight difficulty, I think the former is sustained by the context.

A defect (**vi., 7**).—The translation in the margin, "a loss to you," gives a better sense. Paul had already made it very plain that it was a defect to have lawsuits; but it was much worse, for it involved spiritual loss, causing men to defraud in their eagerness not to be defrauded, and to forget that all unrighteousness excluded from the Kingdom of God. We thus obtain a good connection of thought where at first sight there appears to be a very abrupt transition.

Inherit the Kingdom of God (**vi., 9**), a familiar figure in the Pauline Epistles. In this phrase the Kingdom is regarded chiefly in its future outward realisation. But its more inward and spiritual sense is not forgotten: the Kingdom of God and unrighteousness are for ever incompatible. The list of the unrighteous is given in order to make it quite plain what is meant. Men who lead bad lives cannot get into the Kingdom of God by any legal fiction; their badness proves that they are not of it. Observe once more Paul's absolute refusal to palter in any way with evil living. If Christianity had not brought real righteousness, he would have spurned it as a loathesome sham.

Such were some of you (**vi., 11**).—This form of expression implies that they were so no more, and that the change which had taken place in them was moral. But though they had undergone a moral change, they were in danger of a relapse, and needed to be reminded of the solemn religious sanctions under which the change had taken place.

Ye were washed (vi., 11).—It would be better to keep the strict sense, "Ye washed yourselves," meaning, "Ye submitted yourselves to baptism," for that was a voluntary act. This action implied the acceptance of Christian obligations, and the renouncement of the old heathen life. "Sanctified" and "justified," on the other hand, are Divine acts; for man cannot turn his own impurity into holiness, or acquit himself in the court of supreme judgment. Some are distressed because Paul here places sanctification before justification; but he is not writing a natural history of religious change. No doubt forgiveness long precedes complete sanctification; and yet forgiveness is conditioned by penitence, and penitence implies that the sanctifying spirit is already at work. The man who loathes his sin is sanctified in comparison with the man who loves it, and I know not where it is said that he who loves sin can be justified. The words, "in the name of the Lord Jesus Christ, and in the Spirit of our God," solemnly translate us to the sphere of absolute holiness, where passion is still, and worldly desire ceases to press.

Paul now returns to the subject of fornication, about which there seems to have been some misunderstanding (vi., 12-20).

We must remember that this, if considered a fault at all, was regarded as a very venial one in Gentile society. For this reason it is specially mentioned in the decree of the Council of Jerusalem (Acts xv., 29) along with restrictions about food. Now Paul had taught that meats were things morally indifferent; on what ground, then, did he condemn fornication? This difficulty is answered in the present passage. It was quite true that meats were morally indifferent, so long at least as we did not allow appetite to gain the mastery over us. They were so because they were related only to the physical organ which was necessary for the present life, but was ultimately to perish. In other words, the use of one convenient food rather than another had no moral effect, but left the character untouched. The argument is substantially the same as that used by Christ (Matt., xv., 10 *sqq.*, Mark vii., 14 *sqq.*). The case is different with fornication; for that, though in itself a mere physical act, is a misappropriation of the body, and desecrates the temple of the Holy Spirit. The details of the argument are a little obscure. Paul distinguishes the body from the flesh. The former was the permanent organ of the Spirit, indissolubly connected with our personality, and therefore destined to be raised from the dead; whereas the flesh was corruptible, and doomed to perish. An illicit connection could not be confined to the latter, but handed over to the slave of vice that higher organism which was meant for the Lord. The general lesson is clear: reverence for the body as a Divine organ is inconsistent with all diversion of it from its Divine ends.

God both raised the Lord, and will raise up us (vi., 14).—Observe how Christ is placed with man as dependent on God for his risen life.

Ye were bought with a price (vi., 20).—Explaining this by other passages, we cannot doubt that the reference is to the agonising death of Christ. By a perfectly natural and easy figure Paul represents this as the price which God paid in order to buy man for Himself. To press the details of the figure, and ask to whom God paid the price, is to mistake the nature of figurative language. If we made the general statement that the sinful were brought to God at the cost of suffering to the innocent, everyone who was not a theologian would understand the saying.

We pass now to another section of the Epistle, containing Paul's answers to various questions about marriage which had been laid before him in a letter from the Corinthians (vii.).

In these answers he expresses himself with great care, and frankly says that in certain points he is only giving his own judgment, and not laying down absolute rules of Christian morality. In judging of his views we must in fairness remember that the treatment is conditioned by the questions which are not before us, but which clearly related, not to marriage generally, but to certain definite points connected with it. Nevertheless it would have been quite in accordance with Paul's style to have laid down the great spiritual principles affecting marriage, and to have deduced his rules from these. But he was not a married man, and evidently had no inclination in that direction; and so he lays down prudential rules, and disappoints those who look for the spiritual depth which he displays on other subjects.

He begins with some suggestions, given not by way of commandment, but of concession, about the advisability of marriage and its subsequent duties (vii., 1-7).

We may suppose that the prevailing licentiousness at Corinth had given rise, through reaction, to an ascetic view. Paul expresses his own preference for a state of celibacy, or of abstinence in the case of marriage, as that which in itself was good. But he was a man of the world as well as a Christian saint, and saw the terrible evils which were sure to arise from any unnatural and enforced restraint. He therefore dissuades from celibacy or its equivalent unless a man's special gift of grace leads him to adopt it. We should observe that $v.$ 2 assumes that monogamy is the established and the proper usage.

The next paragraph contains various directions about unmarried and married Christians (for their being such is implied), about mixed marriages, and, as arising out of the latter subject, about the propriety of not changing one's social condition owing to the acceptance of Christianity (vii., 8-24).

On the subject of divorce he appeals to the express command of Christ. In regard to mixed marriages the Lord had left no instructions, such cases not having arisen, and Paul accordingly gives his own advice. He clearly recognises the right of separation in these instances, but thinks that it should not be exercised on the Christian side, though it should be accepted as a dissolution of marriage if the heathen husband or wife thought fit to sever the engagement. It is plainly assumed that the marriages in question were contracted prior to the conversion of the husband or wife to Christianity.

Sanctified (**vii., 14**).—This might be better rendered "consecrated," as it is in the margin in John xvii., 19. The union was holy, and in effect Christian.

Now are they [the children] *holy* (**vii., 14**); that is, counted as belonging to the community of the holy. See the note on Rom. i., 7. The statement indicates that this was an accepted practice. Paul says nothing about baptism, and there is no reason to suppose that infant baptism had been yet established. His views on baptism seem applicable only to converts, and he assumes that the children of a Christian parent belong *ipso facto* to the society of "the saints." This reverses the Roman practice, according to which, under the Latin franchise, the inferior blood prevailed, and "the child of a mixed marriage became a Latin, and not a Roman citizen."[1] But, among the Jews, if a Jewess were married to a Gentile, the nationality of the child was supposed to follow that of the mother.[2]

How knowest thou, O wife, whether thou shalt save thy husband (**vii., 16**).—This may refer to *vv.* 12-14, the intervening verse being parenthetical; and then the meaning is, do not put away the unbelieving husband, for you may convert him. Or it may refer to *v.* 15; do not prevent a separation, for you cannot be sure that you will convert him. You are

---

[1] Merivale, *History of the Romans under the Empire*, ed. 1890, i., p. 8.
[2] Weber, *Jüdische Theologie*, 1897, p. 72.

not bound; your calling has been in peace, and you need not be distressed with anxious scruples. The latter connection seems preferable.

The connection of the following passage is not immediately apparent. Verse 17 checks the statement of 15, and repeats in another form the advice of 12–14: the Christian husband or wife is not bound in the case of mixed marriages; but it is better to remain in the social circumstances which we occupied when we received the Christian call, for the value of the latter is not affected by the former. This was the instruction which Paul gave everywhere; and it is illustrated by the case of circumcision and uncircumcision, and that of slavery and freedom.

As the Lord hath distributed to each man (**vii., 17**).—"The Lord" must, in accordance with Paul's usage, mean Christ. But then I doubt whether "distributed" can refer to men's worldly position, for nowhere else is it suggested that Christ assigns their lot in life to men unconnected with Christianity; and yet this is what the sequel seems to imply. But we may perhaps obtain a good connection of thought by referring it to spiritual gifts (compare Rom. xii., 3, and 2 Cor. x., 13, the only other passages where Paul uses the word in this sense). Then the meaning will be,—direct your lives in accordance with your special gifts and your Christian calling; and then you need not trouble yourselves about outward conditions which have nothing to do with character; keep the commandments of God, and let outward things settle themselves.

Keeping the commandments (**vii., 19**).—This shows how naturally Paul assumes that the commandments of God are moral, and that he had not departed as widely from the teaching of the Sermon on the Mount as is generally supposed. Circumcision was of course prescribed by the Law, but Paul here quietly treats it as lying outside the commandments of God.

Calling (**vii., 20**) must signify the Divine call, not a "calling" in the world, in our sense of the word. The latter idea comes in only by implication: men were called, not to an outward, but to an inward change; let them cling to the latter and not care for the former.

Use it rather (**vii., 21**).—I think the translation of the previous clause, "Nay, even if," is the more correct; so that the meaning must be, prefer to remain in slavery.

Ye were bought with a price (**vii., 23**).—See vi., 20.

Become not bond-servants of men (**vii., 23**).—Ye are Christ's slaves, therefore do not submit yourselves spiritually to any lower mastership, or enslave yourselves to mere human judgments.

In judging of the principle here applied to questions so entirely different (from our point of view) as those of circumcision and slavery we must remember that to Paul the time was short, and it did not seem worth while wasting on earthly concerns the energies which were needed for higher purposes. Moreover, he was so absorbed in the direct action of spiritual power that it probably never occurred to him to consider the different effects which varying social conditions might exercise upon character; and even if it be one-sided, there is something unspeakably grand in that outlook into things infinite and eternal which dwarfed all the cares of the world and of time, and made it a matter of complete indifference whether one was bond or free. This limitation of view was perhaps necessary for the triumph of Christianity. Had the churches become organs of social revolution, and threatened "the rights of property," they would not only have damaged the purity of their own spiritual impulse, but would have been suppressed with ruthless ferocity. The Gospel had principles which were destined to work grand social changes; but remote results of principle are not at once perceived, and before the institutions of the world could be attacked with advantage, the world itself had to be raised to a higher spiritual level. This was the first task which Christianity had to undertake; and for its accomplishment Paul was fitted as well by his limitations as by that transcendent spiritual vision to which his limitations were partly due.

Paul now turns to questions connected with the marriage of virgins, which had doubtless been laid before him in the Corinthian letter (vii., 25-40).

The general sense of the reply is sufficiently clear; but there are a few points of which we should take special note. Paul, having no commandment on the subject, gives his own opinion. This he has formed reverently and faithfully, with a sole view to the good of his readers, and he believes it to be in accordance with the Spirit of God. Thus humble and gentle is an Apostle, when dealing with difficult questions, of which different views might be taken. His general principle is that change of condition is undesirable owing to the distress which was already heralding the close of the present order of the world: the time was so short that all ordinary interests sank into insignificance, and it was better that men should be free from care. But he who felt unable or unwilling to act on this principle did not sin. He treats the marriage of a virgin daughter as entirely at the discretion of her father. Finally, he concedes, in opposition to his own personal preference, that a widow is quite free to marry whom she will, provided only it be within the Christian fold.

The fourth section of the Epistle deals with another question which had arisen at Corinth: What was the proper line of conduct to be observed in connection with the prevailing idolatry? (viii., 1-xi., 1).

A Christian was bound, as a matter of course, to abstain from the worship of idols; but was he to go farther and carefully avoid the use of sacrificial meat—that is, the portion of the sacrifice which was left over for a feast in a temple or at home, or even for sale in the market? Meat could not be really defiled by being offered in sacrifice, and scrupulosity might deprive a Christian of much innocent enjoyment, besides making him appear needlessly hostile to the amenities of social life. This subject is now discussed.

Paul first lays down the true principle of action (viii., 1-13).

In the light of abstract truth the Christian need have no scruple ; but some, through long association with idolatry, were unable to shake off their scruples, and so by eating wounded their consciences. Hence the principle of love came in ; and it was better to abstain than to tempt a man to do what he, though erroneously, considered to be wrong. By so tempting him you inflict moral ruin upon him, and in thus violating love you yourself sin against Christ.

We know that we all have knowledge (viii., 1), said with a slight touch of irony, perhaps quoting the Corinthians' letter ; for in *v.* 7 the proposition is expressly denied.

The same is known of him (viii., 3).—Compare Gal. iv., 9, and Matt. vii., 23. It is a higher thing to be recognised by God as His than to have that loveless knowledge which only ministers to our self-conceit. It is implied that this love contains within it the true principle of practical judgment.

No idol (viii., 4).—Idol must be used technically, to denote an image which actually represented and enshrined a god. This is shown by the antithesis, "There is no God but one."

Called gods, whether in heaven or on earth (viii., 5), referring to the higher Olympian deities, and the inferior gods of grove and stream and home. Their reality seems to be asserted, and only their godhead denied. In x., 20, they are treated as demons. It is possible, however, that the word "god," in a good sense, has a more extended meaning, as it has in John x., 34, 35.[1]

[1] According to Origen, the Father alone is αὐτόθεος, and consequently πᾶν δὲ τὸ παρὰ τὸ αὐτόθεος μετοχῇ τῆς ἐκείνου θεότητος

Lords many (viii., 5).—Clement of Alexandria quotes from an apocryphal book of Zephaniah, "The spirit took me up, and brought me to the fifth heaven, and I saw angels called lords."[1]

To us there is one God, the Father (viii., 6).—This verse, at first sight, seems to contain as plain a statement as it is possible for language to convey that the Father alone is God, and that Jesus Christ is not God. But as such a statement must be got rid of at all costs, it is said that, as the Father may be Lord, so Jesus Christ may be God. This is highly ingenious; but unless the terms here are mutually exclusive, the passage becomes quite incoherent, as is evident if we change "Lord" into "God." "Lord" is a general term, and is applied to the owner of slaves, as in Eph. vi., 5, 9, or to the heir of a property, as in Gal. iv., 1; but Paul obviously employs the word here in a sense not applicable to these; and so, though the word may be applied to God, the terms here are not convertible. The fact is, if we omit the Pastoral Epistles, there is no certain instance in which the term "Lord" is applied to God in the Pauline letters except in quotations from the Old Testament and passages immediately governed by these quotations. Out of 238 instances in which the word may refer to Christ as many as 173 admit of no doubt, and a great majority of the remainder admit of hardly any doubt; so that it is abundantly proved to be Paul's distinctive title for Jesus Christ. On the other hand, the term "God" is used 541 times (of which 366 are in the great Epistles),[2] and unless Rom. ix., 5, be an excep-

---

θεοποιούμενον οὐχ ὁ θεὸς ἀλλὰ θεός. And again, οἱ δὲ κατ' ἐκεῖνον μορφούμενοι θεοί, ὡς εἰκόνες πρωτοτύπου. *Com. in Joan.*, tom. ii., 2, pp. 92 *sq.* (Lom.).

[1] *Strom.*, v., 11, p. 692 (Potter). I owe the reference to Rev. R. H. Charles, *The Book of the Secrets of Enoch*, p. xliii.

[2] The precise numbers may be a little uncertain, owing to differences of reading in certain passages.

tion, it is never applied to Christ. These facts surely speak for themselves. We must also observe that in this declaration of Christian doctrine there is no mention of the Holy Spirit.

All things (viii., 6).—From one point of view it might seem simplest to understand these words as meaning "the universe"; and then it would follow that Paul believed that Jesus Christ was the agent through whom the universe was created. I am anxious not to explain away anything that the Apostle says; but I cannot help doubting whether this is what he meant. The extent of "all things" is frequently limited by the connection. For instance, when it is said that God will freely give us "all things" (Rom. viii., 32), we must understand all things needful to complete our salvation. In the present Epistle, when it is written that "all things are lawful" (vi., 12, x. 23), all things morally indifferent must be intended; and when Paul says he became all things to all men (ix., 22), he does not mean that he ever became a drunkard or a liar. So when he says "all things are of God" (2 Cor. v., 18), although the proposition would be true in its universal sense, I think he refers only to the things of which he has been speaking. For other examples the reader may turn to 1 Cor. xii., 6; 2 Cor. iv., 15; Gal. iv., 1; Philip. iv., 13, 18; Col. iii., 8 (where the translators have inserted "these"); 1 John ii., 20. There are two reasons for limiting the phrase in the present passage. First, the repetition of "us" and "we" seems to require something specially relating to us, and leading naturally to the personal reference. Now the thought is concerned with the objects of religious veneration, so that it is quite in place to say,—as for us Christians, all our religious blessings flow forth from the Father alone, and in turn we are gathered into Him as the sole object of our worship; and all these blessings have come to us through Jesus Christ, through whom also we have been brought

home to God. This gives a coherent sense which is quite
agreeable to the context. Secondly, Paul does not say "the
Son of God" or "the second person of the Trinity," but
"Jesus Christ," and, whatever may be our doctrine, Jesus
Christ is the historic person who taught in Palestine. The
second person of the Trinity was not Jesus Christ prior to
the incarnation, and, though the term is sometimes loosely
carried back, as if the incarnation had taken place from
eternity, it does not seem likely that Paul would have committed such an error of statement. The explanation which
we have suggested suits the historic person, and relieves us
at the same time from the bathos of saying that "we" are
through him, after saying that the universe is through him.

Be emboldened to eat (viii., 10) ; literally, "be edified unto
eating." The word is the same as in *v.* 1, and has an ex-
quisite irony: that is your way of edifying, lifting a man
into a region of knowledge whither his conscience will not
suffer him to go.

The brother for whose sake Christ died (viii., 11).—Compare
Rom. xiv., 15. The man whom you thus ruin is a brother;
yet you will not forego a pleasant dinner for his sake, though
Christ died for him. Christ's death presents the standard
of Christian love, so that in sinning against the brethren we
sin against him.

**Paul now turns aside from the main subject in order to enforce
his advice by appealing to his own example (ix., 1-27).**

The connection of thought is not very obvious, and in the
usual interpretation it is so entirely wanting as to give the
impression that the passage must have been misplaced. The
subject of idolatry is resumed at x., 14 ; and if our text has
been correctly preserved, the Apostle must have had this in
his mind all through, although some other topics, appropriately introduced, may be worked out a little more fully
than their immediate bearing demands. The key to the

connection must be found in the explanation of the words "them that examine me" (*v.* 3). It is generally assumed that this refers to Judaisers, who disputed Paul's right to call himself an Apostle, and thus the whole passage becomes utterly irrelevant. If we had the Corinthians' letter before us, we should doubtless see that the "examination" had nothing to do with Judaisers, but related to the subject in hand. I suppose that Paul had already given general instructions about idolatrous feasts, but that some at Corinth were not satisfied, and pointed out that to them the idol was nothing, so that they could join in the feasts without offence; and they may have put it to him that he was imposing on others a burden that did not affect himself. He, as a Jew, had no temptation in regard to idolatry; but they were surrounded by unbelieving relatives and friends, and did not feel called upon to forego what to them was innocent social enjoyment because some of the brethren were stupid and took offence. Paul's reply is, in effect,—Well, am I not free from the control of others? Have I not the full rights of an Apostle, as much as Peter himself? But I do not avail myself of these rights; I practise the severest self-denial, and make every concession I can to others, that I may win them to the Gospel. Accordingly, though your particular temptations do not affect me, I am only applying to you the same rule as I habitually apply to myself.

Have I not seen Jesus? (**ix.**, **1**); referring to the vision at his conversion, when he was called to be an Apostle. The "seeing" is evidently regarded by Paul as objective, and as something quite different from a mere internal vision. It is clear that nothing in his experience seemed to him more certain.

The seal of my Apostleship (**ix.**, **2**).—The seal is the final authentication. The vision was the source of Paul's faith; the results of his work were the proof to others.

The brethren of the Lord (**ix.**, **5**).—On this subject a long dissertation might be written. Here I can only express my own conclusion that the "brothers" were the real brothers of Jesus, that they were not included among the twelve Apostles, and that they did not become believers till after the resurrection. They must by this time have been known as workers in the Church.

Barnabas (**ix., 6**).—We are not told that he had any connection with Corinth. Still it is assumed that his name will be known, and we thus gain a hint that the affairs of the Church were spoken about among the brethren. It has been suggested that Paul and Barnabas, on the first mission, may have agreed together that they would work for their living.

After the manner of men (**ix., 8**); that is, this is not a mere matter of human opinion, but is supported by the authority of the Law.

Thou shalt not muzzle the ox (**ix., 9**).—This is quoted from Deut. xxv., 4. The allegorical interpretation which Paul gives is quite in accordance with the exegetical rules of the time; but from our modern point of view it is impossible to believe that this is what the legislator really meant. The *principle* of the commandment, however, is retained in the application.

So did the Lord ordain (**ix., 14**); another reference to an express commandment of Christ's, which has been preserved in Matt. x., 10, Luke x., 7.

I write not these things that it may be so done in my case (**ix., 15**): a natural digression from the main point, to guard against all misunderstanding.

I have nothing to glory of (**ix., 16**).—His self-denial could be shown only in relinquishing his just rights; for in simply preaching the Gospel he was not a free agent. If he was doing so of his own will, it must be for a reward, and woe to him if he missed it; if not of his own will, he was fulfilling a trust, and woe to him if he proved unfaithful. No doubt he regarded the latter member of the alternative as the real state of the case. The only reward, then, which he could claim was the privilege of having none, and of renouncing his apostolic privileges for the sake of the Gospel.

Though I was free from all men, I brought myself under bondage to all (**ix., 19**).—He was "free" (as in *v.* 1) so far as human claims were concerned; his adaptation of himself to others was quite voluntary. The whole question relates to things morally indifferent; where principle was involved we know that Paul could stand alone.

The law (**ix., 20**).—There is no article in the Greek, which implies that, though the Law of Moses is intended, it is regarded, not simply as an existing institution, but in its quality of law. This may be added to the reference to the "Jews" because it includes proselytes, and excludes Paul.

Under law to Christ (**ix., 21**).—Release from the law was not the abrogation of law; rather was it the realisation of law in its highest sense.

The weak (**ix., 22**), carrying back our thoughts to viii., 11; I never use my stronger convictions so as to injure a weak brother.

Know ye not (**ix., 24**).—He now appeals to his readers by reminding them of their own Isthmian games. For the sake of winning the prize men would undergo months of severe training, involving, among other things, restrictions in diet. How much easier it was, for the sake of an unfading wreath, to refrain from the indulgence of sacrificial feasts. If Paul was not personally concerned with this immediate question, nevertheless he kept his body in subjection. In running he kept the goal clearly in view; in boxing he did not strike the air. He lived as one who knew that he might fail of a great prize, always on the alert, always repressing those desires that might interfere with his purpose. That was the spirit which he wished to see in his readers; and that would guide them right in dealing with weak brethren.

Examples are here introduced from the Old Testament, to show how men who had received a spiritual baptism and spiritual food might nevertheless fall (x., 1-13).

The argument is thus carried a step farther, and the Corinthians are virtually advised to abstain from idolatrous feasts, not only on account of weak brethren, but for their own sake.

Our fathers (**x.**, 1).—Paul probably uses this expression here from his own point of view, and not with the thought (found elsewhere) of including his readers in the spiritual Israel.

Unto Moses (**x.**, 2); properly, "into Moses," as in Gal. iii., 27, "baptised into Christ." This proves that Paul did not suppose that baptism into a person involved belief in that person's deity. The baptism is necessarily figurative. The whole passage is an example of allegorical interpretation.

The same spiritual meat, . . . the same spiritual drink (**x.**, 3, 4).—The meat and drink are called spiritual on account of their supernatural character, and to establish an analogy with the bread and wine of the Lord's Supper, which are brought into the argument in the next paragraph.

The rock was Christ (**x.**, 4).—In the mention of a rock following the Israelites there may be a reference to a rabbinical tradition. The statement that this rock was Christ seems to me obviously figurative or allegorical; for of course a rock was not really Christ. But it is said that in this case the words would be "the rock *is* Christ." The past tense, however, is required by the context, which throughout throws the allegorical interpretation into the form of history. The cloud and the sea represented the waters of baptism; the manna and the water from the rock represented spiritual nourishment; and so the rock itself represented Christ. It would be very unsafe to assert that Paul here teaches the intervention of Christ in ancient history,—an idea which occurs nowhere else in his writings.

With most of them (**x.**, 5).—To see the full force of this statement we must notice the emphatically repeated "all" in the previous verses: they "all" had every spiritual advantage, and nevertheless most of them fell into sin, and were justly overthrown. The conclusion follows in v. 12: those who think they stand may fall.

Should not lust after evil things (**x., 6**).—This and the following warnings refer to the reluctance of some of the Christians to renounce the pleasures connected with idolatry.

Rose up to play (**x., 7**).—The passage is from Ex. xxxii., 6, and refers to a feast and dance in honour of the golden calf.

Three and twenty thousand (**x., 8**).—The real number was twenty-four thousand (Num. xxv., 9). The change is probably due to faulty recollection.

The Lord (**x., 9**); here probably God, on account of the connection with the Old Testament.

Temptation (**x., 13**), referring to the temptation to join in idolatrous practices. That was not more than a man ought to be able to resist. Such trials of our firmness came from God; and He knows what amount of trial is good for us, and always leaves open to us the way to victory.

From the foregoing Paul deduces the urgent advice to avoid idolatry, and then strengthens his position by showing the complete incompatibility between the special Christian festival and idolatrous feasts (x., 14-22).

Food and drink are nothing in themselves, but both in true and in false religions a religious significance is attached to them, and wherever this is the case we cannot treat them as indifferent. The passage has some difficult points; but the general sense is clear. We may reserve for the next chapter the question of the nature of the Lord's Supper.

The cup of blessing (**x., 16**); that is, the cup over which a blessing is pronounced. This name was given to one of the cups at the feast of the Passover. "Which we bless" might seem tautological; but it is necessary for the argument to point out that all were concerned in and gave their assent to this solemn act.

One body (**x., 17**).—Not only did the broken bread symbolise the body broken on the cross; but the single loaf, made up of scattered grains of wheat, represented the one body of believers who were scattered in many places. This idea is best brought out by the marginal translation; and it is appropriate here because it indicates the obligation of each individual to a corporate brotherhood. Christians could not act as though each man's belief and practice were his own private affair.

Israel after the flesh (**x., 18**); that is, the historic people, distinguished, by implication, from the spiritual Israel (see Gal. vi., 16).

Communion with the altar (**x., 18**).—Eating of sacrifices was not merely partaking of food, but sharing in everything that the altar signified.

That a thing sacrificed to idols is anything (**x., 19**).—This might seem to follow from what has just been said. But it is not so. The meat in itself is nothing, and can do neither harm nor good; and an idol is simply a body of wood or stone. But the religious associations give them a power and meaning which they have not in themselves.

They sacrifice to devils (**x., 20**).—It was the common belief of the early Christians that the gods of the heathen were evil spirits, and Paul here distinctly sanctions this belief. The statement is not inconsistent with the previous verse, or with viii., 4; for these spirits were not gods, and the idols had none of the power ascribed to them. The old belief in demons has passed away from most cultivated men, and I think even the belief of those who consider themselves bound by the letter of Scripture is of rather an antiquarian kind.

Do we provoke the Lord to jealousy? (**x., 22**).—We seem to do so by this divided allegiance. We cannot sanction idolatry and serve Christ at the same time.

The subject is concluded by the introduction of some special rules, succeeded by a final exhortation (x., 23-xi., 1).

All things are lawful; but all things are not expedient (**x., 23**).—The same statement occurs in vi., 12, so that it seems to have fixed itself in Paul's mind as a sort of maxim about things indifferent. Regard must be paid to utility and edification as well as to abstract right. We must think of our neighbours as well as ourselves.

Asking no question for conscience sake (**x., 25**): either, asking no question dictated by conscientious scruples; or, better, refraining from questions, so as not to disturb your conscience by associating the meat with sacrifice. The case seems to be supposed of a man whose judgment is convinced, but who cannot quite get rid of old associations.

The earth is the Lord's (**x., 26**).—The words are from Psalm xxiv., 1. Everything, whether offered to an idol or not, is God's, and therefore pure.

Biddeth you to a feast (**x., 27**); clearly a private one, for at a sacrificial feast the origin of the meat would be known. This is therefore not opposed to viii., 10.

If any man say unto you (**x., 28**).—It is not necessary to limit this reference. If the man was a heathen, the Christian ought to show that he would have nothing to do with idolatry, and so bear his testimony for the good of his unbelieving friend; if the man was a weak believer, then he who was strong in faith ought not to offend, and tempt into violating his conscience, one whose only fault was to be too scrupulous. The allusion to conscience, however, is more suitable in the latter case.

Why is my liberty judged by another conscience? (**x., 29**).— The connection is by no means clear. The words can hardly mean, do not let me act in such a way as to expose my liberty to another's judgment, as I should do if I ate before a weak brother; for in the next verse it is clearly assumed that he does eat. We may perhaps suppose that Paul is referring to the main thesis laid down in 25-27, 28, 29ᵃ being a parenthetical qualification. The meaning is then clear: I must follow my own conscience (except when by so doing I should actually injure another), and no one has a right to blame my conduct in these outward things, so long as I do all to the glory of God. It is thought that Paul's advice here is inconsistent with the decree in Acts xv. Strictly, it is so, and the Apostle nowhere mentions that decree. Still he may have thought it was sufficiently fulfilled by acting on the principle, do not knowingly eat sacrificial meat, but you need not take any pains to know.

I also please all men (**x., 33**), as was fully illustrated in ix. These words confirm the connection in the argument which we assigned to that chapter.

From the subject of idolatry we turn, in the next section, to that of certain disorders which had arisen in the meetings of the church (xi., 2-34).

Paul addresses himself first to the conduct of women (xi., 2-16).

This passage contains the strangest arguments in the Epistle; and it almost appears from *v.* 16 as if Paul himself did not find them altogether convincing, and had to appeal to general practice, and from 11, 12 as if he felt that they might be regarded as inconsistent with his own principles (Gal. iii., 28). But, as he said, "all things are not expedient"; and breaches of social propriety may indicate a failure of moral perception. A glaring violation of usage might have injured the Christian cause.

The traditions (**xi., 2**), not in the modern sense of things handed down through successive generations, but of doctrines delivered by the teachers to the disciples. This indicates an accepted body of teaching.

The head of every man is Christ (**xi., 3**)—This verse contains the one principle in the passage which is permanently regulative. There is a proper subordination in the arrangements of society; and this, when duly recognised, creates that mutual reverence which supplies the moral basis for the observance of social etiquette. Christ was acknowledged by every Christian to be the head of the race; but Paul is not satisfied till he reaches the highest of all: the head of Christ is God, and from Him flow the various orders and relations of human life. This thought is repeated in *v*. 12.

Every woman praying or prophesying (**xi., 5**).—This clearly recognises a public place for women in the services of the Church; for prophesying can only refer to the public utterance of inspired speech. From the connection it seems probable that the "praying" also refers to a public leading of the prayer. Such a practice, however, did not continue in the Church.

The image and glory of God (**xi., 7**).—This statement and the following argument are founded on the narrative of the creation in Genesis. Gen. i., 27, suggests a different view; but this was harmonised with the narrative of ii., 21 *sqq*. Paul may possibly have understood the earlier passage as referring to the archetypal man.

Because of the angels (**xi., 10**).—This is most probably to be explained by the belief that good angels were invisibly present in the services of the Church. Some think bad angels are meant, and that there is an allusion to Gen. vi., 2. Usage favours the former view, "the angels" (without qualification) always standing for good angels. The veil was a mark of respect to them. With the other interpretation, it was a defence against their wiles.

Paul has now to turn to a much more serious subject, and reprove an almost incredible irreverence and laxity in connection with the Lord's Supper (xi., 17-34).

From this passage we learn incidentally several interesting particulars. The disciples already met together in some appropriate building, which is distinguished from the private "houses." Like many Gentile societies, they had a common meal in token of their brotherhood, and of this the Lord's Supper still formed a part. Apparently they followed a practice which was not unusual, of bringing their own provisions. These ought to have been placed in a common stock before the supper began, so that all might share alike; but instead of that each took his supper as he arrived, so that the poor did not get anything to satisfy their hunger, while others were so self-indulgent as to drink to excess. The meeting was held in the evening, but the day is not specified. According to our earliest accounts it was Sunday. The breaking of bread in memory of Christ's death apparently took place during the meal, whereas the cup was handed round "after supper." It is remarkable that the words of institution are reported with considerable differences, the most important being that for the words "This is my blood of the covenant," of Matthew and Mark, Paul substitutes, "This cup is the new covenant in my blood." This shows that more value was attached to the general sentiment than to the precise phrases, and that the reports furnish a very insecure basis on which to erect a dogma.

I praise you not (**xi., 17**), in evident contrast with "I praise you" of *v.* 2. He praises them before blaming them, and reserves his more severe censures till he has disposed of lighter matters.

In the church (**xi., 18**); referring, not to the building, but to the assembly, which the word properly signifies.

Divisions (**xi., 18**).—The context suggests that these were class divisions, or at least unfriendly separations, which turned the Lord's Supper, with its brotherly union, into each man's private supper. The word "heresies," in the next verse, only varies the expression; for there is nothing to suggest its later sense of doctrinal error. The statement that there must be heresies in order to show who are approved (by their not taking part in them) must, I think, be ironical. The words are, however, also explained as a serious statement: divisions must result in parties, it being the Divine intention thus to manifest the approved.

That have not (**xi., 22**); not, that have not houses, but simply those that have no possessions, the poor.

I received of the Lord (**xi., 23**).—The question is raised whether Paul refers to an immediate communication made to himself by Christ, or to something transmitted to him through others. The preposition translated "of" does not determine this question. In favour of a direct revelation we may notice the emphatic "I" (as it is in the Greek) at the beginning of the sentence,—I, as distinguished from others, learned this from the Lord. The emphasis, however, may be due partly to the contrast with the following "you," and partly to the previous context,—I cannot praise you, for *I* learned a very different lesson. It is a more weighty consideration that, if the words refer to the whole narrative, we should expect "in relation to the Lord" instead of "from the Lord." I think it is possible, however, that Paul refers in the first instance only to the words of institution, and then changing his momentary purpose (as he often does) relates the connected facts for the sake of completeness. What he really wanted to bring out was that the words which separated the bread and wine from common food proceeded from the Lord himself. If this suggestion be tenable, it will remove all difficulty from the preposition; for, to this day, we might say "We received from the Lord the commandment to love one another," or, "We received from the Lord the saying, this is my body."[1] Against understanding the words as descriptive of a direct revelation we may plead not only the improbability of such a supernatural communication of matters of fact which could be easily learned, but that Paul himself

---

[1] There is a good example of the Greek use in Origen, *Cont. Cels.*, iv., 44, where, referring to Paul, he says οὐχ ἡμεῖς διδάσκομεν, ἀλλ' ἄνωθεν ἀπὸ σοφῶν παρειλήφαμεν.

never claims such miraculous knowledge; and, further, that, if he had intended this, he would have laid more stress upon it. My own judgment inclines against the view that he referred to a revelation.

This is my body (**xi., 24**).—On these words the doctrine of transubstantiation has been founded, though it seems impossible that the Apostles, without further explanation, can have believed that the bread in Christ's own hand was also the body which was there before their eyes; and even if that particular bread was his body, it would not follow that any other bread would be so. The meal had been symbolical of the first Passover at the time of the Exodus, and now its significance was changed. The word "is," therefore, is quite appropriate, being used as it is in the explanation of a parable, for instance, "The seed is the word of God" (Luke viii., 11). The votaries of literalism ought to believe that Jesus was really a paschal sheep (1 Cor. v., 7).

Ye proclaim (**xi., 26**).—The term seems to imply the use of certain words, but of what precise nature we do not know.

Unworthily (**xi., 27**).—The whole context shows that the reference is not to the general character of the recipient, but to the want of reverence in the manner of celebration.

Shall be guilty of the body and the blood of the Lord (**xi., 27**); that is, shall be guilty of treating them with disrespect. For he who treats a symbol of sacred things profanely profanes the thing symbolized. No one can treat the relic of a beloved friend as if it were only so much common matter; but to the tender spirit it becomes spiritual. So, on every theory, the bread and wine of the Lord's Supper are laden with hallowed associations, and in them the reverent heart of discipleship "discerns" far more than mere physical food and drink. A very moderate amount of "proving" oneself would render impossible such irreverence as was displayed at Corinth.

Many among you are weak (**xi., 30**).—The fact of sickness and death among the Corinthians is referred to as a "judgment."

Wait one for another (**xi., 33**), said in relation to *v.* 21. They should wait, so as to make the meal really one of brotherly communion; and if anyone was so hungry as to require a hearty meal, he should satisfy his needs at home.

The subject once more changes, and, in this sixth section, probably in reply to a question addressed to him from Corinth, Paul deals at considerable length with the subject of spiritual gifts (xii.-xiv.).

First, the general principle is laid down (xii., 1-3).

If we are to judge from the treatment, some of the Corinthians supposed that the manifestations of the Spirit must be of an exceptional and startling kind, and were inclined to attach most importance to those that were of least value. Paul, therefore, begins by pointing out that the grand distinction was between the idolater and the believer, and that no one could make the Christian confession, "Jesus is Lord," except under the influence of the Holy Spirit. We might apply this to differences of opinion among those who confess the same Lord, and then exalt themselves one against another.

"The Spirit of God," " the Holy Spirit" (**xii., 3**).—These expressions are clearly synonymous, and we must therefore interpret the latter by the former. As the spirit of a man does not denote either a distinct person from the man or a second or third person within him, so "the Spirit of God" suggests, not a distinct person, but rather that which is characteristic of the Divine personality, the diffused energy of the Divine life breathed into the hearts of men. It is therefore truly Divine, and the words may be used to denote God Himself, except that they always refer to Him only as operating within the soul of man. This may explain the distinct personal language of *v.* 11, the Spirit carrying with it and executing the Divine will, and so having the

same function as is ascribed to God in *v.* 6. Compare also *v.* 18.

Having laid down the general principle, Paul proceeds to show that the same heavenly Spirit may manifest itself through a great variety of forms (xii., 4-30).

There are diversities of gifts, but the same Spirit (**xii., 4**).—In this passage Paul enumerates the three great objects of Christian faith, but, as usual, with only a religious aim, and without any attempt at philosophical definition. The Spirit and the Lord are both alike distinguished from God, although the Spirit is, as we have seen, the Spirit of God. We learn, however, from *v.* 8, that it is distinct in this sense, that it is regarded as the power "through" which God bestows His gifts. The Apostle begins with the Spirit, perhaps partly for the sake of the climax, but chiefly, I think, because it is the Spirit that enters immediately into human experience, and because the question related to spiritual gifts. The same Divine energy, the same holy character, may manifest itself through every variety of endowment.

Ministrations (**xii., 5**), or kinds of service, are properly spoken of in connection with the Lord, or master. We may serve the same master in different ways.

To profit withal (**xii., 7**); that is, with a view to what is "expedient" (the same word as in vi., 12, and x., 23) and edifying for the community.

The word of wisdom, etc. (**xii., 8-10**).—It is needless to seek for any careful classification of the gifts here enumerated, for the object is simply to give examples of their variety. For "wisdom" see ii., 6 *sqq.* "The word of knowledge" may be more purely intellectual. I see no reason for taking "faith" in any but the ordinary sense; for though all Christians must have faith, it is equally true that all must have some wisdom and knowledge, but in certain persons these attain the rank of special and distinguishing gifts. What "miracles" or powers different from the gifts of healing are intended it is impossible to say. "Discernings of spirits" may refer to the sure perception whether a man was moved by a genuine inspiration or not. False prophets were not unknown in the Church. (See Matt. vii., 15, 1 John iv., 1; also "The Teaching of the Twelve Apostles," xi., 3-12). The speaking with tongues is considered in xiv.

The principle thus laid down is next illustrated by an elaborate comparison of the Church to the body with its many members (**xii., 12-30**). The passage presents a strikingly complete view of the society as an organism, in distinction from a mere aggregate of individuals. For a similar idea in ancient literature reference is justly made to the speech which Menenius Agrippa addressed to the Roman plebs,[1] and to the argument in Plato's *Republic* that the whole body feels the pain of a part.[2]

So also is Christ (**xii., 12**).—At first sight it would seem as though "Christ" stood here for the whole Christian body; but this would be inconsistent with *v.* 27, and it is more likely that Christ is regarded as the animating spirit to whom the body and its members belonged. Compare xv., 45, and 2 Cor. iii., 17.

Were all made to drink of one Spirit (**xii., 13**).—This can hardly refer to the Lord's Supper, owing to the past tense. The comparison of drinking is added to that of baptising to indicate more distinctly that the Spirit entered into vital union with the Christian body.

I am not of the body (**xii., 15, 16**); literally "out of," that is, derived from and dependent on the body, and therefore having duties towards it.

Which seem to be more feeble (**xii., 22**).—This cannot refer to the hands and feet, as the context suggests; for no one could suppose these to be superfluous, or particularly feeble.

---

[1] Livy, ii., 32.   [2] V. 10, p. 462, C.D.

The allusion must be, in a general way, to organs of which the activity is not very obvious, and which, on a superficial view, seem to demand more service than they render.

Upon these we bestow more abundant honour (xii. 23).—It would be better to translate, "We array these in more abundant honour," for then it would be obvious, as it is in the Greek, that the allusion is to clothes and ornaments. The word is the same as in Matt. xxvii., 28, they "put on him a scarlet robe."

Giving more abundant honour (xii., 24).—The reference must still be to clothes, which we use through a God-given instinct.

In the church (xii., 28).—The word is probably used here in its universal sense; for what is said cannot be limited to the Corinthians. Compare xv., 9, Gal. i., 13, Phil. iii., 6.

First apostles (xii., 28).—The first three members of the list are persons who probably exercised continuous functions; and then the functions themselves are introduced instead of the persons exercising them, perhaps because they were of a more fitful character, and not permanently attached to particular people.

Before speaking fully of the gift of tongues, Paul, in order to indicate the right point of view, introduces the praise of love as that without which all gifts are worthless (xii., 31–xiii., 13).

In spiritual as in physical things men are too apt to prefer fireworks to the everlasting stars, and to see God in what is exceptional and startling, rather than in the calm and abiding presence of His eternal Spirit. This is a great danger in times of religious excitement; and nothing shows the grandeur of Paul's mind more clearly than the fact that, while he had a wonderful range of gifts, and spake with tongues more than they all (xiv., 18), he used them only to minister to what was higher and more enduring, and clearly perceived that the life of Christ within the heart, which belonged to every disciple, was the purest gift of the Spirit.

The subject is introduced by a verse which forms a transition from the previous discussion, and may, therefore, be regarded either as the close of the last paragraph, or as the beginning of the new one (**xii., 31**). The admonition implies that the reception of gifts is in part dependent on ourselves. We cannot create any gift, but we may seek for it; and our selfish glorying in lower gifts may unfit us for the higher. The more excellent way of love is open to all, and fits us for whatever it may please God to bestow.

The Apostle begins by declaring that without love all gifts are worthless (**xiii., 1–3**). Men are prone to think that endowment may be a substitute for character. But without love the gift of tongues, of which the Corinthians were so proud, became an unmeaning noise; and equally valueless, at least to the man himself, were higher gifts of inspired speech, of intellectual insight, even of faith before which all obstacles melted away. The extremest acts of self-denial, in property or person, might be purely external, and only the inward spirit of love could profit.

The next few verses describe the characteristics of love (**xiii., 4–7**). These clearly relate to the habitual temper of the mind, and might be absent, though the gifts previously mentioned were present. The meaning of most of the statements is sufficiently obvious. "Rejoiceth not in unrighteousness" is opposed to that malicious self-flattery which takes pleasure in the faults of others. "Truth" is personified, and represented as rejoicing, while love shares in its joy. If this is properly antithetical to the previous clause, the reference must be to the pleasure which truth takes in finding out the righteousness of another. The word "all," as usual, must be limited by the general sense of the passage. Love does not believe all things mean and odious, or hope for the destruction of its enemies. It believes all that ought to be believed, takes a high and generous view of men's conduct, and always hopes for the best.

Lastly, love is eternal, while all gifts are partial and transitory (**xiii., 8-13**). It is highly remarkable that Paul, far from asserting that he has an infallible and final revelation, distinctly declares that knowledge (of the Divine mysteries, see *v.* 2) and even prophecy are only in part, and that that which is perfect is yet to come. He illustrates the growth of spiritual insight by the passage from childhood to manhood, and the vagueness of its perception by the dim images in a metallic mirror.[1] We see the reflection of the Divine form, the glory of God in the face of Christ (2 Cor. iv., 6), but cannot yet look upon Him with direct gaze, and know Him as He knows us. Knowledge must grow and thought must change in spite of the unbelief of bigots; but the spirit of Christianity abides,—faith in God, hope of an immortal sonship, love which is the essence of God. And because love is His essence, it is greater than faith and hope, for these belong only to dependent creatures, whereas love occupies the throne of the universe, and, when it reigns in our hearts, God Himself abides in us, and we in Him.

Having laid down his grand corrective principle, Paul is prepared to deal more particularly with the gift of tongues, which was too highly valued and unwisely exercised at Corinth (xiv., 1-25).

The exalted and powerful emotions of the first Christians gave rise to some strange manifestations, which did not belong to the permanent life of the Church, but on account of their singularity were taken by inferior minds as the most certain tokens of the Holy Spirit. It is apparent from this chapter that the gift of tongues was not the power of speaking foreign languages, of which there is no trace, and which would have been perfectly useless in the circumstances, but an ecstatic utterance, in which the control of the understanding was suspended, and the person thus affected was borne away upon a flood of religious feeling. Why this utterance

---

[1] It was a saying among the Jews that Moses saw in a clear mirror, but all the prophets in a dark one (Weber, *Jüdische Theologie*, p. 82).

was called speaking with a tongue, or with tongues, is doubtful. It may have been because the sounds were taken to be a sort of heavenly *language*, or because the tongue was the organ which the Spirit used for its own purposes. The plural, the kinds of tongues, may refer to various modes of expression, adapted to praying, singing, blessing, giving thanks (see *vv.* 14-17). With this gift, that of prophecy, which was also an inspired utterance, is naturally compared. The speaker with tongues could so far control himself as not to give way to the initial impulse (*v.* 28); but as soon as he began to speak, his own volition apparently vanished. The prophets, on the other hand, retained their self-control throughout (*vv.* 29-33); their understanding rather than their tongue was the seat of inspiration; and they spoke intelligible language, which tended to edify, to exhort, to console (*v.* 3).

After a momentary exhortation to follow the more excellent way of love, the discussion begins (**xiv., 1**) by resuming the advice of xii., 31, descending, however, from the general to the particular, for prophecy is selected as the greater gift, which ought to be preferred to speaking with tongues. The first reason alleged is that the latter was not understood, and therefore did not conduce to the edification of the Church (**xiv., 2-19**).

Understandeth (**xiv., 2**).—The Greek is "hears"; but as the sequel shows that there were audible sounds, the meaning must be that no one hears intelligible words. Consequently, the following clause cannot mean that the man speaks within himself, and not vocally, but that in a state of inspiration he speaks things which are hidden from the by-standers.

Except he interpret (**xiv., 5**).—It is evident from this and *v.* 13 that the person affected sometimes had a distinct meaning, which, when the emotion was past, he was able to explain; and sometimes a sympathetic listener was able to translate the ecstatic sounds into intelligible speech (*vv.* 27, 28).

If I come (**xiv., 6**).—The "I" has no emphasis in the Greek, and accordingly the first person is used here simply as a representative example.

Unless I speak (**xiv., 6**).—The four modes of speech cannot refer to the interpretation of what was spoken with tongues. This verse must therefore be another way of indicating how unprofitable the gift of tongues was if it existed alone. It seems clear that four possible modes of intelligent speech are indicated, and we cannot legitimately say that prophesying was the way in which a revelation was declared, and teaching was the utterance of knowledge. Perhaps revelation and knowledge refer to spiritual and intellectual modes of insight in particular instances, while prophesying denotes prolonged and impressive exhortation, which might include the matter of a revelation, as we learn from *v.* 30, and teaching is the name for continuous instruction in the faith.

Barbarian (**xiv., 11**).—The word ought to be translated "foreigner," for barbarian with us signifies, not a man who speaks a foreign language, but one who is rude and fierce in manners.

Zealous of spiritual gifts (**xiv., 12**).—The Greek is "zealous of spirits," involving the notion that each gift had its own spirit. As Paul pronounced all the gifts to be manifestations of one Spirit, he may be speaking here with a slight irony from the point of view of the Corinthians. Or it is possible that as the one Logos, or Thought, was conceived as resolving itself into innumerable logoi, or thoughts, so Paul may have looked upon each gift as having its own spirit, though all were subsumed under the one universal Spirit of God.[1]

---

[1] Hermas speaks of various evil dispositions as "spirits," πνεύματα (*Mand.*, V. ii. 5 *sqq.*, IX. 11, X. i. 2, XI. 4), and says, πᾶν γὰρ πνεῦμα ἀπὸ θεοῦ δοθὲν . . . ἄνωθέν ἐστιν ἀπὸ τῆς δυνάμεως τοῦ θείου πνεύματος (*Mand.*, XI. 5).

Pray that he may interpret (**xiv., 13**).—The most obvious sense is, pray for the gift of interpretation, which did not always accompany the speaking with tongues (*v.* 28). It is objected to this that "pray in a tongue," in the next verse, must determine the meaning, and accordingly we must understand the phrase thus,—If a man speak in a tongue, let him do so in prayer. But "pray," in the following verse, is simply an example, suggested perhaps by the word just used; and the illustration surely implies that prayer was as little open to interpretation as other forms of the gift.

My spirit prayeth (**xiv., 14**); not the spirit by which I am inspired, but my spiritual as opposed to my intellectual faculty. Though spirit and understanding (or reason) may be used of the same element in our nature, they are not strictly synonymous, the former referring to the organ of our communion with God, the latter to our rational powers. In the case supposed there is a sense of religious satisfaction, which is a precious experience for the man himself, but there is no mental perception of truth which may be told to others, and so the understanding is fruitless for their edification.

The place of the unlearned (**xiv., 16**).—" Place " may be understood literally,—occupies the place reserved for the unlearned,—but may refer to condition,—is classed among the unlearned. The "unlearned" in *vv.* 23, 24, are coupled with the "unbelieving," and yet distinguished from them. They seem to be people who may stray into the Christian assembly, and so far participate in its services as to say " amen " after prayer or thanksgiving, but are not yet enrolled among the believers.

A second reason for preferring prophecy was that the speaking with tongues was not profitable to unbelievers (**xiv., 20-25**).

Be not children in mind (**xiv., 20**).—This address is sometimes taken as the closing of the preceding paragraph; but the appeal, "brethren," points rather to a new line of thought. The connection may be thus indicated: you cannot influence the outside world by unintelligible marvels, but by manliness of understanding and guilelessness of heart.

In the law (**xiv., 21**), here used in its widest sense to mean the Old Testament. The quotation is taken loosely from Isaiah xxviii., 11, 12, where the Prophet threatens the rulers that, as they will not listen to his precepts, they shall be obliged to hear the strange language of the Assyrians; but even then they will not hearken. Bearing this in mind, we may be able to follow the argument of the passage, which is by no means clear; for at first sight v. 22 seems to contradict 23 and 24. The words of the Prophet show that strange tongues were a sign that was intended for unbelievers; but it was fruitless then, and it is fruitless now, because unbelievers, when they hear you, will only think you are mad. But prophecy, which is intended for the edification of believers, may make a deep impression on the unbeliever, when he finds the secret sins and troubles of his own heart laid bare, and feels that he has been brought into the real presence of God.

The discussion of the gifts of tongues and of prophecy is closed with some practical rules to be observed in the meetings of the church (xiv., 26-33).

The general principle is that everything must tend to edification, and that for this purpose there must be a becoming order and quietness.

A psalm (**xiv., 26**), probably an original hymn. "A revelation," a spiritual communication on some particular point. The various members had their several gifts. We may infer that the meetings for worship were still quite informal and spontaneous, and that each contributed what he could to the religious benefit of others, sometimes with an eagerness which led to confusion, and defeated the end in view.

Let him speak to himself (**xiv., 28**); that is, at some other time when he is alone, for the speaking with tongues was loud, and the word for "speak" denotes vocal utterance.

The others (**xiv., 29**); the other prophets, who had the power of discerning the spirits of the prophets.

Let the first keep silence (**xiv., 30**); perhaps on receiving some sign that the other wished to speak, and therefore bringing his own address to a close.

Ye all (**xiv., 31**).—"All" must, as usual, be understood from the context. Here it must mean "all of you who have the gift of prophecy." In the second and third instances of its occurrence in the verse it naturally means all who are present.

The spirits of the prophets (**xiv., 32**): either the prophets' own spirits, the movements of which they can control, or the spirits by which they were inspired (see the note on *v.* 12).

As in all the churches of the saints (**xiv., 33**).—Opinion is divided as to the proper position of this clause, some making it end the previous paragraph, others placing it at the beginning of the new one. It seems to me rather an awkward introduction to a fresh subject, but a suitable appeal at the close of an argument. See the notes on the following verses.

A paragraph is now inserted directing women to be silent in the churches (xiv., 34-36).

It is difficult to avoid the suspicion that *vv.* 34 and 35 are an interpolation. In a few manuscripts they are found after *v.* 40; they completely interrupt the thread of the discussion, which is continuous if we omit them; and, above all, they seem clearly to contradict xi., 5, where the right of women to pray and prophesy is taken for granted. If the verses be retained, we may suppose that the "church" here is used in a limited sense, of the larger and more public meetings; but there is nothing in the context to indicate this. The prohibition seems borrowed from the synagogue, where women were not allowed to speak.

As also saith the law (**xiv., 34**), in Genesis iii., 16.

Was it from you that the word of God went forth? (**xiv., 36**).—An ironical question. By their conduct one might suppose that they were the regulative church of christendom. This fits on exactly to *v.* 33, where Paul appeals to the condition of other churches, in all of which God was the author of peace, and not of disorder; and it forms a natural transition to what follows.

In conclusion a few serious words impress what has been said upon the readers (xiv., 37-40).

Spiritual (*v.*, **37**); here, one endowed with spiritual gifts, with special reference to the speaker with tongues.

Commandment of the Lord (**xiv., 37**).—This can hardly refer to any exact precept, but must be understood in a general sense: everyone with true spiritual perception will see that my instructions are agreeable to the mind of Christ. If a man cannot see this, he must remain in his ignorance, or, with the marginal reading, he is excluded from the Divine recognition and acceptance. Without order and decorum there is no real spirituality.

The last subject discussed in the Epistle is the resurrection, about which doubts and difficulties, in some cases amounting to actual denial, had arisen at Corinth (xv.).

Paul begins by presenting the facts of Christ's death and resurrection as the very basis of his Gospel (xv., 1-11).

This passage contains the earliest account which we possess of the resurrection of Jesus. It seems intended to give in chronological order a list of all the appearances of the risen Christ, at least of those that could be considered valuable as an evidence of the fact. There is no mention of locality or concomitant circumstances. There is no allusion to any intercourse with the disciples, or to any spoken words; and it seems evident that Jesus is not regarded as a resuscitated man, walking about once more upon the earth, but as one who has passed into the immortal life, and now and again manifested himself from the world beyond the grave. Accordingly there is no reference here or elsewhere in Paul to the ascension as distinct from and subsequent to the resurrection. The account is quite different from those contained in the Gospels; and this is the more remarkable because Paul's statement is presented as a fixed tradition which he received from others and handed on to those whom he taught. These facts create serious difficulties; but having stated them, the interpreter must leave it to the systematic theologian to fit them into a scheme of doctrine. Another observation of a different kind requires attention. This account would not be contained in Paul's Epistles unless doubts had arisen at Corinth. The inference is inevitable that his Epistles did not represent his habitual teaching. Naturally that is just what they did not contain; for it is assumed as a matter of course, and is appealed to only where it seems to have been forgotten, or was required to enforce some particular line of instruction.

Make known (**xv., 1**).—It is assumed with some little irony that his teaching was so completely forgotten that he had to make it known once more.

Are saved (**xv., 2**); better, "are being saved," the present tense indicating a process which was not yet complete. This process was conditional on holding fast the substance of the Gospel. This connection, given in the margin by the English revisers, and adopted in the text of the American Version, furnishes a good sequence of thought; the arrangement in the English text makes no very coherent sense.

First of all (**xv., 3**); that is, among the first and most prominent subjects of his teaching; not, I was the first to deliver. The English is ambiguous.

Died for our sins according to the Scriptures (**xv., 3**).— The Greek preposition denotes "on behalf of" our sins. The Apostle does not here unfold his doctrine, but refers simply to the historical fact that Christ died in his effort to vanquish sin: in this supreme instance, as in so many minor instances, the innocent suffered for the guilty. The Scripture alluded to is probably Isaiah liii., which is expressly referred to in Acts viii., 32 *sq.*, 1 Peter ii., 22 *sqq.*

Raised on the third day according to the Scriptures (**xv., 4**). —The reference may be to Psalm xvi., 10, and to 2 Kings xx., 5, Hosea vi., 2, Jonah i., 17, the passages being applied to the Messiah, in the last instance through a symbolical interpretation.

James (**xv., 7**); probably the brother of the Lord, not one of the twelve. I think there is no implication that he is included in "all the apostles." But in any case the word "apostles" is not limited by Paul to the twelve, and the separate mention of the twelve here suggests a wider application. The reference to "the twelve" in *v.* 5, instead of eleven, points to an official designation.

One born out of due time (or *the* child *untimely born*, **xv., 8**). —As Paul's vision was not premature as compared with the others, the figure does not seem very appropriate, and it has been suggested that the term was one of reproach on the part of his Jewish adversaries. But such an allusion is hardly consistent with the seriousness of the passage; and the vision was really premature in relation to Paul himself, for his spiritual eye was suddenly opened to the light of day before he had been fashioned into the Christian form and prepared for this birth from above.

The next step in the argument shows that the denial of a resurrection involves the denial of Christ's resurrection, and the consequent ruin of the Christian faith (xv. 12-19).

The argument throughout this passage has no validity unless Christ be regarded as in the strictest sense a man; for only the resurrection of a man could disprove the universal proposition that no dead men rise. The denial of a resurrection might be associated with the belief in a spiritual immortality, the soul escaping from the body into the upper realms of light and life; and this form of belief might have commended itself to Greeks. But there is no allusion to this, and the argument seems to assume throughout that the question was between resurrection and annihilation, or, if not annihilation, at least that shadowy existence in Hades which was far removed from the life and immortality of the Christian's hope.

Your faith is vain; ye are yet in your sins (**xv., 17**).—If Christ be simply a dead man, and not a glorified and quickening spirit, the Christian conception of an immortal communion of sons of God crumbles to pieces; the belief that we have eternal life abiding in us is a vain dream, and we drop back into the ranks of sinful and perishing men. Then all the brethren whose dying eyes were lighted by the faith of Christ are sleeping to wake no more. We are the most miserable of men, wasting the only life that is ours amid deceitful hopes and mocking ideals.

In opposition to the foregoing the fact of Christ's resurrection is once more asserted; and this is followed by a passage of great sublimity, which carries our thoughts to the final issue of things (xv., 20–28).

The first-fruits (**xv., 20**), *By man* (**21**).—These words justify and emphasise the remark made under the last head, that Paul regards Christ as really and typically human. The first-fruits must be of the same kind as the harvest, for no one could call a sheaf of wheat the first-fruits of a crop of thistles, and unless Christ was regarded as man in the same sense as Adam, the analogy between them breaks down. We should also observe how simply this is taken for granted, without any hint of a different view or of possible or necessary qualifications. Ample qualifications may be found in some commentators, who evidently think Paul's language very inadequate.

Shall all be made alive (**xv., 22**).—The comparison here would clearly fail if we limited the meaning of "all"; and "made alive" can hardly refer merely to the resurrection without its attendant blessedness. We may compare Rom. v., 15–21, where the same universalism is applied to the redemption from sin, and it is maintained that the Christ-nature in us, though appearing at a later stage, is as real as the Adam-nature, and even more certain than the latter to work out its implicit idea. This universalism may be hard to reconcile with some of Paul's expressions, which bring before us moral conditions whereby men may be self-excluded from the blessedness intended for them; but it is certainly remarkable that when he most vividly apprehends the Divine power and meaning of Christ's spiritual humanity, he sets no limits to its saving efficacy.

Order (**xv., 23**).—The word does not mean order in time, but refers to the division or class in which a man is included.

Then cometh the end (**xv., 24**).—Paul does not enumerate all the divisions of men, and the unbelievers and the wicked are not mentioned. But the idea seems to be that at the second advent only believers will rise, and then Christ will reign for an indefinite period, carrying on the war against evil till he is completely victorious. Paul avoids the rabbinical speculations about the length of the messianic period, and says nothing of the way in which the wicked are to be finally delivered from the power of sin; but that deliverance certainly seems contemplated in the abolition of rule, authority, power, words which refer to the sway of the principles of evil. Then Christ will deliver up the Kingdom to God. Spiritual things must be spiritually understood, and I suppose this must refer to the time when all souls will have been brought into direct and full communion with God, like that of Christ himself, and they will no longer need even the Beloved to awaken within them the abiding sense of the Father's love.

He must reign until he hath put all his enemies under his

feet (**xv., 25**).—This is borrowed from Psalm cx., 1, to which a messianic application was given. It is cited to establish the fact that the powers of evil will be subdued. The reign of Christ is service; and the self-sacrificing ministrations of love cannot cease so long as there is one wanderer to be gathered home to God.

The last enemy that shall be abolished is death (**xv., 26**): more correctly, "as the last enemy, death shall be abolished." This is confirmed, in the next verse, by an appeal to Psalm viii., 6. The statement confirms the view that Paul looked forward to the total abolition of evil.

Then shall the Son also himself be subjected (**xv., 28**).—From any point of view this is rather a difficult statement. It can hardly be meant that the Son was not subject, but occupied an independent position, during his messianic reign, when Christians called him Lord; but that afterwards he was made subject to the will of God in a way in which he was not subject before. I think the meaning must be that he will descend, as it were, into the rank of subjects by the elevation of all to the same spiritual height. Through the inworking of his spirit all will have come to the measure of the stature of the fulness of Christ; he will be the first-born of a universal brotherhood; and God will be in all even as in him.

Some further considerations are now adduced in favour of the doctrine of a resurrection (xv., 29-34).

The main thought of the passage is that the denial of the resurrection must have disastrous moral results. It thus resumes the line of thought which was traced in *v.* 19. In opposition to that, Paul described his glorious vision of the future. If these vaticinations of the inspired conscience were but the baseless fabric of a dream, the truth of the moral nature would be shattered, and amid its ruins the doctrine of animal enjoyment would emerge.

Baptised for the dead (**xv., 29**).—This verse has received various explanations, but that which is most generally approved takes it as a reference to the practice of vicarious baptism on behalf of believers who had died unbaptised. Of this practice the traces are very obscure, and the explanation is by no means without difficulties. The verse has no intelligible place in the argument; for it neither proves the resurrection nor points to any evil results from disbelieving it.

I die daily (**xv., 31**); a strong way of saying, my life is in continual danger. The narrative in Acts reports a final, but not a daily danger at Ephesus.

If after the manner of men (**xv., 32**).—The context fixes the meaning,—like a mere perishing man, for whom there is no resurrection. What is the good of my engaging in deadly strife for a future which has no existence?

I fought with beasts at Ephesus (**xv., 32**).—This clearly refers to some event which took place at Ephesus; but it is generally supposed that the expression is figurative, for Paul, as a Roman citizen, would not have been set to fight in the arena, and, if he had, it is very improbable that he would have escaped with his life. The figure, however, is harsh. Paul did not always receive the rights of a Roman citizen, and the beasts at the public shows did not always kill those who were exposed to them.¹

Let us eat and drink for to-morrow we die (**xv., 32**).—This is quoted from Isaiah xxii., 13. The application is Paul's own.

Evil company doth corrupt good manners, or *Evil companionships corrupt good morals* (**xv., 33**).—This is cited from Menander's play, *Thais;* but the line may have become proverbial, and is hardly sufficient to prove Paul's acquaintance with the poet. The warning is directed against the influence of the "some" who denied the resurrection, mentioned in *v.* 12.

¹ See Ramsay, *Church in the Roman Empire*, pp. 312, 404.

Some have no knowledge of God (**xv., 34**).—This points to a deeper source of doubt than mere intellectual difficulties. The Christian's faith in God carries with it the assurance of eternal life; for God will not hand over to destruction the children of His love.

Having now established his doctrine of resurrection, Paul proceeds to remove the chief difficulty which was felt in regard to it (xv., 35-49).

It was clear to the Greek mind that the body which was resolved into its elements in the grave could not rise again, and it was known that Paul himself did not believe that it could. How, then, could the bodily identity be preserved?

The difficulty is met by bringing forward a number of analogies, of which the principal is that of the grain of wheat. This of course does not really die; but it is buried in the ground, and so changed that it may be said to die as a seed, and that which rises above the ground, though retaining the same organic life, is completely different in form. The other illustrations seem intended to show that there are in fact various sorts of bodies, and different degrees even in bodies of the same class. It is not quite clear whether Paul believed that the natural body as a whole would be changed into the spiritual body, or that the latter would be evolved out of an indestructible germ in the former. The latter view was entertained among the Jews, and, I think, suits best the tenor of the chapter. In this case the body of flesh and blood would yield to the corruption of the grave and disappear, and the incorruptible body would rise, like the stalk of wheat, out of the buried germ.

It is sown in corruption (**xv., 42**).—" It " means the body, as is shown by *v.* 44. " Sown " is proved by the whole context to refer to burial.

Natural body . . . spiritual body (**xv., 44**).—" Natural," that is, psychical, a body suited to and governed by the animal principle of life. On account of the parallelism we must similarly understand the spiritual body to be, not one composed of spiritual substance, but one suited to and controlled by the spirit.

It is written (**xv., 45**), in Gen. ii., 7, "first" and "Adam" being added to make the application clear. Adam and Christ are the progenitors of the psychical and the spiritual nature; and for this reason Christ is spoken of as the last Adam because he started that spiritual life which is the culmination of humanity. In saying that he became a life-giving spirit I think Paul means to describe his essential nature, not that he became so at any particular epoch; otherwise the parallelism with the previous clause would be lost. He was the originator of spiritual humanity, and this spiritual humanity must be realised in an organism which is suited to it. According to a rabbinical saying, Adam was wiser than all men, and was the light of the world.[1] From this view Paul markedly dissents.

That is not first which is spiritual (**xv., 46**) either in history or in the individual. Here and elsewhere in Paul we have a very noticeable doctrine of growth or development.

The second man is of heaven (**xv., 47**).—I think this does not describe the place out of which Jesus descended to the earth, but refers to the higher quality of his being, and that therefore it has no bearing on the question of pre-existence. This is shown by the parallelism with other men,—"As is the heavenly, such are they also that are heavenly." Those that share in the spirit of Christ shall share also in his resurrection, and through death cast off the image of the earthy, and assume the image which manifests their more exalted life. In a somewhat similar way Philo distinguishes men of earth, who are devoted to bodily pleasures; men of heaven, who follow reason, the heavenly principle within us; and men

---

[1] Weber, *Jüdische Theologie*, p. 214.

of God, who are priests and prophets, and have their citizenship amid incorruptible and incorporeal ideas.[1]

The chapter concludes by pointing out that even those who have not died before the day of resurrection must be changed, and then at last death will be completely overthrown (xv., 50-58).

Flesh and blood cannot inherit the Kingdom of God (**xv., 50**).—The Kingdom of God is evidently used here, not of the inward reign of God in the heart, but of its perfected result in a society of immortals over whom God is king. This Kingdom was closed against flesh and blood. Although the statement is made in order to show the necessity for a change in those who do not pass through death, it at the same time makes it quite clear that in Paul's view the resurrection-body was not to be one of flesh and blood.

A mystery (**xv., 51**); a thing which they did not know, but was now revealed. The use of the first person in explaining the mystery points to the belief that Christ would return before the end of the existing generation: not all who were then living would die, but all would be changed, whether through the alchemy of the grave or at the sudden blast of the trumpet.

We shall be changed (**xv., 52**).—"We" is emphatic in Greek, and indicates Paul's expectation that he himself would be among the survivors.

Written (**xv., 54**).—The quotation is from Isaiah xxv., 8, and the questions in the following verse are taken freely from Hosea xiii., 14. In Jewish opinion death would cease in the kingdom of the Messiah.[2]

Thy sting (**xv., 55**).—With this translation the figure is

---

[1] *De Gigant.*, § 13. Compare his expression, καταβὰς ἀπ' οὐρανοῦ, said of the νοῦς when it leaves the pure service of God (*Quis ser. div. her.*, §§ 16 and 55). So Origen describes the moral ascent towards God as κάτωθεν ἀναβαίνοντα (*Com. in Joan.*, tom. I. 29, p. 61, Lom.).

[2] Weber, *Jüdische Theologie*, p. 249.

borrowed from an animal such as a scorpion. The word may also mean a goad with which a beast is driven.

The sting of death is sin ; and the power of sin is the law (xv., 56).—This verse receives its fullest explanation in Rom. vii., 7 *sqq.* The thought, however true, does not seem very appropriate to the subject of the chapter, and is not indeed suggested by anything in this Epistle. The conjecture has been made that it may have been a marginal note, and inserted by mistake in the text.

My beloved brethren (**xv.**, 58).—The bigot seeks to destroy error by threatenings and slaughter; the Christian is only moved to a deeper love by men's failure to see the light that shines so brightly on himself. When Paul's indignation is strongly moved against doctrinal error, as in the Epistle to the Galatians, it is against error that made men narrow, exclusive, and arrogant. With the consolation and encouragement of this verse the various subjects of discussion are brought to a close. But the mention of the "work of the Lord" fitly prepares the way for the practical exhortation which follows.

One other topic remains, which, from the manner of its introduction, seems to have been included among the queries of the Corinthians,—a collection for the saints in Jerusalem (xvi., 1-4).

"The saints," without any addition, cannot denote the poor in Jerusalem, so that the reference must be to something already known; and this is confirmed by the article, "*the* collection."

Approve by letters (**xvi.**, 3).—This must mean, "recommend by letters," a meaning which the Greek, I think, cannot bear. The Corinthians were to select men that they approved of, and Paul would recommend them in Jerusalem by a letter from himself,—unless indeed he went himself. Therefore adopt the marginal translation.

They shall go with me (**xvi.**, 4).—It is said that it would have been contrary to Apostolic dignity to say, "I will go with them." I think this mistakes the meaning, which is, in effect, "I will not go alone, but your own approved representatives shall accompany me, and see that everything is properly done."

These directions lead the Apostle to speak of the expected time of his visit, and the rest of the Epistle is occupied with personal references and salutations (xvi., 5-24).

In regard to Paul's movements and intentions see the Introduction.

A great door and effectual (**xvi., 9**).—The last word is hardly applicable to the figure of the door; but the meaning must be that the door is wide enough to admit of effective work. The presence of many adversaries furnished an additional reason for devoting all his strength to the task.

If Timothy come (**xvi., 10**).—As Timothy had been sent on a special mission to Corinth, the doubt probably relates only to the time of his arrival.

Despise him (**xvi., 11**).—The exhortation was perhaps rendered desirable by his youth: compare 1 Tim. iv., 12. Possibly also his gentleness concealed his real strength.

With the brethren (**xvi., 11**): probably those who had been sent with him, though only Erastus is named in Acts xix., 22; perhaps brethren expected from Corinth.

As touching Apollos (**xvi., 12**).—The mode of reference suggests that the Corinthians had asked for a visit. The "brethren" are probably those who were to carry Paul's letter.

For the visit of Stephanas and his friends see the Introduction. They supplied what was lacking on the part of the Corinthians (*v.* **17**) by their own cordiality; and by bringing about a better state of feeling in Corinth they refreshed not only Paul's spirit, but that of the Corinthians.

Aquila and Prisca (**xvi., 19**).—Paul had left them at Ephesus on his journey from Greece to Palestine (Acts xviii., 18, 19). They were probably possessed of some wealth, and so were able to provide a large room in their house for the meetings of a congregation.

Anathema (**xvi. 22**); a thing devoted to destruction. It is not very apparent why this imprecation is introduced; but in view of the many abuses which he has had to notice in the Epistle, Paul may wish to remind his readers of the one qualification of the Christian which carried all else with it, and without which Christianity was a pretence. The following words are Aramaic, and, we must suppose, were for some reason understood by the readers, like *amen*, and *Abba*. It may have been a current phrase of exhortation and warning.[1]

My love be with you all (**xvi., 24**).—He had been obliged to use words of reproof; but there were no exceptions to his love and regard. In the more highly wrought feeling of the Second Epistle he substitutes for this "the love of God." In Christ Jesus all estrangements die away; his followers are bound to one another in mutual affection; and the love of God is supreme over all.

[1] Dr. Neubauer says the words, as they stand, certainly mean "Our Lord has come." He refers to a conjecture of M. Halévy that the words may be differently divided, and signify, "Our Lord, come," corresponding with the invocation in Rev. xxii. 20. (See his article on "The Dialects of Palestine in the Time of Christ," in *Studia Biblica*, I. pp. 57, 73.)

SECOND CORINTHIANS.

ANALYSIS.

ADDRESS AND GREETING, i., 1, 2.

I. DEFENSIVE EXPRESSION OF THOUGHTS AND FEELINGS WHICH AROSE OUT OF INCIDENTS SUBSEQUENT TO THE SENDING OF THE FIRST EPISTLE, i., 3–vii., 16.
  1. Thanksgiving for deliverance from danger, i., 3–11.
  2. Reference to circumstances connected with an unrecorded visit and a lost letter, i., 12–ii., 17.
      a. Defence against the charge of insincerity in his writing or conduct, i., 12–ii., 4.
        (1) General assertion of his conscientious action, i., 12–14.
        (2) His change of purpose in regard to his visit was not due to fickleness, i., 15–22.
        (3) The reason for his change, i., 23–ii., 4.
      b. Advice to forgive a man who had offended, ii., 5–11.
      c. His anxiety for news from Corinth, and his relief on learning its happy character, ii., 12–17.
  3. Defensive description of his Apostolic office, iii., 1–vi., 10.
      a. He has no need to commend himself, iii., 1–3.
      b. His confidence was not in himself, but directed towards God, who made him a minister of a new and glorious covenant, iii., 4–11.
      c. Contrast between Jewish and Christian teaching and learning, iii., 12–18.
      d. Openness and sincerity of his preaching, iv., 1–6.
      e. The preachers of the Gospel are weak and persecuted, but are supported by a conquering faith, which looks to the eternal world, iv., 7–v., 10.
      f. This makes them eager to preach the Gospel of reconciliation, v., 11–vi., 10.
  4. The Corinthians should open their hearts to the Apostle, and not allow themselves to be misled by unbelievers, vi., 11–vii., 4.

5. His comfort on receiving news from Titus, vii., 5-16.
II. DIRECTIONS ABOUT THE COLLECTION FOR THE POOR CHRISTIANS IN JERUSALEM, viii., 1-ix., 15.
  1. Appeal to the example of Macedonia, viii., 1-6.
  2. Exhortation to contribute according to their means, viii., 7-15.
  3. Recommendation of Titus and two other brethren sent to complete the collection, viii., 16-24.
  4. The collection to be completed before his own arrival, ix., 1-5.
  5. Give ungrudgingly, for men reap as they sow, and such a ministration produces thanksgiving and brotherly love, ix., 6-15.
III. DEFENCE OF HIMSELF AGAINST HIS OPPONENTS, AND THREATS AGAINST THE IMPENITENT, x., 1-xiii., 10.
  1. His defence, x., 1-xii., 18.
    a. Pleading that he may not have to be severe when he comes, x., 1-6.
    b. He is determined to maintain his authority by an appeal to plain facts, x., 7-11.
    c. His glorying is only in what he has himself accomplished, not in other men's labours, x., 12-18.
    d. The glorying itself, xi., 1-xii., 18.
      (1) Introduction, excusing his folly in boasting through his zeal for them, xi., 1-3.
      (2) He has as full knowledge of the Gospel as others, xi., 4-6.
      (3) He taught the Gospel to the Corinthians gratis, xi., 7-15.
      (4) Further excuses for his boasting, xi., 16-21.
      (5) His pure lineage, his deeds and sufferings for the Gospel, and his visions, xi., 22-xii., 10.
      (6) He had shown all the signs of an Apostle among them, and had taken no advantage of them, xii., 11-18.
  2. Real reason for his defence, that he might edify his readers, and not have to deal sharply with them when he came, as the impenitent would find that he would do, xii., 19-xiii., 10.
    CONCLUDING EXHORTATION, SALUTATIONS, AND BENEDICTION, xiii., 11-14.

SECOND CORINTHIANS.

COMMENTARY.

The Epistle begins, as usual, with an address and greeting (i., 1, 2).

Timothy here takes the place of Sosthenes, whom Paul couples with himself in the First Epistle; and the salutation, instead of being extended to all Christians, is limited to those "in the whole of Achaia," that is, in the Roman province, which included Hellas and Peloponnesus.

After the greeting Paul enters immediately on the first portion of the Epistle, in which he pours forth thoughts and feelings which were suggested by occurrences that had taken place subsequently to the date of the First Epistle (i., 3–vii., 16).

There is a sorrowful and defensive tone running through these chapters, and the order of the thoughts is determined by the suggestions of feeling as much as by their logical connection. In their course Paul rises to some of his loftiest teaching.

He begins with a thanksgiving for his deliverance from some great suffering and danger, and reflections on the purpose of these (i., 3-11).

It is very uncertain what Paul alludes to. The Corinthians evidently were acquainted with the facts, though they were not aware how terribly they had tried the Apostle (see v. 8). Commentators have naturally thought of the riot at Ephesus. The expression " so great a death " seems most suitable to a tragic situation, and we must not underestimate the horror of being hunted for one's life by a savage mob. It does not, however, appear from the account in Acts that Paul's life was in actual danger, although he may have thought it prudent to hasten his departure from the city; and the references to sufferings and the Divine comfort which alleviated them point to something more than the anxiety of two or three hours. We must be content, therefore, to leave the occasion in uncertainty, but I think the expressions in the passage ("the sufferings of Christ," "enduring of the same sufferings," "ye are partakers of the sufferings") indicate peril and injury from enemies rather than "*a deadly sickness*" (Alford).

We must observe the use which Paul makes of his sad experiences. They were intended, he thought, to enlarge and deepen his sympathies, so that he might pass on to others a Divine gift which he could have received in no other way. The soul that has had no sorrow cannot minister to the sorrowful.

The Father of mercies (i., 3) : that is, He who is the source and author of merciful acts.

Us . . . we (i., 4).—This passage is so full of personal feeling that the plural probably refers only to Paul, though of course it is not impossible that Timothy may have been involved in the same dangers, and experienced the same relief.

The answer of death (i., 9).—"Death" was the answer to the question whether we were to expect life or death.

By means of many (i., 11), through the intercession of many.

It has been questioned whether Paul introduced this paragraph with a distinct purpose. It is no doubt admirably adapted to conciliate the good feeling of his readers, and to prepare the way for the defence which follows; but it is so, precisely because it is such a genuine outpouring of the heart's emotion, and if we could imagine it artfully inserted for a definite end in relation to himself, its beauty and pathos would be destroyed. If there is purpose, it is only such a purpose as springs up spontaneously in a sympathetic mind to meet a particular situation. The need of defence called up the thought of all he had suffered on behalf of Christ, and a yearning love towards the disciples from whom he could not bear to be alienated.

The ground being thus prepared, he enters on a defence of himself against a charge of fickleness or even insincerity because he had changed the plans which in some way he had announced to the Corinthians (i., 12–ii., 4).

For the probable course of the events which are here alluded to see the Introduction.

He first makes a general assertion of his conscientious action (i., 12–14). This is introduced as a reason ("for") why he was entitled to their prayers on his behalf. He was animated by the sincerity which is of God, and not by the wisdom which plots for selfish ends, and he had enjoyed more abundant opportunity of manifesting this to the Corinthians than to others. He had no double meaning in what he wrote; he meant exactly what they read in his letters and what they recognised, and he hoped they would continue to recognise, in his conduct. No doubt there were those in Corinth who misunderstood him; but to a certain extent they had recognised the mutual bond by which they would be united when Christ appeared.

From this general statement he proceeds to the particular charge: it was not through fickleness he had failed to carry out his plan of paying them two visits (i., 15–22).

In this confidence (i., 15) in our mutual understanding and glorying. It is implied that something had afterwards occurred to impair his confidence. He learned that the acknowledgment was only "in part" (*v.* 14). He had intended to visit them "before" going into Macedonia, and then to give them "a second benefit" on his return from

Macedonia, before proceeding to Judæa. There is no reference to the actual number of visits which Paul had yet paid, but only to the number which he intended to pay on this particular journey.

Fickleness? . . . according to the flesh (i., 17).—There is a heightening of the charge. He was fickle, not knowing his own mind; or, worse still, he had unworthy ends, and was deliberately saying yes and no at the same time. The repetition of the words, " yea, yea," and " nay, nay," implies a stronger asseveration, and therefore greater culpability.

Our word toward you (i., 18).—This naturally refers in the first instance to the expressed intention which had been altered; but it immediately receives a wider application, and furnishes an argument in favour of the Apostle's truthfulness. His whole preaching related to him who is the Truth, and in whom all the promises of God had received their solemn affirmation. He as well as they had been established in Christ, and received the earnest of the Spirit; and therefore the use of falsehood would be altogether inconsistent with his character.

The Son of God, Jesus Christ (i., 19).—The Greek throws the emphasis on "God," thus carrying the thought up, as in v. 21, to the supreme source of truth. As God is true, so must be His Son; so too must be the disciples of His Son, who share his Spirit.

We should observe how Paul is careful here to include Silvanus and Timothy with himself as founders of the Corinthian church.

The amen (i., 20); either the absolute affirmation, which would make it simply a strengthened repetition of "the yea," or the solemn affirmation and assent of the Church.

Anointed us (i., 21).—In order to preserve the connection of the words we must translate the name Christ, which means "the anointed." Compare 1 John ii., 20, "Ye have an anointing from the Holy One"; and Theophilus (*Ad*

Autolycum, i., 12), " For this reason we are called Christians, because we are anointed with the oil of God."

Sealed us (**i., 22**), a figure derived from attesting, and so authenticating, a document. "The earnest" is money paid down at the time of a transaction as a pledge of the future payment of the whole sum. The Spirit in the heart is the pledge of all that we are to be.

Having repelled the charge of fickleness, he states the true reason for his change of plan: it was that he might not pay a visit which would only give pain (**i., 23–ii., 4**).

I call you for a witness upon [or *against*] *my soul* (**i., 23**). —Such a strong asseveration seems hardly consistent with the simplicity of Christian speech (see Matt. v., 33–37); but it is after the manner of Paul, and may be explained by the vehemence of his feelings and his painful knowledge that there were some who did not trust him.

Not that we have lordship over your faith (**i., 24**).—These words correct an impression which the previous statement might produce. Their faith, with its various tendencies, was their own, and he claimed no despotic power over it; rather was it his to help their joy in believing, and his censures were directed against moral evils which were inconsistent with the faith that they professed.

I would not come again to you with sorrow (**ii., 1**), feeling and communicating grief. "Again" does not, I think, grammatically necessitate the supposition of a previous visit in sorrow; but this is implied in the whole context, when interpreted by other references to an unrecorded visit (see the Introduction). It would seem that Paul paid a visit to Corinth which filled him with anxiety and distress, and in which apparently someone had even insulted him. He then wrote a lost letter of remonstrance, which, with the great majority of the church, had the desired effect (see vii., 8–13). This letter is alluded to in the present passage, according to the most probable interpretation.

I wrote this very thing (ii., 3), referring probably to the first verse, and therefore meaning that he wrote announcing his change of plan. His reason for doing so was that a better state of feeling might be restored before he again appeared among them in person. It had given him the deepest pain to write this letter; but his object in writing was not to grieve them, but to win them back by an expression of his love. We may suppose that it was too personal, and too closely connected with a passing state of things, to be suitable for permanent use in the Church. Hence we have lost a letter which would have thrown a most valuable light on the Apostle's character and methods.

The reference to a sorrowful visit reminds Paul of one who had given special cause for sorrow, and whom he now forgives (ii., 5–11).

It has been very frequently, but by no means universally, assumed that the offender in this passage, which must be read in connection with vii., 8–13, is the incestuous man of the First Epistle. I agree with those who think that the allusion is to someone who insulted Paul during the painful visit to which he has referred. For, in the first place, this is more agreeable to the context, in which Paul is speaking of an unrecorded visit and a lost letter. To fly back to an event which happened before the First Epistle was written would only disturb the train of thought. Secondly, Paul could not say he had written about such a case simply to prove the obedience and "earnest care" of the church (*v.* 9, vii., 12). Thirdly, if the incestuous man be referred to, the church was not obedient; for this offender, instead of being solemnly excommunicated by the assembled church, was only punished "by the majority" (*v.* 6), apparently without any concerted action. Fourthly, it seems to me impossible that Paul could treat an odious sin in this rather easy way. He would surely have dwelt on its moral gravity, and have intimated the need of Divine forgiveness, and have assured himself that the man had repented, but of this there is no evidence. And, lastly, he treats the whole incident as a personal affair. Evidently he is the one who is supposed to be aggrieved (*v.* 5), and who has to forgive (*v.* 10); and, while his saying that it grieved some of his friends, but not himself, is very noble in regard to a personal affront, it would be anything but creditable in regard to a sin by which he and his friends were not personally injured. He "that suffered the wrong," of vii., 12, is most naturally explained by the "me" of *v.* 5. If the reference is to the case of incest, the injured man must be the father, for whom Paul might have had a little consideration, or at all events might have refrained from boasting that he had none. But the father can hardly be intended, for he was probably dead before his son could contract the incestuous marriage. It is a difficulty that Paul speaks of him who "suffered the wrong" in the third person; but he may do so both for the sake of the antithesis, and in order to avoid emphasising the fact that the wrong was offered to himself. The conditions, therefore, are far better satisfied if we suppose that Paul, during his brief visit, received some gross insult, which was resented by the better men in the church, and against which Paul himself remonstrated in the lost letter, but to which, as being merely a baseless insult, whatever was its nature, he offers no reply.

That I press not too heavily (ii., 5).—The meaning is not very clear; but as the words explain the insertion of "in part," they are probably equivalent to "in order not to exaggerate." The church as a whole was grieved; but still there were some exceptions. Another explanation is, "that I be not too heavy on the offender."

That no advantage may be gained over us by Satan (ii., 11).— Satan gained an advantage through dissensions and ill-feeling in the church. Paul therefore was willing to forgive and forget the affront which had been offered him. If the reference be to the incestuous man, Satan must have grinned with malignant satisfaction that Paul was forced to climb down from his noble moral indignation, and to cover the ignominy of his retreat with the pretence of generosity. This is one of the comparatively few places where the Apostle alludes to diabolical agency. Words may continue to be used after they have ceased to represent a literal belief; but I see no reason to doubt that Paul accepted the current belief about evil spirits, although it enters very little into his great doctrinal passages. It hung upon the fringe of his thought rather than entered into the substance of his ruling and original convictions.

His love for the church is now illustrated by a reference to the anxiety with which he had awaited news from Corinth, and his relief on learning its happy character (ii., 12-17).

The passage throws a vivid light on the eager and passionate nature of Paul; in his solicitude he could not even preach his beloved Gospel though the door of success stood open. The narrative resumes that which was begun in i., 8.

Titus (ii., 13).—The mission of Titus is again referred to in vii., 6, 13, 14, and viii., 6.

Leadeth us in triumph (ii., 14).—Some would give to this phrase a causative meaning, "makes us to triumph," but everywhere else it is used of leading a captive in triumph. Still the context implies that in the present instance the captive shares the triumph; and spiritually this is true. He who is taken captive by God becomes a triumphant power for good in the world.

The savour of his knowledge (ii., 14), referring to the sweet spices which made the streets fragrant during a triumph. The knowledge is the savour.

We are a sweet savour (ii., 15).—The figure abruptly changes, and the Apostle himself becomes the fragrance. In what immediately follows I cannot think that he is referring to his Christian opponents; for though in a later part of the Epistle he uses very energetic language about them, here he is speaking with a view to conciliation, and the antithesis is rather between believers and unbelievers, as in 1 Cor. i., 20–24. The effect here described necessarily accompanies every great advance in spiritual teaching. To those who can receive it it is a source of ever-expanding life; those who are too dead to apprehend it are more tightly clasped by their dead forms and beliefs. We may compare the rabbinical saying, "The words of the Torah have power to kill and to make alive. . . . To those who trust in it it is a means of life; but to those who turn from it it is a means of death." (Weber, *Jüdische Theologie*, 1897, p. 21.)

Who is sufficient for these things? (ii., 16).—No answer is given; but perhaps a double answer is implied: first, no one; secondly, we Apostles, only our sufficiency is not our own (see iii., 5, 6). The second answer is implied by the following verse.

We are not as the many (ii., 17).—Is it possible that Paul means that the mass of Christian teachers were mere corrupters of the word of God? Is it not much more likely that he is contrasting Christian teachers, those who speak "in Christ," with the general run of teachers, whether Jewish or heathen? In the chapters which immediately follow he refers to Jews and unbelievers, and not to doctrinal differences within the Church itself. In opposition to dead forms and self-laudatory wisdom, the Christian ministry was sincere, exercised as in the sight of God from whom it drew all its inspiration.

Paul now enters on a defensive description of his Apostolic office, and of the great subjects of his preaching (iii., 1–vi., 10).

There is no very obvious reason for this, and I know not that we need look for any reason beyond the fact that his "heart was enlarged" (vi., 11), and his thoughts came well-ing up with an irrepressible flow. He seems to have in mind chiefly the unbelieving world, whether Jew or Gentile (see iii., 14, 15; iv., 4; v., 11, 19; vi., 14). He may possibly have thought also of some internal foes, with whom he deals at length farther on; but we must not forget that he was continually beset by external enemies, and the unconverted Jews at Corinth would be influential opponents, who would represent him as a falsifier of the Scriptures, and as a self-interested and unscrupulous agitator.

He opens by disclaiming the need of commending himself (iii., 1-3).

Are we beginning again? (iii., **1**), referring to a former Epistle, perhaps the lost one, perhaps parts of 1 Cor. (parts of v., ix.; xiv., 18; xv., 10).

As do some (iii., **1**); not necessarily a gibe at opponents. Apollos had letters of recommendation (Acts xviii., 27); but Paul, the founder of the church, needed none such.

Our epistle . . . an epistle of Christ (iii., **2, 3**).—The church is compared to a letter of recommendation written by Christ himself, and borne about by Paul, not in his hands, but in his heart. It was read by "all men," not merely by believers; and the high character of the church was the best proof of the genuineness of Paul's preaching. The substance of the epistle, however, was the Gospel written with the Spirit of God in disciples' hearts, and not like the Law on tables of stone. The figure is slightly confused, but the sense is clear.

The confidence thus expressed was not self-sufficiency, but directed towards God, who had made him the minister of a new and glorious covenant (iii., **4-11**). To follow this passage intelligently we must have in mind the account in Ex. xxxiv., 29-35 (in the Revised Version), which Paul assumes is known to his readers. According to his explanation, so long as the face of Moses had the glow of Divine communion, the children of Israel could not look upon its brightness;

and he then put on a veil that they might not see the light fading away. But when he went in to commune with the Lord once more, he took off the veil that the glory might be rekindled.

Not of the letter, but of the spirit (iii., 6).—The contrast is not between the letter and the spirit of a law, but between a written authority and the spirit in the heart. Paul thus sweeps away with a single sentence the whole of the Protestant bibliolatry. A sacred scripture may be of inestimable value when interpreted by, and made to minister to, the spirit; but when used as an engine to crush the spirit, it "killeth."

Ministration of death (iii., 7), *ministration of condemnation* (iii., 9).—For the nature and effect of the law, Galatians and Romans must be consulted. In Paul's view the law was powerless to produce righteousness. It flashed the light of Divine holiness upon the conscience, and so produced the sense of sin, of condemnation, of death. It was a necessary but passing phase in the education of mankind. No doubt, to the ordinary Jew it could not thus present itself; for he was not ripe for the spiritual change which had come over Paul, and the ordinary man seldom goes down to the underlying principles of things. Reformers are born out of the passionate struggles of genius, not from the quiescence of a contented mediocrity.

Ministration of the spirit (iii., 8), *ministration of righteousness* (iii., 9).—As the spirit is opposed to death, so is righteousness to condemnation. The spirit gives life, being the indwelling of Divine and quickening righteousness in the soul, righteousness in its highest sense not being the performance of a deed, but an inward harmony with God.

The thought of the glory of the Gospel leads to further reflections on the contrast between Jewish and Christian teaching and learning (iii., 12-18).

Such a hope (iii., 12) ; the hope of an abiding glory. This produced complete openness of speech, as there was nothing to conceal.

That the children of Israel should not look steadfastly on the end of that which was passing away (iii., 13).—This is Paul's own interpretation. He conceives the light as fading from the face of Moses as soon as he had delivered the commandments, and the veil as put on in order that the termination of the transient glow might not be seen. Thus was symbolised the transiency of the Law, and the inability of the Israelites to look forward to its cessation.

The same veil remaineth unlifted (iii., 14).—The translation is a little uncertain, and an alternative is given in the margin. The general sense, however, is not seriously affected. There is at this point a curious transition in the figure, the veil being transferred from Moses to his hearers.

Whensoever it shall turn to the Lord, the veil is taken away (iii., 16).—Again there is a little confusion in the application of the narrative. There the children of Israel turned to Moses, and Paul wants them to turn to Christ; but it was Moses who had the veil removed when he went in to speak with the Lord. Perhaps the argument, so far as such comparisons contain an argument, is this: the Jews, as disciples of Moses, wear a veil as he did; but as he laid aside the veil in his hours of full communion, so will they when they cease to depend on their tables of stone, and freely commit themselves to the converse of spirit with Spirit.

The Lord is the Spirit (iii., 17).—" The Spirit " must be the life-giving spirit of *v*. 6. Christianity is a spirit of life, not a law or a creed, though it is the source of both; and therefore its essence resides in a living person, not in forms of thought which pass away. The word of God has become flesh, and dwelt among us, and through the death of the flesh has become a universal Spirit, through whom men obtain true and perfect liberty. The glory of law and prophet must fade, but the glory of Divine Sonship cannot fade.

The Spirit of the Lord (iii., 17), after the identification of the Lord and the Spirit, is linguistically inaccurate; but Paul, the seer of grand visions, is not attentive to these niceties of expression.

Reflect as a mirror (iii., 18).—The precise meaning is uncertain. Such usage as exists favours the translation "behold as in a mirror"; but the other translation seems to be allowable, and is better suited to the sense. Moses reflected the glory of God; so the Christian must reflect the glory of Christ. This kind of spiritual reflection implies a change into the same image; whereas merely looking at a reflection in a mirror does not suggest this transformation. And again, "we all" seems to be contrasted with Moses. He alone had the glory of Divine communion on his face; but all Christians have laid aside the veil, and carry a spiritual glory on their countenance.

We have here a further evidence that Paul is not attacking a judaising party within the Church. Had he been doing so he could not have used this emphatic "all."

Still following the line of thought suggested by the veil, Paul asserts the openness and sincerity of his preaching (iv., 1-6). It is quite gratuitous to discover in this passage an insinuation that certain Christian opponents were actuated by the very faults which he disclaims for himself; and if he is repelling suggestions that his Gospel was insincere or obscure, these suggestions came from the "unbelieving" (v. 4), who could not understand the new spiritual power that was rising among them. Perhaps, however, he is not repelling attacks, but simply contrasting the perfect candour of the Christian preachers with the subtle arguments of rabbis and the hollowness of Greek rhetoricians.

We obtained mercy (iv., 1), in our conversion and call to the Christian ministry. The sense of past mercy prevents all faint-heartedness in the delivery of our message.

We have renounced (iv., 2).—This does not imply that he

once had the faults in question, but that he had consciously determined not to have them. He had bidden farewell to the region where men practised cunning tricks which they concealed through shame.

Every man's conscience (iv., 2); literally, every "conscience of man," which is more expressive. Every conscience, Christian, Jewish, or pagan, must recognise the sincerity of his conduct. Paul's life was not only in the Church, but "in the world" (i., 12).

The god of this world (iv., 4), *i.e.*, Satan (ii., 11), who is represented as virtually the god of the heathen world during this present age, which was so soon to make way for the age of the Messiah. The reign of the Messiah was expected to be in this *world*, though in a future, as distinguished from the present, "*age*" (here translated "world").

The image of God (iv., 4).—Man, as such, is described as "the image and glory of God" in 1 Cor. xi., 7. This is the ideal, often latent in him, which ought to govern his actions. Here "the image" is clearly supposed to be realised and manifest. The religious ideal of humanity has become actual, and therefore a revealing glory for all who are not blinded.

For (iv., 5).—The connection seems to be, I mention Christ, for he is the great subject of our preaching; and perhaps also, there is no need to be insincere, for we preach not ourselves.

Lord . . . servants (or rather *slaves*, iv., 5) are correlated terms, though here the Apostles are represented as slaves of those to whom they minister.

In our hearts . . . in the face of Jesus Christ (iv., 6).—Observe the union of inward and outward light to produce revelation. If the heart is blind, the glory of God will for us shine vainly in the face of Christ; if with open eye we gaze into blank space, we discern nothing. The same idea is expressed in detached passages in John: "No one cometh unto the Father, but by me" (xiv., 6); "No man can come to me, except the Father which sent me draw him" (vi., 44). The context shows that the immediate reference here is to the Apostles; but the truth is universal, and is recognised as such, as we see from iii., 18.

The grandeur of the Christian revelation contrasted with the weakness and suffering which Paul had lately experienced leads naturally to a solemn train of reflection. The preachers of the Gospel are weak and persecuted, yet they are always victorious through the Divine power of a faith which looks to the eternal world (**iv., 7–v., 10**). It is needless to account for this passage by supposing that judaising opponents treated Paul's afflictions as a Divine chastisement for his falsification of the Gospel. The sad, yet elevated and triumphant dignity of this noble meditation is wholly unlike his controversial manner.

Earthen vessels (**iv., 7**); referring to the body, the feeble instrument of the Spirit. It is in conscious weakness that the Divine power becomes most manifest. No force of rhetoric can produce the tones of spiritual conviction. These come only when the soul loses itself in God.

Pressed on every side, yet not straitened (**iv., 8**).—The series of contrasts, drawn from that in *v.* 7, are figures from a battle, in which victory is won out of seeming defeat. Compare i., 8, 9, where Paul confesses to a momentary despair, and an expectation of death from which he was delivered only by the mercy of God. This is one of many passages which show that persecution on account of their faith was a familiar incident among the early teachers of Christianity.

The dying of Jesus . . . the life also of Jesus (**iv., 10**).— As Jesus was put to death, so his soldiers are constantly exposed to death, and in a certain sense experience it through the fatigue and stripes and wounds which cripple their powers; but that is only that the principle of Divine and eternal life which came into the world in Jesus, and which is born of self-denial and suffering, may be manifested even through that flesh which seems to belong to death.

Death worketh in us, but life in you (iv., 12).—Rather an unexpected turn; but the life was manifested that others might see and share it, so that the Apostles, like their Master, were giving their lives for the life of the world.

The same spirit of faith (iv., 13), the same as the ancient Psalmist. Paul quotes from the LXX, the Hebrew text of Ps. cxvi., 10 not yielding the same sense. The whole Psalm is admirably suited to the Apostle's state of mind.

Shall raise up us also (iv., 14).—This can hardly be meant figuratively. The words do not necessarily preclude a hope of surviving till the second Advent; but since writing the First Epistle Paul had been face to face with death, and he now expresses his confidence that, even if he died, God would nevertheless present him, along with his converts, to his risen Lord.

For your sakes (iv., 15), referring to the words "present us with you." There was a larger purpose than that affecting the individual; the grace which visited one spread in ever-widening circles, and the gratitude of one heart turned into a multiplied thanksgiving.

Outward man . . . inward man (iv., 16).—The contrast already referred to is resumed in other words. The affliction which wears down the body nourishes the soul. As so often with the saints of God, the might of the spirit flashed from a feeble frame, and the inward eye gazed on eternal things which were impalpable to sense.

Temporal (iv., 18).—The word properly means "temporary," lasting only for a season, and ought, I think, to have been so translated.

The foregoing thoughts are justified by the certain expectation of immortal life, on which the Apostle now dwells (v., 1–10). Commentators are by no means agreed in the interpretation of this passage; but it is impossible in our space to discuss the various opinions. It seems clear that to some extent Paul's view has changed from that which is presented in the earlier Epistles. In things in which we walk by faith, and not by the actual appearance of the facts themselves, we naturally modify our views and the figures by which we express them, according to our varying moods. Paul had been at death's door, and he now contemplates the possibility, almost the probability, of his dying before the coming of the Lord. Could that mean that he was to sink into a "sleep" prolonged for an indefinite time, and so be removed utterly from communion with the Lord whom he loved? He could no longer accept that view; rather would death bring him at once home to the Lord. But if this were so, it must be without the body. Was he, then, as the Greeks supposed, to be a disembodied spirit like the shades in Hades? The answer is uncertain. Some think that he believed in an intervening period, when the spirit, although with the Lord, would be without any bodily organ; and that verses 2–4 refer to the alternative possibility of his surviving till the second Advent, and so not experiencing dissolution at all. This seems favoured by the words "that what is mortal may be swallowed up of life," which suggests a change in the earthly body rather than a parting with it at death. Another view is that the passage throughout assumes the occurrence of death before the coming of the Lord; and then Paul must have abandoned the belief that the spiritual body was to be evolved by mysterious change out of the decay of the grave, and have expected the eternal habitation to descend out of heaven, and to be superinduced at the moment of death, so that the spirit would never be left naked. Neither of these views is easily reconciled with the doctrine of resurrection, which is accepted in iv., 14. But while belief is growing in regard to things which are still behind the veil, we need not look for absolute consistency of expression.

We may observe, as perhaps throwing some light on the subject, that according to a Jewish belief the souls of the righteous went straight to the presence of God, while others were sent into Sheol.[1]

Tabernacle (**v., 1**), a current figure for the human body, derived from its transient character, and here contrasted with a "building," which is permanent. The building is regarded as "in the heavens," waiting for occupancy when the time comes. We are reminded that the figure of the tent is natural to Paul, who was a tent-maker.

In this (**v., 2**) : either "in this tabernacle," as in *v.* 4, or perhaps "on this account." The longing for the heavenly habitation causes us to groan, and the groan is itself an evidence of our destination. Compare Rom. viii., 19–23.

If so be (**v., 3**).—The form of expression in the Greek does not imply doubt, but the contrary.

He that wrought us for this very thing is God (**v., 5**).—Compare i., 21, 22, where also everything is traced up to God, and the Spirit is the earnest of greater things to come. See also *v.* 18.

Sight (**v., 7**), not in the sense of seeing, but rather of that which may be seen, the actual form and appearance of the things apprehended by faith.

Whether at home or absent (**v., 9**) ; that is, in relation to the body. Absence from the body does not necessitate presence with the Lord, except for those who are well-pleasing to him.

May receive the things done in the body (**v., 10**).—This statement is perfectly explicit, and proves that Paul had no notion of substituting a spurious for a real righteousness. Compare Rom. ii., 6, 16; Gal. vi., 7, 8. The fruits of the Spirit are not bad, but good.

The hope of immortality and the certainty of judgment

---

[1] Weber, *Jüdische Theologie*, pp. 338 and 341.

make the Apostles eager to preach the Gospel of reconciliation (v., 11–vi., 10).

The fear of the Lord (v., 11); that is, reverent fear directed towards him, and (as the context shows) arising from the anticipation of judgment.

We persuade men (v., 11).—We need not supply "of our integrity," or "of the truth of the Gospel," or any similar expression. The phrase is used elsewhere in the sense of conciliating or gaining the favour of anyone. In Acts xii., 20, it is translated "having made their friend." In Gal. i., 10, it is equivalent to "seeking to please men." So it may be here. Paul sought to conciliate all kinds of men, that he might win some. But in doing so he was already (before the judgment) made manifest to God, who saw that he had no selfish end; and he hoped that his conduct was equally clear in the consciences of his readers. The word is, however, also used of persuading men to believe the Gospel, Acts xviii., 4, and this meaning would suit v., 20 and vi., 1.

This was not said for the purpose of commending himself, but to supply the Corinthians with an answer when he was attacked (v., 12). Those who gloried in outside distinctions may very likely have been Jews, but we need not here insist on discovering judaising Christians. The words would also apply to those who were proud of their excellency of speech and their wisdom.

We are beside ourselves (v., 13).—The tense is past, and the reference is probably to the ecstatic visions of Paul. These were for the glory of God, not for his own exaltation. His more sober words (which were also for the glory of God) were more distinctly for the benefit of the Church. In neither was there anything selfish or worldly.

The love of Christ (v., 14) must, according to usage, mean Christ's love to us. His love naturally suggests his death as the final proof of love. "Greater love hath no man than this, that a man lay down his life for his friends." The connection seems to be this: the change wrought in us by the love of Christ—the dying to self, and rising into life for him—obliterates all reliance on outward distinctions, and creates a pure sincerity of character. The Christian teacher has not excellence of speech or of wisdom, but demonstration of the Spirit and of power, not a conceited display of personal superiority, but the grace of God speaking in the inimitable tones of convinced and redeemed humanity.

All died (v., 14).—The language is universal. In the thought of Paul the whole of mankind had died and risen in Christ, the second man. The death on Calvary was of world-wide significance, "on behalf of all." It marked a new era in the history of the world. The past was dead, and the heavenly life of sons of God had become a reality. For all men, indeed, to enter individually into this life time would be required; but in Paul's view, no long time. The faith of Christ would sweep triumphantly over the earth, and within a generation the great consummation would appear. The central and spiritual thought remains; but God's times are not as ours.

We know no man after the flesh (v., 16): we pay no regard to merely adventitious distinctions. The cross has destroyed all these, and made the life of self-denying love the sole test. "We" is emphatic in the Greek, and therefore implies a contrast with "them that glory in appearance" in *v.* 12.

We have known Christ after the flesh (v., 16).—From the connection this cannot mean, known him in the days of his earthly life, but known him in relation to earthly grandeur and prerogative. But when was this? Not after his conversion, in which God revealed His Son in him. But if he refers to the time before his conversion, we must understand "Christ" in a general sense: his views of the Messiah took the form of worldly ambition and splendour; but from the time when he recognised Christ in the crucified, such ideas disappeared as a fleshly dream, and spiritual greatness came to his thought in all the majesty and power of humble self-sacrifice under the leading of Divine love. When will Christendom believe?

Wherefore (**v., 17**), introducing the consequence of all that has been said in the last three verses. That implies far more than a change of opinion in embracing Christianity. "If any man is in Christ," having a deep and inward union with him, "he is a new creature," altered in the very essence of his being.

All things are of God (**v., 18**): literally, "out of God," which is more expressive; coming forth, as it were, from His substance as the sole ultimate reality. It is noticeable how this thought recurs as a refrain (i., 21; v., 5). The life of Christ and the spread of Christianity were not mere accidents of human history, but were part of the great world-plan of God; and the mind must continually rise to Him as the ultimate Cause of all, the eternal Source of good, whose righteousness was now made manifest.

Who reconciled us to himself (**v., 18**).—The initiative is with God. It is not man that by meritorious works earned a reward from God, but God who, through the power of love in Christ, drew man up into harmony with Himself, making him the "new creature" just referred to, no longer earthly-minded, but heavenly-minded.

The ministry of reconciliation (**v., 18**): a brief summing up of the purpose of Christianity, to slay the enmity in the human heart, and bring man home to God.

God was in Christ reconciling the world (**v., 19**).—"In Christ" must be connected with the latter words, and not with God; so that it describes here, not the indwelling of God in Christ, but the work which He accomplished in and through him. Paul universalises the reconciliation, as before he had universalised the dying to the past (*v.* 14), not as implying that it had already taken place, but as expressing the purpose and result. Indeed he refrains from saying that God had reconciled the world, and describes instead the process in which He had been engaged in Christ.

Not reckoning unto them their trespasses (**v., 19**), that is, their past offences against the law of right. He was not judging them by a debtor-and-creditor account, but receiving in fatherly love all who turned to Him in faith. Thus the father in the parable did not reckon his riotous living against the humbled prodigal.

As though God were intreating by us (**v., 20**).—This, then, was the way in which God was reconciling the world, intreating men through Christ, and now through Christ's ambassadors. Thus, to refer once more to the parable, the father "intreated" his eldest son. There, however, there is no mediation; yet if it is true that the Father speaks direct to the human soul, still He generally finds us first through the beating of human hearts and the soft words of human lips.

Be ye reconciled to God (**v., 20**).—Man, then, had to respond to the Divine appeal, and lay aside his enmity. But were not the Corinthians already reconciled? We cannot escape from this question by saying that Paul is only describing the general character of his message; for he seems clearly in these words to be pressing it home upon the Corinthians. The great act of reconciliation does not preclude a succession of minor acts before the heart and will are absolutely at one with God.

Him who knew no sin he made to be sin on our behalf (**v., 21**).—This is one of those great sayings of Paul's which suggest so much, and for that very reason leave it uncertain what precise shade of meaning he intended to convey. There is one interpretation, however, which we may confidently set aside. The second "sin" cannot mean a sin-offering, for the word never has that sense, and we cannot attach two meanings to the same word within the limits of the same line. Does the expression, then, mean simply that Christ suffered the punishment of death, as though he had been the embodiment of sin? This may be included, but by itself is hard and unsatisfactory. The proper antithesis of "knew no sin" is "became acquainted with sin," and this Christ did through the sympathy of love, going down into the dark places of human guilt, and bearing on his own heart the grief and shame of others' sin. It is this identification of himself with the sin and misery of his brethren, when he might have lived alone on serene and holy heights of contemplation and communion, which draws men to him, and leads them to identify themselves with the righteousness that was in him. The depth and power of this love were made manifest on the cross, when he submitted to the punishment of a guilty slave; but without a prior manifestation of the love in its redemptive and healing action the crucifixion would be only a painful riddle.

That we might become the righteousness of God in him (v., 21).—"We" is emphatic, in opposition to "him" of the previous clause. The statement may be true of mankind generally; but I think it appears both from the preceding and from the following context that the Christian teachers are those immediately in view. They were to be an embodiment of the righteousness of God in Christ, that they might call on men with the power of a Divine appeal to be reconciled to God. We may, however, universalise the thought; and then we naturally ask, Is the righteousness of God to be as unreal in us as sin in Christ, and is the Apostle only dealing with things falsely imputed? The answer lies in the nature of the things contrasted. The sympathetic identification of oneself with sin only tends to keep the heart more holy, and the anguish of Gethsemane draws the will into more complete self-surrender: the sympathetic identification of oneself with righteousness, through the appeal of love, tends to bring one nearer to righteousness, and to make it a more commanding power in the life.

Working together with him (**vi., 1**).—The words "with him" are inserted by the translators. Probably "with God" is meant, though other explanations have been given. Compare 1 Cor. iii., 9.

Saith (**vi., 2**).—The quotation is from the LXX, Isaiah xlix., 8.

Giving (**vi., 3**).—This agrees with "we" in *v*. i, the intervening verse being parenthetical. He once more enlarges on the self-denial of his ministry, which proved that it was not open to blame, and ought to secure the sympathy of the Corinthians.

Commending ourselves (**vi., 4**).—It has been pointed out that in the Greek "ourselves" here is not emphatic, as it is when he repels the charge of self-commendation. "Ministers of God" is in the nominative. It is as being God's ministers that they strive to commend themselves by their faithful labour and endurance.

Fastings (**vi., 5**).—According to the usage of the word these must have been voluntary. The word gives a momentary, but not unimportant, glimpse into Paul's private religious habits.

In the Holy Ghost (**vi., 6**).—The collocation seems to make it clear that the Holy Spirit is not here regarded as a person. There is no article in the Greek; but this is only in agreement with the rest of the passage, and does not supply a reason for understanding the phrase in any but the usual sense. There was not yet a formulated doctrine.

As deceivers, and yet *true* (**vi., 8**).—It is generally supposed that the first clause expresses the opinion of adversaries, and that this is contradicted by the second clause. Hence the translators have inserted "yet." It is possible, however, that the words may refer to the two kinds of "report" (Alford). A similar remark applies to the succeeding words, "as unknown, and *yet* well known." The subsequent clauses, in either case, seem to describe contrasted experiences in Paul's own life.

As poor, yet making many rich (**vi.**, **10**) ; that is, poor in worldly goods, yet enriching many with spiritual treasure. Some, thinking that both words must be understood literally, suppose that the reference is to alms or collections. But these can never have been sufficient to make the recipient rich. There is a similar contrast in the following words: outwardly he was destitute, and had nothing that he could call his own ; inwardly he held the universe, and appropriated spiritually all the beauty and glory of the world.

In the long description of the nature of the Gospel, and the life of hardship which he so willingly underwent on its behalf, Paul has not forgotten the immediate object which he has in view, to restore perfectly good relations between himself and the church at Corinth; so he now beseeches them to open their hearts to him, and not allow themselves to be misled by unbelievers (vi., 11-vii., 4).

In presenting the subject in this way I assume that the paragraph vi., 14-vii., 1 is genuine. It is apparently so disconnected that many regard it as an interpolation ; but there is no external authority to justify a doubt, and it is difficult to understand how an interpolation which on the face of it is so inappropriate came to be inserted in all the manuscripts. It may be pointed out, too, that, if we are to judge simply by connection, there must be a far larger interpolation ; for vii., 5 is the immediate continuation of ii., 13. But Paul has chosen to insert a number of grand reflections, many of which may have occupied his mind while he was waiting in Macedonia for Titus. The explanation which I have given of these reflections lends some appropriateness to the warning against unbelievers. We are too apt to think of Paul as exercising all his activity within the Church, and of his adversaries as being necessarily Jewish Christians, and we forget that he was in ceaseless conflict with the great worlds of Judaism and heathenism, and that his converts were subject to every kind of extraneous influence that could make them traitors to their faith. Many a gibe against the Apostle may have been uttered by the polished rhetoricians of Corinth, many a charge of double-dealing and religious imposture been made by the worldly-wisemen of the fashionable and immoral city. If we knew all the circumstances to which allusions, to us obscure, are made in the Epistle, we might see that the paragraph was quite in place, much of the coldness towards Paul being the result of an unworthy deference to heathen sentiment and practice. Among those who regard the passage as an interpolation, some, on the alleged ground that it is un-Pauline both in language and sentiment, take it to be a later forgery; others, conceding that it may be Paul's, suppose that it has got misplaced. One of the happiest suggestions from the latter side is that it was part of the lost letter to which reference is made in 1 Cor. v., 9, and that it gave rise to the very misapprehension which is there corrected. We must then suppose that the leaf containing it got accidentally inserted when the Epistles were prepared for publication.

Our heart is enlarged (**vi., 11**), or, more strictly, "has been enlarged," referring to that expansiveness of feeling which led him to take into its embrace all the Christians at Corinth, and pour forth so freely to them his high thoughts and his personal experiences. If there was any narrowness in the matter it was in their affection for him; but as they were his spiritual children, they ought to lay aside their suspicions, and become large-hearted towards him.

Unequally yoked (**vi., 14**), a figure borrowed from placing two unequal animals, as an ox and an ass, under the same yoke. See Levit. xix., 19 in the LXX, and Deut. xxii., 10. The figure, combined with the whole tenor of the passage, seems to me to require more than separation from heathen sins, and to demand a certain aloofness from heathen society and influence. I cannot, however, regard this as un-Pauline. Though in Christ there was neither Jew nor Greek, Paul recognised fully the evils of the Gentile world; and if he did not require his disciples to "go out of the world" (1 Cor. v., 10), he reproves them severely even for going before the civil tribunals (*ib.*, vi., 1 *sqq.*), and insists that they must abstain from everything that could be interpreted into complicity with Gentile worship (*ib.*, viii., 1 *sqq.*; x., 14 *sqq.*). The present passage does not enter into details, but implies clearly enough that the grounds of the needed separation were the idolatrous and sinful practices of the heathen; and the admonition does not go further than we might expect if the Corinthians exposed themselves too freely to Gentile influence, and listened too readily to Gentile arguments and insinuations.

Belial (vi., 15) had become a synonym for Satan. The Greek Beliar indicates, perhaps, not an accidental, but a contemptuous change of pronunciation.

As God said (vi., 16).—The quotation is made up from Levit. xxvi., 12, and Ezek. xxxvii., 27.

Saith the Lord (vi., 17).—The quotation is taken rather loosely from Isai. lii., 11, and Ezek. xx., 34 (LXX).

Will be to you a Father (vi., 18).—The quotation is suggested by the LXX of 2 Kings [Sam.] vii., 8, 14; Isai. xliii., 6.

Defilement of flesh and spirit (vii., 1).—It is needless to drag in here Paul's doctrine of the connection between the flesh and sin. However we may interpret that doctrine, any overt act of uncleanness, such as was common with the Gentiles, would be a defilement. The idea of a defilement of the spirit is more unexpected; for Paul means by the spirit that higher element in us which brings us into communion with God. But such terms are flexible, and here it is applied simply to the conscious element in us, which is distinguished from the flesh. Compare 1 Cor. vii., 34, where we have "body and spirit," or, as we might say, body and mind.

Open your hearts to us (**vii., 2**).—This is connected both in thought and in language (in the Greek) with vi., 11–13 ; and whether the parenthetical paragraph be genuine or not, I cannot regard this as the introduction to a fresh section.

We wronged no man, etc. (**vii., 2**).—He is repelling charges, such as might very well have proceeded from Gentiles, when they saw their friends perverted, as they thought, by Paul. In the improved state of his relations with the church the mere denial of such charges was sufficient.

I say it not to condemn you (**vii., 3**).—He does not refer to these charges in order to condemn his readers for having listened to them, but only to put himself right.

The thought of comfort in affliction (vii., 4) leads him to resume the historical narrative which he broke off at ii., 13, and to speak of the joy which he derived from the coming of Titus with good news about the state of things at Corinth (vii., 5–16).

Our flesh had no relief (**vii., 5**), alluding probably to the bodily restlessness, amounting sometimes to sleeplessness, which is produced by great anxiety. In ii., 13, he says he had no relief for his *spirit*, the conscious seat of his anxieties and fears.

With my epistle (**vii., 8**), now lost : see the Introduction. In his anxiety as to its effect he had regretted sending it. When Titus came, he learned that it really had given pain, but only for a season, and that it had had the desired result of producing repentance and reviving the affection of the brethren towards himself.

That ye might suffer loss by us in nothing (**vii., 9**), indicating the Divine purpose. Sorrow with such blessed results could not be counted "loss."

Which bringeth no regret (**vii., 10**).—Some would connect this with "salvation." But though this is grammatically admissible, it seems inappropriate, for no one could suppose that salvation was a thing to be regretted. There may be an allusion to Paul's present regret that he had ever repented of sending his letter.

The sorrow of the world worketh death (vii., 10) ; the sorrow felt by worldly men, which was selfish and related to material things, as distinguished from "godly sorrow." It is far fetched to interpret "death" of suicides brought about by despair. Death refers to the loss of spiritual vitality, the death of the soul, as contrasted with "salvation."

What earnest care, etc. (vii., 11).—They took the matter much more seriously to heart ; they sought to clear themselves of all complicity in the offence, and were indignant with the offender ; they feared that Paul might be alienated from them, and longed for his return ; they were zealous to inflict proper punishment, and did actually inflict it.

I wrote not for his cause that did the wrong (vii., 12).—See the note on ii., 5-11. If Paul referred in this verse to the case of incest, I am afraid we could only say it was quite unworthy of him. But if he meant that a mere personal affront was not in itself worth notice, but that he wished to bring his friends to a full and clear consciousness of their real affection for him, then he writes as we should expect. He seems to have feared that the insult was acquiesced in by others, and he wished by an earnest appeal to waken into active manifestation the love which he felt sure was indeed there. The letter had the desired result. Titus, who seems to have gone there with some apprehension, was delighted with his visit, and Paul was completely reassured.

We now enter on the second division of the Epistle, which gives full instructions about the collection for the poor Christians in Jerusalem (viii.-ix.).

He begins by appealing to the example of the churches in Macedonia (viii., 1-6).

The grace of God (**viii., 1**).—" Grace " must be used here in its ordinary sense. The Macedonians were moved by the grace of God. Farther on it denotes the gracious gift.

Proof of affliction (**viii., 2**); that is, affliction which put them to the proof. See 1 Thess. ii., 14; iii., 3-5; and for a later time, Phil. i., 29.

Liberality (**viii., 2**); literally, " simplicity " ; and therefore, when connected with giving, denoting the simple generosity, and therefore liberality, with which the gift is made. This meaning, however, is not undisputed, and the word certainly suggests the pure feeling of the giver rather than the extent of his gift.

As he had made a beginning before (**viii., 6**).—This seems naturally to mean " before his last visit," though in the imperfect state of our information we must leave details in uncertainty. It has also been understood to refer to his last visit, in which he began before the Macedonians; but the *collecting* of Titus and the *giving* of the Macedonians do not properly come into comparison, and we must supply something relating to the action of Titus himself.

After this introduction he exhorts them to contribute willingly, and in Christian love, according to their means (viii., 7-15).

By way of commandment (**viii., 8**): that is, I do not command that this collection be made, but only appeal to your love to carry it out.

The grace of our Lord Jesus Christ (**viii., 9**), the gracious spirit of love, which led him to give up so much for others. This verse is frequently explained as referring to Christ's pre-existence : though he was rich in heavenly glory, he renounced it through the incarnation. I cannot persuade myself that this interpretation is correct. For, first, " Jesus " is the name of the man who lived and taught in Palestine; and " Christ " is the official title of a man who was " anointed " for a special work on earth ; so that the pre-existent being (if Paul recognised such) was not Jesus Christ, but incarnate *in* Jesus Christ. Consequently, if the reference here is to pre-existence, Paul must have believed that the human personality pre-existed. He may, as we have already seen, have held the common belief that all souls pre-existed; but this is at all events not the doctrine of the later theology, and it is doubtful whether the earthly names would be applied even to a pre-existent soul. It is true that when these names had come to be habitually employed so as to cover the whole personality of the incarnate Son, people could speak loosely of the pre-existence of Jesus Christ; but I think Paul in such a case would have avoided this misleading language, and have spoken of "the Son of God." Secondly, the Greek, if I am not mistaken, means not "became poor," but "was poor," and implies that the "being rich" was contemporaneous with the poverty.[1] The verse then means, that though he was rich in every spiritual possession (which might have made him great and powerful), he lived a life of poverty, that ye may be spiritually wealthy. We have already seen "poor" and "rich" used with a transition from the literal to the metaphorical meaning in the same verse (vi., 10). We are apt to suppose that the life of Christ, before the closing scenes, did not involve much renunciation, because he came probably of a poor family; but he must have meant something by taking up the cross daily, and not having where to lay his head. It is possible to choose a life of poverty for the sake of some loving service, even though there is not, as in the case of the Buddha or of St. Francis, any store of material wealth to abandon.

[1] See the Epistle to Diognetus, § 5, where it is said of Christians generally, πτωχεύουσι, καὶ πλουτίζουσι πολλούς. The reference seems to be to vi., 10; but instead of πτωχοί the writer uses the verb which occurs in viii., 9. Cyril of Jerusalem says, ὁ δὲ πιστὸς ἀνὴρ . . . ἐν πενίᾳ πλουτεῖ (Catech., v., 2).

This (viii., 10) : that is, probably, completing the collection ; for if it meant " giving my judgment instead of a commandment," " expedient " would not be a very suitable expression. They had anticipated the Macedonians, not only in contributing to the fund, but in expressing their willingness to do so ; and therefore it was expedient to have no further delay.

At this present time (viii., 14), implying that he looked upon the distress in Jerusalem as temporary. The time might come when their relations would be reversed.

As it is written (viii., 15).—The quotation is from Exodus xvi., 18, and refers to the collection of the manna.

Paul now leaves his exhortation, in order to recommend Titus and two other brethren whom he was sending to be recipients of the fund (viii., 16-24).

It is impossible to determine who these brethren were, and the numerous conjectures which have been put forward are only wasted labour.

He accepted our exhortation (viii., 17).—This points back to the statement of *v.* 6 ; but Titus was so zealous that exhortation was unnecessary.

In the gospel (viii., 18).—This has been understood to be a reference to Luke's Gospel ; but it is now generally admitted that the word can refer only to the preaching of the Gospel.

That any man should blame us (viii., 20).—He chose to have representatives of the church with him, so that there could be no suspicion of misappropriation in connection with so large a sum.

We take thought for things honourable, etc. (viii., 21).— This verse is quoted, with slight additions, from Proverbs iii., 4, in the LXX.

Messengers (viii., 23).—The word " apostles " should have been retained, for it is a term which was by no means limited to the twelve in early times.

The commendation of his messengers naturally suggests the object of their mission. It was indeed superfluous for him to write about that, as the Corinthians had shown their readiness so long before. Nevertheless he delicately exhorts them to have every arrangement quite complete before his own arrival, perhaps with friends from Macedonia (ix., 1-5).

In this respect (ix., 3).—His boasting of them covered a wider range than the matter of the collection; on that point he did not wish it to be proved vain.

Extortion (ix., 5), properly "covetousness." If the supposed covetousness were on the part of Paul, the meaning might be fairly represented by "extortion." But I think it is much more naturally referred to the Corinthians, for otherwise there is no true contrast. The Corinthians might be willing to bestow "a blessing" (bounty), and yet Paul might be covetous, and eager to extort all he could. The meaning, then, probably is that they should be willing to bless by giving all they could, and not covetously consider with how little they might get off.

Finally he points out the blessings that arise from cheerful giving: in the providence of God men reap as they sow, and such acts of kindness awaken thanksgiving to God, and create a mutual brotherly affection (ix., 6-15).

This (ix., 6), without any verb expressed, calls attention to what follows;—"this is to be particularly noted."

Bountifully (ix., 6), literally, "with blessings"; but the connection with reaping shows that they are not spoken, but bestowed; hence the phrase is equivalent to "bountifully."

God loveth a cheerful giver (ix., 7), probably suggested by a line in Prov. xxii., 8 a, in the LXX, "God blesses a cheerful man and a giver."

All grace (ix., 8).—The context seems to prove that the word is used here of outward gifts graciously bestowed; but it is not unsuitable to include also the inward grace of generosity.

As it is written (**ix., 9**).—The quotation is verbatim from the LXX of Ps. cxi. (cxii.), 9.

His righteousness (**ix., 9**); that is, the just and kindly temper which leads a man to be helpful and generous in the use of his possessions.

Seed to the sower and bread for food (**ix., 10**).—These words are quoted from the LXX of Isaiah lv., 10.

The fruits of your righteousness (**ix., 10**), an expression borrowed from Hosea x., 12, in the LXX. The fruits are the results of their generosity, which in the following verses are shown to be not only the supplying of the wants of the needy, but the awakening of pious and brotherly feeling. Thus *the ministration* (**ix., 12**) not only served its immediate purpose, but superabounded, and, as it were, poured its overflow through other channels.

Liberality of your *contribution* (**ix., 13**).—These words may be translated "the simplicity of your communion," and in favour of this translation it is urged that the "contribution" was not made "unto all." The Revisers' translation seems best suited to the context, and the Apostle may have added the words "unto all" in order to imply that the generosity of the Corinthians was not confined to this particular occasion. For the rendering of the Greek word by "contribution," see Romans xv., 26.

His unspeakable gift (**ix., 15**).—This naturally points to the blessings of which Paul has just spoken, and especially the drawing together of the Jewish and Gentile churches through the ministrations of love, and it seems rather forced to refer it to God's gift of His Son, though that is indirectly included as the basis of every Christian blessing. The words form a suitable close to this portion of the Epistle, and may remind us that the ability and the will to give are matters, not for boasting, but for thankfulness.

In the third part of the Epistle Paul defends himself against his opponents, and threatens the impenitent with condign punishment (x., 1–xiii., 10).

This part of the Epistle is marked by a very unexpected change of tone, which has given rise to certain hypotheses intended to explain it. These are briefly noticed in the Introduction. Here we may observe that throughout this passage Paul defends his own character and claims against spiteful enemies, and not his Gospel against an adverse (judaising) gospel. In this respect the contrast with the first two chapters of Galatians is very noticeable. Here there is no reference to the Law, and the fear which Paul entertains is not lest the Corinthians should judaise, but lest they should be corrupted from simplicity and purity (xi., 3). This indeed is followed (xi., 4) by the ironical suggestion that if he who was coming preached a different gospel, it might be well to bear with him, the implication being that in fact he would preach the same Gospel, though it might be with subtle interpretations and tricks of speech. There is only one verse which distinctly proves that some of the opponents were of Jewish race (xi., 22). Other allusions are more suitable to Greeks, who set store on philosophical thought and eloquence of expression, and were far more inclined to sensual sin than the Jews (x., 5, 10; xi., 3, 6; xii., 21). These facts seem to render it probable that Paul is now dealing, not with an estrangement resting on doctrinal differences, but with bitter personal manifestations of that factious spirit which he rebuked in the opening portion of his First Epistle. An anti-Pauline faction may very well have included Greeks as well as Jews, though its animosity may probably have been fomented by Jewish-Christian visitors who claimed to be invested with a higher authority than Paul's.

He begins with words of gentle pleading that he may not have to exercise severity when he comes (x., 1–6).

I Paul myself (**x., 1**).—These words show that he is

entering on strictly personal matters, and separate him from Timothy, who was associated with him in the composition of the letter.

By the meekness and gentleness of Christ (**x., 1**), an appeal to their better feelings. They should be gentle, and not make it necessary for him to be more severe than his Master.

In your presence am lowly (**x., 1**), an allusion to the sneer at his bodily weakness, quoted in *v.* 10.

Walked according to the flesh (**x., 2**); that is, "governed my conduct by low and worldly motives." No doubt, like other mortals, he was "in the flesh," and this was an element of weakness; but his armoury was spiritual, and therefore mighty, and would be sufficient to pull down whatever was opposed to the rule of Christ.

When your obedience shall be fulfilled (**x., 6**).—He assumes that the church as a whole will be obedient; and when this result has been secured, then he will be ready to visit every persistent case of disobedience with due punishment.

After this introduction of the subject he asserts his determination to maintain his authority by an appeal to plain facts (x., 7-11).

Ye look at the things that are before your face (**x., 7**).—The sense apparently is,—you judge men by things that are outward and obvious: very well; then look at the fruits of my ministry, which are quite as plain as any advantages of which my adversaries can boast. The meaning is substantially the same if we make the clause interrogative, or if we treat the verb as an imperative. In the latter case he appeals to them to look at the evident nature and results of his labours.

Trusteth in himself that he is Christ's (**x., 7**).—This is clearly a boast on the part of the opponents, and must imply something more than merely being a Christian. It must be a claim to have a closer connection with Christ, and therefore a higher authority, than belonged to Paul. This is proved by the connection with the next verse, which, through its "for," gives a reason for the assertion which is here made.

I shall not be put to shame (**x., 8**), because all my glorying will be borne out by facts. A spurious authority would not have established so many churches.

That I may not seem as if I would terrify you (**x., 9**).—The connection of this verse is by no means apparent, and must be found in some suppressed thought: I will not say too much of my authority, and such authority as I possess was given me, not to injure you, but to build you up. There is of course an allusion to the sneer of his enemies: he is very valiant at a distance, and frightens you with letters; but when he actually comes he turns out to be a poor creature.

His bodily presence is weak (**x., 10**).—We do not know in what this weakness consisted; but it is clear that Paul was not the stalwart orator of popular imagination. We can readily suppose that his public speaking lent itself to this gibe at a time when oratory was studied with as much care as professional singing is among us, and when men cared more for outward grace and finish than for spiritual insight and depth of conviction; and yet, if his modulation violated the rules of the rhetoricians, his tones may have reached far into the sanctuary of hearts that were prepared.

Such are we also in deed (**x., 11**).—Whatever differences there might be in the impressiveness of his letters and his speech, his conduct was always directed by the same principles.

A rather obscure passage follows, of which the general purport is that he glories only in what he has himself accomplished, and not (like some) in other men's labours (x., 12-18).

We are not bold (**x., 12**); ironically,—"we do not venture to do such a thing." It is probable that the men whom Paul treats so contemptuously were really very vain and paltry. In great religious movements the leaders are often compelled to assert themselves pretty peremptorily, in order that their work may not be wrecked by conceited and incapable upstarts. These fussy creatures sometimes make a strong, though temporary, impression; and it is only to a later generation that their relative magnitude becomes clear.

But they themselves, etc. (**x., 12**).—The words as they stand give a good sense. The antithesis is with the sense implied in the previous clause: they seem to be very fine fellows; but shutting themselves up in a clique given to mutual admiration, and having no standard beyond themselves, they do not understand the real state of the case. Some, contending that an antithesis containing Paul's mode of judgment is required, omit the words "are without understanding. But we"; and then we must translate in the first person, the sense being,—we will not compare ourselves with some, but, measuring our condition by our ideal, we will not glory beyond our measure. The change is not necessary, and has far too little support in the ancient authorities to be safely adopted.

Beyond our *measure* (**x., 13**).—"Our" is inserted by the translators. The Greek rather suggests, "we will not go off into unmeasured boasting," like the vain men who have no standard with which to compare themselves.

Province (**x., 13**).—This is an interpretation, not a translation. The Greek means the rule or line with which the measure is taken.

In the Gospel of Christ (**x., 14**); that is, in preaching the Gospel. It is implied that his was the preaching which first reached them.

In other men's labours (**x., 15**), *in another's province* (**x., 16**).—Paul implies that his opponents were intruding on his ground, where they could have made no impression unless he had been there before them. For his own part he was anxious not to interfere with other men, but to seek always untrodden fields.

He that glorieth, etc. (**x., 17**), a saying quoted also in 1 Cor. i., 31. It is a motto which he tried to make the rule of his life.

He now enters on the glorying itself; and first, in a few introductory verses, states his reason for descending to this apparent folly. It was due, not to pride in himself, but to zeal for them (xi., 1-3).

The division of the paragraphs is uncertain; but I think the comparison of himself with the false teachers begins with *v.* 4.

Nay indeed bear with me (**xi., 1**).—I think the marginal translation does more justice to the Greek construction. It also suits the sense: in asking for their forbearance he does not forget that they already bear with him, though he is going to try their patience a little further. The imperative, on the other hand, gives a feeble repetition of the same sense.

One husband (**xi., 2**).—"One" is specified in order to emphasise the purity and simplicity of the attachment which they ought to feel. All their love ought to go to one, and suffer no distraction.

As the serpent beguiled Eve (**xi., 3**).—The comparison may seem a little far-fetched; but as Christ was the second Adam, the Church might be regarded as standing to him in the relation of Eve. There may possibly be an allusion to the rabbinical notion that Eve was seduced into idolatry.

The first point in his boasting is that he has as full a knowledge of the Gospel as his rivals (xi., 4-6).

For (**xi., 4**).—With the connection which we have suggested this word does not introduce the reason for *v.* 3: I am afraid you may be corrupted, for these men are really preaching another Jesus. It refers rather to the general implication of the previous passage: I have a better claim upon you than my opponents, for, first, I have as much knowledge as they.

He that cometh (**xi., 4**), the coming man, whoever he may be. Paul need not be referring to any particular individual; but it is clear that he has in mind, not members of the church itself, but one or more visitors from abroad, who were extolled by their partisans for their eloquence and knowledge. In what follows it is disputed whether Paul is charging these men with really preaching another Jesus or is ironically making an impossible supposition. We may to some extent combine these views by supposing that they boasted of giving a truer representation of Jesus, and preaching a far finer gospel than Paul, but that Paul treated this as mere pretence. The sense may then be given thus:—If you find that these men really do as they say, it is all very well to put up with them; but in fact their claim is baseless, for my knowledge (*gnosis*) is as good as theirs. If, however, Paul is stating what he believed to be a fact, the connection is as follows:—I am afraid you may be corrupted; for if the coming man preach (as he does) a gospel different from mine, you bear with him splendidly. There is a various reading at the end of the verse, which is supported by most of our authorities, though one manuscript of the greatest weight gives the reading in the text. With the variation the sense would seem to be:—If the man preaches another Jesus (which is impossible), you would do well enough in bearing with him.

The very chiefest Apostles (**xi., 5**).—I prefer the translation in the margin; for there can be little doubt that the phrase is a sarcastic description of the false teachers, and contains no reference to the Twelve. The latter, to say the least, would be as " rude in speech " as himself.

Rude in speech (**xi., 6**).—This phrase, in the original, only implies that he was not a professional speaker. For this he cared little; for he did not want to win applause, but to melt the heart. The claim, however, to possess a higher *gnosis* was a different thing, and this he could not admit. He had indeed no wish to indulge in speculations which corrupted the simplicity of the Gospel; but he knew the Gospel in all its height and depth, and made it manifest in every particular, and among all, reserving no esoteric secrets.

As a second point in his boasting he dwells on the fact that he preached the Gospel gratis (xi., 7-15).

Did I commit a sin (**xi., 7**).—This is partly ironical, but partly also a reference to the charge of not venturing to claim his apostolic rights, or of being cold and distrustful towards the Corinthians in not choosing to do so (see *v.* 11).

I robbed [better, *despoiled*] *other churches* (**xi., 8**), namely, those in Macedonia. See Phil. iv., 15, where the bounty is attributed to the church at Philippi alone. The plural here may be rhetorical; or possibly the Philippians alone contributed on his departure from Macedonia, but "the brethren" afterwards brought contributions from other churches as well.

When I was present with you (**xi., 9**).—Two occasions are specified. He had brought supplies with him with a view to his ministry; afterwards, during his residence in Corinth, his wants were supplied from Macedonia. "The brethren" were either Silvanus and Timothy or Macedonian visitors, whom the Corinthians would remember.

That I may cut off occasion (**xi., 12**).—The interpretation of this verse is very uncertain. Two facts, however, are pretty clear, and these must control our judgment. The false teachers were willing to receive support from the churches; for Paul excepts only himself and Barnabas from what he regards as an established right of maintenance (1 Cor. ix., 6 *sqq.*). Secondly, they were anxious to have the appearance of real Apostles (xi., · 13-15). Accordingly, "that wherein they glory" is most probably their assumed apostleship; and the "occasion" is (less certainly) the opportunity of making a plausible comparison of themselves with genuine Apostles. If this be correct the final clause may be taken as a definition of the "occasion";—they seek an occasion, in their apostolic pretensions, of placing themselves on an equality with Paul; and this they could not have so long as Paul's labour was entirely without emolument. If this connection be not accepted, we may perhaps regard the last clause as a challenge from Paul to become as disinterested as himself; for we cannot well regard it as expressing his real purpose. Even a pretended following of his disinterestedness would only have served to increase their repute. Some commentators think that this was the course which they were actually pursuing, making public professions of being completely disinterested, but receiving gifts in a private and underhand way. This does not seem probable.

Fashioning (**xi., 13**); better, "transforming." It is unfortunate that we do not know who or what sort of men these were. Simply to say that they were Judaisers may be exceedingly unjust to Paul, who in that case would be guilty of pouring abuse upon serious, if narrow-minded, opponents, instead of meeting them in fair argument. But there is no reason for this assumption. They were much more probably the parasites who bring danger and disgrace on new movements, and belonged to the class that is described in Rom. xvi., 17-20.

Satan fashioneth himself (**xi., 14**).—There is probably no reference to any particular incident, but only an allusion to the general belief that Satan sought in this way to gain his ends.

Before proceeding to details in his own life which were a subject for glorying he once more excuses himself for descending to such foolishness as boasting (xi., 16-21).

I say again (**xi., 16**).—The reference must be to *v.* 1, although the form of expression is changed. He is not a fool; but he craves at least as much attention as would be granted to a fool. It is only in the assumed character of a fool, and not as one under the direction of the Lord, that he indulges in boasting (**xi., 17**).

Glory after the flesh (**xi., 18**); that is, boast of mere outward distinctions, such as their descent from Abraham. To boast of such things Paul regarded as sheer folly.

Being wise yourselves (**xi., 19**): strongly ironical; in the calmness of their superior wisdom they are ready to bear not only folly, but violence.

If he bringeth you into bondage (**xi., 20**).—Even here the reference is to the grand airs and overbearing conduct of the men who are attacked, and not to the error of their teaching. The "bondage" might indeed be to the law; but the law is not mentioned throughout, and bondage to the imperious demands of the men themselves is probably what is intended.

I speak by way of disparagement, as though we had been weak (**xi., 21**).—It is difficult to extract any meaning from this translation, and the Greek is also obscure. Two things are plain in the original. The word translated "I speak" requires an object, and would be better rendered by "I say"; and the second clause is so expressed as to indicate, not a fact, but someone's (here the Corinthians') conception of a fact. The passage may then be understood as purely ironical, thus: I say to my own disparagement that (as you suppose) I was too weak to do things of that sort. Or the words may refer to the previous verse: You bear with such men (I say so to your disparagement) on the ground that I [whom you ought naturally to have obeyed] was weak and insignificant.

He now proceeds to enumerate the various circumstances in his history which might form a subject for boasting (xi., 22-xii., 10).

Hebrews, etc. (**xi., 22**).—The word "Hebrews" is here used in its widest national sense, not, as sometimes, to denote Palestinian as distinguished from Hellenistic. "Israelite" is the theocratic, and therefore a higher, designation. "The seed of Abraham" points out the heirs of the Messianic promises. The term is extended by Paul to the believing

Gentiles (Gal. iii., 29; Rom. iv., 16), but is here confined to literal descent.

Are they ministers of Christ? (**xi., 23**).—It is not denied that they are really such, even though their labours were not equal to Paul's. We need not identify these with the "false Apostles" of *v.* 13. In the number of Paul's opponents there may have been men of various character, and he may now be referring to the more respectable among them. In the interesting list of his experiences which follows there are several particulars which are not recorded in Acts, showing how very imperfect the historian's narrative is.

Forty stripes *save one* (**xi., 24**).—This punishment was inflicted by the local Jewish courts, to which the Romans allowed a certain jurisdiction over their own community. According to Deut. xxv., 3, an offender might receive forty stripes, but that was the extreme limit. As a precaution, therefore, lest the number should be inadvertently exceeded, only thirty-nine were inflicted.

Beaten with rods (**xi., 25**), by the order of Roman magistrates. It was against the law to scourge a Roman citizen; but several instances are cited in which the rights of Roman citizens were disregarded.

Perils among false brethren (**xi., 26**), such as are alluded to in Gal. ii., 4. Considering the nature of religious bigotry, we can believe that some of these were willing to use violence against Paul. However shocking such a supposition may be, it certainly seems implied in the present passage.

Who is weak, and I am not weak? (**xi., 29**).—" Weak " must be used here in quite a general sense. The verse expresses Paul's profound sympathy, which in itself was a drain upon his feelings. He was consumed in the failings and struggles of other men.

I will glory of the things that concern my weakness (**xi., 30**).—As there is no mark of transition to a fresh subject, the connection may perhaps be thus supplied: Since I must boast, I will boast of the very weakness of body which is made a reproach against me; for it is due to the hardships which I have undergone, to the intensity of my feelings, yea to the visions which have been vouchsafed to me, and on this very weakness my spiritual power depends. He is going to speak of his holiest experiences, and hence the solemn asseveration with which he begins, and which we must not limit to the incident in Damascus. That incident, however, may have made a deep impression upon him, for not only was his life in the greatest danger, but it was his first experience of being the persecuted instead of the persecutor. It was an instance of his weakness, having to slink away like a hunted animal; and yet it was something to boast of that he dared to encounter such risks. This explanation attempts to remove the chief difficulties of the passage. Some, however, are so impressed with the irrelevancy of the strong asseveration in *v.* 31, when applied to the event at Damascus, that they regard the latter as interpolated, and so bring *v.* 31 into immediate connection with the second part of xii., 1, or even with xii., 2. This undoubtedly would remove a difficulty; and the variety of reading in xii., 1 is thought to give it additional plausibility. But the interpolation would be very difficult to explain; and Paul's style, especially when he writes under strong feeling, is not so finished and connected as to call for these heroic remedies.

In Damascus (**xi., 32**).—For the event see Acts ix., 23-25.

Visions and revelations of the Lord (**xii., 1**); that is, granted by, or proceeding from, the Lord. These are mentioned, not as subjects of boasting, but as the reason for the "thorn in the flesh."

I know a man in Christ (**xii., 2**).—It is clear, in spite of *v.* 5, that he means himself. He adopts this form of expression in order to disclaim all personal merit. The phrase "in Christ," implying a spiritual union with him, is richer in meaning than "a disciple of Christ" or "a Christian."

Fourteen years ago (**xii., 2**).—This, according to the usual chronology, gives the year 43 or 44. The date shows that Paul refers to a single occasion.

In the body . . . out of the body (**xii., 2**).—Whether Paul meant this quite literally may perhaps be doubted. It implies that he was in an ecstatic condition, and unconscious of his bodily surroundings. If he meant it literally, it shows his acceptance of the belief that the soul could wander away for a time from the body, and then return.

The third heaven (**xii., 2**).—The prevailing belief in seven heavens was founded on astronomical appearances, a sphere being assumed for each of the seven planets. These heavens, or some of them, were assigned, in Jewish speculation, to various orders of spirits. In the curious *Book of the Secrets of Enoch* paradise is placed in the third heaven, and with this view the present passage seems to agree.[1]

Unspeakable words (**xii., 4**); that is, too deep and holy for human utterance,—an expression derived perhaps from the Greek mysteries.

I shall not be foolish (**xii., 6**).—The word "foolish" is now used without irony. If he did boast of his revelations, he would speak only the sober truth; but his object was to boast of his weaknesses, and he wished to be judged, not by these exalted experiences, which were in the privacy of his own soul, but by what men could see and hear for themselves.

That I should not be exalted (**xii., 7**).—Even Paul required to be kept humble, and painfully reminded that all spiritual power was a gift of grace.

There was given to me (**xii., 7**).—Clearly not by Satan, who is here regarded as an agent employed to bring about a purifying adversity.

---

[1] See chapters viii. and ix., and Mr. Charles' interesting review of the ancient belief, in the Introduction, pp. xxix. *sqq.*: *The Book of the Secrets of Enoch*, translated and edited by Morfill and Charles, Oxford, 1896.

A thorn in the flesh (**xii., 7**).—This apparently refers to some painful malady, which attacked him in the times of his greatest spiritual exaltation. Whether or not it was epilepsy, it was probably induced by the nervous exhaustion following on his spiritual transports. It seems to have been distressing, and even repellent, to those who witnessed it (see Gal. iv., 13, 14). With some other saints, too, the fire of the spirit has consumed the bodily strength, and a force that has shaken the souls of men has issued from a feeble frame.

I besought the Lord thrice (**xii., 8**).—" The Lord " is proved by the next verse to be Christ. As the number of times when he made his petition is stated, he probably refers to particular occasions of spiritual vision, when, in the utmost recesses of his soul, he exchanged words with his heavenly Guide. The third time the answer came, and remained, for him and for others, as an abiding truth.

My *power is made perfect in weakness* (**xii., 9**), for then there is nothing but the spiritual power, nothing to attract false admiration, no distraction of worldly gifts and graces. And in the Apostle himself all vain ambitions are killed, and he can only cling in trust to that power without which he must sink back into the ranks of ordinary and weak humanity.

Again the tone changes, and he once more apologises for his boasting, reminding them that the signs of an Apostle had attended him, and he had taken no advantage of the disciples (xii., 11-18).

I ought to have been commended of you (**xii., 11**).—" I " is emphatic in the Greek, in antithesis to " the superlative Apostles,"—a further proof that these " Apostles " were the pretenders at Corinth, and not the Twelve.

Though I am nothing (**xii., 11**).—This is probably not ironical, but a genuine expression of his feeling,—nothing apart from him who used him as an instrument.

Signs and wonders and mighty works (**xii., 12**).—These words refer to the same class of phenomena, but describe them under different aspects. The first regards them as evidences of the Divine presence; the second refers to their extraordinary character; and the third traces them to their source in superhuman power. Some commentators, in order to get rid of this testimony, treat them as an interpolation; and some reject with them the whole verse, together with the end of the last verse. This, however, is mere arbitrary hypothesis. Paul himself, no doubt, may have thought there were higher evidences of his apostleship than these outward and surprising tokens; and still he might not scruple to appeal to them in reply to his adversaries, and might even have been perplexed if others had them while he had not. Elsewhere he thanks God that he speaks with tongues (1 Cor. xiv., 18). He refers to "gifts of healings" as well known in the Church (1 Cor. xii., 9); and in one of the most certainly attested narratives in Acts (xxviii., 7-9) we are assured that Paul himself had this gift. It does not belong to a commentary to discuss the nature and credibility of these events. Suffice it to say that similar phenomena are guaranteed by strong evidence at various periods, and physiologists are not prepared to fix precisely the limits where the emotions of the mind cease to affect, for good or ill, the condition of the body.

I myself (**xii., 13**).—The implied contrast is not with his companions, who followed the same rule (xii., 18). It must therefore be with "signs of an Apostle": these I wrought among you, but was not myself a burden to you.

This is the third time I am ready to come to you (**xii., 14**).— The plain meaning of these words is that Paul was about to pay a third visit. To evade this by laying the emphasis on "ready" gives a very unnatural turn to the passage. If he had been *ready* fifty times, it would be nothing to the purpose; for the point is that in his coming visit he will follow the same rule which he had already observed (on two previous occasions).

Lay up (**xii., 14**), or, to give the meaning more fully, "lay up treasure." Paul regards himself as the father of the church.

If I love you more abundantly (**xii., 15**), than I do other churches, as I have shown by not making myself a burden to you.

I caught you with guile (**xii., 16**).—Such an insinuation, we must suppose, was actually made. It can, however, hardly refer to a misappropriation of the collection; for we have no reason to suppose that any of this was yet in the hands of Paul or his companions, and a charge of theft would be treated with greater indignation. The suggestion rather is that Paul's messengers not only lived at the cost of the community, but exacted, or at all events received, gifts which they handed over to Paul.

I exhorted Titus (**xii., 18**).—It is obvious from what follows that this is not the epistolary past tense, as in viii., 6, but refers to a visit which had been already paid.

By the same spirit (**xii., 18**).—I think, from the tenor of the passage, the reference is not to the Holy Spirit, but to the temper of the mind: the conduct of Titus was animated by the same spirit as Paul's own. It is implied that Titus, like Paul, chose to be no burden to the church. "The brother" with him is unknown.

The defence is now at an end. Was it real boasting? Was he trying to excuse himself to the Corinthians? No, he had been speaking with the deepest sense of responsibility for the good of the community, lest, when he came, he should have to exercise his authority in a way that would be painful both to him and to them (xii., 19-xiii., 10).

Strife, jealousy, etc. (**xii., 20**).—Observe, he dwells solely on moral faults, and says not a word about false doctrine or subjection to the law. The faults he attacks are pre-eminently the faults of the Greeks, a factious and jealous temper, and sensuality.

Should humble me before you, and I should mourn (**xii., 21**).—"Humble," because he had not sufficient spiritual power to raise them above such sins; "mourn," because no one who loves righteousness can have a deeper sorrow than springs from the guilt of those whom he loves.

Many of them that have sinned (**xii., 21**).—"Many," not "all," because he might hope that some would repent when he personally appealed to them.

This is the third time I am coming to you (**xiii., 1**).—The natural meaning of this statement is that he had already paid two visits to Corinth. In order to get rid of this plain testimony it has been twisted into the meaning, This is the third time I am thinking of coming to you. Paul may not have been skilled in the arts of rhetoric; but he was not likely to expose himself so needlessly to the obvious rejoinder that he was always making grand plans, and never had the courage to carry them out.

At the mouth of two or three witnesses (**xiii., 1**), conformably to the law in Deut. xix., 15. This has been strangely interpreted as figurative, the witnesses being his two or three visits, or things repeated two or three times in his letters. It is clear that Paul intends to act as a judge over the members of the church, and of course he would not do so without having the facts properly established. We must take note of this paramount authority which he claimed. Great reformers are often compelled to exercise a little judicious despotism.

I have said beforehand (**xiii., 2**).—The obvious meaning is that he had actually said this when he was present with them during his second visit, and he now repeats it in his absence. This is evaded by translating, "as though I were present the second time," or by connecting "the second time" with "I say beforehand." The accumulation of forced interpretations in order to get rid of the unrecorded visit adds to their improbability when taken one by one.

Them that have sinned heretofore (**xiii., 2**).—The Greek is simply "sinned before," so that "before the second visit" may be meant; and then "all the rest" may refer to those who have sinned since, or who may sin before Paul's arrival.

A proof of Christ (**xiii., 3**).—The sense seems to be that Paul's vigour in punishing will be an evidence of the power of Christ, whose word rather than his own the Apostle is uttering. Christ is not weak, but is powerful amongst them for the infliction of chastisement.

He was crucified through weakness (**xiii., 4**).—I cannot suppose that this is said in reference to the belief of Judaisers, who could see nothing but weakness in the crucifixion. Even Judaisers must have seen some Divine purpose in it, or they would not have embraced Christianity at all. Surely Paul refers to the great example simply to make clear the enigma of his own life. Weakness and strength belong to the essence of Christianity. Christ was weak so far as regards all worldly power, and sank under the frailty of death; yet he lives through the power of God. So the Apostle abjures in him all worldly strength, but he too will live through the power of God, and prove the presence of this Divine life and power by his conduct towards the Corinthians.

Try your own selves (**xiii., 5**).—The sense might be thus supplied: instead of seeking a proof of Christ in me, prove yourselves. But I think it is rather: prove yourselves instead of waiting for me to put you to the proof; see whether you retain your Christian faith, for, if you do, you will find Christ in yourselves, bringing your evil into judgment. "The faith," according to Paul's usage, must mean, not the objective system of belief, but the inward sentiment,—are you within that region of faith which is the basis of the

Christian life? If that is gone, and you have no sense of Christ in you, you are reprobate, rejected as not satisfying the test. This is put as an improbable hypothesis: the means of Christian self-judgment are really there.

But I hope (**xiii., 6**).—However this may be, I hope you will see sufficient proof of Christ in me.

Not that we may appear approved (**xiii., 7**), as we should do if our admonition prevailed, and you refrained from all evil. Our desire is simply that you should do what is right, and we should be, as it were, reprobate, having no occasion to exercise our judicial and punitive authority.

We can do nothing against the truth (**xiii., 8**): the truth of the Gospel, according to some; the truth of the facts, according to others. We may perhaps to some extent combine these explanations: my whole life is devoted to the interests of truth; therefore I cannot act against it in any particular case.

This we also pray for, even your perfecting (**xiii., 9**).—That was his one supreme object in his dealings with them. He had no wish to "deal sharply"; for the very purpose of his apostolic authority was that he might build up the Church. For this reason he put his admonitions in writing, that they might quietly produce their effect, and there might be nothing to estrange the feelings of the Corinthians, or interfere with his power of edification, when he himself appeared upon the scene.

The subject is now concluded, and Paul closes the letter with a few words expressive of the deepest affection, and still suited to the themes of which he has been treating. He exhorts them to be perfected, forsaking all the sins of which he has had to complain; and to be of the same mind, giving up their factions, and the mutual jealousy from which they sprang. And then God whose highest attributes are love and peace would be with them, and dwell within their hearts (xiii., 11-14).

All the saints (**xiii., 13**): that is, all the members of the church in the town where Paul was writing, as well as the companions of his travels.

The grace of the Lord Jesus Christ, etc. (xiii., 14).—The grace of Christ is placed first. This may be due to the fact that Paul generally speaks only of the grace of Christ in his closing benediction; and so here he begins in the usual way, and out of the fulness of his feelings adds the other clauses, which are so suited to the circumstances of the church. Or, if the whole benediction was already in his mind, he may have placed the grace of Christ first as being the basis of Christian experience. "God," standing without any defining term, such as "the Father," is clearly distinguished from Christ and the Holy Spirit. We may compare Jude 20, 21, where the Holy Spirit, the love of God, and the mercy of Christ are in similar juxtaposition, and presently (v. 25) the doxology is made "to the only God our Saviour, through Jesus Christ," the Spirit being not again mentioned. "The communion of the Holy Spirit" may mean participation in the Holy Spirit, or communion with one another effected by the Holy Spirit. Both ideas may be included; for the latter would be brought about by the former, the Spirit in the heart being the firmest and closest bond of union. This most comprehensive and sublime benediction came from the depths of Paul's love for a church which sorely needed it. He pronounced it upon "all" the members. He may have to speak severely; he may even have to expose his enemies; but there can be no exceptions in that large and profound religious love with which he would embrace both friend and foe, in order to lead them to their perfection.

THE EPISTLE TO THE GALATIANS.

INTRODUCTION.

THE Epistle to the Galatians is here placed between those to the Corinthians and that to the Romans, not because I am satisfied that that is its true chronological position, but because, that position being quite uncertain, we may conveniently locate it according to its literary affinities, and combine it with Romans, to which it is most closely related in thought and argument. The prevailing opinion has been that it was written during the same missionary journey as the Corinthian and Roman Epistles; but there has been no uniform judgment as to its place within the group, nor has it been settled whether it was written from Ephesus or Corinth, or on the journey between the two cities. Owing, however, to the want of clear chronological indications within the Epistle itself it is possible to take very different views; and it has been regarded both as the latest and as the earliest of the Pauline writings. The variety of opinion as to the date is partly connected with a difference of view as to the locality of the Galatian churches. Eminent scholars have sought for these churches in the district occupied by the horde of Gauls who forced their way into Asia Minor towards the close of the third century before Christ, while others have argued with great force in favour of the churches founded by

Barnabas and Paul, during the first missionary journey, in the southern part of the Roman province of Galatia, which embraced a much wider territory than Galatia proper. The latter view has recently been brought into prominence by the able discussions of Professor Ramsay. It is by no means free from difficulties, and the question must, I think, be regarded as still *sub judice*. It is impossible to discuss it in this small commentary; but happily the decision does not in any way affect the main purport of the Epistle.

It seems clear from the letter itself that the churches addressed were composed of Gentiles, who had passed straight from polytheism into Christianity (see iv., 8 and v., 2–4). Certain Judaisers made their way into these churches, and endeavoured, only too successfully, to persuade the people that Paul's was a very imperfect Gospel; that he knew nothing about Christianity but what he had learnt from the authorities in Jerusalem, to whom alone he could owe his title to be a missionary; and that, if they wished to enter into the full enjoyment of the promises made to Israel, they must receive the sign of the covenant. It is not surprising that such men should produce a marked effect among fickle and excitable people, who might feel awed by the grandeur of the ancient claims of Judaism, and who would think at first that, in adopting Jewish rites, they were only adding to the perfection of the Gospel which they had received from Paul.

The mind of the Apostle was deeply stirred by the accounts which reached him; for the principles laid down by the Judaisers seemed to be directly antagonistic to the Gospel which he preached. He wrote the Epistle in order to check the mischievous results which were so quickly manifesting themselves in the community. It gives a vivid picture of the activity of Judaisers among the Gentile churches, and lays down in broad lines, and with sharp incisiveness, the arguments on which Paul relied to confute their false principles. There is a tone of indignation, which now and again melts into tenderness, running through its glowing sentences. It is evident that the Apostle himself had been attacked and misrepresented; and this leads him in the first two chapters to defend his authority and independence. In doing so he gives us most interesting glimpses into his personal history. The account of a remonstrance which he addressed to Peter brings him into the doctrinal argument, which runs through the third and fourth chapters; and this is succeeded by a hortatory portion, in which the main theme constantly recurs. The Epistle closes with some ardent sentences written with the Apostle's own hand.

The subject of the Epistle is identical with that which occupies a large part of Romans, and the argument occasionally follows the same lines; but the style of treatment is exceedingly different, and, when we make a careful comparison between the two Epistles, several instructive contrasts present themselves. These are due to the general fact that in the one he is indignantly repelling an insidious and dangerous attack; in the other he is calmly endeavouring to confirm sympathetic readers, and sometimes, probably, resolving difficulties which had arisen in his own mind. The study of Galatians is a useful preparation for the wide outlook and the lofty treatment of the whole question in the larger Epistle.

GALATIANS.

COMMENTARY.

THE Epistle begins, as usual, with an address and greeting (i., 1-5), which are, however, distinguished by some special features, the insistence on the Divine origin of Paul's apostleship, the coldness of his description of the "churches" (or "congregations"), and the doctrinal allusions, which are suited to the general subject of the Apostle's communication.

Not from men, neither through man (i., 1).—We may infer that his opponents represented his apostolic commission as derived from the Twelve, and therefore possessing no independent authority; and accordingly he devotes the first part of his letter to an assertion of his independence. He was a high example of those who, without any official authority, are led by the Spirit of God. His commission was not derived ultimately "from men," nor conveyed to him through the mediation of man. "Jesus Christ" is here contrasted with "man," not because Paul denied the humanity of Christ, but because Christ in his heavenly condition, and as head of the Church, was raised above the world of men living on the earth. Hence the allusion to the resurrection: it was not through the earthly but the heavenly Christ that Paul was called to be an Apostle. The extension of the preposition "through" to God seems to indicate that Paul received his apostleship, not only through the mediation of Christ from God as its ultimate source, but through the immediate operation of God Himself. (Compare *v.* 15.)

All the brethren which are with me (i., 2), that is, his companions in travelling and teaching, who were unanimous in supporting his doctrine.

Grace to you and peace (i., 3).—The word grace, χάρις, which begins the greeting, is one which requires our attention in connection with the Pauline theology. It is obvious to every reader of the Epistles that this ancient Greek term has acquired under Christianity a theological signification. Its English equivalent is grace, a word which we must retain; for though it is sometimes desirable, when practicable, to find a substitute for the ancient expression, so as to restore the freshness and vigour of the original thought, there is no other term in English so suggestive as grace, or capable of conveying the necessary ideas.

Χάρις (grace), in what we may term its theological sense, as distinguished from its use in ordinary speech, is, though not distinctively Pauline, yet so characteristic of his language and his thought that we may probably ascribe to the Apostle of the Gentiles its introduction into Christian phraseology. In Matthew and Mark it is not found at all. Luke uses it eight times (besides the preposition χάριν, once), but of these in four instances it denotes thanks, and in the other four, if the theological sense is present, it is certainly not prominent. In John it occurs four times in the proem, but never afterwards; nor does it appear in John's First Epistle. In the other non-Pauline Epistles it is most frequent in 1 Peter, where it is used eight times, besides twice in a different meaning. In Hebrews it is much rarer than might have been anticipated. In Acts it is, as we might expect from the appearance of Paul upon the scene, and from the Pauline tendency of the writer, more common than in the Gospels, and in about nine instances we may attach to it the specifically Christian sense. But in the Pauline Epistles it presents itself not less than a hundred times; and though its import is not invariably theological, Paul's fondness for it, due probably to its religious value, is evident from its being so copiously employed. Selecting the instances of its theological use, it will be sufficient if we refer to the more important Epistles. In Romans it is met with 22 times; in 1 Corinthians 8 times; in 2 Corinthians 9 times; in Galatians 7 times; in Ephesians 12 times. The verb χαρίζομαι is confined to Luke, Acts, and the Pauline Epistles, where it is used not only of the gracious gifts and forgiveness of God, but also of human forgiveness proceeding from a like gracious spirit: see Luke vii., 42, 43; 2 Corinthians ii., 7, 10, xii., 13; Ephesians iv., 32; Colossians iii., 13. Χάρισμα is confined, with the single exception of 1 Peter iv., 10, to the Pauline Epistles, where we meet with it 16 times, of which 6 are in Romans and 7 in 1 Corinthians. We may, then, I think, safely affirm that the introduction of the word χάρις, with the ideas it involves, into Christianity is, if not exclusively, at least very largely, due to Paul's peculiar spiritual experience, combined with his remarkable powers of speculative thought. That others should to some extent have echoed his language is no more than was antecedently probable; but it is only in his Epistles that the term stands out in bold relief, and seems to express a characteristic doctrine. We now pass on to ascertain its sense.

The classical use of the word lies at the root of Paul's special application of it. From denoting outward, generally personal, grace or beauty, it came to express the gracious or kindly feeling of either the bestower or the recipient of a favour. The classical writers use it most commonly of the recipient, and then it signifies gratitude or thanks. In this sense it is occasionally employed by Paul. See, for instance, Rom. vi., 17, χάρις δὲ τῷ θεῷ. From the inward feeling of kindliness it is easily transferred to the outward favour or gift by which the kindliness is expressed. Now Paul deviates from classical usage by ascribing to the word predominantly the meaning of goodwill felt by the bestower of a favour. This is an inevitable result of carrying the idea over into the Divine realm. The χάρις of God cannot be gratitude for a benefit received, but only the gracious feeling of the all-bounteous Giver. Here, then, it receives a distinctly theological stamp. It so habitually refers to the grace of God that it may even be used by itself to represent an abstract principle of Divine government, as in Romans vi., 14, οὐ γάρ ἐστε ὑπὸ νόμον ἀλλὰ ὑπὸ χάριν, "you are not under law, but under grace." As on the human side faith stands over against legal works, so on the Divine side the grace which showers down its benefits on men is opposed to the law which only demands their obedience. If we ask in what respect this differs from love, we are introduced to another important element in Paul's thought. It excludes the notion of desert in its object. Love does not of course necessarily include this notion, for it is possible to love the unworthy; but it does not exclude it. Χάρις, however, implies an unconditioned freedom in the Divine action. This is seen most clearly in Romans iv., 4, "to him that worketh, the reward is not reckoned as of grace, but as of debt," which shows that just in proportion as the idea of debt towards the meritorious comes in, the idea of grace retreats. See also Romans iii., 24, "being justified freely by his grace" [*cf.* further Eph. ii., 8, 9].

We must next observe that the grace of which Paul speaks is exercised in the *spiritual* sphere, in relation to the *soul* of man; and consequently, when the word passes on to the meaning of a benefit or favour conferred, it denotes the effect of God's gracious operation in the soul, or the form of spiritual character which is determined by the free bounty of God. We may illustrate the extended use of the term by referring to 1 Corinthians xvi., 3, where the money collected in the church at Corinth for the poor Christians in Jerusalem is called τὴν χάριν ὑμῶν, "your grace," that is, your gift spontaneously presented as a simple offering of good-will. Paul does not use it, however, of the outward gifts of God, but reserves it for the higher and spiritual graces which flow from Him. An instructive example is furnished by 1 Corinthians xv., 10, "By the grace of God I am what I am: and His grace which was bestowed upon me was not found vain; but I laboured more abundantly than they all: yet not I, but the grace of God which was with me." Here the grace is a Divine power communicated to the soul, preparing it for a special office, and then continuously working through it. This use is further illustrated by Galatians ii., 9, where we are told that Peter, James, and John knew, or, as the Revisers have it, perceived, the grace that was given to Paul. The grace, therefore, was something which was given, and which might be recognised by its results. We get a clearer insight into its nature from the previous verse. It was an inworking of God, fitting Paul with the needed gifts to make him an Apostle to the Gentiles. The varying nature of this grace is apparent from Romans xii., 6 *sqq.*, where Christians generally are represented as having χαρίσματα (gifts of grace) differing according to the χάρις given to each. The χάρις seems to be the type of spiritual excellence which is bestowed by the grace of God, the χάρισμα the resulting aptitude for some special kind of work. In Ephesians iv., 7 *sqq.*, if we may venture to appeal to that Epistle in stating the belief of Paul, the varying character of grace is attributed to its being given in partial measures, and the hope is held out that in time this partiality will disappear, and all will attain to a complete man, to the measure of the stature of the fulness of Christ.

These remarks may suffice to make clear to our thought the Pauline meaning and use of χάρις as the grace of God. The doctrinal application of the ideas which it contains we must reserve for consideration as the occasion arises. Paul, however, speaks not only of the grace of God, but of the grace of Christ. The notion is thus modified, by introducing the great agent through whom the Divine grace manifested in the Gospel was dispensed; but its contents remain essentially the same. As we have just seen from a passage in Ephesians, Christ was regarded as the full receptacle of all the grace that was possible for man; and if Paul could say of himself that it was not he, but the grace of God, that did the work, much more was it the free and boundless love of God that lived and poured itself forth in Christ. The grace of Christ, then, was still the grace of God, not indeed in its immediate and untraceable operation in the soul, but as visible and active in one who was wholly surrendered to the guidance of the Spirit. It was his gracious influence upon the heart, an influence essentially Divine because uncontaminated by human self-will; and its result upon him whom it affected was to lay upon him the same spiritual impress, and make him consciously a child of God. Thus the grace assumed in Christ a definite and intelligible form; and Paul's thought would not be complete without this reference to Christ, which brings to a clearly defined focus what would otherwise be a vague and cloudy image.

We must now ask whether we are to attach to χάρις its rich theological meaning in this and similar salutations in the other Epistles. Fritzsche, in his note on the salutation in Romans, is for reducing it to a mere compliment, "May God and Jesus Christ favour you, and prosper your affairs." I think this explanation misses altogether the earnestness with which Paul writes. His deep religious feeling colours all his language, and he was not likely to use in an empty formula two words so fraught with spiritual meaning for himself. He would naturally have preferred the ordinary χαίρειν ("greeting"). Fritzsche's objection that the Roman Christians had not still to be brought to Christ, but must already have received grace and peace in their higher sense, is of little weight; for these spiritual gifts are not fixed quantities, given once for all, but influences which, with most of us, come and go, and for which we may pray daily. I therefore suppose that Paul in his salutations used χάρις in its profoundest and richest religious significance. The same reasoning will apply to the word which is coupled with χάρις, εἰρήνη (peace). It has been observed that the former answers to the Greek salutation, χαίρειν, and the latter to the Hebrew term used in a similar connection. It is difficult to say whether this is intentional; but at all events we must look for the meaning of "peace" in Paul himself, and not in the Hebrew greeting. Though not of such frequent occurrence as χάρις, it is still found sufficiently often to arrest the attention; but there is no passage where its meaning is very clearly defined. There can, however, be little doubt that it expresses primarily an inward, spiritual peace, the consciousness of a calm and reconciled mind. "The fruit of the Spirit," we read, "is love, joy, peace," and so forth (Gal. v., 22); and, as all the other words in the list denote mental qualities, we must ascribe a corresponding meaning to "peace." Again, "the kingdom of God is not eating and drinking, but righteousness and peace and joy in the Holy Spirit," not mere liberation from ceremonial restraints, but the possession of certain spiritual sentiments (Rom. xiv., 17, with the context). A mind at peace with itself involves peace towards God, for peace can be obtained only by the reconciliation of the lower with the higher. The law in the members wages war against the law in the mind; but the law in the mind is the law of God, and hence the inward war does not stop within, but the "mind of the flesh" is enmity against God, and on the other hand "the mind of the spirit" is peace, that is, if we are to judge from the context, peace with God (Rom. vii., 22, 23; viii., 6, 7). "Peace towards God," therefore, is one of the ends of the Christian life (Rom. v., 1). But the holy calm of a reconciled heart not only reaches upwards, but spreads around, and creates a peaceful community. "God is not a God of confusion, but of peace" (1 Cor. xiv., 33), preventing all disorders in the Church wherever His Spirit truly reigns; and it is therefore incumbent on us as Christians to "follow after things which make for peace, and things whereby we may edify one another" (Rom. xiv., 19). If this be a true sketch of what Paul meant by peace, we can understand with what serious and loving purpose he placed the word in his salutations. His strong, passionate nature knew full well the violence of inward strife, and the agony of a heart which could not feel itself at one with God; and when the power of Divine grace cooled the fever of his heart, and through the spell of a new spirit placed him on the side of God, he must have known with rare intensity the sweetness and blessedness of peace, and what better could he have wished for his most beloved friends than grace and peace, the peace of a crucified self-will, and of childlike rest in God? In this connection it may be worth while mentioning that Philo also was acquainted with "the war of the soul," and with the peace which "God graciously confers on the mind"; and he assigned to peace a most exalted rank, making it a leader among the many-named powers of the Self-existent, for God alone, as possessing absolute volition, was also absolute peace.[1] But in Philo the subject wears a colder and more philosophical aspect. We do not find in him the profound religious experiences which shook the soul of Paul; and it is needless to say that the peace which he discovered did not detach him from his fealty to Judaism, or convert him into the missionary of a higher faith.

Who gave himself for our sins (i., 4).—In life as in death Christ " gave *himself*," and not mere outward gifts; and in his death on the cross the sacrifice of love was made complete. It was "in relation to" or "on behalf of"[2] our sins that he gave himself. The conquest of sin was the object of his self-devotion. It is the spirit of the life that gives value and significance to suffering.

This present evil world (properly *age*, i., 4).—Paul accepts the customary Jewish division into two ages, the pre-Messianic time, and the future, when the Messiah would have come and established the Kingdom of God. But he seems in the present passage to turn the temporal into a moral distinction, for only thus could men pass out of the "present age." To the Christian, looking for the speedy return of Christ, the new age had virtually come. There is here an anticipation of the subject of the Epistle; for when men had left all evil behind them, the Law would thereby have given place to the Spirit.

According to the will of our God and Father (i., 4).—The self-sacrifice of Christ was an expression of the Divine will, the will of one who is "our Father," and therefore does all things in love. The idea of the Divine fatherhood is reiterated in this passage; for the doctrine of human sonship is fundamental in the Epistle.

Amen (i., 5), a Hebrew word, "so be it," uttered as a response in the synagogues at the end of prayers. From the

---

[1] *De Somn.*, II. § 38, I. 692 (Mangey). See also *De Gigant.*, § 11, I. 269; *De Ebriet.*, § 18, I. 368; *Quis rer. div. Her.*, § 58, I. 514.

[2] The reading is uncertain.

synagogues it passed to the Christian assemblies, and, when Greek churches were formed, was retained as a solemn expression which they did not wish to translate.

He introduces the subject of the Epistle by expressing his astonishment at the speedy defection of the Galatians (i., 6-10).

These strongly condemnatory expressions take the place of the usual thanksgiving.

Quickly (i., 6).—It is doubtful whether this means so soon after their conversion, or after Paul's second visit, or after the coming of the false teachers. It is not necessary to limit the reference very strictly; and the second and third explanations may coalesce, for Paul had to speak a word of warning on his second visit (see *v.* 9).

Him that called you (i., 6); that is, God. The defection was not merely from an opinion, but from God Himself, whose call they had acknowledged.

In the grace of Christ (i., 6).—The "in" is partly, but not purely instrumental. The call was contained within the grace, and so came in and through it. The grace is specially mentioned here as antithetical to the Law, and involving deliverance from it, so that subjection to the Law was a renunciation of the Gospel.

Which is not another (i., 7).—The false teaching was quite "different" from Paul's, but it was not a second *gospel;* it was a mere turning of the Gospel of Christ the wrong way about.

We or an angel (i., 8).—In this verse he supposes an impossible case; in the next he introduces hypothetically a fact which was actually taking place. We ought to reject the highest imaginable authority if it perverted the best that we have seen and known.

Anathema (i., 8, 9), a thing devoted, used in the New Testament in a bad sense, devoted to destruction. Hence it came to be used of excommunication; but it probably does not refer here to any formal act. It is a strong way of saying, "reject utterly all such false teachers."

We have said before (i., 9).—The contrast with "now" shows that the reference is not to the previous verse, but to Paul's last visit to Galatia.

Ye received (i., 9): an important statement in the argument. Having "received" the Gospel, they must have been conscious of its superiority to the teaching of the Judaisers.

Am I now (i., 10).—The words seem to imply that Paul had been charged with being a mere man-pleaser; and this is his excuse for using such vehement language. He became all things to all men that he might gain some to Christ, but not that he might win their favour. The service of Christ was wholly inconsistent with the principle of selfish man-pleasing; and since his opponents mistook his gentleness and courtesy, he would use language which could not be misunderstood.

Still (i., 10).—It is probable that this word is used hypothetically, and not of Paul's pre-Christian state; for even then man-pleasing was not his characteristic. He says in effect:—" If, as you affirm, I once curried favour with men, you cannot say that I am doing so now. If I continued to act on that principle, I should not be Christ's servant."

After this introduction Paul enters on his personal defence (i., 11-ii., 21); and first he states his case by affirming that he had received his Gospel through direct revelation (i., 11, 12).

The Gospel which was preached by me (i., 11).—This probably refers, not to the outward facts, which would be learned through the ordinary channels of information, but to the spiritual significance of the facts. The "different gospel" of the Judaisers must have presented the same facts; but Paul's Gospel was distinguished from theirs by its spiritual depth and universalism.

Not after man (i., 11), not conformed to the ordinary

thoughts and ways of men, and therefore not such as would proceed from a man-pleaser.

I (i., 12), emphatic in the Greek, probably meaning "*I* was not more dependent than other preachers of the Gospel on human instruction."

Receive . . . taught (i., 12).—The former word refers to that which is handed on from one to another, as in the rabbinical schools; the latter to the systematic teaching by which the tradition was driven home, and fixed in the memory.

Revelation of Jesus Christ (i., 12).—The contrast with "man" requires the meaning, revelation communicated by Jesus Christ. The idea in i., 16 is different, but not inconsistent with this. Compare the similar statement of St. Francis of Assisi: "No one showed me that which I ought to do; but the Most High Himself revealed to me that I ought to live according to the form of the holy Gospel."[1]

The Apostle now proceeds to his proofs. First, his Gospel was directly opposed to the tradition and teaching of his early years, and no mere human learning could have brought about so complete and sudden a change in his convictions (i., 13, 14, in connection with what follows).

Traditions of my fathers (i., 14).—Paul belonged to a Pharisaic family, and was therefore particularly attached to the "traditions," which were handed down in the schools as an oral interpretation of the written law, and were observed with peculiar care by the Pharisees.

As a second proof he affirms that after his conversion, which was due to an immediate Divine act, he did not confer with other men (i., 15-17).

Separated me (i., 15), set me apart even from my birth. Little as he knew it, it was the design of Providence that he should become an Apostle, and that by means of the law

---

[1] *Testamentum Fr.*, quoted by Sabatier, p. viii., note.

which he loved so fanatically he should die to the law, and rise into the new spirit of life which came through the Crucified.

Through his grace (i., 15).—The change in him was not through the teaching of others, or through his own effort, but through the call of Divine love, which came to him with overpowering appeal.

To reveal his Son in me (i., 16).—Jesus, the Crucified, was revealed within him as the Son, who was to lead mankind into the new life of sonship, where the distinction of Jew and Gentile ceased to exist. The Gentile mission was involved in this inward illumination, and already Paul saw more deeply into the spiritual bearing of the Gospel than the primitive Apostles themselves.

Immediately I conferred not (i., 16).—There was no hesitation; immediately he decided not to confer.

Arabia (i., 17): possibly the regions adjoining Damascus. He probably retired into a lonely place, to meditate on the great change which had taken place within him. The duration of his stay cannot be fixed, for he does not say how long he remained in Damascus. According to Acts (ix., 20) he preached there, and from his own account in 2 Cor. xi., 32, 33, we may infer that his labours lasted for an appreciable time, since they excited the enmity even of the Governor.

As a third proof he states that three years passed before he went to Jerusalem, that then he went to pay a private visit to Peter, and saw no other leading man except James, that he remained only fifteen days, and then removed to a distance from the Jewish capital (i., 18-24).

After three years (i., 18); most probably, not after his return to Damascus, but after his conversion.

Cephas (i., 18), an Aramaic word, of which Petros (Peter) is the Greek equivalent.

Save James (i., 19).—There is great difference of opinion

about this James, which it is not necessary to discuss here. I think the most probable view is that he was a son of Joseph and Mary, and not one of the Twelve. The word "Apostle" may then be understood in the wider sense in which it includes not only Paul, but Barnabas and others.

Before God, I lie not (**i., 20**).—This strong asseveration guards against the possible notion that at that time he received his apostolic commission from the church at Jerusalem. The account in Acts ix., 26-30, though it does not affect this particular point, gives a very different impression of the visit.

Syria (**i., 21**), meaning, no doubt, the part contiguous to Cilicia, and remote from the influence of Jerusalem.

The churches of Judæa which were in Christ (**i., 22**).—The churches are so described to distinguish them from Jewish congregations. These churches were no doubt Jewish, and observed the law; but Paul fully recognises their Christian position, and they, on their side, glorified God in Paul, although he had received no commission from them. The change from a persecutor to an Apostle of the faith was a sufficient evidence that God was working in him, and that he had a Divine right to preach.

A fourth proof was afforded by the fact that only after a very long interval did he lay his Gospel before the authorities in Jerusalem, and they, so far from communicating anything further to him, fully accepted it (ii., 1-10).

After the space of fourteen years (**ii., 1**).—This naturally means fourteen years after the last event, and therefore seventeen years after the conversion. This date leads us to identify the visit with the one recorded in Acts xv., which, according to the usual reckoning, took place about the year 51. Other coincidences which point to the same conclusion are the following:—*a.* The connection of Paul with Antioch (see *v.* 11). *b.* He was still co-operating with Barnabas, but seems by this time to have taken the lead. *c.* Barnabas was not his only companion. *d.* The occasion was due to the efforts of Judaisers. *e.* The subject of controversy was the circumcision of the Gentiles. *f.* James and Peter are prominent (Paul adds John). *g.* The decision is given in favour of Paul. These coincidences seem to be decisive, especially when we remember that one visit of this kind would render a second superfluous. Professor Ramsay, however, is strongly of opinion that the visit is the one briefly referred to in Acts xi., 30. He has not convinced me; but as the question relates to the historical value of Acts rather than to the interpretation of our Epistle, we cannot here examine his arguments.[1]

Titus (ii., 1) is specially mentioned, as being a Greek. To take a Gentile with him was to challenge a decision in the most practical way.

By revelation (ii., 2); in accordance with what he felt to be the Divine leading. This does not necessarily preclude the supposition that Paul may have laid the matter before the church at Antioch, and received from them the authority of an embassy.

Before them (ii., 2) refers indefinitely to the Christians of Jerusalem; and then the added clause, "but privately before them that were of repute," is either an explanatory limitation or a description of a second meeting, in which matters may have been discussed more in detail with the leaders of the church. So far as we can judge from the condensed and rather confused account, the latter seems the more probable. The result of the first, more public meeting was doubtful, owing to the efforts of the false brethren, and it seemed for a moment as if Paul's efforts might be fruitless. He therefore sought for a more private interview, and from the "pil-

---

[1] See some further considerations in my little commentary on Galatians, published by the Sunday-School Association, 1893, before the appearance of Professor Ramsay's discussion.

lars" of the church he received a complete acknowledgment of his Gentile Gospel.

Who were of repute (ii., 2).—There is nothing sarcastic in this phrase; but from its repeated use (*vv.* 6 and 9) we may perhaps infer that it is quoted from his opponents.

Should be running, or had run, in vain (ii., 2).—It is clear that things had reached a crisis which gave Paul considerable anxiety. An adverse decision on the part of the primitive Apostles, though it would not have shaken his own faith, would probably have reduced the Gentile mission to a nullity, and changed the fortunes of Christianity.

Was compelled to be circumcised (ii., 3).—The obvious meaning is that an attempt was made to have Titus circumcised, but did not succeed. The implication is that Titus, a complete Gentile, was received as such into brotherly communion, and thus the whole principle of the Gentile mission was practically conceded by the Jewish Church, with the exception of a small fraction.

And that because of the false brethren (ii., 4).—The construction is uncertain; but it seems best to begin a new sentence here, "But on account of the false brethren," in which, however, the construction is lost in the endeavour to make this parenthetical statement as brief as possible. The sense apparently is that Paul and Barnabas were obliged to contest the point owing to the action of false brethren; that they would not yield to their demands even for a moment; and that they were successful in maintaining their ground. If we are to interpret the words strictly, Paul believed that these opponents only pretended to be Christians, and were really Jewish spies.

To spy out our liberty (ii., 4); hoping perhaps to find some immoral practices, to which they could point as a result of abandoning the law.

With you (ii., 5).—If taken strictly, this implies that the Galatian churches were already founded, and is in favour of the South-Galatian theory; but it may mean generally "you Gentiles," whether already converted or not at that particular time.

From those who were reputed to be somewhat (ii., 6).—This resumes the account in *v.* 2, which was interrupted by the reference to Titus.

When they saw (ii., 7).—Their minds were open to conviction, and they saw that Paul was under the Divine guidance as much as Peter. It is neither said nor implied that it was difficult to convince them. Paul, on his side, assumes that God wrought for Peter as truly as for himself.

Gentiles . . . circumcision (ii., 9).—This implies a distinction in the field of operations and not a radical difference of principle. The Jews, of course, would not be taught to abandon their law; but the acceptance of Paul's position reduced the law to a thing religiously indifferent, and made its observance simply an affair of national custom,—a great and momentous change.

The poor (ii., 10), meaning no doubt the poor Christians in Jerusalem. How far Barnabas carried out this proviso we are not told; for in the next clause Paul changes the verb into the first person. The "I" is not emphatic; so that there is no implication to the disadvantage of Barnabas. The two Apostles parted company in undertaking their next missionary journey.

As a final proof of his independence Paul relates how he rebuked Peter himself at Antioch (ii., 11-21).

In reproducing the substance of what he said to Peter he passes into the doctrinal portion of the Epistle, and fails to tell us the result of his remonstrance. He begins his account as though the Galatians must already have heard of Peter's visit; and if so, they probably knew something of his subsequent conduct. Paul was alone in his protest, and, if he remained alone, this occurrence must have seriously damaged his cause. We cannot doubt that the defection of Barnabas was temporary; and if Peter's conduct was really due to fear, we must believe that he returned to a better mind. The event may have made the more spiritual principle, on which he had been half unconsciously acting, clearer to his thought.

He stood condemned (ii., 11); that is, by his conduct. It has also been explained as referring to the condemnation pronounced by the wiser members of the church. But there is nothing in the context to suggest this.

He did eat (ii., 12).—The Greek tense implies continuance, "he was in the habit of eating." He thus disregarded legal scruples about things clean and unclean. Pious Jews would not eat with Gentiles, who were regarded as sinners; and especially they were forbidden to partake of the bread, oil, and wine of Gentiles, lest they should be brought into connection with idolatry.[1] It was necessary, however, to religious unity for Jewish and Gentile Christians to eat together in their love feasts, and if James meant to prohibit this absolutely, there was little meaning in giving the right hand of fellowship to Paul. The account in Acts relieves the difficulty. The Gentiles were required to observe some small rules in regard to food, so as not to offend Jewish scruples. The Jewish Christians at Antioch, including Peter, may have had no such scruples, and hence the agreement arrived at in Jerusalem may have become a dead letter. Some supposition of this kind seems needed to explain the defection of Barnabas, who had so lately stood side by side with Paul in the battle for freedom.

Dissembled . . . dissimulation (ii., 13).—The original charges them with hypocrisy,—a word which our translators did not hesitate to apply to the Pharisees. It was the hypocrisy that roused Paul's indignation; with a genuine

---

[1] Weber, *Jüd. Theol.*, p. 59.

scruple he would have dealt tenderly. No language could assert more strongly Peter's agreement in principle with Paul.

Livest as do the Gentiles (ii., 14), referring not to the present moment, but to Peter's habitual manner of life before the men came from James.

How compellest thou the Gentiles? (ii., 14), as he was doing indirectly by refusing to eat with them unless they judaised.

Not sinners of the Gentiles (ii., 15).—Paul speaks from the Jewish point of view. Gentiles were outside the covenant; but he and Peter had all the advantages that Judaism could give, and still they had come to recognise the futility of the law for justification.

Knowing that a man is not justified by the works of the law (ii., 16).—I think the marginal reading "works of law" is better. No doubt the Mosaic law is meant, but it is regarded in its character of *law*, so that the proposition is in principle made universal. Works done merely to fulfil a law cannot justify, that is, cannot make a man truly righteous in the judgment of God. The full meaning of this statement will become apparent in the course of the Epistle, and still more in the Epistle to the Romans.

Save through faith (ii., 16).—These words must not be connected with "works of law," but only with "not justified."

Faith in Jesus Christ . . . faith in Christ (ii., 16).—The Greek is "faith of Jesus Christ . . . faith of Christ." See the note on Rom. iii., 22. This is the only verse that seems strongly to support the meaning "faith in Jesus"; but it does not require this, for in order to acquire the faith of Jesus one must have faith in him. If Jesus gives us his own faith, he bestows the power of a Divine life, and we need no outward law. The commentators are adverse; but I must judge of Paul's meaning by Paul's usage.

By the works of the law shall no flesh be justified (ii. 16), a phrase repeated in Rom. iii., 20. It is perhaps borrowed, as a Christian interpretation, from Psalm cxliii., 2, "in thy sight shall no man living be justified," and is brought forward both here and in Romans as an accepted principle.

While we sought to be justified in Christ (ii., 17).—The argument is intended for Peter, but is expressed in the first person so as to make it less offensive. The meaning is,—if, as your conduct implies, we have been misled by Christ to become mere sinners like the Gentiles, it must follow that Christ is the minister of sin, and we were wrong in thinking we could find justification in him; but such a supposition is quite inadmissible.

I prove myself a transgressor (**ii., 18**).—As this verse states a principle in the most general terms, without any mention of the law, I think it must be taken as a parenthetical explanation of "were found sinners": If a man build up what he pulled down, he thereby admits that he was wrong in pulling down; and so you, by insisting on observances which you previously disregarded, are declaring yourself a transgressor in disregarding them. There is, however, another explanation: Christ did not lead you into sin, but you are now a transgressor, for you are violating the deepest principle of the law itself in returning to it for justification. This is favoured by the "for" of the following verse, which may, however, have a general reference to what is implied in the preceding passage,—the law is really superseded for all who truly apprehend the life in Christ and the inability of the law to justify; for I, etc.

I through the law died unto the law (**ii., 19**).—Again the absence of the articles in the Greek shows that we must look for something in the quality of law as such to lead to the dying to law. It is its characteristic effect to give the knowledge of sin (Rom. iii., 20), but not the power of righteousness; and therefore it proclaims its own transitory nature, and points to something beyond itself; and that is, a living unto God, life in the abiding consciousness of His presence and under the leading of His Spirit, the life of faith.

I have been crucified with Christ (ii., 20), a very strong figure to express the completeness with which the believer shares the self-renunciation of Christ. He has died to the old self, to the world, and to the law as completely as if he had been nailed with Christ upon the cross, and passed with him into the life of glorified spirits.

Yet I live (ii., 20).—I think the preference must be given to the translation adopted by the American Revisers in their text, and by the English in the margin. It is no longer "I," the old self, following my own will, that live; Christ is the source and rule of my activity, reproducing his life in mine. Paul was still, however, "in the flesh," and therefore had to live the life, not of vision, but of faith. That faith was the faith "of the Son of God" (so it should be translated), that triumphant faith which led him through the agony of the cross into the glorified life beyond. This faith was communicated through the persuasive power of love, felt and appropriated individually,—"loved me," spoken out of the fulness of grateful devotion. "Gave himself," the utmost that anyone can give.[1] "For me" means "on my behalf." The preposition is the same as when Peter says "I will lay down my life for thee" (John xiii., 37).

I do not make void the grace of God (ii., 21), as I should do if I insisted on the law as necessary to acceptance with Him; for legal exaction and forgiving love are antithetical to one another. The following clause makes this clear. If the law was the sufficient source of righteousness, then the

---

[1] As St. Gregory says, "et fortasse laboriosum non est homini relinquere sua; sed valde laboriosum est relinquere semetipsum." Quoted by Père Grou, *Hidden Life of the Soul*, in the Library of Spiritual Works for English Catholics, p. 177.

manifestation of Divine love on the cross was futile. Paul saw that Christ had done much more than call men, as John the Baptist had done, to repent and fulfil their moral obligations: he had introduced a new spirit of life, the spirit of holy love and self-renunciation in communion with God, and through this life he had made manifest the love of God, who freely forgives those who turn to Him in faith. Before this life of filial communion the whole structure of mere legal righteousness collapsed. If this was not so, if men after all had everything they required in the law, then Christ threw away his life for nothing,—a conclusion which the warmhearted Peter could not accept any more than Paul.[1]

We now enter on the doctrinal argument of the Epistle (iii., iv.).

It is immediately suggested by the preceding passage, and the transition is marked by the direct appeal to the Galatians.

The Apostle begins with an appeal to the spiritual experience of his readers (iii., 1-5). They owed all their higher life to faith; yet now they are sinking into law.

Foolish (iii., 1).—The Galatians were a quick-witted people, but often acted foolishly because they did not apply their understanding steadily to the question before them.

Bewitch (iii., 1).—Their folly in the present case was so extraordinary that it seemed like enchantment from an evil eye. From this they might have kept themselves by fixing their eyes on the Crucified, who had been presented so vividly before them. The word "crucified" takes us back to the words "I have been crucified with Christ." There was the Divine love beseeching them; there the secret of eternal life: how could they turn from it?

Received ye the Spirit (iii., 2).—We read in Acts how the

[1] Compare Ignatius, Tral. x., δωρεὰν οὐν ἀποθνήσκω.

Holy Spirit fell on those who were moved by the preaching of the Apostles; and so Paul refers here to the vivid moment when the reality of God and the nearness of His love were first keenly felt. The new, exalted faith came in those days with overwhelming force.

The hearing of faith (or *the message of faith*, iii., 2).—Whichever translation we adopt, the general meaning is the same. It was not by doing works of law, but by hearing the tones of faith, as the Christian preacher delivered his message, that their own faith was kindled, and the Spirit received.

Are ye now perfected in the flesh? (iii., 3).—The force of the present tense should be given more distinctly, " are ye now being made perfect?" The force of the antithesis may be thus expressed in modern language: Having begun with the higher life, are you seeking perfection through the lower? Having known the power of inward and spiritual religion, are you giving yourselves up to that which is formal and external? " The flesh " need not refer to circumcision, but denotes generally that side of our nature which is opposed to the spiritual.

He therefore (iii., 5); that is, God, who does not give His Spirit through carnal ceremonies (for it was to these that the Galatians were falling away), but through the hearing of faith.

Worketh miracles among you (iii., 5).—I think the Greek rather implies " works within you " (compare 1 Cor. xii., 6), and that the reference is to the supernatural exaltation which manifested itself through unusual " powers " (translated " miracles ") in the first believers.

We now proceed to an argument founded on the case of Abraham (iii., 6–18).

To him the promise, which was to be fulfilled in the advent of the Messiah, was made. Who, then, were his true children and heirs, the men of faith or the men of law? The Judaisers maintained the latter, and thought the Gentiles could be brought within the covenant only by submission to the law. In controverting their position Paul uses arguments which in form are much less adapted to our time and modes of thought than to his own, but which rest ultimately on great spiritual principles. The argument is introduced abruptly, but is founded on the implied answer to the previous question:—You know in your own experience that the Spirit comes through the hearing of faith; it was always so, even in the case of Abraham.

Believed God (iii., 6).—This translation conceals the connection of thought. The Greek is the verb of which "faith" is the noun, and implies more of moral trust than of intellectual assent. Abraham had such trust in the truth and power of God that he believed His promise. This quotation from Gen. xv., 6 is introduced as one which must be quite familiar to the Gentile readers. The Old Testament was the first Christian Bible. Faith is reckoned for righteousness, not because it is an arbitrary substitute for it, but because it is the source and power of real and inward righteousness, and shows, in spite of external faults, that the heart is right with God. What God judges to be so is so; for His "judgment is according to truth."

They which be of faith (iii., 7), or, to give the sense more fully, those who find in faith the source and principle of their life. The spiritual children of Abraham can be only those who share his characteristic attribute. The "faith" referred to must be the same as his, a childlike confidence in God, which hears His word speaking within, and implicitly trusts it.

The Scripture, foreseeing (iii., 8).—This personification of the Scripture is without a parallel in the New Testament, though it occurs in Jewish writings. "The Scripture saith" is hardly analogous, though the expression "the Scripture saith to Pharaoh" (Rom. ix., 17) should be noticed. There is a personification, but not so marked, in *v.* 22.[1]

Would justify (iii., 8) ; more correctly, "justifies," stating a general principle of the Divine action.

In thee shall all the nations [better, Gentiles] *be blessed* (iii., 8).—The quotation blends Gen. xviii., 18, and xii., 3. Compare "in thee" with the phrase "in Christ."

Are blessed (iii., 9).—This is an important word in the argument, being opposed to the curse of the law. It is virtually to faith that the promise of blessedness in Abraham is given.

Are under a curse (iii., 10).—By this verse all except the men of faith are excluded from the blessing. Paul does not notice the fact that in the very next verse (Deut. xxviii., 1) to the one which he quotes (*ib.*, xxvii., 26) a blessing is pronounced on those who observe all the commandments. But it was an axiom that "by works of law shall no flesh be justified," and therefore the blessing seemed to be offered on impossible conditions. No doubt the mass of men would take these words in a large sense, and indeed it was admitted in the schools that God would strike a balance between good and evil deeds. But to a keenly sensitive conscience, with its visions of ideal perfection, the offer of a blessing on the condition of absolute obedience could only be a source of despair, and the curse pronounced on disobedience stood out in all its horror, a haunting vision of intolerable judgment. The curses threatened in Deut. xxviii., 15 *sqq.*, should be read if we wish to understand Paul's experience of spiritual agony. In the Apostolical Constitutions the Jews are repre-

---

[1] We may notice the strong personification in Clem. Al., *Strom.*, i., 28, p. 425 (Potter), ἡ γραφὴ τοιούτους τινὰς ἡμᾶς διαλεκτικοὺς οὕτως ἐθέλουσα γενέσθαι παραινεῖ. Compare Cyril. Hieros., προεῖδεν ἡ γραφὴ τὰ πράγματα (*Catech.* xiii., 10), and προβλέπουσα ἡ προφητικὴ χάρις (*Catech.*, x., 12).

sented as under the curse because, in the Dispersion, it was impossible to fulfil all the commandments.[1]

By the law (iii., 11); literally, "in law," a universal proposition: when everything is measured by strictly legal requirements, justification is impossible. This is proved by the statement of Habakkuk ii., 4, in which it is laid down that the principle of life is faith. The prophet referred only to the time of the Chaldean invasion; but the Apostle regards it as the expression of a general principle.

By faith (iii., 11); literally, "from faith." The same preposition is used in the following sentence, "the law is not from faith" (iii., 12). The verbal connection is lost in the Revisers' translation. This statement is proved by a quotation from Levit. xviii., 5. The law aims at the regulation of outward acts, and there its function ends. Real righteousness springs from a deeper source.

Christ redeemed us from the curse of the law (iii., 13).—This verse affords a fruitful theme for controversial theology. We can do no more here than endeavour to trace a probable line of thought in the Apostle's mind. The fundamental fact is that as a Pharisee, seeking for perfect righteousness, he felt himself under a curse; as a Christian, longing for the fulness of the Spirit, he felt this no more, but only the love of God shed abroad in his heart. How, within his own spiritual experience, did the change come about? We must start with the quotation from Deut. xxi., 23, which, in the original, is, "he that is hanged is cursed of God" [literally, "the curse of God"]. To the Pharisee this was conclusive proof that Jesus was not the Messiah, for the Messiah must be "blessed" not "cursed." But when the Son of God was revealed within him, and he saw in the crucifixion at once the most absolute submission to the Divine will and the indwelling of God's love in the heart of a man, he had

---

[1] vi., 25.

in some way to reconcile this new view with the ancient curse. The simplest way was to follow out a line of thought which was suggested by many other considerations. The Beloved could not be really cursed by God; and therefore it followed that the law, however Divine in its origin and purpose, was introduced to meet a temporary condition in the spiritual progress of the world, and, when the Christ came, its course was run. "The curse of God" had become merely "the curse of the law," a thing of no validity for those who shared the self-renunciation of faith and love, and spiritually were crucified with Christ.

Redeemed (iii., 13): see the note on Rom. iii., 24.[1] *Us* (iii., 13); that is, Jews. See iv., 5.

That upon the Gentiles might come the blessing of Abraham (iii., 14).—The blessing pronounced upon Abraham could come to the Gentiles only through the abrogation of the law, whereby Jews and Gentiles were placed upon the same spiritual level, and the Kingdom of Heaven was opened to all believers.

That we might receive (iii., 14).—This clause is co-ordinate with the preceding, and opens a yet wider view. All Christians alike were to receive the fulfilment of the promise.

Having reached this climax, Paul meets an objection which might be readily urged, that the promises made to Abraham had been superseded by the coming of the law (iii., 15-18). The reply is that, when once a covenant is ratified, its conditions cannot be altered. This is true of a human covenant; much more, of the Divine. It was a Jewish belief that the generations before the giving of the law lived through the

---

[1] Compare the Letter on the Martyrdom of Polycarp, § 2, $διὰ\ μιᾶς\ ὥρας\ τὴν\ αἰώνιον\ κόλασιν\ ἐξαγοραζόμενοι$, said of martyrs generally. Such figures are of common occurrence. In § 10 Polycarp is compared to "a noble ram for sacrifice, a whole burnt offering," and he himself said $προσδεχθείην$ . . . $ἐν\ θυσίᾳ\ πίονι\ καὶ\ προσδεκτῇ$ (§ 14).

grace of God, but afterwards men had to earn their reward by keeping the commandments.[1]

I speak after the manner of men (iii., 15) : that is, in what follows I avail myself of a human analogy.

To Abraham . . . and to his seed (iii., 16).—Reference is made to the "seed" in order to show that the promise was not fulfilled before the coming of the law. It was given long before the law, but the fulfilment was much later, and therefore the law could only be regarded as an episode which did not alter the conditions. "Promises" is in the plural because the promise was repeated on different occasions. The reference to the "seed" shows that the passages in Paul's mind are Gen. xiii., 15 and xvii., 8. The argument is objected to because "seed," in the sense of posterity, is a collective word (in Hebrew and Greek as well as in English), and in the plural it is used only in the literal sense of seeds. Paul himself follows the proper usage in *v.* 29; and when he reconstructs the argument in Rom. iv., 13 *sqq.*, he does not repeat this portion of it.

Four hundred and thirty years (iii., 17).—In giving this number as including the residence "in the land of Canaan" Paul follows the LXX rendering of Exodus xii., 40. The Hebrew limits this period to the sojourn in Egypt.

Law . . . promise (iii., 18).—These are antithetical in principle, law throwing the conditions entirely upon the voluntary efforts of men, the promise being an unconditional expression of a gracious purpose. The expected blessing was *promised* to Abraham as a gift of grace,—for this is the force of the word translated "granted." We should observe that Paul sets aside in a most emphatic way the idea that Christ or anyone else had to fulfil certain legal obligations in order that grace might have free course to act. If he became man's substitute, and had to bear the curse of the law as

---

[1] Weber, *Jüd. Theol.*, p. 304.

a condition of the fulfilment of the promise, Paul's whole argument falls to pieces.

Paul now proceeds to deal with a question which arises very naturally out of the foregoing views. Was any room left for the law in the providential purpose of God? Was it adverse to His promise, and introduced perhaps by some alien power? (iii., 19–iv., 7).

At a later time an extreme party actually maintained that the God of the Old Testament was not the God of the New, and thus completely broke the continuity of history. But Paul never lost his faith in the Divine origin and authority of the law. History was one continuous unfolding of a providential plan, a Divine evolution of the "natural" into the "spiritual." His answer to the question, then, is, in substance, that the law was a necessary instrument in the education of mankind, but, being adapted to a state of minority, became obsolete as soon as men entered upon their full-grown sonship.

It was added (iii., 19), not as a new condition of the promise (which he has just shown to be impossible), but as a subsidiary and temporary measure.

Because of transgressions (or, more strictly, *for the sake of the transgressions*, iii., 19).—Transgression, in Pauline language, is the violation of a commandment. Sin, as the principle of moral evil, may exist apart from law; but "where there is no law neither is there transgression" (Rom. iv., 15). The immediate effect of introducing a law, therefore, is (except on the impossible supposition of its perfect fulfilment) to turn unconscious sin into wilful transgression. From this moment begins the moral struggle which ends only with a cry of self-despair as the man commits himself in faith to God, and receives a new birth from the Spirit. Thus by means of law men died to law, and entered the serener life brought into the world by Christ.

Through angels by the hand of a mediator (iii., 19).—It was a common Jewish belief that the law was communicated through angels (see, in the New Testament, Acts vii., 35, 38, 53; Heb. ii., 2). It is said that God came down to Sinai, the one mountain that had remained free from idolatry, attended by 22,000, or according to others 600,000, angels, each holding a crown wherewith to crown the Israelites, at least those who, on being asked, voluntarily accepted the law.[1] The mediator is of course Moses. This mediation distinguishes the law from the promise. The latter was made to Abraham and his seed (Christ) without any mediation, and therefore its fulfilment depended solely on the faithfulness of God. The law was a compact between two, God imposing and man accepting certain conditions through their respective representatives. There is nothing in the context to indicate that Paul intends by these words either to magnify or to depreciate the law.

Now a mediator is not of one; but God is one (iii., 20).— The words are clear; but the argument is so obscure that there are said to be no less than 430 different interpretations of it. Here I can only suggest the following: Mediation implies two parties and an agreement between them. But God, the author of both promise and law, is one. Consequently it might be argued that the law was God's own proposed supplement to the promise, and became, through mutual consent, the condition under which alone the promise could be fulfilled. This has at least the advantage of explaining the following question, "Is the law then," since it rests on a mediated agreement, "against the promise of God?"

God forbid (iii., 21).—This strong negation of the question shows that Paul looked upon the promise and the law as alike Divine. The difficulty arising from their apparent antagonism is set aside by maintaining that they had different

---

[1] Weber, *Jüd. Theol.*, pp. 268 *sqq.*

ends in view. Law was intrinsically unable to produce the highest spiritual life. If it could have done so, then righteousness would really (as the Judaisers imagined) have its source in law, and the promise would have a rival, or indeed be superseded, for righteousness cannot spring from two fundamentally different principles. We may compare the express rabbinical teaching, that the words of the law give life to the world.[1]

Howbeit (iii., 22) : better, "but," introducing the opposite of the previous clause. On a certain supposition righteousness would have been of the law; but the contrary is the case, and therefore the supposition falls.

All things (iii., 22).—The neuter gives greater universality to the statement, as though sin had been the one dominant fact in the universe.

Promise by faith in Jesus Christ (iii., 22).—"Promise" here is equivalent to "the promised blessing." The following words are literally "out of faith of Jesus Christ"; that is, arising out of Christ's faith (see the note on ii., 16). The promise was made to Abraham, the man of faith, and to his seed, Christ, who restored the life of faith, and thereby made the realisation of the promise possible. Through him, then, the blessing came, and was extended to all who, by believing on him, shared his faith.

Before faith came (iii., 23).—This clearly refers not to a mere transference of belief from one thing to another, but to a new principle of life which came into the world in Christ. It had appeared, indeed, in Abraham; but then withdrew, awaiting "the fulness of time" for its perfect revelation.

Kept in ward (iii., 23).—The law acted the part of a gaoler, imposing restraints, but not liberating from the prison-house of sin. Yet all was a preparation for the faith which was to be manifested to the world in Christ. Paul includes the Gentiles as "kept in ward under law," and in so doing

[1] Weber, *Jüd. Theol.*, p. 22.

follows the rabbinical doctrine that the law was given, not only to the Israelites, but to all nations, and was therefore communicated on neutral ground, outside of Palestine, and in such a way that every nation heard the voice of God in its own language.[1] The Gentiles, however, did not receive it, and consequently were excluded from communion with God.[2]

The law hath been our tutor (iii., 24).—The same idea is expressed under a gentler figure. The "tutor" was a slave who had the care of children, and, among other duties, conducted them to school. Christ, however, is not here regarded as the schoolmaster, for there is no allusion to his teaching, and the words "to bring us" are not in the Greek. The phrase briefly suggests that the law kept Christ in view, as the one to whom we should come when the time of pupilage was past.

Justified by faith (iii., 24).—"Faith" is emphatic,—"that from faith we may be justified," and not from the law. This follows from our attaining to Christ, and thereby entering into that spiritual principle of faith which was the root of his life.

Now that faith is come (iii., 25).—This is a solemn assertion of the advent of a new principle of life into the world. It is one in which the soul is no longer under leadership, but rises by faith into direct communion with God, and therefore lives out of its own free conscience and judgment, under the guidance of the Spirit of God.

In Christ Jesus (iii., 26).—The Greek preposition shows that Christ is not here regarded as the object of faith, for which reason the Revisers have inserted a comma. We may connect the words with the whole clause,—"In Christ Jesus you are all sons of God through faith,"—or, if we connect them with faith, the meaning will be "the faith which exists

---

[1] Weber, *Jüd. Theol.*, pp. 18 *sqq.*   [2] *Ib.*, p. 57.

Baptised into Christ (iii., 27).—Christ is here represented as the spiritual element into which believers were plunged, as it were, by baptism; and then again, by a figure which is found in other writers, he is compared to a garment with which a man is clothed. In Rom. xiii., 14, the readers are exhorted to put him on, as though they had not already done so in baptism. Spiritual conditions are ideal, begun at some definite moment, yet needing constant faithfulness to bring them to their perfection.

Ye are all one man (iii., 28).—*Man* is inserted to show that the Greek word for "one" is masculine. All believers are blended, as it were, into a single personality, so that the old distinctions cease to exist. In 1 Cor. iii., 8, "he that planteth and he that watereth are one," the word is neuter, implying not so much the complete union and harmony of inward life as identity of aim and function. Each was simply an instrument in the hand of God, employed for the same great purpose.

We should notice the emphatic way in which Paul here places man and woman on the same spiritual level, and we should check by this statement passages in which he assigns to woman an inferior position. He asserts unequivocally the ideal result of his principles. But in practice ideals must be slowly realised, and an attempt to grasp them outwardly often only violates them inwardly. A servile war to maintain the equality of slave and master would have horrified him; and he was repelled when women asserted their equality with men through a breach of feminine decorum. The expression of his views is qualified by the occasion, but the varying expressions are due to his strong grasp of the same spiritual reality.

Then are ye Abraham's seed (iii., 29).—He returns for a moment to the case of Abraham, in order to state as a conclusion the proposition with which he started, "the men of faith (whether Jews or Gentiles) are the sons of Abraham." The Galatian believers were such by virtue of being in Christ, and belonging to him. He and all who were his were the true spiritual seed, and therefore heirs of the blessings which were promised to Abraham. This accorded with the special promise, "in thee shall all the Gentiles be blessed."

Paul concludes this portion of his subject by unfolding more distinctly some thoughts implied in the previous paragraph (**iv., 1-7**). The spiritual, like the natural, life had its fixed times, and regulations adapted to the stage of its development.

A child (**iv., 1**), or rather "a minor." Though by right of birth he is owner of the whole property that has been left to him, yet, till the time appointed for entering into full possession of the inheritance, he is virtually in the position of a slave, being subject to guardians of his person and stewards of the property.

We (**iv., 3**), emphatic, in contrast with the heir just spoken of. That the reference is not confined to Jews seems proved by the changes of person in *vv.* 5-7, and by the question in *v.* 9. Paul uses Jewish history to interpret the history of the world.

Rudiments [or, *elements*] *of the world* (**iv., 3**).—Various interpretations are given. Probably the reference is to an elementary state of religion, such as was observed in the common world of men. It is clear from *vv.* 9, 10 that he has chiefly in mind a ceremonial religion, with its recurring festivals. As these were determined by the observation of celestial phenomena, it has been often supposed that "the elements" are the heavenly bodies. These, however, would hardly be described as "weak and beggarly."

The fulness of the time (**iv., 4**), the moment which filled up and completed the appointed period. The idea of a gradual providential growth is clearly implied.

God sent forth his Son (iv., 4).—Commentators say that these words imply the pre-existence of Christ, and it has even been said that they can only mean "sent forth from Himself," and so involve the divine essence of the Son. The latter is sufficiently refuted by the fact that the word translated "sent forth" is applied to Paul himself in Acts xxii., 21, and is several times used of prophets in the LXX (see, for instance, Jud. vi., 8; Ps. civ. [cv.], 26; Jer. i., 7; Ezek. ii., 3, iii., 6), to say nothing of serpents (Jer. viii., 17), and of an evil spirit (Jud. ix., 23). Sending, however, logically implies the pre-existence of the thing sent; but this is quite disregarded in ordinary speech. No one infers the pre-existence of John the Baptist from the fact that he was "sent from God" (John i., 6); and in the LXX God is said to have "sent forth" many things which cannot well be regarded as pre-existent; for instance, "satiety" (Ps. cv. [cvi.], 15); "signs and wonders" (Ps. cxxxiv. [cxxxv.], 9; "famine" (Ezek. v., 17, xiv., 13; Amos viii., 11); "corn and wine" (Joel ii., 19); a "curse" (Malachi ii., 2). Further to exemplify the use of language, we may quote a modern writer. Tolstoy says, "I am urged to what I do . . . only by fear to fail in what is required of me by Him who has sent me into this world, to whom I am hourly expecting to return."[1] But though the words do not point to pre-existence, they seem certainly to imply that Jesus Christ was the Son of God in a very special sense, that he was sent into the world for a very high purpose, and that he came at a time when the world had grown sufficiently mature to profit by his advent.

Born of a woman (iv., 4).—The Greek word does not mean "born," but conveys the idea of "becoming," and might be translated "sprung from." The same word is used in Rom. i., 3, where it is said, not that the human nature, but that the "Son of God," was "sprung from the

[1] "The Christian Teaching," in *The New Age*, July 14, 1898, p. 218.

seed of David according to the flesh." It seems to me that these passages, so far from implying a pre-existent Son, identify the Son with the man Jesus. This identity is essential to give coherence to the argument. "Sprung from a woman" is a phrase which simply indicates the reality of his human nature, with perhaps some reference to the weakness and lowliness of that nature. We may compare Mt. xi., 11, and Job xiv., 1, xxv., 4, and a rabbinical saying, "Well for him [Jacob] who has been born of woman that he has seen the King of kings."[1] The Greek word for "woman" is generally, though not necessarily, used of a wife. If Paul meant a virgin, he would almost certainly have used that term, for he himself distinguishes the "woman" from the "virgin" (1 Cor. vii., 34, where our translators render "wife").[2] This clause connects Christ with mankind, as the subsequent one connects him with the Jews. As Paul conceives it, only one placed under the law could break the power of the law, and so redeem those who were under it.

That we might receive the adoption of sons (**iv., 5**).—"We" is general, including both Jewish and Gentile believers. Paul's argument and illustration seem to imply that men were sons by right of birth, though hitherto they had been in a state of infancy. If so, "adoption" must refer to the formal recognition and full bestowal of the privileges of sonship.

The word υἱοθεσία ("adoption") is not very common, but it undoubtedly means adoption, referring to those who are sons οὐ κατὰ φύσιν, ἀλλὰ κατὰ θέσιν.[3] But this distinction is nowhere clearly

---

[1] Weber, *Jüd. Theol.*, p. 175.

[2] Cyril of Jerusalem, referring to John the Baptist, says, οὐκ ἐν γεννητοῖς παρθένων, ἀλλὰ γυναικῶν. *Catech.*, III., 6. In connection with this passage, however, he says, ἡ παρθένος is also called γυνή, XII., 31, but does so only under the compulsion of his argument. See also Philo, ἡ ἐπὶ γενέσει τέκνων σύνοδος τὰς παρθένους γυναῖκας ἀποφαίνει (*De Cherub.*, § 14).

[3] Cyril Hierosol., *Catech.*, III., 14.

indicated by the Apostle; and it would be no great straining of the usage of the word, and none, I think, of its etymological force, to give it the meaning suggested above. This meaning is suitable also to Rom. viii., 15 and 23, and ix., 4.

Because ye are sons, etc. (iv., 6).—The sending forth of the Spirit is the act of adoption; and this takes place, not because men are not sons, but because they are. The Spirit is the Spirit of God's Son, exalting men from their state of infancy and subjection into full and perfect sonship. Here the Spirit is represented as crying; in Rom. viii., 15, it is we who, under the influence of the Spirit, cry, "Abba, Father." "Abba" is Aramaic; "Father," Greek. Thus Jew and Greek are united in an invocation which expresses the sum and substance of the truest and highest religion.

Thou (iv., 7), in the singular, so as to bring the truth home to each individual. Sonship is no longer collective, as with Israel, but distributed. Consequently each man is an heir of the promised blessing, and ought to enshrine within himself the Divine life of sonship, which is far above the perishing forms of thought and practice suited to the childhood of the race; and he is an heir, not through his own efforts, but through God, whose grace is therefore despised when men fall back upon the weak and beggarly elements of a sensuous religion.

Having concluded his argument, the Apostle now pleads with the Galatians not to turn back, in principle, to what they had forsaken, reminding them of the strong affection which they had displayed towards himself, and warning them against the narrow aims of the false teachers (iv., 8-20).

At that time (iv., 8), the time when you were bond-servants. The Galatians were then attached to a polytheistic religion. It is implied that they had come straight from heathenism to Christianity.

Or rather to be known of God (iv., 9), taken, as it were,

into His knowledge, suggesting that the initiative was on the side of God. Compare the words addressed to the wicked, "I never knew you" (Mt. vii., 23).

How turn ye back again, etc. (**iv., 9**).—By these words Paul places Judaism and heathenism, not indeed on the same level, but within the same category of weak and elementary religions. He is, however, viewing them here purely on their ceremonial side. The Galatians were returning to the principles they had forsaken, and in adopting Jewish rites they must have been moved by the superstitious feelings by which they had been actuated in their heathen condition. This sort of ritualism was "weak," because it imparted no moral strength. It was "beggarly," because it was not rich in spiritual gifts. It was rudimentary, because it was adapted only to a childish and undeveloped state. Childish men desire to be thus in bondage, instead of walking in the responsible freedom of Christ.

Ye observe days, etc. (**iv. 10**).—"Days" are sabbaths and fast-days; "months," either new moons, or months esteemed especially holy; "seasons," the annual festivals; "years," sabbatical years. To Paul all time was holy; and special times might be so observed as to be a denial of this universal truth. Such he assumes to be the case with the Galatians; for they could have no reason for adopting foreign rites except a belief in their special sanctity, and in their own merit in observing them.

Be as I am (**iv., 12**); literally, "become as I am," that is, become free from the law, as I once, a born Jew, became like you Gentiles.

Ye did me no wrong (**iv., 12**), at the time of his first visit, of which the previous words have reminded him.

Because of an infirmity of the flesh (**iv., 13**).—He was detained in the country by illness, apparently not having intended to preach there.

A temptation to you (**iv., 14**).—The illness evidently had something repulsive connected with it, which might have tempted the Galatians to treat him very differently.

Your eyes (iv., 15).—They were ready to give him what was most precious. There is no implied reference to Paul's eyes, as though his disease was in them.

Have I become your enemy? (iv., 16).—This seems to refer to some charge made by his opponents. On his second visit he must have had occasion to use some plain speech, and this was misinterpreted to his disadvantage.

They desire to shut you out (iv., 17); to make you into an exclusive clique attached to themselves alone, for which purpose they court and flatter you.

It is good to be zealously sought, etc. (iv., 18).—This seems to be a qualification of what he has just said. He does not want to keep the Galatians all to himself, so that they should be zealously sought only during his presence. He does not object to the seeking provided it be in a good cause.

My little children (iv., 19).—This is the only place where Paul applies this term to his readers. It expresses his affection and their immaturity. He compares himself to their mother, and is again suffering for them till Christ become the inmost principle of their being, when all their reliance on externals would drop away of itself.

To change my voice (iv., 20), to speak more gently and persuasively.

With a sudden change of feeling Paul now adduces rather abruptly an argument from the history of Abraham, leading up to the hortatory portion of the letter (iv., 21–v., 1).

This is the most elaborate instance of allegorical interpretation in the Epistles. It was a method of explaining ancient writings which was common at the time; but it is applied by Paul with great reserve, and with none of the arbitrary fancy which so abounds in other writers. The present example we might almost describe as an application of history to illustrate a spiritual truth, though no doubt in calling it an allegory he implies that the story was intended to convey that truth. The question was whether the heirs of Abraham were only Jews and those who had been incorporated with Judaism. Paul contended that the promised heirs were those who possessed his spiritual faith. So we are told that he had two sons, the natural one born from a slave, the spiritual born through Divine promise from the freewoman. Here we see typified two covenants, of bondage and of freedom, and two lines of descent, the servile and the free. The free-born child of promise alone was the heir.

This Hagar is Mount Sinai in Arabia (**iv., 25**).—There is no "this" in the Greek. The proper translation is "the word Hagar," meaning that this was a local name for Mount Sinai, and thus justifying the connection of Hagar with the covenant which is associated with that mountain. The reading, however, is uncertain; and if we adopt the reading in the margin, the connection will be this,—Hagar represents the covenant from Sinai, for she is the mother of the Arabians, and Sinai is in Arabia. This answered to the present Jerusalem, which was the central city of the law, and was in bondage spiritually, and in subjection politically.

Jerusalem that is above (**iv., 26**).—The Jews believed in a heavenly or ideal Jerusalem, which had existed with God from the creation of the world.

It is written (**iv., 26**), in Isaiah liv., 1. The passage refers to the revival of the Israelites after a period of subjection. Paul applies it to the Church, the promised seed which would soon outnumber the Jews.

Persecuted (**iv., 29**).—The reference is to Gen. xxi., 9, where it is told that Sarah saw Ishmael mocking Isaac. A rabbinical story says that Ishmael shot arrows at Isaac under the pretence of playing with him; and it is possible that Paul may have had this in mind. The present persecution was from the Jews. The war is thus carried into the enemy's camp. The Jews as a nation, instead of being the promised seed, were, spiritually, the children of Ishmael, and, therefore, as the next verse shows, were not to share the inheritance. The Scripture quoted, with a change of words, but not of sense, is Gen. xxi., 10.

Wherefore (iv., 31); a conclusion drawn from the allegory, but serving also as a fitting close for the whole argument.

Christ set us free (v., 1).—This verse forms a transition to the more hortatory portion of the Epistle. It sums up in a few words what Paul has shown to be an essential characteristic of the Gospel, spiritual freedom. To abandon this, and place oneself in subjection to a mere outward authority, however grand and imposing, was to renounce Christ.

Having begun with an exhortation to stand fast, Paul subjoins an authoritative statement of the reason why they should do so; to be " in Christ " and to be " under law " were incompatible (v., 2-6).

I Paul (v., 2): an appeal to his personal authority,—I, your father in the faith, an apostle of the Gentiles; I, who admit that circumcision is in itself a matter of indifference, and have even been charged with preaching it (see *v.* 11); I, the Pharisee, who know all about the law and its failure to satisfy the deepest needs.

If ye receive circumcision (v., 2).—These words do not, of course, apply to Jews, for Paul himself had received circumcision. But Gentiles could have no motive in receiving it, except a belief that it was necessary, or at least useful, for justification; and to receive it for any such reason was to accept the whole principle of the law, and abandon the spiritual faith of Christ. The Jews, on their side, taught that, if a Gentile kept the whole law, that would profit him nothing without circumcision.[1]

I testify again (v., 3).—He probably had occasion to do so on his second visit. This verse gives the reason why Christ

---

[1] Weber, *Jüd. Theol.*, p. 67.

would profit them nothing. Circumcision involved the entire acceptance of Jewish legalism, and bound a man to the law as completely as baptism bound him to Christianity.

Fallen away from grace (**v., 4**); because law judges everything by extraneous conformity to its precepts; grace is able to forgive, and accepts the faith and devotion of the heart.

Through the Spirit (**v., 5**).—There is no article in the Greek, and the stress is thrown on the quality of spirit as such, in implied contrast with "the flesh," to which the law appealed. Whether the reference is to the Spirit of God, as distinct from the human spirit, may be questioned. Paul may include the whole of the spiritual domain, where the spirit of man holds communion with the Spirit of God.

By faith (**v., 5**): literally, "out of faith," denoting the source from which the waiting springs, and co-ordinate with "through the Spirit."

The hope of righteousness (**v., 5**).—"Hope" stands for the fulfilment of the hope. The words might mean the hope generated by righteousness, for righteousness is elsewhere looked upon as a present Christian possession. But they more naturally imply that righteousness is the object of hope. This is not inconsistent with the present possession; for the grandest Christian gifts are both present and future. We have received "the adoption," and yet we wait for "the adoption." We have received "the reconciliation," and yet we are exhorted to be reconciled. We have communion with God, and righteousness; but perfect communion, absolute righteousness, are in the future.

In Christ Jesus (**v., 6**).—Paul speaks both of our being in Christ and of Christ being in us. These things are not local, but spiritual, and imply a communion whereby his life becomes the principle of our life. Then mere outward forms become indifferent; and the principle of our life is faith, using love as the instrument of its activity. Here, as elsewhere, we have the triad, faith, hope, and love.

Paul now turns to the Galatians with a personal appeal, reminding them that they had followed a good course, and warning them against the change that was taking place (v., 7-12).

This persuasion (v., 8) ; either the act of persuasion which was exercised upon them, or the doctrine which they were being persuaded to adopt.

Him that calleth you (v., 8) ; that is, God, as always in Paul. The present tense indicates a permanent attribute of God: He calls, but men do not always hear.

A little leaven, etc. (v., 9) : a proverb quoted also in 1 Cor. v., 6. The reference is either to the little band of Judaisers or to their false principles.

None otherwise minded (v., 10) : they will not think otherwise than according to the doctrine which he has just taught. But though the troubler may fail in his efforts, he must bear his judgment. It is clear that Paul did not regard it as a slight thing to interfere with the spirituality of the Gospel, however honest might be the narrow zeal which thrust itself in where other men had laboured.

If I still preach circumcision (v., 11), as I did before my conversion. This seems to imply that Paul himself was said to be preaching circumcision. Such a statement must appear to us very absurd ; but Paul became as a Jew to the Jews, and if, in conformity with this practice, he circumcised Timothy (Acts xvi., 3), we can understand how the zealots might misrepresent him, as though he really did believe in the advantage of circumcision, and omitted to impose it on the Gentiles merely to gain their favour. They could thus appeal to his authority against himself. This allegation, however, was sufficiently refuted by the fact that the Jews continued to persecute him ; for the cross was without offence, if it was not a rival to the law. One who merely added to his Jewish belief the acceptance of a crucified man as the Messiah might be looked upon as comparatively innocent ; one who saw in the crucifixion the source of a great religious revolution, and the downfall of Judaism, was in a very different position, and was hated with all the hatred that only a religion of forms is able to generate.

Cut themselves off (or, *go beyond circumcision*, **v., 12**).—The meaning, cut themselves off from intercourse with you, is not without defenders. This suits the tone of the passage:—I wish they would go of themselves, and not render harsher measures necessary; for you have been called to mutual love. But the other sense is generally preferred, though it introduces a very bitter piece of sarcasm.

A necessary caution is now introduced. Freedom from the law implied spirituality of life (v., 13-26).

The Judaisers would naturally charge Paul with teaching antinomianism; and in doing so they pointed to a real danger. It is so easy to accept freedom as an outward gift, while knowing nothing of its spiritual source, and neglecting its obligations.

For ye (**v., 13**).—The connection is not very clear, and "for" must be referred to the general sense of the previous passage. It is particularly suitable to *v.* 8. "Ye" is emphatic, in contrast with the disturbers.

The flesh (**v., 13**): the lower and animal portion of our nature, which is innocent in its primitive instincts, but is naturally self-regarding, and, when adopted as a principle of life, makes the character selfish and impure. It is therefore the source, not only of sensual sins, but of anger, jealousy, ambition, worldliness, which minister to an unspiritual gratification.

The whole law is fulfilled (**v., 14**).—Love was the highest principle of the law; and therefore he who loved had virtually fulfilled all that lay beneath it, and had risen into that life of freedom with which the law did not interfere.

Walk by the Spirit (**v., 16**).—As in *v.* 5 (which see), there is no article. The contrast with "the flesh" certainly suggests that the Spirit is in some sense ours. On the other hand, *v.* 18 may fairly be compared with Rom. viii., 14, where the Spirit is expressly called the Spirit of God. But did not Paul believe that the Spirit of God so dwelt within us as to enter into our consciousness, and to become as it were a part of our personality, while yet bearing witness to its Divine source and essence? Hence, while recognising the distinction, we cannot always mark the precise limits between the Divine and human spirits. The latter may indeed be defiled (2 Cor. vii., 1); but it is in itself the organ of Divine communication, and its end is perfect union with God. When we walk in this realm of spirit, where the Divine and human meet, we are raised above the misleading desires of the flesh.

These are contrary the one to the other (**v., 17**).—This points to a contrariety in our own nature, which arises as soon as that nature is quickened on its higher side. This contrariety exists as a condition of moral life, which would not arise if we could do without check whatever we might for the moment wish. This internal conflict, by creating a sense of moral weakness, prepares us for the redemption in Christ, when the soul rises through faith into communion with God. See Romans vii. and viii.

If ye are led by the Spirit, etc. (**v., 18**).—"Spirit" and "law" have no articles in the Greek, so that the emphasis lies on their contrasted qualities.

In evidence of the contrariety, the works of the flesh are contrasted with the fruit of the Spirit (**v., 19-23**). The former are utterly opposed to the righteousness of God, and exclude from His kingdom. They belong to a wholly different realm, and no freedom from the law can ever make them Divine.

Parties (or, *heresies*, **v., 20**) are referred to here as springing from factious preferences and self-will. Heretics, therefore, are not those who gravely and conscientiously form opinions different from those of the majority, but those who cause divisions by their want of love.

Fruit of the Spirit (**v., 22**), not works of the Spirit; for the list contains only dispositions. These dispositions have their appropriate actions, but do not move in obedience to fixed rules.

Faithfulness (**v., 22**).—This is the word which is usually translated "faith," and Paul ought not to be saved from apparent contradiction by altering his expression. If the Spirit comes by the hearing of faith, it is equally true that faith is a fruit of the Spirit. Paul is not under the law of a rigid dogmatic any more than a law of works.

Against such there is no law (**v., 23**); and therefore the law ceases to be a restraint, and we live freely out of the resources of the Spirit within us.

Crucified the flesh (**v., 24**).—This, taken in connection with the whole passage, shows that Paul is dealing with something far more profound than an imaginary forensic imputation. The flesh is not of course literally crucified, but self-denial is real, and those who are Christ's live a life above and beyond the cravings of the animal nature.

Live . . . walk (**v., 25**).—The former word refers to the inward principle of life; the latter, to the outward conduct. It depends, at least in part, on our own will whether the latter is a true expression of the former. Hence the exhortation.

Let us not be vainglorious (**v., 26**).—It is one of the frequent results even of serious differences of opinion that they stir up all that is vain and petty in men, and controversy begets party spirit, and mutual jealousy and alienation. Against this the Galatians are warned. Christian freedom is the freedom to serve others, under the leading of love.

The exhortation is continued by supposing a case of real trespass, and showing how we ought to deal with it (vi., 1-5).

If we are really spiritual, the fault of another will make us humble; for the fault is in a nature which we share. We shall therefore seek gently to restore him, instead of making the fault an occasion for pride and ill-nature. If we want a law and a burden there is the law of Christ, whereby we help to bear the weight of a brother's burdened conscience. To puff oneself up in comparison with others is mere self-deception. His own work is what each man ought to test, instead of sitting in judgment on that of his neighbour; and then, if it be really good, his satisfaction will not be due to comparison with someone else, who may have had fewer opportunities. For each man must carry his own load, and can neither shuffle off his own responsibility on another, nor gain credit for carrying what might crush his neighbour, but is easy for him. The "load" here is not the same as the "burden" of *v.* 2. We cannot shift responsibility; but we can, through spiritual sympathy, relieve the weight with which a sense of sin presses on a brother's heart. We must note the importance which Paul here attaches to "work." Faith works through love, and we can test the character and power of the faith and love by the quality of the work.

An exhortation follows of a more general kind. They must seek to be and to do good in all things and to all men; and this is enforced by a very solemn statement (vi., 6-10).

Let him that is taught (**vi.**, 6).—The word translated "taught" means orally instructed, and thus an interesting light is thrown upon the practice of the churches at that time. This is generally taken as a direction to the taught to communicate of their temporal blessings to the teachers; but some prefer an ethical meaning,—let the taught share with the teacher in everything spiritually good.

Be not deceived, etc. (**vi.**, 7, 8).—This is a most emphatic statement of the unalterable law of retribution, and sweeps away the whole system of forensic make-believe which has been thrust upon the Apostle. From one point of view it might be said to be the very principle of the law itself, and undoubtedly the law bore witness to it. But the observance of the law had become, in Paul's apprehension, a piece of mere externalism. In turning to it, the Galatians were simply sowing to the flesh, deserting the spiritual substance and reality for the sake of forms and shadows. Of course the application extends far beyond this, and probably the reference is more immediately to the "works of the flesh," which have been already condemned. These can end only in corruption, physical and moral, and no descent from Abraham, no outward ceremony, can alter this imperious fact. Eternal life, the gift of God, comes only from the Spirit, and he who would have it must sow to the Spirit.

Opportunity (**vi., 10**), the same word as "season" in the last verse. Now is the season for doing good; the season for reaping will come. Observe the stress laid on "doing" and "work," and the desire to extend our beneficence to "all," though a preference may be given to those who are sharers of our faith.

The Epistle concludes with a summing up which Paul wrote with his own hand, and which is expressed in strong and concise words (vi., 11-18).

With how large letters I have written (or, *I write* **vi., 11**).—The past tense is used from the point of view of the readers, so that the reference need not be to the whole Epistle, but only to this concluding section. Paul either dictated his letters or caused a fair copy to be made (Rom. xvi., 22), and then authenticated them by adding a few words in his own hand (1 Cor. xvi., 21; Col. iv., 18; 2 Thess. iii., 17). Here the gravity of the subject leads him to make a longer addition than usual, which was easily distinguished by its large characters from the neater text of the scribe.

Make a fair show in the flesh (**vi., 12**), make an outward display of religion, which will gain a reputation for sanctity. Compare Christ's own warnings in Mt. vi., 1 *sqq*. This sort of outward religion is apt to end in insincerity, not necessarily hypocrisy in our sense of the word, but a want of reality and simplicity. Paul adds, however, a further motive, the fear of persecution. We may infer from this that the party who insisted on the observance of the law were much less obnoxious to the Jews than Paul. The ascription of such motives to his opponents constitutes a very serious charge; but Paul may have known the men he was dealing with, and had good grounds for making it. Of his unbelieving countrymen he bears witness elsewhere that they had a zeal for God (Rom. x., 2).

They who receive circumcision (vi., 13).—If this reading be correct, the reference must be to Gentile believers who were submitting to the rite; but then there is no proper contrast with "you"; and the whole statement seems inexplicable unless Jewish believers are meant. This is an argument in favour of the other reading, "those who have been circumcised," which is not without good authority. The words, then, are to this effect: Even the Jews who are troubling you do not consistently carry out the obligations of the law. Circumcision has ceased, for them, to be a sign of incorporation with Judaism, and all they want is to be able to boast among their unbelieving countrymen that, at their instigation, you have accepted the rite.

Far be it from me to glory save in the cross (vi., 14).—Outwardly and in the eyes of men the cross was a thing to be ashamed of, and to glory in it then brought nothing but scorn and persecution. But spiritually it was the symbol of redemption, and through the spirit of him who suffered on it Paul had been delivered from all worldly thoughts and aims.

Neither is circumcision anything, etc. (vi., 15).—These outward distinctions are nothing. There is just as little merit on one side as the other; and the only serious matter is the "new creation," the life of faith and love within the heart, bringing forth fruits of well-doing.

The Israel of God (**vi., 16**), the true, spiritual Israel, whether Jewish or Gentile.

Henceforth (**vi., 17**).—Now he has fully expressed himself, and there can be no further ambiguity as to his position. No one can have a right to interfere with him; for he, whatever may be the case with others, is the slave of Christ, as is proved by the branded marks, the stigmata, which he bears in his body, the scars left by stoning and scourging. It was thus that he who wore the crown of thorns, and whose hands and feet were pierced with nails, stamped the Apostle as his own.

The Epistle concludes with a benediction, suitable to any of the Pauline letters, but especially appropriate to this, which contrasts grace with law, and the spirit with the flesh. It is the only Epistle which ends with the word "brethren." He has had occasion to speak plainly and even severely; but he has not become their enemy by telling them the truth. They were still dear to him as members of the new brotherhood in Christ.

THE EPISTLE TO THE ROMANS.

INTRODUCTION.

THE Epistle to the Romans is Paul's most elaborate and systematic work. To attempt to discuss with any fulness the numerous questions which are raised in an Introduction to this letter would carry us far beyond the limits assigned to this Commentary, and I must be content with touching very briefly on the principal points which require investigation, and leaving my own opinion without adequate defence.

From Macedonia, whither he had gone from Ephesus after the riot, Paul proceeded to Greece, and the Epistle was written at Corinth during his three months' residence there. This appears from the following facts. He was about to set out for Jerusalem with the contributions for the poor to which we have already referred, and he intended afterwards to visit Rome.[1] It had been his purpose, when he came to Greece, to take up his abode in Corinth[2]; and Corinth is clearly indicated in this Epistle as the place of composition. Phœbe, a deaconess of the church in Cenchreæ, is commended to the readers, and Cenchreæ was one of the ports of Corinth.[3] After this reference to the port "the city" can have but one meaning; and Erastus, "the steward of the city," sends his greeting.[4] It is also a coincidence that

[1] xv., 25-28.
[2] Cor. xvi., 5-7; 2 Cor. ix., 4; xii., 20-xiii., 2.
[3] xvi., 1, 2.
[4] xvi., 23.

Gaius, the host of Paul and of the whole church, sends his salutation,[1] and a certain Gaius was one of the few whom Paul had baptised at Corinth.[2] We may add that internal indications of style and thought place this Epistle in the same period as Corinthians and Galatians. This view is generally accepted, and we need have little hesitation in placing the composition in the early part of the year, shortly before Paul left Greece for his final visit to Jerusalem. Whether this year was 58 or a few years earlier depends on the chronology of Paul's life as a whole. Relatively to the events of his life the date is admitted.

The evidence on which we have chiefly relied is contained in the last two chapters of the Epistle. This reminds us that the genuineness of these chapters, and especially of the sixteenth, or of part of it, has been called in question. The letter, in the ordinary printed text, closes with a long doxology; but the greater number of our authorities place this doxology at the end of xiv. A further difficulty is occasioned by the recurrence of what seems to be the closing benediction; and the salutations present some features which are thought to be perplexing, and to point to Ephesus rather than Rome. A variety of hypotheses have been started which, without denying that these chapters are the composition of Paul, suggest that certain portions were meant for another church, and through some mistake got attached to Romans. Baur, however, and some of his followers deny altogether the genuineness of these chapters, and think they are the work of a Pauline Christian who wished to soften down the anti-Judaic spirit of the Epistle in the interests of catholic unity. The arguments rest on a subjective conception of what Paul is likely to have written in conformity with the Tübingen scheme. These various difficulties and conjectures furnish material for a prolonged examination; but in this brief Introduction I can only say

[1] xvi., 23.   [2] 1 Cor. i., 14.

that my own judgment is in favour of the genuineness of both chapters, as this appears to me to involve fewer difficulties than the rival hypotheses.

The origin of the Roman church is wrapped in obscurity. The traditional ascription of its foundation to Peter and Paul may apply to its final constitution by apostolic authority, but certainly not to the assembling of the first groups of Christian believers. When the Epistle was written there had been a church in Rome for many years,[1] and it certainly seems implied that no man of the first rank had yet paid it a visit. It had probably grown up gradually, without any formal or organised effort. Christians from the provinces may have settled in Rome for various reasons, and gathered little congregations into their houses from among neighbours whom they were able to interest in the new faith; and others who were permanently resident in Rome may have come in contact with Christianity and been converted in journeys abroad. If the church grew up in this way, and not through a definite appeal to the Synagogue, it was all the more likely to present that predominantly Gentile and Pauline appearance which particular passages as well as the whole tenor of the Epistle indicate. On this subject, however, opinion has been sharply divided. At one time it had become almost a critical dogma that the church was mainly composed of Jewish Christians, of a mildly anti-Pauline type. Opinion, however, has undergone a considerable change, and many who would be reckoned as belonging to the critical school have yielded to the force of evidence, and regard the church as principally Gentile.

The Epistle bears more resemblance to a treatise than any other of the Pauline letters, probably because it was not called forth by any immediate requirement in the church itself. After the introductory portion it falls into two great divisions, of which the first[2] is mainly doctrinal, and the

[1] xv., 23; cf. i., 8, and xiii., 11.   [2] i., 16-xi., 36.

second[1] is mainly ethical and hortatory. The rest of the Epistle relates to personal affairs, and lies outside of the principal theme. The first division again falls into two strongly marked subdivisions: in i.–viii. it is shown that the Gospel is the power of God unto salvation to Jew and Gentile alike, irrespective of the observance of the Law; in ix.–xi. it is proved that, in spite of the unbelief of most of the Jews, the ancient word of God had not failed. A full analysis of the argument must be reserved. Suffice it to say that in the course of it the Apostle goes down into the most hidden depths of spiritual conflict, and soars to the sublimest heights of Christian redemption. The theme bears a close resemblance to that which is discussed in the Epistle to the Galatians, as though the subject had been running and elaborating itself in the writer's mind; but the treatment is larger and more abstract, and much may be learnt by a study of the parallels and contrasts between the two Epistles.

Opinion has been greatly divided as to the occasion and the object of the Epistle, the principal dividing line being between those who regard it as a systematic exposition of Christian truth, or at least of Pauline Christianity, and those who, with Baur, would trace it entirely to historical conditions and the great controversy of the time. We cannot pause to examine these various opinions. I think there is some truth on both sides. It was a sufficient reason for writing to the Romans that Paul was expecting to visit them, but was obliged once more to postpone an event to which he had long looked forward. There was nothing in the circumstances of the church that required his intervention, and, as he was therefore free to choose his subject, he wrote out of the fulness of his heart that grand defence of the Gospel which, though shaped by the conditions of the time, is animated by the timeless Spirit, and has proved to be a possession for ever.

[1] xii.–xv., 13.

ROMANS.

ANALYSIS.

THE GREETING, i., 1-7.   INTRODUCTORY REMARKS, i., 8-15.

I.

DOCTRINAL PORTION, EXTENDING FROM i., 16, to xi., 36.

THE SUBJECT STATED, i., 16, 17.

A. GENERAL EXPOSITION OF THE SUBJECT, AND DEFENCE OF THE VIEWS ADVANCED, i., 18-viii., 39.
  (i). Universal sinfulness, showing universal need of salvation, i., 18-iii., 20.
    1. The case of the Gentiles, i., 18-32.
      a. Statement of the subject of this section, i., 18.
      b. Source and character of heathen iniquity, i., 19-23.
      c. The moral corruption resulting from this, i., 24-32.
    2. The case of the Jews, ii., 1-iii., 20.
      a. General principles, ii., 1-16.
      b. Jewish claims, and disobedience, and consequent futility of circumcision, ii., 17-29.
      c. Objections refuted, iii., 1-8.
      d. Scriptural proof that the Jews as well as the Gentiles are under sin, iii., 9-20.
  (ii). Announcement of the Christian principle of salvation, iii., 21-31.
  (iii). Proofs of the Christian principle, iv.-v.
    1. Argument from the Old Testament, iv.
    2. Argument from spiritual experience, v., 1-11.
    3. Argument from the antithesis of Adam and Christ, v., 12-21.

    (iv). Moral and spiritual results of the Christian position, **vi.-viii.**
        1. Argument against dangerous inferences, vi., 1-vii., 25.
          (1). False inference that we may continue in sin, vi., 1-vii., 6.
            a. We must not continue in sin, for we have entered a new life, vi., 1-14.
            b. We must not sin, for we cannot serve sin and righteousness at the same time, vi., 15-23.
            c. We must not sin, for we have died to the law, and become the property of another, vii., 1-6.
          (2). False inference that the law is identical with sin. In answer, its true nature and purpose shown, vii., 7-25.
        2. Positive spiritual results, **viii.**

B. DIFFICULTIES ARISING OUT OF THE ACTUAL COURSE OF EVENTS, **ix.-xi.**
    INTRODUCTION: Paul's expression of his feelings in regard to the Jews, ix., 1-5.
    Statement of the proposition to be proved: the word of God has not failed, ix., 6a.
    (i). Nature of the original word to Israel, and its application to the existing state of things, ix., 6b-29.
        1. Original character of the Divine election, ix., 6b-13.
        2. This does not imply injustice in God, ix., 14-29.
          a. Generally, ix., 14-21.
          b. In its special application to the Christian Church, ix., 22-29.
    (ii). General conclusion, and spiritual law on which the facts rested, ix., 30-x., 13.
    (iii). The application of this spiritual law not prevented by ignorance of the Gospel, x., 14-21.
    (iv). God had not cast off His people, for a remnant received the Gospel, xi., 1-10.
    (v). The rejection of the Gospel was only temporary, being part of the Divine plan of salvation, xi., 11-32.
    Concluding expression of praise, xi., 33-36.

II.

ETHICAL PORTION, EXTENDING FROM xii., 1 TO xv., 13.

GENERAL PRINCIPLE OF CHRISTIAN CONDUCT, xii., 1, 2.

A. UNIVERSAL RULES OF DUTY, xii., 3-xiii., 14.

- (i). Personal intercourse of Christians with one another, xii., 3-17a.
- (ii). Conduct of Christians towards the outer world, xii., 17b-xiii., 10.
    1. Towards its injustice, xii., 17b-21.
    2. Submission to magistrates, xiii., 1-7.
    3. General social intercourse, xiii., 8-10.
- (iii). Personal purity, xiii., 11-14.

B. MUTUAL DUTIES OF DIFFERENT PARTIES IN THE CHURCH. THERE MUST BE MUTUAL RESPECT FOR PRIVATE CONVICTIONS, xiv., 1-xv., 13.
- (i). Because we are all responsible to God, xiv., 1-12.
- (ii). Because intolerance is a violation of Christian love, xiv., 13-xv., 13.
    1. By driving a brother away through offence given to his scruples, xiv., 13-18.
    2. By inducing him to act against his scruples, xiv., 19-23.
    3. By not using one's strength for the benefit of the weak in accordance with Christ's example, xv., 1-13.

CONCLUSION: Passage relating to personal affairs, xv., 14-33; commendation and salutations, xvi., 1-16; warning against false teachers, xvi., 17-20; more salutations, and doxology, xvi., 21-27.

ROMANS.

COMMENTARY.

Address to the readers, modified and expanded from the usual Greek mode of beginning a letter ("So-and-so to So-and-so greeting"), and full of allusions to the theme of the Epistle (i., 1-7).

A servant [better, *a slave*] *of Jesus Christ* (i., 1).—Paul does not generally so describe himself; but in writing to a church which he had never visited he naturally begins by placing himself upon the common Christian ground, and in doing so selects a word which at the same time suggests the dependence of his activity on a higher command. The expression reminds us of the relation between a rabbi and his pupils.[1]

Called to be an Apostle (i., 1),—an Apostle who is such by virtue of a Divine call. Compare Gal. i., 15, and contrast with it the controversial statement in Gal. i., 1. Here there is no controversial object, but he refers to his call partly to justify himself in addressing a strange church, and still more because the whole subject of a Divine call to mankind was uppermost in his thoughts. His readers too had experienced a Divine call (*vv.* 6, 7). This word answered to a vivid experience in Paul's life, a change which affected the inmost springs of his being, and coloured all his subsequent thought. The conscientiousness and zeal of his early years now appeared to him ignorant and misdirected, and he felt

[1] Weber, *Jüd. Theol.*, p. 132.

that there must be something imperfect and weak in the principle which had guided them. This principle he described as Law; the new principle which swayed him after his conversion, he called Faith. The meaning of these terms will be unfolded as the Epistle proceeds.

Separated unto the Gospel (i., 1),—set apart, according to Gal. i., 15, even from his birth (compare Jer. i., 5). The whole of his life, not least his experience of the awful requirements and condemnation of the law, prepared him for his office of Apostle to the Gentiles.

The Gospel of God (i., 1).—"God" is the genitive of the subject, the author of the message. The word "Gospel" is without the article in Greek, and this omission throws the stress upon the quality, so that we might translate thus: "set apart to preach glad tidings from God."

The holy scriptures (i., 2).—In the Greek there is no article. The Old Testament is alluded to; but the emphasis is laid on its distinctive character. The statement brings out two facts: the promise was preserved in writings; these writings were holy. Paul thus connects the Old and New Testaments. In spite of the antithesis of principle between Law and Faith, they were both parts of one providential plan, and what was explicit in the New Testament was implicit in the Old. The Old Testament is frequently appealed to by Paul in writing to Gentile churches; it was in fact the Bible of Christendom before the New Testament was written.

Concerning His Son (i., 3).—There is, I think, very insufficient evidence that "Son of God" was an accepted designation of the Messiah among the Jews. At all events Paul does not use such terms as mere equivalents for something else. The doctrine of sonship enters deeply into this Epistle, and we must suppose that that doctrine was in his mind when he selected this particular term as a designation of Christ.

Who was born of the seed of David according to the flesh (i., 3).—Some commentators here make "flesh" equivalent to "the human nature," in contrast with "the Divine nature" of Christ,—language which is quite foreign to the writings of Paul. I must here express my opinion once for all, that, whatever inference the dogmatic theologian may legitimately draw, it is highly improper for the interpreter to introduce theological terms, such as "trinity," which are not found in Christian literature till long after the time of Paul. The Apostle's antithesis is that between flesh and spirit. Compare his allusion to his brethren, "my kinsmen according to the flesh" (Rom. ix., 3), and the statement, "it is not the children of the flesh that are children of God" (Rom. ix., 8). Sonship to God is not determined by mere physical relationship. So far as race or physical lineage was concerned, Christ was sprung from the seed of David; but in the inner spirit of his life, in all that constituted the reason or spirit, he was not the son of David, but owned a higher parentage. We are therefore dealing not with metaphysical, but with spiritual conceptions. Paul accepted the Messiah of prophecy, belonging to the royal line of David; but his Christ was no longer an ideal David. Rather was he the lofty type of spiritual humanity, drawing his essential life from God, and thereby entering those universal relations in which questions of race and kindred disappear.

Declared to be the Son of God (i., 4).—The Greek word rendered "declared" properly means "to appoint" or "institute," and is correctly translated "ordained" in the only other passages in the New Testament where it is applied to Christ (Acts x., 42; xvii., 31). This undoubtedly creates a difficulty, for Paul does not seem elsewhere to treat the sonship of Jesus as beginning after the resurrection; and accordingly the meaning "declared" has been invented[1] for the word. I venture to make the following suggestions.

[1] Not in modern times, for it is given by Greek commentators,

We have an analogy in Paul's view of the spiritual man. Men *are* sons of God, though in their minority they differ not from slaves; but it is only after their minority that they receive the spirit of God's Son, and this crisis is described as "adoption," because it is only then that they are ordained to the full privileges which inherently belong to them (Gal. iv., 1-7). Now let us look at Rom. vi., 9, 10, and we shall see that Paul regarded Christ's death and resurrection as an important turning-point in the conditions of his spiritual being. This may be analogous to the adoption. The consciousness of sonship may have been the pervasive power of Christ's earthly life; but he took upon him here the "form of a slave" (Philip. ii., 7), and only by passing to the life beyond the grave did he receive the full freedom and power of his sonship. It is instructive to compare the speech of Paul at Antioch in Pisidia, where the resurrection is connected with the idea of holiness, and is represented as constituting Christ's birth into his Divine relationship (Acts xiii., 32-35). See also Lk. xx., 36, they "are sons of God, being sons of the resurrection."

With [better *in*] *power* (i., 4).—This is perhaps best taken as a supplementary statement,—ordained the Son of God, and ordained so in full possession of that power which is characteristic of his Gospel.

According to the spirit of holiness (i., 4).—"Spirit" is here contrasted with "flesh," and the words clearly indicate the ground of sonship. On the physical side Jesus was the son of David; by reason of his holy and exalted mind he was raised above the rank of a national hero, and could be adequately described only by the highest term that is applicable to man. Sonship as here defined is ethical, not metaphysical. Compare Romans viii., 14, "As many as are led by the Spirit of God, these are sons of God." Christ's holiness, instead of separating him from humanity, was the norm for all his disciples, who are accordingly habitually spoken of as "the holy ones" (commonly translated "saints"). The Romans are exhorted to present their bodies "a holy sacrifice to God" (xii., 1), and the Corinthians to "perfect holiness [the word here used] in the fear of God" (2 Cor. vii., 1). Paul did not look upon the sinful, earthly man as the type of humanity; *that* he found in the spiritual, heavenly man, and he believed that as is the heavenly man such also are the heavenly men (1 Cor. xv., 48). But Christ was the first man of the new creation, "the first-born among many brethren" (Rom. viii., 29).

By the resurrection of the dead (i., 4).—This cannot be legitimately interpreted as referring only to Christ's resurrection. That, in Paul's view, was not a miraculous exception to the fate of mankind, but an anticipation and example of the universal destiny. The idea of sonship was bound up with the idea of eternal life; and it was through the general fact of raised humanity, already begun, but not completed, that the son of David was ordained the Son of God.

Through whom (i., 5).—Here, as elsewhere, Christ is expressly represented as the medium, not the ultimate source, of Divine gifts; and among these "grace" is included.

Unto obedience of faith (i., 5).—This phrase is of rather uncertain meaning. It points out the object with which his apostleship was conferred upon Paul; and as it was Paul's peculiar task to preach "faith," and this preaching involved the inclusion of the Gentiles, and as moreover this Epistle largely deals with faith in opposition to law, I think we must attach to it here the high and spiritual sense in which it is generally used by the Apostle. The words may then mean "the obedience which consists of faith," or (less probably) "obedience to the principle of faith." Some would make "faith" mean the Christian religion; but this is contrary to usage.

Among all the nations (i., 5).—"Gentiles" would be a better translation; for the word is technically used by Paul in a sense that excludes the Jews.

Among whom are ye also (i., 6).—This verse places the Roman Christians among the Gentiles, and suggests the reason why Paul, the Apostle of the Gentiles, thought himself justified in writing them an Epistle, though the church was not of his own foundation.

Called to be Jesus Christ's (i., 6).—Better, I think, "Jesus Christ's called ones," persons called by God, and belonging to Christ. The clause is added to give greater completeness to the description; they were not only Gentiles, but were called from the great Gentile world into a higher fellowship.

To all that are in Rome (i., 7).—"All" is repeated in the next verse. Paul may have wished to make it clear that he had no partial preference, but extended his good-will to the entire church, known and unknown.

Beloved of God (i., 7), an expression found only here, denotes those who know that they are loved by God, and return His love. The Divine love is one of the themes of the Epistle, and is naturally touched on here.

Called to be saints (i., 7); rather, those who are saints by virtue of a Divine call. The "calling" applies to the readers as well as Paul. It implies that the higher spiritual life originates with God, and not with man; that it is the product, not of human will, but of Divine grace; and is therefore a response to a heavenly invitation. It had an inner and an outer side. Outwardly it was the invitation spoken by man to man, the voice of the Christian preacher, which might fall on heedless ears. Inwardly it was the awakening of an unknown faith in the reality, the nearness, and the love of God, which could be ascribed only to the direct action of His Spirit upon the soul. Paul always includes the latter.

The word translated "saints," properly "holy ones," has been interpreted by very able writers so as to deprive it of all moral significance. I believe that this is quite erroneous, and that the word means simply what at first sight it seems to mean. But as the question goes into the very heart of Pauline theology, it is necessary to subjoin a somewhat technical discussion.

In considering the meaning of "saints"[1] we encounter a divergence of view which affects our whole interpretation of the Epistle. Fritzsche puts one view in its extremest form. Following, as he thinks, the analogy of the Hebrew,[2] he contends that the term means simply men consecrated to God, or united with Him by an unusually close bond, and that Christians are so called in the New Testament neither as men who have obtained pardon for their sins through the benefit of Christ, nor because they are really holy and innocent in their morals, nor because they ought to become so. As Meyer expresses it, the word must be understood in a Christian theocratic sense, and not of individual moral holiness, as appears from the fact that *all* Christians *as* Christians are "holy." According to this view the theocratic or objective relation becomes all-important, and the subjective realisation of any nobler life is quite a secondary thing; the drama of salvation passes from the hearts of men, and is acted out amid the distant scenery of heaven. The question thus raised is of the highest moment, for it affects our entire conception of Pauline theology; and we must therefore pause to test the accuracy of Fritzsche's assertion. We may observe, in the first place, that Meyer's argument is far from having the conclusive force which he ascribes to it. It rests, I think, on a forgetfulness of the very different conditions surrounding the Church in early times and in our own day. *Now* the Church has become the world, and it would no doubt be quite absurd to say that all nominal Christians were holy; and we have accordingly dropped the ancient name of saints. But in the primitive age it was not so. Men had to be in earnest in order to make a profession of Christianity; and though there were great evils and great misunderstandings even then, yet it seems clear that personal purity and elevation of character was one of the real notes of the Church in opposition to the surrounding heathenism. It might consequently be assumed in a large way that all Christians as such were holy; and though men of depraved life found their way into the Church, they were not regarded by Paul as genuine members of it, for he himself says, "If a man has not the spirit of Christ, he is none of

---

[1] Ἅγιοι.   [2] קָדוֹשׁ.

his" (Rom. viii., 9). If it be said that numbers even of sincere disciples must have fallen far short of holiness, we may reply that this fact would not render the word inapplicable to the general body of Christians so long as holiness, however imperfectly realised, was an essential ingredient in their character, and marked them off from the profligacy around them. It is possible, then, that Paul may have used the word in a strictly ethical sense, and we must determine by a comparison of instances whether he actually did so.

Let us look first at the application of the Hebrew word to the Israelites. In Lev. xi., 44, 45, we read, "Ye shall sanctify yourselves, and ye shall be holy, for I am holy." This sums up a number of prohibitions against the use of unclean food. A similar commandment occurs in xix., 2, as the introduction to a series of precepts, ceremonial and moral, but chiefly the latter; and after many more precepts of a similar kind the commandment is once more repeated in xx., 26. These passages, which furnish the key to the sense in which the Israelites are called "a people of saints"[1] (Daniel viii., 24), prove beyond question that the Hebrew term contains an ethical meaning. The people are to be holy because God to whom they belong is holy, a statement which surely implies that they were to imitate the sanctity of God. The context confirms this interpretation; for the sanctity was to be exhibited in a life of purity and rectitude. The fact that the purity was to some extent ceremonial does not affect our present question; for even a ceremonial sanctity involves personal qualities in men, and not merely a judicial relation between man and God. That this natural meaning of the commandment had not been lost in New Testament times may be inferred from the appeal which is made to it in 1 Peter i., 13-16, where, as in the Old Testament, it is introduced to enforce the claims of personal holiness. The parallel term in Hebrew, therefore, affords no excuse for emptying the Greek word of its genuine significance.

When we come to the New Testament, although the word translated "saints" or "holy" is used an immense number of times (79 in the Pauline Epistles alone), there is yet some difficulty in fixing its meaning, because, when it is applied to men, it is always possible to say that it refers to their dedication, and not to any quality in their character. Nevertheless I think the ethical meaning would be naturally regarded as fundamental if we had no theological purpose to serve. Its constant use in the phrase "the Holy Spirit"

---

[1] Translated "the holy people" in our Versions.

seems to determine its deepest sense in Christian teaching. Whatever our doctrine of the Spirit may be, no one, I presume, will maintain that this phrase means "the dedicated spirit." The epithet surely denotes the attribute of holiness; and it would be absurd to describe a man as full of the Holy Spirit if his mind were a chaos of brutal and sensual passions, even though he were a High-priest or a Pope. Such a description applies only to a pure, exalted soul, refined from the common dross of earth and self. Does, then, the word change its meaning when it is predicated of a man? John the Baptist is spoken of as a "just and holy man" (Mk. vi., 20), where the union of "holy" with "just" induces us to look for a moral quality. So Christ himself is "the Holy One of God" (Mk. i., 24; Lk. iv., 34); and as this is the terrified confession of a man with an unclean spirit, we immediately think of the serene, unclouded purity with which the uncleanness was confronted. Again, he is called "the Holy and Just One" (Acts iii., 14) and God's "holy Servant" (Acts iv., 27, 30). No one will wish to lower the meaning of the word when applied to Christ, and we have just seen an elaborate metaphysical dogma raised upon an ascription to him of a spirit of holiness. If this can denote, after all, only a spirit of dedication, then, so far as the passage in question is concerned, Christ's sonship ceases to be grounded in his essential being, and expresses only an official relation; and thus the warm life of Christianity is frozen at its source, and instead of the bread of spiritual reality our hungry hearts receive the stone of theological fiction. Let our commentators at least be consistent, and not strain the sense of the word to its most abstract perfection when applied to Christ, and then, when this strained sense is found inapplicable to men, insist on abolishing it altogether, and introducing a new one adapted to their theories.

Let us see, however, how Paul applies the term to others than Christ. In 1 Cor. vi., 1, he contrasts "the saints" with "the unrighteous," that is, the Christians with the outlying unbelieving world. There is no true antithesis unless "saints" contains an idea of moral excellence; and that a moral contrast is very prominent in Paul's mind is evident from what follows; for he resolves the "unrighteous" into fornicators, idolaters, adulterers, thieves, drunkards, and so forth, whereas the Christians, though they were such before their conversion, have washed and been sanctified and justified in the name of Christ and in the Spirit of God. This surely ought to satisfy us that Paul regarded the disciples as holy in a far higher than a merely judicial and imputative sense. We may refer also to Eph.

i., 4, where we have "holy and without blemish." (Also in Col. i., 22.) See, further, v., 27, where the same epithets are applied to the Church when without spot or any such thing. The force of the word in its application to persons may, then, I think, be regarded as sufficiently established.

Nevertheless it is evident that in its application to things it must undergo some modification, but even in regard to things it does not mean simply "dedicated," apart from any quality attaching to them, but represents a sanctity and purity corresponding as closely to the personal attribute as is possible in that which is not personal. Thus the Scriptures are called holy, as being intrinsically good, and an expression of God's holy will. This is apparent from Paul's reply to the question, "Is the law sin?" No; "the law is holy, and the commandment holy and just and good" (Rom. vii., 12). The injunction to present our bodies a holy sacrifice (Rom. xii., 1) is a demand for personal purity, the body sharing as it were the sanctity of the spirit. The "holy kiss" with which the brethren were to greet one another (Rom. xvi., 16; 1 Cor. xvi., 20; 2 Cor. xiii., 12; 1 Thess. v., 26) must represent the temper with which the kiss was to be given. So, in the Old Testament, if the Sabbath, the temple, the priesthood are holy, I do not think that the meaning is satisfied if we merely say that they were dedicated to God; it is rather that God has chosen them to represent, as it were, His own holiness, so that they ought to awaken in men's minds the reverential awe which is due to Him. Things do not become holy in our belief until, through an association of ideas, we transfer to them some of the feeling which is strictly applicable only to character, just as we entertain feelings of tenderness and affection towards a relic or a memento of some beloved friend. This transference of the meaning to things may enable us to explain the one passage to which Fritzsche is able to appeal, 1 Cor. vii., 14. Paul is here discussing the question whether in the case of mixed marriages the Christian ought to divorce the unbeliever. He decides that separation should not proceed from the Christian side, because the unbelieving husband or wife "is sanctified"[1] by union with the believer. Now the Greek word does not necessarily mean "to make holy," but may signify, as no doubt it does here, "to devote to a holy purpose." This is illustrated by John xvii., 19, where Christ says, "for their sakes I sanctify [or, consecrate] myself." But it does not follow that this meaning can be

[1] Ἡγίασται.

transferred to the adjective, and a comment of Theophylact's on the passage in Corinthians[1] is very instructive as showing that the adjective, in contradistinction from the verb, carried with it the idea of personal holiness: "Not that the Greek becomes holy; for he did not say that he 'is holy,' but, 'he has been consecrated,' that is, has been overcome by the holiness of the believer." Paul gives a proof that the heathen husband or wife must be thus sanctified: if it were not so, the children would be "unclean," whereas in fact they are "holy." Now I think we must admit at once that Paul does not refer here to the personal holiness of the children. For the purposes of his argument he must refer to some obvious fact, and I presume that fact must have been simply this, that the children of mixed marriages were treated as Christians. They are called "holy," therefore, as members of a holy community, persons to whom the characteristic quality of the community may be presumed to belong, just as the children of heathen parents are called "unclean" because they are born into an impure and corrupt society. There is thus a reason for the imputative use of the word in regard to children; but this reason would not exist unless the children belonged to a corporate society of "holy ones," and therefore this single example, instead of determining the universal sense of the term, presupposes its higher ethical significance in its application to the collective Church. To use a simple illustration: in a brave army we impute bravery to every soldier till he has proved himself a coward, but we do so only on account of the real and proved bravery of the army as a whole. It deserves notice, however, in this connection that it is only to the collective Church or quite indefinite members of it, and never to particular individuals, that Paul assigns the epithet "holy." This might be merely accidental; but it is not difficult to find a reason for it. The sanctity of the Church as a society might stand out in sharp contrast to the heathen depravity around it; and yet one might hesitate to call this man or that man holy lest we should be ascribing to him a personal character of higher perfection than really belonged to him. So far as he was imbued with the characteristic spirit of the Church he was holy; and yet you might shrink from pronouncing upon his individual possession of that spirit, unless he possessed it in a very eminent degree. Hence Paul admits the possibility of individual corruption in the midst of corporate sanctity. He says, "Know ye not that ye are a temple of God, and the Spirit of God dwells in

---

[1] Quoted by Alford.

you? If any man spoils the temple of God, him will God spoil; for the temple of God is holy, which temple ye are" (1 Cor. iii., 17). A living temple wherein the Spirit of God dwells must be distinguished by real, and not imaginary, holiness; and if any professing Christian has none of this Spirit, he only mars the sanctuary with his sacrilegious presence.

Our discussion, then, brings us to the following result. In the Pauline use of "holy" the notion of imputation is present only to a very limited extent; and so far as it is admitted, it is based on the actual holiness of the Church. Holiness enters essentially into the ideal of the Christian character; and in the first age this ideal was, at least approximately and comparatively, realised.

For the meaning of the salutation (i., 7) see the note on Gal. i., 3.

Introductory statements: Paul's thanksgiving for the faith of the Roman Christians, and mention of his desire to visit them, and labour among them (i., 8-15).

I thank my God through Jesus Christ (i., 8).—The phrase "my God" is found also in 1 Cor. i., 4; 2 Cor. xii., 21; Philip. i., 3, iv., 19; Philem., 4, and expresses a deep feeling of God's intimate presence and His care for the individual life. It may show that "my Gospel" does not necessarily denote a distinctive Gospel of Paul's. Compare Christ's use of the words "my Father."

"Through Jesus Christ" has been explained of the mediatorial function of a priest. Usage does not sustain this. Paul exhorts his disciples "through Jesus Christ" (Rom. xv., 30, where "through the love of the Spirit" is added; 2 Thess. iii., 12), "through the name of our Lord Jesus Christ" (1 Cor. i., 10), "through the meekness and gentleness of Christ" (2 Cor. x., 1), and says that he gave injunctions "through the Lord Jesus" (1 Thess. iv., 2). Christ was not the medium through whom the exhortations were conveyed; and such expressions must therefore denote the influence from which the exhortation proceeded, and under which it was likely to be received. Similarly, it is as quickened by Christ's spirit, through him as the inspiration of his life, that Paul gives thanks.

The rest of this paragraph speaks for itself. Notice Paul's deep interest in the Roman Christians, and his purpose, long entertained, of visiting them; also his including them once more among the Gentiles.

Statement of the subject of the Epistle, for which the declaration of his readiness to preach the Gospel in Rome has prepared the way (i., 16, 17).

I am not ashamed of the Gospel (i., 16).—Paul's experience had shown him that to the wise and powerful of this world the Gospel was an object of scorn, and he might well feel some timidity as he thought of bringing the tidings of the Crucified to the proud capital, where all that was majestic and imposing in the old civilisation was united with boundless power and the haughtiness of imperial supremacy. But he was not ashamed of his message, which alone was capable of saving the Empire from the demoralisation that was eating out its life.

The words which follow resolve themselves into several important statements. The Gospel was a power, a living force in the individual and in society, in contrast with the Law, which was "weak," and unable to effect the righteousness which it enjoined (viii., 3). The power was of God. The Gospel was no mere human device, but God Himself was working in and through it upon the hearts of men. The object is salvation, deliverance from sin, resulting in the immortal life of sons of God. The salvation is extended to him who has faith, to him who spiritually apprehends the Divine love manifested in Christ, and, trustfully surrendering himself to it, accepts the Spirit of God as the fountain of his life. It comes to the Jews first, both because as a fact the Gospel was first preached among them, and because they were the chosen line through whom the Messiah was to come; but it includes the Greeks because the life of faith was the universal life of redeemed humanity, and was in no way hampered by national or legal restrictions.

A righteousness of God (better, ***God's righteousness***, **i., 17**).
—The word translated "righteousness," and other cognate words, enter so deeply into the theology of Paul that a right understanding of them is absolutely essential. But a full discussion of their meaning would be too long and technical for this small commentary, and I must be content with presenting here only the briefest summary of the results of an investigation which I must hope to find some other opportunity of publishing. In opposition to the view that righteousness, in the Pauline Epistles, does not refer to any moral or spiritual condition, but only to an objective relation between God and man, established by a forensic judgment, whereby God imputes righteousness which has no reality, on the condition of faith in the atoning death of Christ, I believe that when Paul says "righteousness" he simply means "righteousness." But he had come to see that there were two antithetical ideas of righteousness. There was legal righteousness, which consisted in outward conformity to a law: the man that *did* what the law required was righteous, the law being confessedly the Divine rule of conduct. This law was for the Jews the Mosaic code; for the Gentiles the commands of conscience. But conformity to a law, even if perfect, which it never was, was not real righteousness as it is in the sight of God. In contrast with this was the "righteousness of God," the eternal reality, God's own Spirit of holiness, justice, and love, which, instead of being subservient to a law, is the source of law. This righteousness man receives through faith; and then, instead of standing over against God as a subject, he is on the side of God, and, being led by the Spirit, is a son of God. Hence there is room for forgiveness, which has no place under a strict administration of law; and God is able to justify the ungodly, not through a false, but through a true judgment. For as soon as the sinner turns in faith to God, and opens his heart to the inflowing of Divine love, the reality of righteous-

ness begins to dwell within him, the promise and potency of perfect holiness. Thus he is emancipated from subjection to the law by rising into the Spirit of which law is the expression; and thereby law is not annulled, but established, and its righteous requirements are for the first time fulfilled.

It was the revelation of this righteousness in the Gospel that made the latter "the power of God unto salvation." The preaching of the Christian missionaries awakened the world's faith, and, as they set forth the righteousness of God manifested in the love and self-devotion of Christ, many a sin-burdened soul turned heavenward, and the revealed righteousness began to work as a new leaven within.

All this is confirmed by an appeal to ancient Scripture, Hab. ii., 4, and if Paul finds here a deeper meaning than was clear to the Prophet, he only follows with reverent caution the principle, which was often grossly misapplied, of finding in Scripture ideas which were not apparent on the surface. This and other passages must have glowed for Paul with a new significance when he read them again with Christian eyes.

The evidence of universal sinfulness, showing the need of universal salvation, is presented as the first step in the Apostle's argument, extending as far as iii., 20. The case of the Gentiles is taken first, and then that of the Jews: and the whole subject is introduced by a reference to the wrath of God (i., 18).

"For the wrath of God is revealed from heaven." "Wrath" is the word used to denote the Divine displeasure and punitive judgment against sin. "For" gives a reason for the foregoing statement: God's righteousness is being revealed because His wrath is being revealed. It seemed to Paul that a decisive crisis in human affairs was manifest. God's righteousness was dawning on the world in the "spirit of holiness," which dwelt in Christ. In antithesis to this were the unnatural vices and crimes of heathenism, which displayed themselves with unblushing openness, and which proved that God had "given men up" (a phrase thrice repeated) to the loathsome results of their inward iniquity. These, if unchecked, could end only in a great catastrophe of merited retribution. This was becoming apparent, was being "revealed," to every unspoiled conscience. The two revelations, accordingly, helped one another; and the darkness of sin made all the more splendid the righteousness which had come to seek and save.

The deplorable character of heathenism is now painted in detail in the darkest colours (i., 19-32).

In considering these verses it must be sufficient here to notice certain important implications. Observe:

1. That men have by nature a sufficient knowledge of God and of His will to leave them without excuse (i., 20).

2. That God's power and divinity (rather than His goodness and love) are the attributes most clearly revealed by the works of creation (i., 20).

3. That the loss or perversion of faith is the source of unrighteousness (i., 24, 26, 28). This is the other side of the doctrine of righteousness by faith, and may help to illustrate it. Depraved morals must spring sooner or later from a lowered spiritual vitality.

4. That the punishment for our departure from God is that we are given over to the sensual and brutal nature (i., 24 sqq.). This is the only punishment which the Apostle mentions in this passage.

5. That the outward deterioration of our life, with all its attendant misery to the individual and to society, as the consequence of the repudiation of faith, is of *Divine* appointment (i., 24, 26, 28).

There is nothing in the present passage to indicate that Paul regarded this description of the state of morals as universally applicable. Though tracing, as he proceeds, delicate moral laws, he is now dealing with men in the mass, and describing the general appearance of the heathen world as it must have presented itself to every pure and noble-minded man. It seemed full of moral corruption, and, owing to the falsity of its principles, to have no recuperative power. But no one would have admitted more joyfully that in every nation there were some who feared God and worked righteousness. This indeed is implied in ii., 14.

Again, it deserves notice that in condemning the religious position of the Gentiles he does not trace all their aberrations to faulty doctrine, but insists that they knew God; and the one falsity which he ascribes to them is the practical falsity of worshipping the created instead of the Creator. Accordingly his sad picture of the state of society is drawn, not from the absurd notions which he might have found in such abundance, but entirely from the domain of the affections and the will, along with the practices which spring from their depraved condition.

Knowing the ordinance of God, that they which practise such things are worthy of death (i., 32).—We have here the first intimation, in the Epistle, of any connection between sin and death. It is a connection known to sinful Gentiles, known therefore to the common conscience of mankind. What, then, does conscience testify? Is it not precisely what Paul says, that, if we live a selfish and sensual life, we *deserve* to die? Such a life is a blot upon the universe; and no man can solemnly place himself before the Divine judgment, and maintain that it is and ought to be the *eternal* life.

Statement of principles, partly deduced from the foregoing passage, and leading clearly up to the case of the Jews (ii., 1-16).

These principles, when thus stated in the abstract, are of such a character that it is impossible not to accept them. The dependence of this chapter on the preceding is indicated by *wherefore* (ii., 1), and the connection may be thus given: if the knowledge which the Gentiles possess of God and of the doom pronounced by conscience upon moral depravity leaves them without excuse, it follows that everyone who, by judging his neighbour, lays claim to a knowledge of moral distinctions, *a fortiori* leaves himself without excuse when he practises the very things which he condemns.

The principles may be enunciated as follows:

1. Moral judgment is virtually an acknowledgment of moral obligation (ii., **1**).

2. All men, Jew as well as Greek, are subject to the Divine judgment (ii., **2, 6–16**).

3. This judgment is according to truth, answering to the reality of things, and not guided by any conventional standard (ii., **2**). We may observe in passing that this principle is as luminous in statement as it is obviously just in fact, and any interpretation of Paul's teachings which contravenes it must be wrong.

4. The Divine judgment is conducted without respect of persons: all will be judged impartially by the same standard (ii., **11 sqq.**).

5. Its sentence is given in accordance with every man's work, according to the whole scope and tenor of the life, including the most secret acts (ii., **6–10, 13–16**). It has been supposed that this is inconsistent with Paul's polemic against justification by works of the law, and that therefore he is here speaking as a Jew to Jews. But in order to see that the principle is, in his view, of universal application we may compare 1 Cor. iii., 13–15, 2 Cor. v., 10, Gal. vi., 7, 8, and, if we accept these Epistles as Paul's, Eph. vi., 8, Col. iii., 25. We see from these passages that it was no part of Paul's Gospel to offer men a substitute for the duty of living well. The difficulty is solved by Christ's principle, "The tree is known by its fruit" (Mt. xii., 33). A few good works, and many ritual works, may be done while the heart is bad; but bad works cannot proceed from a good heart, and "patience in well-doing," giving its rich quality

to the whole outward manifestation of life, cannot proceed from an evil spirit.

The goodness of God leadeth thee to repentance (ii., 4).—The danger of abusing the patience of God is here pointed out. We may think that He is indifferent to the sin of ourselves or of others; but His goodness is intended to lead us to repentance, and, if we obstinately resist it, we only accumulate greater condemnation when the time for forbearance is over.

Gentiles which have no law (ii., 14).—Though the Greek word for law has no article, Paul probably refers here to the Mosaic Law. All civilised Gentiles, and not least the Romans, had laws, so that the Apostle must refer to a written law which furnished the Divine standard of human life. Most Gentiles did not govern their daily conduct by reference to such a law, but, if they were virtuous men, trusted to the natural conscience as their guide. It is clearly implied that the natural conscience might lead them right.

One with another (ii., 15).—The reference is uncertain. Either the "thoughts" are personified, and represented as holding mutual debate, or the allusion is to the judgments which different men pass on one another.

The Jews not justified by the Law (ii., 17–iii., 20).

They had not kept the commandments which they imposed upon others; and the true and only valuable distinction of a Jew was in the spirit, not in the form, which is worthless unless it represent an inward reality (ii., 17–29).

Dost thou rob temples? (ii., 22).—Reference is made by commentators to Deut. vii., 25,—"The graven images of their gods shall ye burn with fire: thou shalt not covet the silver or the gold that is on them, nor take it unto thee, lest thou be snared therein: for it is an abomination to the Lord thy God";—to Josephus, *Ant.*, IV., viii., 10, who refers to a command not to rob foreign temples; and to Acts xix., 37, where the town clerk says that Paul and his friends were not "robbers of temples."

Even as it is written (ii., 24).—The reference is to Isaiah lii., 5, where, however, the blasphemy is on the part of oppressors, who scoff at the afflictions of the people. Paul, adopting the words as suitable to his purpose, gives them a totally different application from that intended by the Prophet.

Judge thee (ii., 27).—Observe the use of the word "judge," referring not to the exercise of judicial functions, but to the standard of judgment. So when Paul says that God will judge men through Jesus Christ (*v.* 16), though he probably expected Christ formally to exercise the office of judge, we must include the idea that in him resided the principles of judgment by which men's lives would be tested.

He is not a Jew which is one outwardly (ii., 28).—Observe the spiritual sense which is here attached to the word "Jew," as elsewhere to "Israel" (Gal. vi., 16).[1]

In the spirit, not in the letter (ii., 29).—Circumcision was supposed to have a symbolical or spiritual meaning. Philosophical Jews defended the practice by dwelling on its spiritual significance, but at the same time thought it necessary to observe the letter of the commandment. Paul, on the other hand, contended, not only that the literal observance was worthless if it failed of its spiritual end, but also that, if the latter were secured, the need of the symbol dropped away.

We must pause here for a moment to reflect on this impeachment of Judaism. It seems extraordinarily feeble in comparison with the scathing exposure of heathenism. Thefts and adultery are the only moral faults which are directly attacked; and we cannot suppose that they were so common as to give an obvious taint to the whole of the popular life. On Paul's own showing, therefore, the moral life of the Jews, if it fell far short of the Divine require-

---

[1] Compare *Apost. Const.*, v., 18; Christ was crucified ὑπὸ τῶν ψευδωνύμων Ἰουδαίων.

ments, nevertheless was incomparably superior to that of the heathen world; and to this extent the Law had not failed. We must also remember with sorrow that if Christianity were subjected to this line of argument, it would be utterly condemned; for we may find in so-called Christian countries all the moral faults which are here ascribed to Gentiles. We may ask, then, have the promises of Christianity failed? We answer, no; but their fulfilment is immeasurably slower than Paul anticipated. He felt that for him the Law was dead, and that a higher principle of life had found him, which he thought was speedily to conquer the world. It is the mistake of all noble enthusiasms; and it will be well if we who have learned from history the slow operation of Divine causes can retain our enthusiasm, and an unshaken faith in the power of that Christian ideal which is still working as a hidden leaven in the heart of society.

Consideration of difficulties arising out of the foregoing contention that Jews as well as Gentiles would be judged according to truth, on precisely the same principles (iii., 1-8).

This is a very obscure passage, and its meaning cannot be determined with certainty. It evidently consists of objections and replies, and our first question is, Who makes the objections? I think they may be difficulties which the Apostle himself felt, and which may have existed in the minds of other Jewish Christians, and even of Gentile Christians who were imbued with the teaching of the Old Testament. This view is favoured by the following considerations: (1) The argument, though relating to unbelieving Jews, is not addressed to them, but to Christians who needed to be confirmed. Paul is most likely to meet their difficulties and his own. (2) The objections as coming from an unbelieving Jew are very obscure, and the answers unsatisfactory. (3) Paul felt a deep interest in his people; and their being apparently cast off, while the tide of religious life and thought swept past them, may well have perplexed him, when taken in connection with ancient promises, which were certainly true, but might have been misinterpreted. (4) The difficulties arise naturally out of the great truth at which Paul had arrived, of God's impartial judgment, and of the dependence of responsibility on privilege. (5) In his more elaborate argument, ix.–xi., he seems to attribute the calling of the Gentiles to the unbelief of the Jews; and historically it was so to a great extent, so that, in the words of the present passage, the unrighteousness of the Jews commended the righteousness of God.

We may now present the substance of the difficulties and their solution in the following way: (1) The real distinction of the Jew consisted in his means of instruction, not in exemption from the general standard of judgment (iii., 1, 2). (2) Could the want of faith, not of the whole people, but of some, make void the faith of God, and cancel the distinctions which He accorded to the Jews? Surely not: sooner than admit the least stain on the truthfulness of God we must suppose that every man has been false, through self-will and presumption maintaining the falsehood of God's favouritism, so that the ways of God are justified in placing all on one level, agreeably to the words of Psalm li., 4 (as they stand in the Greek translation) (iii., 3, 4). (3) But if true righteousness, shown in the justice and impartiality of God, is proved by the Jews' unrighteousness, if this dream of favouritism is dissipated by the sad spectacle of Jewish sinfulness, ought not this fact at least to exempt them from condemnation and punishment? That cannot be admitted; for then there would be no fixed principle by which God could judge the world, it being the function of a judge to punish sin (iii., 5, 6). (4) To put the matter more clearly: if the truth of God's impartial justice is so gloriously established in the world precisely by means of the false assumption of the Jews, which falsehood was in part the parent of their sin, then ought they to be punished as sinners? Yes; or else the maxim would be established that we may do evil that good may come. A man is equally guilty, though God may overrule his evil for good (iii., 7, 8).

The character of the Jews is painted (in words which apply also to Greeks) in the darkest colours by their own writers (iii., 9-19).

Are we in worse case than they? (iii., 9).—This translation is approved, not only by the Revisers, but by other modern scholars. It is, however, by no means certain, and it does not appear suitable to the context; for the object is to show that the Jews are in as bad a case as the Greeks, and there has been nothing to suggest that they were in a worse case. The old and ordinary way of understanding the expression is, "Are we better than they?" The form of the Greek verb is opposed to this; and still it is some support of this more satisfactory meaning that the word was so explained by men who spoke Greek. We must be content here to leave it undecided.

The string of scriptural quotations which follows might seem inapplicable to the existing generation; but Paul's object is to show, not that Jews of any particular time were sinful, but that the fact of their being Jews did not exempt them from liability to sin and punishment, and descriptions of their past condition by contemporary writers would fairly answer this purpose.

The law (iii., 19), here used of the Old Testament as a whole, the Prophets and Hagiographa being regarded as an extension of, or commentary on, the Law.

Every mouth, . . . all the world (iii., 19).—The citations from Scripture applied to the Jews; and therefore as the sinfulness of the Gentiles was conceded, it followed that all the world was placed upon the same level before the Divine judgment. Observe the generalisation that man as man is sinful. Thus the Law is made to obliterate the very distinctions which it was commonly used to foster.

We should notice the phrase *To them that are under the law* (iii., 19)—The Greek is "in the law," so that it exactly corresponds with the expression "in Christ," and points out the principle in which men lived.

Enunciation of the principle on which the foregoing depends, and of the function of law (iii., 20).

The principle is that by works of law shall no flesh be justified in the sight of God. "Law" has no article in the Greek; and if the Law of Moses be intended, still it is regarded simply in its character of law, and the statements made are applicable to all law as such. The principle is affirmed like an accepted Christian maxim, which involves the previous contention, that Jew and Gentile are on the same level in the Divine judgment. The inability of law to justify is due to the fact that its function is not to reveal the absolute nature of righteousness or to communicate moral power, but through its Divine prohibition of evil-doing to give a clear knowledge of sin. Mere law can never awaken the higher affections and aspirations, but by standing in our way it makes us conscious of something in us which runs counter to its requirements, which requirements we are nevertheless constrained to approve.

Manifestation of the righteousness of God; its manner and result (iii., 21-26).

This passage introduces the new Christian principle, on which Paul bases his opposition to Jewish legalism. It is one of extreme difficulty, not only on account of the brevity of expression and the ambiguity of some of the leading terms, but because it is encrusted with the ideas of a later age, and with the associations of doctrinal controversy, so that the mind involuntarily reads into it notions which it does not contain. It would be impossible in our space to attempt an adequate discussion of various views; and I must be content to sketch out certain lines of suggestion, which appear to me to indicate with the greatest probability the real meaning of the Apostle. We must attend first to the principal terms.

A righteousness of God (iii., 21).—The indefinite article here seems to imply that God had different kinds of righteousness; but as there is nothing in the Greek to suggest this, it would be better to translate either "*the* righteousness of God," or simply "God's righteousness." In interpreting this phrase the following points should be observed:— (1) It must have the same meaning throughout. (2) It stands in opposition to "sin" in the previous verse; and as sin so far has had a purely ethical meaning, it is probable that "righteousness" also is used in a strictly ethical sense. (3) It resumes the statement of i., 17, and therefore must have the same meaning,—real righteousness, as it is in God, in contrast with legal, or merely external righteousness. (4) For these reasons it cannot mean punitive justice. This is made certain by verse 22, where it is explained that this righteousness is "unto them that believe," and by the fact that Paul has a distinct word, "wrath" (see i., 18), to denote punitive justice and its effects. (5) It must satisfy several characteristics which are distinctly laid down:—(a) It must be something that had been manifested at a particular time, and was being continuously revealed (iii., 21; i., 17). (b) The manifestation must be "apart from law"; not depending on a written code or communicated by legal teaching. (c) Yet this righteousness was borne witness to by the Law and the Prophets, which testified to an inward law of righteousness, written in the heart, though they did not perfectly reveal it. (d) It was shown by the death of Christ. (e) It was apprehended through faith. (f) It was needed by all, inasmuch as all had sinned, and fell short of the glory of God. All these conditions are satisfied when we take the words in their natural sense of real and eternal righteousness. The inner essence of this righteousness is love. It was His love that God commended towards us in the death of Christ (v., 8); and the Christian's life consists in the love of God shed abroad in his heart through the Holy Spirit (v., 5). Paul uses the word righteousness here instead of love, because the question in dispute was, What is the nature of real righteousness, and when is a man accounted righteous in the sight of God?

Faith in Jesus Christ (iii., 22).—The Greek has simply the genitive and might be translated "Jesus Christ's faith." The other translation, however, does no violence to Paul's thought (for see Gal. ii., 16), and is admissible by the usage of classical Greek. There is, however, only one certain instance of this construction in the New Testament, Mk. xi., 22, "have faith in God." There are a few examples of the use of the genitive of a *thing* which is the object of faith; but these do not fix its usage with the genitive of a *person*. Now in the Pauline writings "faith" is used with the genitive of a person other than Christ at least twenty-two times,[1] and always in the sense of the faith belonging to the person, even in the one case where we find "the faith of God" (Rom. iii., 3); so that if we are guided by Pauline usage, we must interpret the genitive similarly in the eight cases where the phrase is used of Christ. This result is confirmed by the following considerations. Paul might have removed all ambiguity by the use of certain prepositions, which are actually used in later Epistles. An expression of similar import is found in later Epistles, which, even if they are not Paul's, may be quoted as belonging to the Pauline school,—"Faith which is in Christ," that is, the faith (sometimes combined with love) which exists in him, and must be appreciated by the disciple. And lastly, the words rendered "faith in Jesus" in iii., 26, are identical with the words in iv., 16, except that in the latter verse we have "Abraham" instead of "Jesus." For these reasons I am obliged to depart from the prevailing view. A deeply interesting result follows: Paul attached a vital importance, not only to faith in Christ, but to Christ's faith, and could not regard the former as complete without the appropriation of the latter.

✓ This leads us to the consideration of another significant fact. In this great Epistle about Justification by Faith the word "faith" occurs 38 times, and of these it is used absolutely (*i. e.*, without any defined object) 36 times, or, if the foregoing remarks have been correct, always.[2] Surely the natural inference from this is that Paul did not mean by faith belief in some definite object or event or doctrine, but rather a vital principle which was related to the whole realm of spiritual thought. The same result follows from the use of the verb "to believe, or have faith, in"; for not only is this also used absolutely several times, but it is followed by a variety of objects, agreeably to the question under discussion. In its Christian sense it has for its object sometimes God (Rom. iv., 5, 24), sometimes Christ (Gal. ii., 16, the only doctrinal passage where the expression occurs; Philip. i., 29; 1 Tim. i., 16), sometimes a fact ("we believe that we shall live with

---

[1] Of which 5 are in Rom., 5 in Corinth., and 5 in 1st Thess.

[2] 141 times in all the Pauline Epistles; 122 times absolutely.

him," Rom. vi., 8; "believe that God raised him from the dead," Rom. x., 9; "so ye believed" [the facts connected with the resurrection], 1 Cor. xv., 11; "we believe that Jesus died and rose again," 1 Thess. iv., 14). We must therefore understand faith in a large sense, as denoting spiritual apprehension and religious trust. No doubt the Christian believed enthusiastically in Christ; but this belief was itself the source and inspiration of that larger faith which dwelt in Christ himself, and which permeated the whole character of the spiritual man. It is thus that men of faith and men of law form an antithesis; not that they believe in different things, but that the whole quality of their inward life is determined by different principles. Thus, too, the righteousness of law and the righteousness of faith form a contrast, the one being obedience to an outward rule, the other an inward surrender to the leading of the Spirit of God. If we overlook these distinctions, we lose the spiritual coherence of Paul's thought, and are unable to follow him as he traces the permanent laws of the religious life.

Being justified freely by his grace (iii., 24).—This perfectly explicit statement sets aside not only the notion that men are justified through the merit of their works, but every doctrine which represents justification as purchased by the full payment of a substitute. Every denial of the perfect freedom of Divine grace and forgiveness is fundamentally anti-Pauline, and inadmissible in the interpretation of the present passage. It does not follow, however, that there is no condition; for man may resist the grace of God. The condition which Paul lays down is faith, trustful surrender to the love of God, that He may pour into us His own life.

Through the redemption that is in Christ Jesus (iii., 24).—These words indicate the historical medium through which the free justification came. "Redemption" is a figurative term, and properly denotes the purchasing of anyone out of slavery by the payment of a ransom. Accordingly, though the term might be applied metaphorically to sacrifice, it belongs in itself to a wholly different region of thought. The simple verb[1] from which this word is formed is used repeatedly in the LXX., several times in a figurative sense. We may refer to a few illustrative passages. It describes the delivery of the Israelites from slavery in Egypt (see for instance Ex. vi., 6; Deut. vii., 8, xiii., 5). David speaks of God as having redeemed him out of all affliction (2 Kings [Sam.] iv., 9). Isaiah represents God as saying, "I

[1] λυτρόω.

redeemed thee, I called thee by thy name, thou art Mine" (xliii., 1); and again, "I wiped out . . . thy sins; turn to Me, and I will redeem thee" (xliv., 22). The Psalmist also says, "With Him is plenteous redemption, and He will redeem Israel out of all his iniquities" (Ps. cxxix., 7, 8). These passages not only illustrate parallel expressions in the New Testament, but remind us of a rule which is often forgotten, that we must not press figures of speech beyond the immediate purpose for which they are introduced. The slavery in Egypt was real; but no ransom, even of the most figurative kind, was paid to the Egyptians. In other cases the slavery is metaphorical, and the figure denotes nothing more than release from any kind of oppression.[1] In the present passage the figure is somewhat more complete than in the Old Testament passages. What was the slavery which is implied in redemption? Paul answers that men were the "slaves of sin" (Rom. vi., 16, 17). Is any ransom implied? This is not stated with equal clearness; but we may fairly accept as the answer Christ's own declaration that he gave his life as a ransom (Mt. xx., 28); for this almost inevitably suggests itself, and is sufficiently implied by the reference, which immediately follows, to his blood. Christ's death was the price which was paid for the accomplishment of the Divine purposes of love, just as, if Moses had fallen a victim to the rage of Pharaoh, his life would have been the price paid for the redemption of the Israelites. How easily such a figure was used when slavery was a marked feature of society we may illustrate from an early Christian work, *The Teaching of the Twelve Apostles*. The writer, in urging the duty of giving, says, "If thou hast, thou shalt give through thy hands a ransom of thy sins."[2] A later writer says that deacons must act like Christ, who gave his life as a ransom, and must not hesitate, if need be, to lay down life instead of a brother.[3] If we pass on to the further question, and ask to whom the price was paid, we are pushing the use of figurative language beyond its legitimate limits. Paul gives no answer, and it is not necessary that there should be any answer. Origen, however, answers that Christ delivered himself up to the enemies of the human

---

[1] For instance, αὐτῶν λύτρωσιν [simply "deliverance"] ἀπὸ τῆς Αἰγυπτίας (*Test. of the Twelve Patriarchs*, Joseph., § 8).

[2] iv., 6. Λύτρωσις is the word used.

[3] *Apostolical Constitutions*, iii., 19. Cyril of Jerusalem says, λύτρωσίς ἐστι τὸ βάπτισμα Ἰωάννου πυρὸς ἀπειλῆς (*Cat.*, iii., 7). Philo says, πᾶς σοφὸς λύτρον ἐστὶ τοῦ φαύλου (*De ss. Ab. et Caini*, § 37).

race who were thirsting for his blood,[1] or, more definitely, "to the prince of this world."[2] This is the only reasonable answer; for a ransom must be paid to the enemy who detains the captive. I think, however, that in Paul's mind the figure had exhausted itself before reaching this stage.

Whom God set forth (iii., 25).—The word translated "set forth" elsewhere means "purposed" (Rom. i., 13; Eph. i., 9). In classical use, however, it signifies not only "to purpose," but "to set forth publicly"[3]; and this seems to be the most suitable meaning here.

This statement is of great importance in connection with the interpretation of the passage. In the first place, God is represented as the agent in whatever transaction is referred to. If any sacrifice was offered, it was He that offered it; if any propitiation was made, it was He that propitiated. In the second place, the word translated "set forth" is not a sacrificial word; and accordingly, though it does not forbid a reference to sacrifice, it does not lead us to anticipate such a reference.

A propitiation (iii., 25).—So our revisers render a word,[4] the meaning of which is extremely doubtful.

The word may be a neuter adjective, with the word "sacrifice" understood. Three instances in which it has this meaning of a propitiatory sacrifice are cited from late Greek writers; but the use is so rare that we cannot be sure that this sense would suggest itself to the readers apart from a context which necessarily implied it.[5] An objection to this interpretation arises from the fact that only in one other passage in all the Pauline Epistles is Christ described as a sacri-

---

[1] *Com. in Ep. ad Rom.*, iii., 7, p. 203 *sq.* Lom.

[2] *Ib.*, iv., 11, p. 308. See also Irenæus, v., 1. Cyril of Jerusalem puts it rather coarsely: "The devil would not have dared to approach, if he had known him. . . . Therefore the body became a bait for death, that the dragon, having hoped to swallow it, might vomit out those also who had been already swallowed" (*Cat.*, xii., 15).

[3] It has this sense also in the LXX., where it is not of frequent occurrence. Lysias uses it of exposing a corpse (*Contra Eratosth.*, § 4).

[4] Ἱλαστήριον.

[5] It may have this sense in Fourth Maccabees, in a sentence which is otherwise instructive,—διὰ τοῦ αἵματος τῶν εὐσεβῶν ἐκείνων καὶ τοῦ ἱλαστηρίου τοῦ θανάτου αὐτῶν ἡ θεία πρόνοια τὸν Ἰσραὴλ προκακωθέντα διέσωσε (§ 17). I cannot, however, help suspecting the article before θανάτου.

fice,—" Christ . . . gave himself up for an offering and sacrifice to God for an odour of a sweet smell " (Eph. v., 2),—and this although the figure of sacrifice is used five times in relation to others (Rom. xii., 1, xv., 16; Philip. ii., 17, iv., 18; 2 Tim. iv., 6). The mention of the sweet smell clearly proves the figurative nature of the term when used of Christ; and this indeed is sufficiently evident from the fact that sacrifices were not crucified. There is also the comparison of Christ to the Paschal sheep which was sacrificed or slain (1 Cor. v., 7). Such metaphors were almost inevitable when sacrifice so generally formed a part of worship; and indeed, down to our own day, the usage is so inwrought into ordinary language that we almost forget that it is figurative. Now, let us suppose that the sacrificial figure is used here. Then it is God that offers the propitiatory sacrifice; and as men do not offer sacrifice in order to propitiate themselves, the intention must be that God, in His infinite and saving love, reversed the expected relation, and sought to win men from their enmity by this gracious offering. I know that this result is too startling to be immediately accepted. Yet it is quite in harmony with Paul's thought. " God commendeth His own love towards us in that, while we were yet sinners, Christ died for us (Rom. v., 8); so, then, Christ's death was a manifestation, not of God's punitive justice, but of His love. " He that spared not His own Son " (Rom. viii., 32); the sacrifice then was on the side of God. " All the day long did I spread out My hands unto a disobedient and gainsaying people " (Rom. x., 21); it was God accordingly that offered supplications to sinful men. " God was in Christ reconciling the world unto Himself, . . . as though God were entreating by us, we beseech you . . . be ye reconciled to God " (2 Cor. v., 19, 20); so it is men that are enemies of God, and have to yield up their hostility in reverence for the great sacrifice of love. Nevertheless, if Paul intended here this fulness of meaning, I cannot but think that, in spite of the very condensed language, he would have been more explicit, and I doubt whether the true key of the interpretation is to be found in the sacrificial metaphor.

Again, the word may mean a mercy-seat, comparing Jesus to the mercy-seat which covered the Ark in the Temple. This explanation has been adopted by many commentators, but has met with less favour in recent times, on the ground that the figure is not very appropriate, and that it becomes quite confused if we regard Christ as at once the mercy-seat, the priest, and the victim, as Origen expressly does.[1] I long acquiesced in these objections, but can no longer find

[1] *Com. in Ep. ad Rom.*, iii., 8, p. 213.

them convincing. We have to ask ourselves what meaning Paul and his readers would naturally attach to the word. I think Origen[1] is right in assuming that the Apostle borrowed from the treasures of the Old Testament. The term is not established in classical speech, whereas in the LXX., which was well known to Paul, and probably to his readers, it is the regular name for the mercy-seat.[2] It has this meaning in the only other place where it occurs in the New Testament, Heb. ix., 5. It seems almost inevitable, then, that the word should immediately suggest this sense. The supposed confusion of metaphor is not made in the passage itself, where Jesus is not compared to either the priest or the victim, or, if there be a reference to the victim in the allusion to "his blood," it is not such as to force on the reader a sense of incongruity. The metaphor is satisfied when we understand that Christ stands to the Christian in the same relation as the mercy-seat to the ancient Hebrew. The Greek reader, however, would not think only of the material object, but would attach to it some notions connected with the fundamental meaning of the word in his own language. Now Philo, in his allegorising way, says that the "propitiatory" mercy-seat) was an imitation of the propitious power of God, and he defines the propitious power as that whereby the Divine artist compassionates His own work, and represents it as standing in relation to beings who will sin.[3] If similar thoughts occurred to Paul, he here describes Christ as the seat of the Divine mercy, through which God commends His love to sinful men. We should also remember that in Exodus and Numbers there is no mention of the sprinkling of blood upon the mercy-seat, but it is regarded as the place where God made Himself known to Moses, and communed with him. In this sense also the figure would be applicable to Christ.

Through faith (iii., 25).—It is not immediately apparent what it is that is accomplished through faith, and least of all in the ordinary interpretation, where the setting forth and the sacrifice are supposed to be entirely objective. Then faith can only be regarded as the organ by which the benefits are appropriated; but nothing in the passage suggests this idea of appropriation. In the interpretation which I have suggested, the meaning must be that it is only through faith that

---

[1] *Ib.*, p. 206.

[2] Several times in Ex., Lev., and Numbers. It is also found in Ezekiel xliii., 14-20, where our translators render the Hebrew word "settle," and once in Amos ix., 1, where the reading is doubtful.

[3] *De Prof.*, §§ 18, 19, i., pp. 560, 561.

Christ becomes to us an expression of the Divine mercy, and that to the heart hardened against spiritual apprehension he ceases to be so. Compare 2 Cor. ii., 15, 16, for the different effects of the Gospel on opposite characters.

By his blood (iii., 25).—This is so translated and punctuated by our revisers as to suggest that the propitiation was made by Christ's blood. The Greek is literally "*in* his blood," and the preposition need not have an instrumental force. The words connect themselves quite naturally with "set forth," and describe the fact that Christ endured a violent death, in which his blood was shed. It is mentioned here because it was the final proof through which God commended His love towards us (Rom. v., 8). It is so common to refer to a violent death under this term that it is noticeable how seldom Paul uses it. In the great Epistles it occurs in only one other place (Rom. v., 9), if we except the allusions to the Lord's Supper, which belong to a different region of thought. Elsewhere it is found only three times (Eph. i., 7, ii., 13; Col. i., 20). We may compare the common saying, "the blood of the martyrs is the seed of the Church," and Origen's statement that the sacrifice and blood of the martyrs were akin to the sacrifice of Christ, and like that sacrifice weakened the power of the enemy.[1] Similarly the author of Fourth Maccabees, speaking of those who were martyred for the law, says, "Such ought to be those who as priests administer the Law with their own blood."[2] In such expressions "blood" briefly describes the fact of a violent death, and the yielding up (the sacrifice) of that which is physically most precious for the sake of a higher spiritual good. Such deaths may have a various and wide-reaching efficacy; but the notion that, among its effects, God is appeased by blood is one for which Paul is not responsible.

To show his righteousness (iii., 25).—This resumes, in the form of a purpose, the fact of manifestation mentioned in verse 21.

Because of the passing over of the sins done aforetime, in the forbearance of God (iii., 25).—One of the sources of doubt about the reality of moral distinctions is found in the apparent moral indifference of Providence. This is referred to in ii., 4, 5, where it is suggested that the forbearance of God may be abused to harden men in their impenitence. Such men must expect a "revelation of the

---

[1] *Com. in Ev. Joan.*, tom. vi., 35, 36.

[2] § 7. See also *Apost. Const.*, v., 9, the genuine martyr δυνηγωνίσατο τῷ λόγῳ τῆς εὐσεβείας διὰ τοῦ οἰκείου αἵματος.

righteous judgment of God." But a revelation of a different kind, not of righteous judgment, but of righteousness, of which the essence is love, may be made to men of a different stamp, who, amid the decay of morals, and in the absence of clear providential government, had begun to be sceptical about the reality of goodness, and to fancy that instead of being an eternal principle it was a fleeting human convention, for which it was not worth while to make any sacrifice. As an historical fact, one result of the life and death of Christ was a clearing of the moral perceptions and a kindling of moral enthusiasm in the minds of believers; for it was seen once more that righteousness was Divine, and demanded the absolute fealty of men.

That he might himself be just, and the justifier of him that hath faith in Jesus (iii., 26).—In order to preserve the similarity of expression which is apparent in the Greek it would be better to translate " Be righteous and receive as righteous "; and the final words should be " him who is of the faith of Jesus." For the latter words see verse 22. Observe that "righteous" and "receive as righteous" (or justify) are connected by the simple copula, so that they do not separate into antithetic ideas, but combine into one idea. He who is righteous accepts, for that very reason, the man who comes to Him in faith. This was the end toward which the manifestation of Divine righteousness was directed. Through it men's faith was awakened; and sharing the faith of Jesus they came home to God, and found peace in His forgiving grace.

We are now prepared to paraphrase verses 21–26. To give the connection we must include the latter part of verse 20.

The great function of law is to create a clear knowledge of sin. In doing so, however, it bears witness to the righteousness of God (whose will it expresses), though it is not able to reveal its intrinsic nature. This righteousness has accordingly been manifested apart from law, through its presentation in living form in Christ, and comes through the faith that inspired Christ upon all without exception who have that faith. There is no difference between Jew and Gentile, for spiritually men all stand upon the same level of failure and need. As men have thus failed in the past to earn their acquittal, and are condemned before the bar whether of revealed law or of natural conscience, they are now receiving forgiveness and acquittal freely through the grace of God, the great instrument in this work of grace being the emancipation from an evil conscience and from the power of sin which men find in Christ, whom God set forth to take the place, through the agency of faith, of the ancient mercy-seat, where He made Himself known and displayed His propitious feelings towards His people,—set forth in his blood, exposing him to the agonising death of the cross, in order to exhibit the reality and nature and depth and power of His righteousness, the inmost meaning of the eternal spirit of goodness, the existence of which men had begun to doubt, because they interpreted the long-suffering of God into an evidence of moral indifference. This long-suffering, however, was exercised with the intention of exhibiting His righteousness clearly and persuasively at the present time, with this end in view, that being righteous He may receive as righteous those who have the faith of Jesus, not passing the inevitable sentence of the law upon their past deeds, but freely forgiving all who turn to Him in faith, and open their hearts to the inflowing of His love.

Rapid statement of results suggested by the previous argument. These results are more carefully worked out in the succeeding chapters, and relate to Jewish boasting, to justification by faith, with its spiritual consequences, and to the establishment of law (iii., 27-31).

The glorying (iii., 27), that is, the Jewish boasting. Dependence on an external religion, and the idea that we are more favourably regarded by God on account of our compliance with certain forms either of thought or action, always lead to boasting. The religion of the spirit, on the other hand, "the law of faith," is inseparably connected with humility.

Law (iii., 27) is clearly used here in a wide sense, and cannot possibly mean the Law of Moses. Observe that in Paul's view faith too has a law. It is a principle of order, and not of anarchy; but it is a law of inward life, not of extraneous obedience.

Therefore (iii., 28).—Another reading is "for." If we retain "therefore," we must regard the verse as a general conclusion of the whole argument. If we read "for" it explains and justifies the previous statement.

Yea, of Gentiles also (iii., 29).—We may contrast with this the saying of the Midrash, "I am the God of all who come into the world; but I am not called the God of all peoples, but the God of Israel."[1]

God is one (iii., 30).—This verse indicates the spiritual meaning of the doctrine of the unity of God: there was no truth in the supposition of national Gods; and He who is God of Jew and Gentile alike would not use different principles of government towards different peoples; if He is one, His rule of justification also is one.

The change in the use of the prepositions and of the article here, ἐκ πίστεως, διὰ τῆς πίστεως, has occasioned some difficulty. It has been suggested that the latter expression relates to the whole clause, while the former is connected immediately with περιτομήν, so that the meaning is, "who will justify through faith believing Jews, and also Gentiles."[2] Compare οἱ (ὁ) ἐκ (τοῦ) νόμου, iv., 14, 16, ὁ (οἱ) ἐκ πίστεως, iii., 26, iv., 16; Gal. iii., 7, 9. On the other hand we have ἐκ πίστεως δίκαιοι, Gal. iii., 8.

Do we make the law of none effect? ... Nay, we establish the law (iii., 31).—Some able commentators regard this verse, not as the conclusion of the preceding argument, but as the introduction to the argument in the next chapter:—Do we make void the Law of Moses? No, we establish it by producing an argument from Genesis. In order to judge of this we must remember that the word "law" has no article in the Greek, and it would properly have one here if it denoted

---

[1] Weber, *Jüd. Theol.*, p. 58.
[2] *The Epistle of Paul to the Romans Analysed*, by John Jones, Halifax, 1801.

the Law of Moses. Again, the opening words of the fourth chapter naturally form the introduction to a new argument, and if they were meant to begin the proof of the last statement, we should expect to read "*For* what shall we say?" But the most serious objection is that the statement would be not only a mere evasion, but would be directly counter to the very object which Paul had in view. I therefore think that this verse briefly describes, and summarily dismisses an objection which is treated more fully afterwards: Does this new principle of faith abolish law, and sanction antinomianism? Quite the contrary; it places the Divine principle of order on a surer basis, and brings in the righteousness which the Law has failed to secure.[1]

From the announcement of the Christian principle we now proceed to its proof, in which, however, exposition is always mingled, so that the force and bearing of the principle become more evident as we advance. The arguments are of three kinds, and fill the next two chapters. Chapter IV. is occupied with an argument from the Old Testament. From this arises an exhortation, which is at the same time an appeal to spiritual experience (v., 1-11). And lastly, in the light of this experience, a contrast is drawn between Adam and Christ, and it is contended that the universality of sin must guarantee the universality of redemption (v., 12-21).
The first argument is founded on the case of Abraham (iv., 1-25).

The argument may be briefly analysed. It was Abraham's faith that was reckoned to him for righteousness. This faith was prior to circumcision, which is therefore nothing more than a seal of the righteousness of faith. Abraham accordingly is the spiritual father of all who have faith. For the promise is not limited by law, which might make it of none effect, the office of law being the imposition of punishment. The promise, then, having been given independently of law, no transgression can make it void; but it rests on the cer-

---

[1] In the *Apost. Const.*, vi., 22 *sq.*, it is said that Christ did not abolish, but confirmed the natural law.

tainty of Divine grace, and is extended to all who have faith. Therefore as Abraham's faith in God strengthened his body which was as good as dead, so we must have faith in Him who raised Jesus from the dead, and such faith will be reckoned to us for righteousness, whereof we have an assurance in the death and resurrection of our Lord.

Our forefather according to the flesh (**iv., 1**).—The reading of this verse is uncertain; but it seems to me quite impossible that the words can be connected as they are in this translation. They would imply, in the Pauline usage, that Abraham was not our father spiritually; but that he was so is precisely the point that the Apostle is anxious to prove. If we connect " according to the flesh " with " hath found," we obtain a suitable sense: had not Abraham, then, who received the rite of circumcision, some outward and fleshly advantage? The answer is implied, that even Abraham, with all his works of obedience, could not boast towards God, the Scripture having expressly declared that it was his faith which was reckoned for righteousness.

The reward (**iv., 4**).—There may be a reference here to Gen. xv., 1, where the LXX. reads, "thy reward shall be exceedingly abundant," a promise which is immediately followed by Abraham's act of faith, and which was not fulfilled by the rendering of so much work in return for so much pay. The principle so clearly stated in this verse is not universally admitted in Jewish teaching. According to a Midrash man acted under an obligation to keep the commandments; but God was under no obligation to the creature, and bestowed His gifts, though not unconditionally, nevertheless from grace.[1] Only the law, the lights of heaven, and the rain, were given without previous human merit.[2]

Justifieth the ungodly (**iv., 5**).—Law can only pronounce a man guilty for sins which he has committed; God can ac-

---

[1] Weber, *Jüd. Theol.*, pp. 303 *sq*. [2] *Ib.*, p. 307.

quit, for He can look into the heart, and see the faith that trusts Him, and has brought the man, however imperfect he may still be, over to the side of goodness. Compare the parable of the Pharisee and the Publican, where the latter, knowing only that he is a sinner, commits himself to the mercy of God, and so is "justified" rather than the Pharisee, who could only pride himself on his outward virtue, and was unconscious of the hollowness within. The justification of the publican was not due to arbitrary imputation, for we ourselves feel the justice of this judgment. It surely is that humble trust in the Divine love is the right attitude towards God, and, as soon as the heart is open to the inflowing of the Holy Spirit, real and eternal righteousness begins to take possession of it, whereas the arrogance of the Pharisee placed him in a wrong relation to God, and, in spite of his virtuous deeds, shut up his soul against the only fountain from which true righteousness can proceed.

The quotation (iv., 7, 8) from Psalm xxxii. is admirably appropriate. The Psalm shows how alienation and misery arose from pride and self-reliant impenitence; but blessedness from confession and penitent self-surrender to God.

A seal of the righteousness (iv., 11).—This view is different from the Jewish doctrine, according to which Abraham fulfilled the commandments, and was made perfect through circumcision.[1] The circumcision of a Gentile was called "the seal of Abraham," or "the sign of the holy covenant."[2]

Calleth the things that are not as though they were (iv., 17). —This must refer primarily to the promised posterity; but there is probably an allusion to God's power of quickening the dead soul, and anticipating the perfect righteousness in us which as yet we see only through a glass darkly.

Who believe on him that raised Jesus our Lord from the

---

[1] Weber, *Jüd. Theol.*, pp. 37, 264 *sq.*   [2] *Ib.*, p. 76.

dead (**iv., 24**).—Observe that in this doctrinal exposition the faith which is to be counted for righteousness is faith in God, and it is clearly implied that it is faith in Him as the giver of life. The resurrection of Jesus is ascribed wholly to the agency of God.

Who was delivered up (**iv., 25**).—This is the word which is used of the betrayal, but it is also used by Paul to denote the action of God in giving Christ up to death (Rom. viii., 32). This delivering up was "on account of" (better than "for") our transgressions. An historical (but not less a religious) fact is thus described. It was in the struggle against sin that Christ fell, and in a sinless world the tragedy of Calvary would never have taken place. We need not thrust into the words a recondite theological idea. It would not be wrong to say that on account of the sin of slavery the United States were delivered up to a terrible civil war, in which many an innocent man was given up to die. But it was "on account of" (that is, for the sake of) our justification that Christ was raised from death. What precisely Paul meant by the resurrection has been considered elsewhere (under 1 Cor. xv.); but whatever obscurity there may be in some parts of his doctrine, he was certainly convinced that Jesus was living and glorified, and had thus become the pledge to man of a divine and immortal soulship. Faith might have perished at the foot of the cross, but the resurrection drew it heavenward, and created that reliance on the vivifying energy of God which, on the human side, was the medium of justification.

The Apostle, starting off from the word "justification" at the close of the last chapter, now introduces a hortatory argument founded on spiritual experience (v., 1-11).

Let us have peace (**v., 1**).—The fact of justification is assumed; but it does not follow that men who had been forgiven, and had entered on a new life, might not relapse into enmity against God. Hence the exhortation to "have," that is, to hold or retain the peace which at the moment existed. The tribulation which their faith involved might tempt some to murmur against God. Observe, enmity, peace, reconciliation, are always represented by Paul as on the side of man. In sinning men fight against the will of God ; and they *must* become reconciled to that will if they are to reach their true end. God can never become reconciled to their sin, else He would cease to be righteous. Yet He is not their enemy, who has to be appeased, but their Father who awaits, and in Christ entreats, their return. But this love is, of course, not inconsistent with the truth of judgment which recognises an enemy as an enemy. The love which a good father feels towards a hardened and dissolute son is different from the love which he feels towards the pure and dutiful ; but it is the son who has to be reconciled.

In hope of the glory of God (**v., 2**).—This verse introduces a thought which recurs throughout the passage, and is found elsewhere, that the new life is not one of finished excellence, but is a blending of attainment and hope : the presence of spiritual peace, a laying aside of all hostility towards God and goodness, and along with that a looking forward to a glory to be revealed.

Tribulation, hope, love (**v., 3, 5**).—In contrast with this hope is our present lot. But afflictions are the inevitable pangs of a higher birth. It is a mystery of the spiritual life that the more we suffer the more profoundly conscious we become of the meaning and power of that Holy Spirit which was given us when first our hearts were awakened to these things, and through this indwelling Spirit we feel more deeply the Divine love ; and thus our hope of glory, though it may seem to the heathen a shameful folly and fanaticism, makes us not ashamed, for we see a glory which they know not of, and have already in rich stream that which we seek, God's love within our hearts.

In due season Christ died for the ungodly (**v., 6**).—Christianity, not being a mere miraculous irruption into human affairs, but part of a great providential plan, had its proper season for appearing in the world, a season when men were still weak, and yet ready for another forward step. God's love was brought home to them, and the mystery of sorrow broken by Christ's death. It was not unknown that men should die for the good; but the love that sought out the vilest, that despaired of none, and gave up life in order to redeem the fallen and degraded, this was something new and Divine, and revealed the meaning and power of that love of God in communion with which Jesus lived.

Being now justified by his blood (literally, *in his blood*, "in" being instrumental, v., 9).—This partly resumes, in another form, the thought of verse 1: since, as a fact, we have been justified, the rest must follow. "Justified in his blood" is explained in the next verse as "reconciled to God through the death of His Son." That complete self-sacrifice of love was the means by which men's hearts were touched. If, in the parable of the Prodigal Son, the offender had not wished or had not dared to return home, and if the elder son, knowing his father's love, had gone to seek him, and, having entreated him to come back, had been murdered by the youth's dissolute friends; if, further, the prodigal had been overcome by this proof of affection, and sought once more his father's home, might he not have said that he had been reconciled by his brother's death, that his redemption from sin had been at the cost of his brother's blood, and that the love which had given up so much would give all else that was needful? Such phrases as we have here sound harsh and strange when we treat them as some theological mystery, but become intelligible as soon as we turn to the natural springs of gratitude and affection.

Much more (v., 9, 10).—The argument is *a fortiori* as in viii., 32. When so much has been given we need not fear about the rest.

The wrath of God (**v., 9**).—As this is something future it probably refers to some great display of Divine retribution which Paul expected to come upon the earth at no distant date. When that crisis came the men who had already been reconciled would surely be safe amid the terrors of judgment that were to fall upon the wicked.

Rejoice in God (**v., 11**).—This translation hides the connection with ii., 17, and iii., 27, and it is not very apparent why the translators have changed the word. The Christian as well as the Jew gloried in God; and the glorying that was excluded by faith can have been only glorying in oneself or one's fancied distinctions.

Reconciliation (**v., 11**).—See verse 1 for the meaning of the term, and verse 9 for the way in which reconciliation came through Christ.

Argument founded on the antithesis between Adam and Christ, and the effects which flowed from their acts (v., 12-21).

In order that we may do justice to Paul's thought in this passage we must consider what is the central idea which he intends to illustrate. The paragraph stands in close connection (indicated by "therefore") with the preceding, the main thought of which is the certainty of the triumph of good through God's reconciling and saving love. Exactly the same thought is repeated here under a different aspect. The doctrine of sin is not the main doctrine, but is brought in to exhibit with greater distinctness the extent and power of the spiritual life which is given to man by the mercy of God. Again, in estimating the weight of the teaching we must distinguish between what the Apostle positively lays down as his own doctrine and what he simply accepts from the theology of the time. Now the positive and original doctrine relates to the effects of Christ's life; the part about Adam is introduced by "as," indicating a view which was well known and accepted, and which in fact is substantially accordant with what is found in rabbinical and other Jewish writings.[1] Paul's use of the doctrine shows that he did not reject it; but it occupies a very different position from a doctrine which he had elaborated in his own thought, and under the influence of his own spiritual experience. Accordingly the idea that Adam's sin had any connection with that of mankind never recurs in the Apostle's writings, whereas the influence of Christ's life upon the soul of man is continually dwelt upon. A similar remark applies to Paul's inevitable acceptance of the early chapters of Genesis as a record of actual events. The height of inspiration is disclosed, not by the extent of historical and scientific knowledge, but by insight in the interpretation of man's spiritual nature.

Bearing these cautions in mind, we may indicate several principles of great importance which are here set forth:

1. It was through *man* that sin entered into the world. He first was endowed with the full responsibility of a moral nature.

2. Mankind is not composed of a multitude of isolated individuals, but is a community of members mutually interdependent, and animated by a common nature.

3. Sin and death are an inheritance into which, by virtue of our common nature, we are born. These, at least in the past, were universal facts.

---

[1] According to the prevalent conception Adam was created pure and blessed (not as Paul's earthy and psychical man), but by disobeying an express command entailed death on himself and his posterity. But as sin was a matter of the individual will, it could not be inherited, and it was therefore assumed that everyone brought death on himself through his own offences. Even great saints, however, experienced the common lot, lest the wicked should manage to escape death by hypocritical acts; but they received compensation, and their soul was taken away, not by the angel of death, but by the kiss of God. Further, some of the sinners, like Enoch and Elijah, passed from the earth without dying.[2]

[2] Weber, *Jüd. Theol.*, pp. 213 *sqq.*, 246 *sqq.*

4. We may distinguish between sin as a principle of evil which affects the race, and its results in actual transgressions committed by the individual will.

5. Sin in the former sense produces its appointed outward results even in cases where we may suppose there was no wilful violation of a known law. For instance, the indulgence of a depraved appetite, although through ignorance the indulgence may be morally innocent, will nevertheless destroy the health.

6. There is a connection between sin and death. *a.* The fact of death has an important bearing upon character, placing before the conscience of all men a solemn close to their present career. *b.* Death ceases to be death in the Apostle's sense in proportion to men's goodness. It is only the dissolution of an earthly tabernacle, and a being clothed upon with our house which is from heaven. "The sting of death is sin"; but to sleep upon the bosom of God is not to die.

7. By reason of our intercommunion the obedience or disobedience of one man is a power for good or for evil in the world, and, according to its degree, affects the whole mass.

8. The spiritual life is the inheritance of man as man even more certainly than sin and death. For the latter are a violation of the normal or ideal nature of man; the former belongs to him in the Divine idea and purpose,—but everything in its own order, the higher succeeding the lower.

9. Christ is a far truer representative of the special endowments of human nature than Adam. The one is the type of the psychical, the other of the spiritual man.

10. From the last two statements we may infer (agreeably to the general thought of the Apostle) that sin and death are the elements which are to be conquered and destroyed, while the spiritual life is to rule with ever increasing power.

11. The loving providence of God is ever working against sin and death, and will at last surely bring in the reign of righteousness and love.

Sin entered into the world (**v., 12**), *Sin reigned* (**v., 21**), *Death reigned* (**v., 14, 17**), *So might grace reign* (**v., 21**), *The law came in beside* (**v., 20**).—Observe the personifications, which prove that not everything to which personality is ascribed is forthwith to be regarded as personal in the thought of Paul. Sin here takes its place with death, grace, and law; and therefore, although it is a power which corrupts us, and is not the creation of the individual will, it does not follow that Paul looked upon it as personal, and identified it with the devil. His allusions to satanic power elsewhere may be sufficient to prove that he held the current belief; but it is remarkable that where he expressly lays down his doctrine of sin, he omits all reference to diabolical agency.

The one man, Jesus Christ (**v., 15**).—Here Paul applies the word "man" to Jesus without any qualification; and not only so, but his whole argument would become incoherent unless he regarded him as being a man in quite as strict a sense as Adam.

The many were made sinners, Shall the many be made righteous (**v., 19**).—I see no reason for understanding these words of mere imputation, apart from reality. In relation to the effect of Adam's transgression Paul says expressly "all sinned," though they did not all, like him, violate an express commandment. And so men are not to be put off with a mere illusory righteousness. Every act of disobedience lowers, every act of righteous self-sacrifice heightens the spiritual vitality of mankind; and this universal law receives its grand exemplifications in Adam and in Christ, with whom, in a special sense, the race are organically united.[1]

That the trespass might abound (**v., 20**).—Law came in for a temporary purpose. Its immediate effect was to turn into

---

[1] A Midrash puts the case thus: The world is half guilty, half pure. If one man commits transgressions, so as to give transgressions the preponderance, the world becomes through him guilty. If one fulfils a commandment, and so gives the preponderance to good actions, he

transgression the instinctive movements of sinful impulse, and so create that consciousness of sin which must precede redemption from its power. This thought is elaborated at a later stage of the argument.

Having completed the first portion of his argument, Paul now proceeds to unfold the moral and spiritual results of the Christian position (vi.-viii.).

First, he finds it necessary to set aside certain dangerous inferences (**vi., 1-vii., 25**), of which the most serious was the notion that we might continue in sin, relying upon the superabundant love of God to save us at last. His doctrine of faith, as indeed every doctrine which insists that the entire moral value of actions is dependent on the inward sources from which they spring, was liable to be misunderstood by less spiritual minds, and might even be abused by the vicious into a justification of their offences. We know from 1 Cor. how Paul had to urge upon the attention of some of the Gentile converts what seem to us quite elementary lessons of moral decency; and there may have been some ground for apprehending similar abuses in Rome. The argument is so mixed with exhortation that it is rather a warning to the readers than a reply to opponents, though of course it obviates at the same time an objection which might have been brought against the Pauline doctrine by those who viewed it only from the outside.

The question is, Shall we continue in sin? The first answer is that that is impossible, because in Christ we have died to the old life, and risen into a new one (vi., 1-14).

We who died to sin (**vi., 2**).—This contains the central thought of the passage, which is expanded in the following

makes the world thereby righteous (Weber, *Jüd. Theol.*, p. 283). The fathers of Israel, however, were able to leave to their children a share of their own reward, and by their merit to make good the deficiencies of their descendants (*ib.*, pp. 292 *sq.*).

verses. The very meaning of the Christian's faith was that he had escaped from the old propensities to sin as completely as if he had died, so that the life of faith and the life of sin were absolutely incompatible. This dying to sin reminds Paul of baptism, the solemn act by which the renunciation of the old life was sealed. We must remember that at that time baptism was administered to adult converts, and therefore it had a very practical significance. It formally committed men to their Christian profession; it was a final breaking up of the past heathen life, and an acceptance of the Christ-life. The form, then, in which it was administered, by immersion, not unnaturally suggested a comparison with the death, and burial, and resurrection of Christ, with whose spirit of self-denying righteousness and love every true believer was imbued. Therefore, as Christ left behind him this sinful world when he suffered on the cross, and through death entered on the glorified life, so the soul, rising in faith into a new empire of the Spirit, had passed forever from the domain of sin. We see very clearly from this passage how completely faith was an inward principle of life, in contrast with everything external, whether in the domain of action or of intellect; it was an incorporation of Christ's life of devoted faith, an indwelling of his Spirit, and without this a man was not a genuine member of the Christian brotherhood.

The body of sin (**vi.**, 6) means most probably the body which belongs to or serves sin, the body with its passions being the medium through which sin works. This body is "done away" or rather "rendered powerless," being, in a figure, crucified with Christ, the believer sharing the great act of renunciation.

He that hath died is justified from sin (**vi.**, 7), a legal principle, that one who is dead is *ipso facto* no longer amenable to the law; and so sin can no longer lay claim to one who has died to all his evil past.

We shall also live with him (**vi., 8**).—Having dwelt on the death to sin, he now proceeds to notice more particularly the nature of the new life, as a living to God.

The death that he died he died unto sin once (**vi., 10**).—The words in regard to Christ's dying to sin are strictly parallel with the expression used in verses 2 and 11 of believers generally. Yet the ideas which have grown up around the person of Christ oblige the commentators to assign them very different meanings in the two cases; and instead of referring them, in connection with Christ, to any spiritual conquest, they explain them simply of his passing from a world in which he came in contact with sin. But I think the contrast, dying to sin, living to God, will hardly bear this interpretation, to say nothing of the utter inapplicability of Christ's case to ourselves which is thus introduced. Yet the Apostle believed that Christ "knew no sin" (2 Cor. v., 21), and cannot have supposed that he had ever lived in subjection to sin, from which he was released only by death. But he may have believed that "the man Jesus Christ" had real spiritual struggles, that he had painfully to repress the claims of self, of the wearied body and the anxious brain, that his exalted life required a voluntary conquest of opposing forces, and a clinging in faith to God, that it was in short a continual losing of the lower life in order to find the higher; and the death on the cross, which was the final and complete abnegation of self, was also a dying once and forever to sin, and entering upon that life where sin has no more power. We die to sin whenever we decide against a wrong course which lies temptingly open to us; and in this sense we may, with the Apostle, "die daily." Understanding the words thus we attach, if not the same, at least an analogous meaning to them in both their references, and find the light of Christ's experience shed into our own souls. We may with Christ die to sin, but we can do so only through Christ's faith.

In Christ Jesus (**vi., 11**).—Paul's expressive phrase for being a Christian. Farther on, he says "Christ is in you" (viii., 10). The two expressions denote an intimate union and identity of life, and this life is forever irreconcilable with sin.

Paul now introduces an **exhortation** (**vi., 12, 13**), showing, as often elsewhere, that while he insists on the Divine conditions he never forgets the human condition of fidelity. The inward life may be changed; but it still requires all our vigilance to be faithful to the new principle. The reasoning may be thus exhibited: faith can be no encouragement to sin, for its essential spirit is a dying to sin and living to God; see, then, that you carry this out in action, and remember that you *can* do so, that sin is no longer your master, because you are not under law, but under grace. The meaning of this last statement is found in the following chapters.

The mention of grace suggests a repetition of the question *Shall we sin?* (**vi., 15**); but the point of view is changed, and a more subtle danger is exposed. It is no longer suggested that we may indulge in sin, trusting in God's love to overlook it, but that if the dominion of sin is broken, and we are no longer judged by the formal rules of the law, we may allow ourselves to remain in sin, and yet retain our mastery over it. The answer is that you cannot voluntarily place yourself in subjection to any power, and then leave its service whenever you please; if you make yourselves slaves, slaves you are, and must take the consequences; and this is true both of the sin which ends in death and of the obedience which ends in righteousness.

I speak after the manner of men because of the infirmity of your flesh (**vi., 19**).—This is an apology for using such an expression as "Ye became servants [or rather, slaves] of righteousness." The words seem to imply a doubt whether the readers were sufficiently advanced spiritually to see that in following righteousness there was no slavery. Seen from the opposite sides each life is a life of slavery; but he who has found his life in God, and relinquished the claims of self, is not a slave, but a son (see Gal. iv., 7).

The wages of sin (**vi., 23**), that is, the wages paid by sin to its servant, sin being personified.

In Christ Jesus (**vi., 23**).—This has not exactly the same meaning as "through Christ Jesus," the latter more clearly implying agency on the part of Christ. We may perhaps best understand the words by asking, What did God give to the world in Christ? The answer is "eternal life," the life which was with the Father and was manifested to us. Paul felt with clearer consciousness than is always felt now that it was in Christ that he had received this gift.

Paul, reverting to the thought of vi., 14, advances a third argument to show that the Christian state cannot be one of sin: you died to the law in order that you might be united to Christ, and bring forth fruit unto God (vii., 1–6).

In entering on the life of the spirit we leave behind us that lower and carnal life, where sin has its seat, and which the law at once prohibits and excites. The latter thought is worked out in the second portion of the chapter.

The law (**vii., 1**).—As there is no article in the Greek, the Law of Moses need not be specially referred to: the principle belongs to law as such. But we can hardly doubt that Gentile as well as Jewish Christians were acquainted with the Old Testament, which at that time was the only Christian Bible, and which has always continued to be part of the Christian canon.

The illustration drawn from marriage is rather confused; for the principle was that law has authority over a man only as long as he lives; the example shows that law has authority over a person only so long as someone else lives. In the fourth verse the original principle is resumed, but blended with the idea of marriage drawn from the illustration, so that the law seems to take the place of the dead husband. The general thought, however, is sufficiently clear: death dissolves legal obligations; but you are dead to the law, and therefore your obligations towards it are at an end.

Through [or *by means of*] *the body of Christ* (**vii., 4**).—This expression, if we are to judge from the previous reasoning, must refer to Christ's death, in which the disciple spiritually shares. The body may have been selected as the mortal part, or, as Jowett suggests, "to express the necessary idea of a communion of many members in one body." It was only through connection with the community of believers, who formed figuratively the body of Christ, that a man could have the fulness of Christian experience.

When we were in the flesh (**vii., 5**), when our lower and animal nature was the principle of our life, contrasted with being "in the spirit."

Which were through the law (**vii., 5**).—These words anticipate the next section, and are explained in verses 9-11.

In newness of the spirit, and not in oldness of the letter (**vii., 6**).—The letter and the spirit are contrasted, as in 2 Cor. iii., 6, "The letter killeth, but the spirit giveth life," where Paul refers to the deadening effect upon the higher powers of servile adhesion to an authoritative document; here he traces the consequences of this deadening down into the moral life. When he wrote these words there was no New Testament, and he was not substituting a new "letter" for the old, but committing men to their own faith, to be taught by the Spirit of God in their hearts. In the light of a profound spiritual experience he cleared himself at once from that bibliolatry, that bondage to the letter, from which in our age men are reluctantly dragging themselves by the slow efforts of a laborious criticism.

Paul next proceeds to unfold the nature and action of Law (vii., 7-25).

The foregoing discussion might easily give rise to an erroneous view of the Law, and lead men to identify it with the principle of evil; for Paul seemed to be treating subjection to sin and subjection to the Law as synonymous. This was far from his intention. The two conditions were not identical, but simultaneous; and they must always remain so; for the moment a man ceases to be spiritual, and falls under sin, he is confronted by the Law which is Divine and spiritual. It is impossible to escape from it by sinking below it; deliverance comes only when we are drawn up into the sphere of the Spirit, from whose intrinsic life the moral law has emanated. The honest man is independent of the commandment, "Thou shalt not steal"; but the moment he becomes dishonest it resumes its sway, and so by falling under sin he falls under the Law. Paul, however, is more concerned at present with the thesis that the austere purity of the Law, coming with the check of a merely external command, aggravated the sin which it was meant to curb, so that escape from the Law into the life of Spirit was at the same time an escape from the dominion of sin.

Howbeit (vii., 7).—The Greek means "but," and expresses the opposition between Paul's view and the view implied in the question,—this is not my view, but——.

I had not known sin except through the law (vii., 7).—The emphatic "I" in verse 9 (for in the Greek it is emphatic) proves, I think, that Paul is speaking in his own person throughout this passage; but it is also clear from the whole drift of the argument that his object is not to convey information about himself, but to use his own experience for the establishment of general principles, so that the intense glow of his inward strife sheds a revealing light into the dim interior of ordinary men.

The first point is that Law brings the knowledge of sin. This has been already announced in iii., 20; and we have also been told that sin was in the world even when there was no law, and when, therefore, it could not be imputed (v., 13).

We now see the meaning of these statements. Covetousness, considered in itself, has the nature of sin; nevertheless before the conscience wakens we innocently covet whatever naturally excites our desire, and it is only when the Law comes that we recognise our selfish desires as covetousness, and know that they ought to be repressed. In its absolute sense this condition belongs only to infancy; but many men can distinctly remember the time when the light of Divine Law first awoke the sense of sin, and made them conscious of the wild and disordered state within them. According to Jewish teaching, a child, innocent up to the tenth year, contracts from that time " the evil impulse." [1]

Sin, finding occasion (vii., 8).—The awakening, just mentioned, is always a critical period, and gives sin its opportunity. It is a time when hitherto innocent pursuits may contract the taint of guilt, and yet be too deeply rooted in the habits to be abandoned in obedience to a law which inflames their rebellious selfishness. "Apart from law sin is dead." There is no depraving sin in the cruelty of the tiger; but a man who, knowing the Law, yields to the temper of a tiger becomes corrupt and an enemy of God.

I was alive apart from the law once (vii., 9).—Paul now enters more distinctly into a statement of personal experience. The meaning of this and the following verse has been explained in the remarks already made.

Beguiled [or *deceived*] *me* (vii., 11).—Sin may deceive one in many ways. It may suggest that the Law is too ethereal to be observed by frail mortals, or that it is more manly to take one's own course, or that at all events it will be time enough to obey when the keen blood of youth is sobering into age. Paul may possibly have thought of the fury of his mistaken zeal; for to reach powerful minds sin must clothe itself in a garb of virtue.

The law is holy (vii., 12).—This states the conclusion

[1] Weber, *Jüd. Theol.*, p. 213.

from the preceding exposition, and is the complete answer to the question, "Is the law sin?"

Did then that which is good become death unto me? (**vii., 13**).—The difficulty recurs in another form. Grant that the Law is not sin, yet it seems equivalent to death. The answer is that it is sin alone which is the source of death, and it was allowed to work through the holy Law in order that its heinous character might become perfectly clear.

I am carnal, sold under sin (**vii., 14**).—Sin finds its seat, not in the Law, which expresses the order of the spiritual realm, but in the carnal or animal nature of man, which is not legislative, but the subject of legislation.[1] The question is raised whether Paul refers to the time before or after his conversion. "Sold under sin" seems quite inapplicable to one who was "redeemed." The inward strife is inconsistent with the "peace" which belongs to a believer. And further, a great revulsion of feeling takes place between chapters vii. and viii. But how, then, are we to explain the present tense, which continues to be used throughout the passage? The parallelism with "the law is" almost necessitates "I am," as Paul is now stating a general principle without reference to particular times. The present, being once introduced, is naturally continued, and is particularly appropriate since the strength of feeling may have made the old conflict live again like a present fact. We must remember, too, that the description is not intended to be merely personal and historical, but to be typical of a wide experience.

I consent unto the law that it is good (**vii., 16**).—The fact that the will accepts the commands of the Law is a proof that we admit its excellence.

---

[1] The more approved reading, σάρκινος, instead of σαρκικός, does not properly denote "carnal" in the moral sense, but "composed of flesh." If this distinction is strictly observed, the meaning must be, "I am composed of flesh, and therefore under the dominion of sin," which works through the lower, material nature.

It is no more I that do it, but sin which dwelleth in me (**vii., 17**).—Doing wrong through the violence of desire, in opposition to the bent of the will, seems due to the prompting of a foreign power within us. Independently of deliberate transgression there is an obliquity of nature, a vehemence of the lower and a weakness of the higher elements, which constitute the incentives to transgression; and which Paul calls by the name of sin.

In me, that is, in my flesh (**vii., 18**).—Instead of representing human nature as corrupt in every part, Paul recognises here and in verse 22 a higher and a lower nature. The latter is not the seat of good, but acts as a check upon the aspirations of the former. Hence we find a law, or rule, that when we wish to do good evil is present (**vii., 21**). Moral choice presupposes a lower in conflict with the higher, and the lower is apt to gain the victory when there is nothing but strength of will to oppose it. The misery of the inward struggle reaches its height when the mind is full of admiration for righteousness (**vii., 22**), but passions wild and strong, which sometimes beset the noblest minds, drag us captive to the law of sin (**vii., 23**). The anguish of this division in our nature, and the feeling of helplessness and self-contempt which it brings, extort the cry for a deliverer (**vii., 24**); and the emotion which produced this highwrought description subsides, as it were, with a sigh of thanksgiving, for the deliverer has come (**vii., 25**).

The body of this death (**vii., 24**), that is, probably, the body which is subject to this death, the spiritual deadness just described, to which physical death owes its terrors. The Greek may also be translated, "this body of death," *i. e.*, which is subject to death. Compare viii., 11.

I thank God (**vii., 25**).—God, then, is the source of deliverance, to whom our gratitude is due. It is noticeable that in the preceding passage the religious element does not appear. There is no mention of faith, love, the communion of sons, Divine strength made perfect amid conscious weakness. The impersonal Law has no sympathy, abates no claim, and imparts no strength. But He who gave the Law may be a strong Deliverer, and through Christ we will give thanks to Him, for His love has entered our hearts, and a heavenly peace reigns within.

I myself with the mind serve the law of God, but with the flesh the law of sin (vii., 25).—These words calmly sum up the previous description. The present tense is retained as it has been used throughout. The expression "I myself" is not easily understood; but we may perhaps explain it from Paul's state of mind in dictating the passage. He was presenting a picture of the highest results of the legal position, even in one who had lived in all good conscience. May he not have remembered the proud self-righteousness of the young Pharisee, who breathed out threatenings and slaughter against the disciples of Jesus, and was rapidly rising to a position of eminence through his zeal for the Law? Is it not possible that the thought of this, seen now in the light of more recent self-knowledge, may have made him utter the words "I myself"? I myself, so vain of my training in the Law, I, so noted for severity of conduct, I, a Hebrew of the Hebrews, brought up in the strictest sect, am after all miserable, torn by inward strife; and in spite of the adhesion of my mind to the Law of God, the flesh drags me into subjection to the law of sin.

Paul now proceeds to unfold the positive spiritual results of the new principle of faith (viii.).

The rich and numerous suggestions of this chapter hardly admit of very precise divisions. It is an outpouring of high and glowing thoughts, celebrating the power, the glory, and the triumph of the Gospel. In the earlier part the present spiritual facts are most dwelt upon, and afterwards the eye is more directed towards the future, the sympathetic interaction of the lower and the higher creations, and the purpose of Divine love ruling over all. The chapter, which concludes the first part of the Epistle, closes with the assurance of faith that God's purpose must prevail, and that nothing can "separate us from the love of God which is in Christ Jesus our Lord."

There is therefore now no condemnation (viii., 1).—From all that had been said this primary fact in the Christian's faith followed—there was no condemnation. The disciple had left behind him his guilty past, and with a subduing sense of Divine forgiveness and love made a new start, no longer struggling hopelessly towards the perfection of an outward standard, but living out of the resources of the implanted spirit of holiness within.

The law of the spirit of life in Christ Jesus (viii., 2).—Thus, and not by the usual word "faith," is the new principle described; but if we have been right so far, the two expressions are practically synonymous. The change is probably made because Paul is still guarding his doctrine against Antinomianism. The new life has a law of its own, and, though it may be long in working out its perfect results, it at once lifts a man above that lower law in the animal nature (described in vii., 23) which has hitherto kept his will in captivity.

What the law could not do (viii., 3).—The construction is imperfect, but the meaning is clear,—what the law could not do was accomplished in another way.

It was weak through the flesh (viii., 3).—Being simply an outward rule, enforced by outward sanctions, it did not attempt to produce any radical change of character, but left the fleshly passions in their full force. This is the radical defect of all systems which seek to control human conduct solely by the principle of self-interest.

God sending his own Son (viii., 3).—As Paul is our earliest witness, we must interpret these and similar words through himself, and not through the doctrine and phraseology of a much later time. In the Epistles ascribed to Paul Jesus is spoken of as the Son of God seventeen times, of which eleven are in Romans and Galatians.[1] Eight times the term "son" is applied to others.[2] Five times the expression "children of God" is applied to others.[3] Our space does not allow us to examine these passages here; but the following appear to me to be legitimate results: (1) The Son is always distinguished from God, and is identified with Jesus, the historical man. (2) Jesus was the Son of God in a spiritual, in contradistinction from an official or metaphysical sense, by possession of the Spirit of holiness, and not by the mode of his generation in time or eternity. Whatever may have been Paul's view of the pre-existence of Christ (or of all souls), he nowhere connects sonship with ideas of that kind. (3) Christ's sonship was the same, in essence, as that which belongs to other men; to all potentially; to those who are led by the Spirit of God, in its full sense. (4) Nevertheless to Jesus is assigned a marked pre-eminence, as the predicted Messiah, the one who historically, in God's providence, wakened the human soul to the realisation of this relationship, and for the accomplishment of this purpose was endowed with the spirit of Sonship from the first in unique fulness. Hence he is "*the* Son," God's *own* Son, the Son of His love. Paul may have had a metaphysical explanation of these things, and have derived all souls from the very substance of God, but he never enters into these philosophical speculations. Everywhere the religious in-

---

[1] Rom, i., 3, 4, 9, v., 10, viii., 3, 29, 32; 1 Cor. i., 9, xv., 28; 2 Cor. i., 19; Gal. i., 16, ii., 20, iv., 4, 6; Eph. iv., 13; Col. i., 13; 1 Thess. i., 10.

[2] Rom. viii., 14, 19, ix., 26; 2 Cor. vi., 18; Gal. iii., 26, iv., 6, 7 (twice). Two of these are in quotations, which are applied in a Pauline sense.

[3] Rom. viii., 16, 17, 21, ix., 8; Philip. ii., 15.

terest is dominant. He is content with the reality of filial communion between man and God which he had found in Christ; but he will have nothing less than this, and will not be put off with a legal or dogmatic substitute which might separate him from the love of God.

In the likeness of sinful flesh (viii., 3), literally, "flesh of sin," which need not imply that the flesh is intrinsically sinful, but that it is the element in us through which sin works. These words imply a distinction between the permanent spiritual personality and the flesh which was its earthly organ. The same distinction is recognised in the case of men generally,—"We that are in this tabernacle do groan, being burdened" (see 2 Cor. v., 1 *sq.*). The flesh is mentioned in order to show that sin was defeated in its own stronghold; and to bring out this latter idea it is called "the flesh of sin." But to have said that Christ came in the flesh of sin might seem to imply his sinfulness; and so the longer phrase is chosen, implying that his flesh was like ours, except that it never belonged to sin.

As an offering for sin (viii., 3).—The Greek is simply "in relation to sin," and though a sacrifice may be made in relation to sin, the words do not contain in themselves the notion of sacrifice, and there is nothing whatever in the context to suggest such an idea. It was not primarily with man as ignorant, but with man as sinful, that Christ's mission was concerned.

Condemned sin in the flesh (viii., 3), passed sentence against it within that very element in which its power seemed to reside. God also condemned sin in the Law; but this condemnation only drives the thought in upon the passions which we want to forget, and thus gives strength to sin. How different is the effect if someone comes with commanding character, whose pure spirituality lifts him above all polluting thought. Through him sin is condemned in the flesh, and in his strength we become strong. Of this he was the typical instance whose whole mission was in relation to sin.

That the ordinance of the law might be fulfilled in us (viii., 4).—The object of Christ's mission was to bring about that obedience to the righteous requirements of the Law which the Law itself was powerless to secure. This and the following verses explain how this end is secured. It is by a change from the fleshly to the spiritual mind; or, to revert to the language previously used, it is only when the righteousness of God dwells within that we can fulfil externally the requirements of that righteousness.

The Spirit of God, The Spirit of Christ (viii., 9), *Christ* (viii., 10).—These expressions are used here as equivalents: how is this? The Spirit of God comprises those attributes of holiness, justice, love, which have their reality and source only in Him. But these are precisely the attributes which shone forth from Christ, and constituted the essence of his being; and therefore in speaking of the relationship of men to Christ Paul might substitute for his first expression " the Spirit of Christ," or simply " Christ." This spiritual indwelling of Christ is the indispensable mark of those who are his. That Paul meant spiritual rather than what we should call personal indwelling we may infer from his statement that " while we are at home in the body we are absent from the Lord " (2 Cor. v., 6). Nevertheless in the realm of spirit this distinction may, perhaps, be unreal, and it may be relative only to the present dimness, in which we walk by faith, not by sight.

The body is dead because of sin (viii., 10).—Notwithstanding the indwelling of Christ the body remains under the power of that death which, as Paul believed, was entailed upon the race by sin. But the higher spiritual part was full of life on account of that righteousness in which believers participated. And finally, through the power of the indwelling Spirit of God, even the mortal bodies would be quickened. This shows that the body, though, as we learn from 1 Cor. xv., it was to be totally changed in its qualities, was nevertheless expected to preserve its identity.

With verse 12 we enter on practical deductions from the foregoing principles. There are two ways, which lead respectively to life and death. The reference cannot be to mere physical death, as that affects good and bad alike, but to the deadening of all the higher powers which is the result of the carnal mind. Further, the new principle of life does not supersede the efforts of the will. Deeds lie within the domain of the will, and we must mortify the doings of the body if we would have true life; and now we are able to do so through the power of the Spirit. For (viii., 14-17) the sons of God must have true life in them, and all who are led by the Spirit of God are His sons. We have here a clear definition of what constitutes sonship, and there could be no broader or more universal rule for testing our spiritual relationship. Its negative aspect is given in verse 9. This great principle has been treated with almost invariable contempt by churches and sects. Once, however, it was a living bond of brotherhood, and it might be assumed that the Roman readers came under it; for when they accepted the Gospel they had received the Spirit of adoption. The Greek word for "adoption," here and in Gal. iv., 5, denotes, I think, the recognition of men as sons, a reception of them into the full privileges of sonship, without any implication that they were not really sons; for the previous verse says that they *are* sons, not that they are *counted* such. There is a twofold witness to our sonship. Our own hearts rise up to seek a Divine original; and in answer to this yearning there is a response, or even prior to it an appeal, which is not adequately described as our better nature, but comes with the majesty and grace of something that is higher than we. The lower experience may give us elevated thought, but may also minister to our pride; the higher alone can impart an uplifting life, and temper with the sense of dependence and humility our conviction of human greatness. As sons we are heirs of God. We have here a good illustration of the principle insisted on in another connection, that a metaphor must not be pressed beyond its immediate application; for God does not die and leave an inheritance. Observe the clear distinction between God and Christ, and the way in which the latter is put wholly on the human side of the relationship. But if we would be glorified with Christ, and become full and perfect organs of the Divine Spirit and Will, we must be ready to suffer with him. The cross is the way of life.

The mention of suffering leads the Apostle off into a new train of thought in the following paragraphs (**viii., 18–30**). We must bear our sufferings and infirmities here patiently, for, first, the future glory is out of all proportion to them (*vv.* 18–25); secondly, we have the aid of the Spirit (*vv.* 26, 27); thirdly, everything conspires to further the good of those who love God (*vv.* 28–30). Observe the lofty strain of thought throughout. Paul believed in the return of the Messiah; but there is no allusion to any compensation in kind for present suffering; the ordinary messianic pictures are totally absent; and he stoops to nothing lower than the liberty of the children of God.

Waiteth for the revealing of the Sons of God (**viii., 19**).— Creation is here personified, and regarded as looking forward to an ideal end. There is a constant stress and struggle, from which even the Christian, with the first-fruits of the Spirit, is not exempt. We are sons, and have received the Spirit of adoption, and yet we must wait for the adoption, for a fuller realisation of the Divine thought, which it pleases God to work out slowly from the original vanity of the world. Such is Paul's conception of the final cause of creation, so that the Divine sonship which is just breaking in light upon the world goes back into the eternal counsels of

God, and that which is last in the order of nature was first in the creative mind. Throughout this passage hope is represented as the instrument of progress, and it is even said, "By hope were we saved," where hope takes the usual place of faith. The two must co-exist, and sustain one another; but we may note that Paul does not bind himself to his own language with the strictness of a dogmatist. According to Jewish conception the world was made for the sake of Israel, and the fulfilment of the law was its goal. The world-plan proceeded from the fathers to the sanctuary and the people devoted to the law, and finally to the kingdom of the Messiah. Its continuance was conditional on the obedience of Israel; but God foresaw that Israel would accept the law.[1]

The Spirit himself maketh intercession for us (viii., 26).—The word "Spirit" in Greek is neuter, so that the pronoun may be rendered at the discretion of the translator either "himself" or "itself." Intercession is undoubtedly a personal act: but considering how many personifications we have already met with, and what a lofty strain the language has now reached, it would be rash to assert that Paul here expresses his belief in the separate personality of the "Holy Spirit." If he did, he regarded him as one who offered prayers to God, in accordance with the Divine will, and therefore as distinct from God. But the language is fairly applicable to those inarticulate aspirations which are not the self-raising, but the Divine uplifting of our hearts. The Holy Spirit, in Paul's view, is, I conceive, the manifestation and power of God in the human soul, that in God of which we become immediately conscious, and which blends with our own personality to an extent which it is impossible to define. This Spirit, in us, but not of us, helps our natural infirmity. Our special prayers may be unwise; but there are sighings which are unutterable, aspirations which we

[1] Weber, *Jüd. Theol.*, pp. 196 *sqq.*

cannot throw into definite petitions, and these have a Divine source, and are an intercession for us, bringing down, not what in our ignorance we ask for, but what is conformed to the will of God.

Called according to his purpose (**viii., 28**).—Religious love is not the offspring of human volition; and however needful the operation of our own will may be, the Apostle, since he is here dealing with the providential government of the world, retreats from the human manifestation of piety to the Divine purpose which prepared and worked it. "Called" does not necessarily imply "chosen," but Paul uses it only of those who respond to the call.

Foreknew (**viii., 29**).—By this word Paul guards himself against being supposed to deny the possibility of faithlessness in the human will.

Forcordained to be conformed to the image of his Son (**viii., 29**).—We cannot choose the possibilities of our own nature. These are given to us, and their end can be reached only in fulfilment of our destiny. It is not by human choice that we are drawn through successive grades towards the perfection of sonship. Observe that the Son, Jesus in his highest aspect, is here classed "among many brethren," of whom he is the first-born, the leader of the new spiritual humanity. The following verse touches very briefly the steps by which the providential purpose is fulfilled. "Glorified," the past for the future, indicates the certainty of the result, future glory being involved in present justification.

The succeeding paragraph closes the whole argument in an outburst of assured and triumphant faith, suggested by the words just used (**viii., 31-39**).

Spared not his own Son (**viii., 32**).—See verse 3. "Own" is a mark of endearment, needful to give force to the argument,—if God so earnestly desired to bring men to true holiness that He gave up His best beloved for them, He will give everything else which is necessary to make them perfect. Some think that to talk of sparing is quite out of place unless Paul looked upon Jesus as God; but with Him without whom not a sparrow falls to the ground it may be otherwise, or at least Paul may have thought so, as doubtless he remembered that "precious in the sight of the Lord is the death of His saints," and that "He shall spare the poor and needy, . . . and precious shall their blood be in His sight."

The structure of the following verses (33-35) is rather uncertain. Probably the best way is to take the question in verse 33 as covering the whole passage. The first answer is found in the statement and question, "God is He who justifies; who is he that condemns?" A more remote answer is given in another statement and question, "Christ is he who died, . . . ; who shall separate us from his love?"

Elect (**viii., 33**), chosen ones, a conception to be fully dealt with in the succeeding chapters.

At the right hand of God (**viii., 34**), a figurative expression, as we have no reason for attributing anthropomorphism to Paul. It may refer simply to the exaltation of Christ or it may include his instrumentality in the administration of the world. But this high office is not regarded as changing the old affection: he still loves and prays for man.[1]

Principalities (**viii., 38**) refers to a certain class in the angelic hierarchy.

The love of God which is in Christ Jesus our Lord (**viii., 39**). —Paul began by asking, "Who shall separate us from the love of Christ?" He may here change the form of expression because this is the solemn conclusion of the great argument which constitutes the first part of the Epistle. He has now escaped from the Law which placed us over against God, and spoke the language of reproof and condemnation, into the Love of God which draws us to its own side, folds

---

[1] In the Sanhedrin the president, Nasi, had a representative, Ab-Beth-Din, who sat at his right hand (Weber, *Jüd. Theol.*, p. 140).

us in its inseparable embrace, and forms the inspiration of our lives. This love was in Christ. Christ's love was not one thing, and God's another; for all true love is of one substance, and wherever we see it, but most of all in Christ, it is the love of the Father moving amid our finite conditions.

We come now to the second main division of the doctrinal portion of the Epistle (ix.-xi.).

The subject of which it treats was suggested by the circumstances of the period. It had become evident that, at least for the time being, the Jews as a nation had rejected the Gospel, and that in place of the Jewish theocracy known to history, in place of the Messianic kingdom with its centre at Jerusalem, which had been dear to popular expectation, a new Church was arising, composed, so far as its principles were concerned, of Jews and Gentiles indifferently, but in fact accepted by the latter in numbers becoming ever more and more preponderant, and threatening to assume the aspect of a Gentile institution. This state of things might be regarded in the Church itself with very different feelings according to the nationality of the believer. To any Christian of Jewish race who still loved his people, and was not under the dominion of mere reactionary impulses, it must have been fraught with pain; to one who still reverenced the Old Testament as the oracles of God, and believed in the ancient promises, it must have seemed full of perplexity till fresh lights of interpretation, kindled by the spirit of Christ, exhibited old and new as parts of one great providential plan. A Gentile, on the contrary, who retained his former contempt for the Jews, and was willing to minimise his indebtedness to Judaism, would rather exult in the flowing tide of Greek superiority, declare with satisfaction that the Jews as a people were outcasts from the Kingdom of God, and sometimes treat the Jewish members of the Church with a supercilious tolerance, or openly ridicule their scruples. To either of these states of mind the subject of the present chapters would have a deep interest, removing from the Jewish Christian difficulties which might cloud his faith, and presenting to the Gentile a larger and truer view of the slow and progressive unfolding of the purposes of God.

Paul introduces the subject by expressing his profound attachment to his people, and his willingness to incur the utmost self-sacrifice for them (ix., 1-5).

The strong asseveration in **ix., 1**, shows that Paul was well aware that the motives of an apostate were open to suspicion, and also that he exercised a solemn judgment upon his own feelings.

Anathema from Christ (**ix., 3**).—An anathema is a thing devoted, and has come to be used in a bad sense, of a thing devoted to destruction. It must denote here a complete separation from Christ; but whether it includes the idea of eternal damnation may well be doubted. In any case the language is simply that of strong emotion. A man may feel willing to forego his own deepest life in order that a nation may share it; but such renunciation is not possible in fact, for here, too, he that will lose his life shall find it.

Who are Israelites (**ix., 4**).—The word is used in a higher than a mere national sense (compare Jn. i., 48; 2 Cor. xi., 22; Gal. vi., 16). Paul enumerates the high privileges of his race as a reason for his devotion to them, but also as an introduction to his argument, the difficulty lying in the contrast between their past and their present condition. Observe that the giving of the law is classed with the adoption and the promises.

Who is over all, God blessed for ever (**ix., 5**).—The connection and translation of these words are much disputed. A full discussion of them is much too technical for the present commentary; but I think the main points may be made intelligible without resorting to Greek. There is no doubt that, so far as the grammar is concerned, the words may be connected with Christ. There is also no doubt that a full stop might be placed at "flesh," and the following words translated, "He who is over all, God, is blessed for ever." Other modes of punctuating and translating have been suggested; but on the whole the question resolves itself into these two modes. The names of distinguished scholars are found on both sides.

The following are the principal objections urged against placing the full stop at "flesh." (1) In ascriptions of blessing the word "blessed" is always placed first, as in 2 Cor. i., 3. This is not absolutely correct as a matter of fact, though it is undoubtedly the general rule. The order of words, however, depends entirely on the emphasis; and as the emphasis is usually on "blessed," that word occupies the first place. We have an instructive example in another word which is also translated "blessed," as in the beatitudes. In forty-two passages in the New Testament this word is placed first; but in one instance (James i., 25) the emphasis is on the subject, and the order of the words is accordingly reversed. It follows that if we place the emphasis on "He who is over all," the order of the words is perfectly correct. As we shall see, these are precisely the words which the sentiment of the passage requires us to emphasise. (2) The expression "he who is" would be altogether superfluous, and we ought to have simply "the supreme God is blessed." But this depends entirely on the shade of meaning which the writer wished to convey. If he desired to call attention to the fact of the Divine supremacy, which ordered all things, giving and taking away, he would express himself in the words before us, and the delicate sentiment of the passage would be destroyed by any alteration. So far, then, as grammar and the use of words are concerned, I think there is nothing to incline our opinion one way or the other, and we must appeal to more general considerations.

Appeal is made on both sides to antiquity; but there is no doubt that the greatly preponderant view is in favour of referring the words to Christ, though I think there is room for hesitation in the case of one or two of the authors who are cited. On the other hand we must notice that some of the oldest and best manuscripts have a point at "flesh."[1] This of course only represents an opinion, because it is not probable that the original copies had any punctuation; but it supplements our other evidence that opinion was not unanimous. However, the judgment of early writers must be taken simply for what it is worth in itself; for we have no reason to suppose that it represents a traditional interpretation coming down from apostolic times.

We must inquire next into Pauline usage. On the one side, it is said that the words "as concerning the flesh" require an antithesis. But the antithesis suggests itself, as we can see by going back only a few lines, to verse 3. Paul, like his Master, was now related to the Jew only by race, and not in the spirit of his life. Besides, the following words do not express an antithesis, but only add a description. An antithesis would have to assume some such form as, "but not according to his Godhead." On the other side it may be mentioned that the word "blessed" is nowhere else applied to Christ; but, as it occurs only in four other passages in the Pauline writings, we have too few instances to establish a usage. A more serious, if not absolutely decisive consideration lies in the fact that the application of such an expression to Christ would be quite unique in the writings of Paul. Jesus is mentioned 66 times in the present Epistle, 225 times in all the Pauline Epistles. How is it that in this immense number of references he never uses a similar expression? If he held the doctrine involved in this mode of understanding his words, his mind must have been full of it, and we should expect it to be flashing perpetually into vivid phrases. But not only is this the case, not only does he speak of Christ as "man" without any qualification (Rom. v., 15. Compare 1 Tim. ii., 5, where the absence of any higher description is almost startling), not only does he say that "Christ is God's" (1 Cor. iii., 23), and "the head of Christ is God" (1 Cor. xi., 3), and is careful to explain that Christ's universal dominion must be understood to have been given, and given only for a time (1 Cor. xv., 24-28); but, when he uses his most elevated language, he always markedly distinguishes Christ from God, "the image of God" (2 Cor. iv., 4; Col. i., 15), "in the form of God" (Phil. ii., 6), "God highly exalted him" (*ib.*, 9). With this usage, it is not easy to believe that Paul would in such a passage as the present omit all reference to God the

---

[1] Professor C. R. Gregory says that the larger number of Greek MSS. have a full stop after "flesh." See *The American Journal of Theology*, January, 1897, p. 33.

Father, and adopt words which, standing by themselves, could only suggest that Jesus was the sole supreme God. This consideration is, to my own mind, decisive.

How, then, are we to interpret the sentiment of the passage? It is true that a triumphant thanksgiving would be totally out of place; but this is not contained in the translation which we have given, and which, in my opinion (if we place the full stop at "flesh"), is required by grammar and usage. It will be admitted that the word "Christ," if it stood alone, would have fitly terminated the list of Jewish privileges. But it at once occurs to Paul that the Jewish descent of Christ is true only in a limited sense; in spirit he was no national hero or the prophet of a single people, and the Jews' rejection of him showed that they were separated spiritually by a wide chasm. Here are blended the two notes which dominate the passage, that of patriotic affection as the Apostle thinks of the glory of Israel, that of sorrow as he remembers that the Kingdom of God has passed from them. With the words "as concerning the flesh," he is plunged into grief; but he cannot end with an expression which might seem to imply that all had ended in disaster, and that God's promises were broken. So he strengthens his own and his readers' hearts by the thought of One who is over all, guiding the vicissitudes of nations, and working towards His own glorious ends, even God, who, however mysterious and painful may be His methods, is blessed for ever. We thus reach a sentiment of resignation and trust which is precisely suited to the context, and which has the advantage of giving a satisfactory account of every word and of the arrangement of every word. It also suits the following verse. The words of devout acquiescence might almost seem to suggest a doubt whether the Divine purpose had not changed. In a moment Paul throws off the implied difficulty,—"But I do not mean that the word of God has failed"; and he then proceeds with his close and unimpassioned argument.

He begins by stating clearly the proposition that has to be proved, *It is not as though the word of God hath come to nought* (**ix., 6**).

That this proposition contains the determining subject of the three chapters is apparent from the recurrence of the same thought in different forms as the argument draws to its close: "God did not reject his people" (xi., 1); "they stumbled, but not that they might finally fall" (xi., 11); "all

Israel shall be saved" (xi., 26); "the gifts and the calling of God are without repentance" (xi., 29); "in order that they also may now obtain mercy, for God shut up all unto disobedience that He may have mercy upon all" (xi., 31, 32). Thus the fulfilment of the Divine word to Israel recurs as a refrain, till it ends in a burst of praise, "O the depth of the riches both of the wisdom and knowledge of God!"

"The word of God" does not mean the Scriptures generally, but something mentioned in the Scriptures as having been spoken by God, as appears clearly from verse 9.

Paul appeals, first of all, to the original character of the Divine election (ix., 6-13).

For they are not all Israel who are of Israel (**ix., 6**).—Israel is used here in the highest sense of the Israel of God. These words contain the first step in the argument. From the first the heirs of the promise were determined by a providential selection, which set aside the claims of fleshly descent. This general principle is proved, in the following verses, by particular instances. Abraham had a son Ishmael, but the promise was limited to the line of Israel. But there is a stronger case: Jacob and Esau had the same mother as well as the same father; yet before they were born the promise was restricted to Jacob, the younger of the two.

This is a word of promise (**ix., 9**).—The emphasis is on "promise." The passage cited (according to its sense) from Gen. xviii., 10, proves that Isaac was a child of promise, and the whole incident shows that the children of God are not determined by mere physical lineage.

The purpose of God according to election (**ix., 11**).—This verse does not assert that nothing in human life depends on human volition. The election refers to the choosing of nations to fulfil a certain providential purpose in the spiritual development of mankind. The mental characteristics of the Greeks, the Romans, and the Jews were not created by the will of the individuals composing these nations; and if Israel has impressed its religion upon the world, while Edom has been spiritually barren, we can ascribe this fact only to the selective purpose of God. How far nations are faithful to their calling and election, and what happens to the unfaithful, are questions which are not at present raised. We should bear in mind that the Jews had the strongest belief in responsibility, and therefore in free will. God determined the circumstances of men, but left it to themselves whether they would be righteous or godless.[1] Abraham himself was chosen on account of his righteousness.[2] A curious Haggada even relates how Jacob and Esau conversed, before their birth, about the two worlds, and that Jacob there and then chose the future world, while Esau, denying the resurrection, chose the present.[3]

Jacob I loved, but Esau I hated (**ix., 13**).—This quotation from Malachi i., 2, 3, states concisely, in Scriptural words, the historical fulfilment of the promise in the previous verse; God's blessing had never rested on the Edomites. It would be hypercritical to insist that Paul here ascribes hatred to God. He who so dwells upon God's love can hardly have intended to do so, and at another time would maintain that God hates nothing that He has made. The word is in a quotation which suited his purpose; and had he been using his own language he might have expressed himself differently.

An objection has now to be met, and Paul proceeds to prove that the elective action of God, including especially the present application of it, is not unjust (ix., 14-29).

Is there unrighteousness with God? (**ix., 14**).—"Unrighteousness" is here used in its stricter sense of injustice. Why should anyone think the mode of action which Paul has described unjust? No one thinks it unjust that God distributes intellectual gifts as it pleases Him. Two answers

---

[1] Weber, *Jüd. Theol.*, p. 216.   [2] *Ib.*, p. 264.   [3] *Ib.*, p. 401.

may be given. Character is so much more implicated with the will than is intellect that we often forget that religious power and originality are as much a gift as the inspiration of a poet. And further, the cry of injustice is never so sedulously raised as when long-established privileges are attacked. To the Jew his privileges seemed a sort of Divine right; and though to us the placing of Jew and Gentile on the same level may seem an act of justice, to the ordinary Pharisee it would seem an outrage on the order of the universe; and Paul himself may have found it hard to realise his new position when he first felt that he was simply one of the great family of God, to whom he owed everything, and from whom he could claim nothing.

I will have mercy on whom I have mercy (more correctly, I think, " whomsoever," **ix., 15**).—The quotation is from Ex. xxxiii., 19, of which the context should be read, as Paul assumes that his readers are acquainted with the passages to which he refers. The point of the narrative is that the Israelites were threatened with desertion by God on account of their sins, and that the Lord consented to remain with them on the pure ground of His pity. The Jews, then, had forfeited their spiritual privileges even in the time of Moses, and retained them, not on account of their birth or legal works, but solely on account of God's undeserved compassion.

It is not of him that willeth (**ix., 16**).—This deduces a general principle from the special instance. All our eager running after spiritual superiority will never bring us to it; and he who simply waits upon God's infinite love, and is content to take the lowest post of self-denying service which He may appoint, shall enter His kingdom before us. Any eminent position that a man may hold in that kingdom has been given, not earned.

For the Scripture saith unto Pharaoh (**ix., 17**).—This is generally taken as the introduction of an opposite instance to the foregoing, an example of God's unconditioned wrath. But in this view the "for" has no meaning; and the example ought to prove that something had proceeded, not from man's desert, but from the mercy of God. Now the verse makes two important affirmations: that it was God who raised up Pharaoh, and that He did this with a special purpose. As Pharaoh did not contemplate this purpose, he illustrates "not of him that willeth." As the purpose, the publishing of God's name in all the earth, is a benevolent one, we have an example of the mercy of God, overruling the willing and ruining of a bad man, and bringing good out of evil. Thus Paul touches on what he conceived to be the true principle of Divine action: it was a world-embracing mercy, selecting and rejecting with a view to the most beneficent results. This foreshadows the close of his argument: the Jews were hardened, for a time, that the world might come in; God shut up all unto disobedience, that He might have mercy upon all (xi., 32).

Whom he will he hardeneth (**ix., 18**).—This verse sums up the first reply to the question, "Is there injustice with God?" It points out two modes of dealing with undeserving men, but does not mention the motive to which allusion has been made, and which is worked out at a later stage of the argument. "Hardened" has in English a moral implication which, I think, is absent from the Greek. It means "to make obstinate," and is applied to men who are not easily convinced.[1] Here it refers to that blindness of judgment which ended in a disaster that might have been prevented by a little political sagacity. Paul, we can hardly doubt, had his countrymen in his mind. They were hard-

---

[1] This meaning suits Acts xix., 9; Heb. iii., 8 (also 15, and iv., 7) and 13, where also the word is found. There is a good example in Eusebius, *Hist. Ec.*, ii., 17, εἰ δ' ἐπὶ τούτοις ἀντιλέγων τίς ἔτι σκληρύνοιτο, where the reference can be only to intellectual obstinacy or dulness, a δυσπιστία, as it is presently called.

ened so that they could not read the signs of the times; and this hardening was necessary (to speak from an historical point of view) in order that the Gospel might have free course among the Gentiles, and work out its own independent life.

Why doth he still find fault [or blame]? For who withstandeth his will? (**ix., 19**).—The difficulty started in verse 14 is presented in another form; but it is not obvious what the precise point of the difficulty is. It is generally assumed to be in effect this,—If God chooses to harden me, why does He blame me for being hardened? or, as "hardened" is understood in a moral sense, if God makes me sinful, why does He blame me for sinning? To this there are serious objections. (1) If our interpretation so far has been correct, there has been nothing to suggest such a question. (2) This question expresses one of the most serious doubts that can affect the human mind; and if this is what is meant, Paul has treated it with a frivolity which is quite out of keeping with his character. To say that a potter has a right to make an ugly dish does not prove that he would be right in blaming it for being ugly. (3) The doctrine implied in this interpretation is inconsistent with Paul's belief in human responsibility. In order to find the true meaning let us recall the point established in the last section. It was this, that the favours which God bestows upon the guilty are an offering of pure mercy; and that the same mercy, taking a more comprehensive range, may see fit to prepare the guilty for their fall; but in either case God works out His own beneficent plan. Now is it not a natural, though not a wise or devout retort for the guilty man to say, "Well, then, why am I to be blamed? If, whatever I do, I am working out God's purposes, what right has He to find fault with me? Even Pharaoh caused God's name to be declared throughout the earth, in accordance with the Divine will; who is there, then, that resists that will?" This question and the reasoning on which it is grounded are similar to those in iii., 5 and 7, so that our interpretation is not only suggested by the context, but is agreeable to a known train of thought in the Apostle's mind.

Nay but, O man, who art thou that repliest against God? (**ix., 20**).—In the ordinary interpretation this is simply an attempt to browbeat an opponent who presents an unanswerable difficulty. As we have understood it, the question amounts to this: If God brings good out of our evil, why should that evil be found fault with? In the third chapter Paul dismisses this as an illegitimate question, simply pointing out its inconsistency with the fundamental fact of human responsibility, and intimating that it involves the principle of doing evil that good may come. Here he does not feel called upon to give any reply to a query which seemed to him immoral; and he therefore throws it off, and turns it round to the main subject of discussion. The connection may then be presented thus: Instead of asking why God should blame you, it would be much more fitting to ask why you should blame God, as though He had not an absolute right to assign your place in the world, and to give you a position of honour or lack of honour as He sees to be best. This, accordingly, is not intended to be an answer to the question in verse 19, but is the second answer to the question in verse 14: God is not unjust in His elective action, because, as their Creator, He may assign men their various posts of service according to His own good pleasure. One difficulty, however, remains: why does Paul propose a question which he does not condescend to answer? Simply, I believe, because the question was actually proposed by his calumniators, to whom he alludes in iii., 8. This is indicated by the change of form. In verse 14 we read, "What shall we say then?" and a serious difficulty is seriously met. Here the question is transferred to an opponent, "Thou shalt say then unto me"; and as it has its origin in malice rather than in real perplexity of thought, Paul turns on his opponent and shows that in claiming spiritual privileges as a right he is denying the free sovereignty of God.

Honour, dishonour (**ix., 21**).—These words confirm our interpretation. The question is not of making good or bad vessels (for no decent potter would be so foolish as to make a bad vessel), but of making vessels of various degrees of dignity in the household economy. The moral question does not come in at all; for the scullery bowl may be quite as good in its kind as the drawing-room vase.

In the following verses Paul indicates what he believed to be the real state of the case in relation to the growing Gentile Church (**ix., 22-29**). The construction is broken, and the grammatical connection a little uncertain; but the general sense is clear. God had a perfect right to distribute His spiritual gifts as He pleased; but in fact the Jewish nation had forfeited its prerogative, and was ripe for destruction. God had long borne with them, wishing, as in the case of Pharaoh, to make His indignation against sin more conspicuous. This is not inconsistent with the teaching of ii., 4, that the long-suffering of God leads to repentance; for in that very passage the two ideas are combined. The man who remains impenitent lays up an accumulating store of wrath for the day when God's righteous judgment will be revealed. But God had another purpose in the Christian movement, "to make known the *riches* of His glory." That glory was not so poor and narrow as some of the Jews supposed, but shone also upon the Gentile world; and if He had prepared Jewish hearts through the Law and the Prophets, He had prepared pagan souls as well through the consciousness of deeper needs and the faintness of a strange thirst for the unknown God. To show His glory He prepared a new race for glory; for our spiritual glory is a ray from the Divine, an indwelling of that Spirit which alone can constitute us in the highest sense sons of God.

The position thus reached is illustrated by quotations from the Prophets (**ix., 25-29**). Those from Hosea ii., 23, and i., 10, refer originally to the Israelites of the northern tribes. Here they are applied to the Gentiles; and the Apostle may cite them as evidence of the general principle that, although at one period a people might be rejected, yet at another they might be accepted, and to show that the claim now made on behalf of the Gentiles was no more than had once been required by the Israelites themselves. In the quotation from Isaiah x., 22, 23, the emphasis must be laid on "the remnant." As in Assyrian, so was it in Roman times; the flood of justice was flowing over the Jewish people, and only a remnant should be saved. The quotation from i., 9, contains, by implication, a terrible indictment of the moral corruption of the people, and an appalling picture of the fate which their sins deserved. This brings the original question round to an unexpected issue. Is there injustice with God? No, there is justice; and therefore a seed of evil-doers may tremble. Punishment may seem long delayed; but God is not mocked, and at last it shall come down as upon the cities of the plain.

Having vindicated the righteousness of Divine election, Paul next proceeds to state the existing facts in regard to Jew and Gentile, in order to reach the spiritual law on which the facts depended (ix., 30-x., 13).

He assumes as a fact that the Gentiles, as represented by the scattered groups of believers, had accepted the Gospel, and that the Jews as a nation had rejected it; and this shows, I think, that the Gentiles in the Church already far outnumbered those of Jewish birth.

The case of the Gentiles is taken first (**ix., 30**). In saying that they did not follow after righteousness, Paul is simply referring to a general characteristic of heathen life and religion. We know that there were splendid exceptions; but with these he is not at present concerned. In every church which he founded he must have known of numbers of instances in which the spiritual power of the Gospel took possession of hearts which had never before aspired after a Divine life. The righteousness thus attained was a righteousness which sprang out of faith, in the sense which has been already explained. Observe how the attainment of genuine righteousness is the goal of Paul's thought, and he reduces the rival claims of religions to a great practical test.

The case of Israel is considered more fully (**ix., 31–x., 3**). They followed after "a law of righteousness": that is, they made a written law their supreme rule of life, pursuing the outward form and not the inward reality of goodness. So pursuing, they did not even attain to law, the external seemliness of a well-ordered life. The word "*that*," which our translators have inserted before "law," has nothing in the Greek to justify it; and I think it impairs the sense.

The reason for the failure of the Jews is now stated: they followed a wrong method (**ix., 32**). To pursue righteousness by works is to seek it in obedience to the letter of an outward rule. The natural effect of this is to harden, or, as Paul says, "to kill," the inner life of man. It imposes fetters on the free forces of the mind, places the judgment in leading-strings, and chills the fresh and glowing instincts which turn to the good and true wherever found. The operation of faith is different: it opens the soul to the free inpouring of the Divine Spirit; and if the Jews had committed themselves to the faith of Isaiah instead of the legalism of Ezra, the results on the national character would have been of a far higher order. Historically, however, the legalism was necessary to prevent the nation from being absorbed in the surrounding heathenism. The Law thus fulfilled a Divine purpose; but nevertheless it caused the Jews to stumble when Christ called them to the righteousness of God. A characteristic result of legalism, whether of works or of creeds, is the inability which it lays upon the mind of appreciating anything excellent which lies outside the prescribed rule. Goodness must appear in one particular garb, and express itself in one familiar language. Whatever lies beyond the pale is the world of sin, and the seeming beauty of holiness that may be found in it is only the deceitful ray that lures men to their destruction. The zeal of the Jews, then, for their "*law* of righteousness" would, just in proportion to its intensity, disqualify them for the recognition of an original goodness, which lived calmly out of its own depths, and drew its inspiration from the Father, and not from the Law. While many a poor Gentile, who had nothing but mother nature to trust to, was drawn by the God-given emotions of the heart to feel that this was indeed the life from heaven, the Jew, with his artificial training, could see no beauty in the inner soul of goodness, nor acknowledge, when it lived and breathed before him, that "righteousness of God" which is itself the fountain and the judge of Law. But besides this, the Jew felt, and felt correctly, that there was in principle an irreconcilable antagonism between the spirit of Christ and the exclusiveness of his own system. In such circumstances how many were likely to be found who would leave the path which, if a narrow one, glowed with the fervid memories of a thousand years, and had been trodden by judges, and kings, and prophets, which marked a track of verdant life amid the pagan desert, and which alone promised to guide the chosen few into God's glorious kingdom, and all to follow, in obedience to unauthorised dreams, an upstart teacher to a bloody doom? Thus it was that seeking righteousness, not from the deep and inner wells of a Divine communion, but from the unyielding mechanism of an outward system, their hearts were hardened against the appeals of Christianity. In devotion to the form they lost the substance, and "stumbled at the stone of stumbling."

The quotation in **ix., 33,** is made up from Isaiah xxviii.,

16, and viii., 14. "On him" is inserted by Paul, for it is not in either the Hebrew or the LXX. The insertion suits the immediate context, in which the Apostle is dwelling, not upon the want of faith generally in the Jews, but upon the special exemplification of it in their rejection of Christ, with all that that rejection involved.

Having reached a sad conclusion, Paul's tender affection and solicitude once more seek expression (**x., 1**). The Jews really had a zeal for God; but as it was misdirected, it produced mischievous results (**x., 2, 3**). They were ignorant of real righteousness, as it exists in the nature of God Himself, and sought to establish righteousness as it existed in, and was conceived by, themselves, that is, their own peculiar system, their own narrow views, of righteousness, which they regarded as final and unchangeable. Hence "they did not subject themselves to the righteousness of God," of which men can become the organs, not by devotion to their own sect or law or creed, but only by committing themselves to God in the submissiveness of faith.

The foregoing remarks suggest the abolition of the Law, and therefore of the distinction between Jew and Greek, under the new principle of faith (**x., 4-13**).

For Christ is the end of the law, or, more exactly, *Christ is an end of law* (**x., 4**).—If we understand "Christ" merely of the historical person, we shall only have a conflict of opinion, and no advance in spiritual thought. With Paul "the Lord is the Spirit" (2 Cor. iii., 17), and I think we often miss the full depth and force of his meaning if we refer his words only to Christ's historical and official relations, and not to the enthronement of the "life of God" within the life of man, which was realised in Christ. To the heart that loves him this one name comes laden with a world of spiritual thought, which being presented in a concrete form, and vivified by the affections, makes its appeal with a power which abstract speculation has never succeeded in attaining.

Thus Christ is the end of law for righteousness, not merely by historical position and by special work, but by what he was, the Son of God with power, whose Spirit in the heart of man makes all questions of form, comparatively speaking, indifferent.

To everyone that believeth (**x.**, 4).—As usual, no object is expressed; and though faith in Christ must be included, it is best to understand the word in the high spiritual sense which we have all along attached to the word: those who had faith recognised in Christ the end of Law, and sought for righteousness by a new principle. It was not a question of transferring belief from one object to another, but of receiving that trustful apprehension of inward realities which freed men from the impotence of outward symbols.

We now see the connection between this and the previous verse. The Jews did not subject themselves to the righteousness of God; "for," had they done so, they would have recognised in Christ the realisation of that goodness of which all law is but the imperfect expression, and which therefore, when it appears, puts an end to the principle of legal obedience. When the perfect comes, the partial vanishes.

In what has been said a principle has been laid down which opened the door for the free admission of the Gentiles. Paul proceeds to show that the Law itself described not only the legal form of righteousness (**x.**, 5), but also a righteousness more inward and spiritual (**x.**, 6-8). The first quotation, from Leviticus xviii., 5, does not imply the impossibility of keeping the Law, but rather assumes the contrary. But it refers simply to outward conduct, and does not describe that righteousness which is the root of the Law, and can alone be called the righteousness of God. The following quotation, from Deut. xxx., 11-14, is adapted by Paul to his own purposes, and we need not suppose that the parenthetical explanations are intended to represent the original meaning of the passage. The point is that it describes a word which is very different from the word of a statute-book. It is worth noticing, though this part is omitted by Paul, that in Deut. "doing" is as clearly mentioned as in the previous quotation; but the order in which it occurs is reversed. There the life followed the doing, as its reward; here the word is in thy heart that thou mayest do it. The whole spirit of the passage, therefore, is adapted to Paul's purpose; and it is fairly used by him as the language of the righteousness which is of faith. Observe the personification, a figure which we have met with several times before.[1]

We must now ask why Paul, if he is dealing with principles, introduces Christ. One reason is that the whole inquiry has arisen from an historical difficulty, the rejection of Christ by the Jews, and the consequent opening of the Kingdom of God to the Gentiles. And again, as in verse 4, Christ stands for the embodiment of Divine righteousness in humanity, and was the historical realisation of the love, and obedience, and cleaving unto God, which are insisted upon in the chapter from which the quotation is taken. And lastly, the ancient saying had become true in a fuller sense than formerly. It was not now necessary to look up to heaven for a Christ that was still to come, or dig among the graves of buried wisdom to find some living word. Men had *seen* the eternal life, which death could not hold, and never more should its impression be effaced from the human soul. The word which proclaimed faith in these sublime realities was not far off, written in some remote title-deed, but in each believer's mouth and heart.

Whether we translate "*because*" or "*that*" in **x.**, 9, the following words contain a broad description of Christian life

---

[1] A rabbinical interpretation deduces the eternity of the law from this passage: none of it has been left in heaven, so as to require another Moses to arise, and bring another law from heaven (Weber, *Jüd. Theol.*, p. 18).

and faith, thrown into this special form to suit the above quotation. Here at last Paul seems to define what he means by faith, and he throws its object into the form of a proposition, which announces simply that God raised Jesus from the dead. This, however, does not invalidate the explanation which we have hitherto given of the word faith ; for from time to time Paul isolates some special point in the contents of faith for closer consideration. Thus in iv., 24, he makes it consist in believing " on Him that raised Jesus our Lord from the dead," a belief akin to that referred to here, but larger, rising from the single fact to the quickening power of Him to whom the fact was due. But no doubt he selected what seemed to him of vital importance. The confession of Christ before a hostile world, and the belief in his immortal life, carried with them all the depth and power of that spiritual confidence in Divine things which he summarises under the word faith. In those days the decisive step of acknowledging the Crucified as Lord in a sense far transcending the lordship of the Cæsars required an enthusiasm of conviction which saved men by lifting them out of their old life into the communion of the immortal children of God. We must not leave this verse without remarking on the grand simplicity of the Apostolic terms of salvation, from which most of the doctrines insisted upon in later times as the essentials of Christianity are entirely absent.

The principle thus laid down was not limited by race, and Paul now reverts (**x., 11**) to the quotation of ix., 33, in order to call attention to its universality. The connection may be thus given :—I am justified in making the above broad statement about salvation, for the Scripture, in the passage which I have quoted, has no limiting clause.

The same Lord is Lord of all (**x., 12**).—It is commonly assumed that the Lord here is Jesus, since the term is applied to him in verse 9. This argument does not seem to me convincing ; for there is a transition of thought in verse

11 which carries us back to the end of the last chapter, and great confusion is introduced into the quotation from Isaiah by referring the word to Christ. According to that quotation the Lord God lays in Zion a stone; and, in Paul's interpretation, those who trusted in this stone should not be ashamed. This suggests the idea that those who trusted in that stone should, on that sole condition, experience the mercy of Him who laid it, and who is rich towards all, without distinction, who may call upon Him. But in the interpretation the stone becomes Christ, who must therefore be distinguished from the Lord God; whereas the ordinary view represents Christ as being both the stone and Him who laid it; quite contrary to the sense of the original passage. I am therefore of opinion that the word "Lord" here refers to God, and that it is employed simply because it is the word adopted by the LXX. in the passages which are quoted. We must remember that the Gentiles had to learn from the Gospel to call upon the name of God, and that believing on Him was for them, in form as well as substance, a new experience. Also compare iii., 29, 30.

The quotation from Joel ii., 32 (**x., 13**) serves to express a universal truth, though in the prophet it is of more limited application. We must observe how completely free the Apostle is from the fetters of dogmatism. Here he accepts a statement of the conditions of salvation which is totally different in form from that which he presented only a few lines back. He accepts as sufficient the most universal ground of simple piety that it is possible to discover. This is confirmatory of our whole line of exposition.

> The following passage (x., 14-21) shows that the application of the spiritual law which has been just set forth is not prevented by mere ignorance, for to Gentile and Jew alike the Gospel has been preached, and the present acceptance of it by the one and rejection of it by the other have been clearly described in the ancient Scriptures.

How then shall they call on him in whom they have not believed? (**x., 14**).—If we have understood the previous context correctly, the person referred to must be God. This is still more obvious from the sequel; for it is clearly God who is found of those who sought Him not, and stretches forth His hands to Israel. It may be objected that the Jews at least had faith in God. But this was not so in the Christian view: they had neither heard His voice at any time, nor seen His form (John v., 37); in Paul's language, they had not faith. A self-confident dogmatism is only the sorry counterfeit of faith. In order to have faith men must have heard the voice of God within their own hearts; and in order to hear this voice they must catch the tones of awakened faith in the speech of another.

How shall they preach except they be sent? (**x., 15**).—Unless an inner word of God send them with imperative command, they cannot so preach as to bow down the conscience before a new-found holiness, or fire the heart with spiritual emotion. The language which Isaiah (lii., 7) uses in regard to the return from the captivity occurs to Paul's mind as applicable to the present deliverance from spiritual servitude. We need not suppose that he looked upon this and the succeeding quotations as predictions of the particular events of his own time, or, on the other hand, that he merely wished to express his own thoughts in well-known language. Words are often used in relation to special circumstances, which nevertheless embody a universal principle, and hence become full of illumination for analogous circumstances which were not originally contemplated.

There is now a transition in the thought (**x., 16**). The sentiment has been full of joy, resulting from the comprehensiveness of the announced conditions. But there is another side to the picture. The conditions are indeed universal; but nevertheless they are conditions, which may be accepted or rejected, and in fact the rejection of the glad tidings by the Jews is due to a "disobedient and gainsaying" spirit which has run through all their history. It was true in the time of Isaiah (liii., 1) that they would not believe what they heard. So it was now. They had heard the word of Christ through his preachers (**x., 17**), calling them as the prophets had called, to a nobler faith. Wherever they were scattered over the world the voice of the preacher had addressed them (**x., 18**). And they could not plead ignorance; for as long ago as the time of Moses (Deut. xxxii., 20, 21) they were warned that if they moved God to jealousy with that which was not God, He would move them to jealousy with those who were not a people (**x., 19**). So at the present time they saw Gentiles pressing into the Kingdom of God, and cleaving to Him with a faith to which they themselves had become strangers. It was the same in the days of Isaiah (lxv., 1, 2). The careless heathen had found God (**x., 20**); but Israel had refused to listen to the Divine pleading (**x., 21**). Let us try for a moment to apprehend the grandeur and originality of the thought. Here we have the image of One who seeks to make His name known throughout all the earth, and sends His messengers to the ends of the world, One who stretches out beseeching hands to the sinner, and often comes even to the indifferent with such visions of glory that the dead soul trembles into unexpected life. Such is the vision of Christian faith, invisible only to those who have been blinded by their endeavours to establish their own righteousness. To Him who is in Christ Jesus Gentile and Jew, Christian and pagan, are no more; the sects are lost in the Church of the children of God, who, in the spirit of Christ, listen in faith to the living word within and feel that nothing but their own self-willed pride and want of submission can separate them from that infinite Love which has chosen all men for itself, though all have not obeyed.

The train of reflection in the last few verses might seem to im-

ply that God had finally cast off His people; and Paul, to whom as himself an Israelite such a thought was abhorrent, proceeds to show that this was not the case; for, first, to resume the position of chapter ix., there was a select remnant (xi., 1-10).

God had not chosen His people without foreknowledge, and therefore could not cast them off (**xi., 2**). It was the old story. As in the days of Elijah seven thousand had remained faithful (**xi., 2-4**), so it was now. There was a remnant, while the mass of the people had lost their spiritual discernment, so that to them might once more be applied the words of Isaiah (xxix., 10, combined with Deut. xxix., 3, 4) and of David (Psalm lxix., 23, 24).

If it is by grace, it is no more of works (**xi., 6**).—If the people were rejected for their disobedience, nevertheless the remnant were not chosen as a reward for any meritorious works. Faith itself, in its lower and higher stages, the initial point of all spiritual life, is a gift, which we may indeed forfeit, but cannot earn. Responsibility is connected with problems that are *given*, and is confined to the spiritual plain to which only the grace of God can lift us. Man is not responsible for being human and not angelic; but he is responsible when he is brutal and not human; for our humanity is a gift, and determines the nature of our duty. The same truth holds good of the various degrees of spiritual elevation and insight.

The rest were hardened (**xi., 7**).—The word "hardened" here differs from that in ix., 18, and refers less to obstinacy than to an intellectual obtuseness. Compare Mark vi., 52, viii., 17; John xii., 40; 2 Cor. iii., 14, where the context makes the meaning plain.

In his usual manner Paul now resumes in another form the question with which he started in verse 1, in order to return a different answer: the lapse of the nation was temporary, and, while it lasted, it was made contributory to the merciful designs of Providence (xi., 11-32).

As an historical fact, the preaching to the Gentiles was largely due to the opposition which the Jews offered to the Christian preachers. The latter were forced to turn to those who would listen to them, and the logic of events made the Church conscious of its world-wide calling. But when this purpose was accomplished, and the Gentile harvest was gathered in, the partial hardening of Israel would pass away, and the complete nation would once more contribute to the world's riches out of the fulness of its spiritual life. Such was Paul's vision of the course of history, which he must have expected to be realised at no distant date, when Christ would return, and reign over a regenerated world.

By their fall (**xi., 11**).—This is a most unfortunate translation; for Paul has just stated in effect that the Jews did not fall, but only stumbled. The word elsewhere is translated "trespass," and always denotes the wilful violation of a commandment. Here it naturally refers to the disobedience alluded to in x., 21.

In the remainder of the passage the Gentiles are specially addressed, and warned not to be arrogant towards the Jewish race. After all, they were only grafted on to the stem of Israel; and if some of the branches were broken off by their unbelief, this was not a reason for exultation, but for fear; for Gentiles too might fall, and the natural branches once more be grafted in.

If thou continue in his goodness (**xi., 22**).—Note once more the conditional character of the Divine gifts. We cannot create them, but may necessitate their withdrawal.

Mystery (**xi., 25**), a hidden truth, which may be plain to more advanced minds. Here it refers to the secret meaning of Israel's rejection. That rejection really affected only a portion of the people, and it was to last only till the entire body of Gentiles came in; and then all Israel would be saved. So Isaiah had foretold (lix., 20, 21, and xxvii., 9).

They are enemies . . . they are beloved (**xi., 28**).—It is said that on account of the antithesis "enemies" must be understood in a passive sense: "hated by God." But you cannot both hate and love a man at the same time, though you may be obliged, on certain grounds, to treat as an enemy one whom, on other grounds, you love. I think we shall reach the true sense if we subordinate the active sense of hostile (though that is included), and understand the statement thus:—in relation to the Gospel which they have rejected, they are looked upon as enemies, in order that the Gentiles may be drawn in; but as regards the Divine election of Israel, they are beloved for the sake of their fathers, and as the purpose of God cannot change, and He does not repent of bestowing His gifts (**xi., 29**), the estrangement must be temporary. There was a Jewish doctrine that the Israelites, having fallen into sin through the worship of the golden calf, were allowed, owing to the merit of their fathers, to remain the people of God.[1]

God hath shut up all unto disobedience (**xi., 32**).—This can hardly mean that God makes all men disobedient; for that would be a self-contradictory proposition. But men being in fact disobedient, God has shut up all alike in disobedience, as in a prison (see Gal. iii., 22, 23), making no difference in that respect between Jew and Gentile, that all, having the same need, may experience the same compassion.

The great argument closes with a burst of adoring praise (xi., 33-36), in which glory is ascribed to God alone, the source and the end of all that moral discipline and providential leading by which the whole family of man is to be gathered home into the Divine love.

The doctrinal portion of the Epistle being concluded, we pass on to its ethical application (xii., 1-xv., 13).

This larger section falls into two well-marked divisions, the first dealing with universal rules of duty (xii., 3-xiii., 14), and the second referring especially to the mutual duties

---

[1] Weber, *Jüd. Theol.*, pp. 274 *sqq.*

of different parties in the Church (xiv., 1–xv., 13). The first two verses, which have not been mentioned in this partition of the subject, lay down the general principle of Christian conduct.

Paul, having traced the course of events to the Divine pity, sets before us, in accordance with this view, the principle of action in the new life of faith (xii., 1, 2). Its motive lies in the apprehension of God's "mercies," His feelings of compassion towards us; its essence, in the offering of ourselves as a holy sacrifice to God, and the transformation and renewal of our minds in accordance with His will.

Your reasonable service (**xii., 1**).—" Service " relates to the temple-worship; and " reasonable " means " belonging to the reason," in contrast with outward ceremonial. Nothing could be more natural than to borrow figures from the established ritual; and in a case where their own bodies are concerned commentators are content with a metaphorical explanation. In the early Christian assemblies praise and prayer took the place of the ancient offerings; and here Paul would extend the underlying and spiritual meaning of sacrifice to our own persons, and to every part of our lives.

This world (**xii., 2**); rather, " this age," referring to the Jewish division of time into the present and the future age, divided from one another by the advent of the Messiah.

Paul deals, first, with the personal intercourse of Christians with one another (**xii., 3-17ª**).

A measure of faith (**xii., 3**).—This expression shows once more that faith was not mere belief in either a fact or a proposition. It had various grades, and ramified in various directions. In some it was bold and venturous; in others it was timid and conservative. In some it was luminous upon this point, in others upon that.

One body in Christ (**xii, 5**).—This figure is worked out much more fully in 1 Cor. xii. It admirably expresses the subordination of each member to the good of the whole spiritual community, from which its own vitality was fed, and to which it owed the unselfish discharge of its appropriate function. Everyone had his own particular gift, the result of Divine grace, and this was to be used, not with haughty self-satisfaction, but with that soundness and sobriety of mind which *we* describe as judgment and good sense.

Prophecy (**xii., 6**), the gift of inspired utterance of spiritual themes. *Ministry* (**xii., 7**), the administration of funds, for helping the poor and the sick. *Teaching* (**xii., 7**), the regular instruction of the less advanced in Christian truth. *He that ruleth* (**xii., 8**), perhaps the president of a congregation or of any other body; possibly the patron of poor dependents.

The Lord (**xii., 11**).—This naturally refers to Christ as the animating soul of the entire body, or the Master to whom all Christian service is due. We should expect this precept to dominate the whole section, instead of appearing as one of many miscellaneous injunctions; but the thought flows forth without any very clear line of suggestion. As is stated in the margin of the Revised Version, " some ancient authorities read the *opportunity*," the two Greek words being written in a very similar manner.

Bless them that persecute you (**xii., 14**).—This most naturally refers to persons outside the Church; but from its position we should expect it to apply to the conduct of Christians towards one another. Yet if the latter were intended, some advice would surely be given to the persecutors. The thought may be suggested by contrast with " the saints ":— not only to be hospitable to your fellow-believers, but extend your blessing to those who persecute you.

We now pass almost imperceptibly into the second subdivision, which relates to the conduct of Christians towards the outer world (xii., 17ᵇ–xiii., 10).

First, we must exhibit a peaceful attitude towards the injustice of the world (**xii., 17b–21**).

Give place unto wrath (**xii., 19**).—" Wrath " is a technical word with Paul; and the context shows that the reference is not to our own anger, but to the punitive action of God, to which our resentment must give place, as He alone can judge with perfect justice.

It is written (**xii., 19**), in Deut. xxxii., 35, more nearly in the Hebrew than in the LXX.

Thou shalt heap coals of fire upon his head (**xii., 20**).—This verse is cited from Proverbs xxv., 21, 22. The figure suggests something painful; but it is obvious from the context that the infliction of pain is not the object. The best explanation seems to be that which refers it to the burning sense of shame which is kindled by kind and gentle conduct, and which leads to repentance and reconciliation.

From the general principles of Christian conduct we now proceed to the particular duty of loyal submission to the constituted authorities in the state (**xiii., 1–7**). There must have been some special reason for enforcing so obvious a requirement. The proclamation of a Kingdom of God was not only suited to arouse the jealousy of the ruling powers, and to afford a plea for persecution, but may have sometimes produced a dangerous ferment among the more excitable spirits in the Christian community. At Thessalonica the preachers of the Gospel were charged with acting " contrary to the decrees of Cæsar, saying that there is another king, one Jesus " (Acts xvii., 7), and Jesus himself had been put to death on a charge of treason. The new religion, moreover, required the believers to separate themselves from all idolatrous practices, and therefore to withdraw from a large part of the social life around them; and this in itself would excite suspicion of revolutionary designs and secret conspiracy. It was therefore necessary to be peculiarly scrupulous in the fulfilment of civic duties, and to hold in check the more fanatical minds who might have wished to precipitate a political crisis. Paul himself believed that the outlying world was under the dominion of an evil principle, and we must admire all the more the large and balanced judgment which recognised a Divine ordinance as the basis of civil society, and insisted on keeping the new movement strictly within the spiritual realm. If any think it strange that Paul should write thus in the time of Nero, we must remember that the Epistle was composed during those early years, so full of promise, when the savage character of the tyrant had not yet displayed itself.

A minister of God (**xiii., 4**).—The word here translated "minister," one who acts as the servant of another to administer his affairs, is used technically of the deacons in the Church. The word with the same translation in verse 6 is different, and means one who discharges a public duty. It is specially applied, but not limited, to a priesthood.

An avenger for wrath (**xiii., 4**); that is, he executes the punitive judgment of God against the evil-doer.

The following verses relate to general social intercourse (**xiii., 8-10**). There is a verbal connection with the seventh verse in the Greek, which is lost in the translation. We may represent it thus:—"Render to all what you owe: owe no man anything but love."

Hath fulfilled the law (**xiii., 8**).—"Law" is without the article in Greek, so that the phrase is equivalent to "has fulfilled all the requirements of law." Although the following examples are naturally drawn from the law of Moses, the connection of thought demands the wider sense: love pays all lawful debts, not only to rulers, but to your neighbours. This confirms our interpretation of the general doctrine of the Epistle. When the righteousness of God, of which the essence is love, takes possession of the heart, the commandments become obsolete, for they are fulfilled through the spontaneous energy of the indwelling life.

These more general admonitions close with an exhortation to personal purity, founded on the nearness of the expected day (xiii., 11-14).

Salvation (**xiii., 11**) is here used of perfect security, a final deliverance from the evils of the present age.

The day is at hand (**xiii., 12**).—This is one of the many evidences of Paul's belief in the speedy establishment of the Messianic reign. He uses this as a reason for following the course of conduct which need not be ashamed to appear in the open day.

Put ye on the Lord Jesus Christ (**xiii., 14**).—This expressive figure is used also in Gal. iii., 27, where, however, the putting on of Christ is represented as having taken place at the time of baptism. This shows once more how little Paul is bound by the rigid phraseology of dogmatism. Spiritual life moves from grace to grace.

A section now follows which sets forth the principles that ought to be observed by different parties in the Church towards one another (xiv., 1-xv., 13).

The directions are so pointed and so earnest that Paul was probably aware of some circumstances in Rome which rendered the admonition desirable. It is clear that the bulk of the Church held the freest possible position. They were ready to eat everything, and placed every day upon the same level. They were sure that nothing was unclean of itself, and vaunted their faith which made them superior to silly scruples. On the other hand there were men who were addicted to an ascetic life or the observance of particular days. To what extent these formed a party it is impossible to say; but men of similar tendencies would naturally draw together, and the admonition to receive one another (xv., 7) indicates at least the danger of division. It is generally assumed that these "weak" men were Jews, and this view is supported by the reference to Jews and Gentiles at the end of the discussion; but it is by no means certain, for the ascetic tendency existed far beyond the confines of Judaism. Whatever the precise facts may have been, the principles laid down remain equally clear and important, and admit of wide application. The plea for brotherly communion is supported by two main arguments. First, we must not interfere with the private convictions of others, because we are all immediately responsible to the supreme Judge (xiv., 1-12). Secondly, the conduct complained of is a violation of Christian love (xiv., 13-xv., 13). This forbids us to give needless offence; but we do so when we fail to respect the scruples of a brother. We may virtually destroy him in one of two ways: by driving him out of the Church through his repugnance to our apparent laxity (xiv., 13-18); by inducing him to act against his scruples, while his conscience is not convinced (xiv., 19-23). We further violate love when we do not use our strength for the benefit of the weak in accordance with Christ's example (xv., 1-13).

Not to doubtful disputations (**xiv., 1**), literally, not with a view to decisions of thoughts, which probably means, not to pass judgment on the thoughts of the brother weak in faith.

God hath received him (**xiv., 3**).—Whom God has received we are bound to receive, and have no right to exclude others through personal dislike or owing to conscientious differences of opinion or practice. A church of God must act in accordance with the judgments of God, or it sinks to the level of a private club.

The Lord (**xiv., 4**).—Throughout this passage (except in the quotation in verse 11) I think "the Lord" denotes Christ. This appears from verse 9. Whatever differences there may be, all disciples alike are servants of Christ's and act, according to their several convictions, in reference to him. Living or dead, they are his, and ought to form one fellowship in him.

To this end (**xiv., 9**).—Observe how Christ's lordship is represented as acquired by his death and resurrection. Compare Philip. ii., 9–11.

The judgment-seat of God (**xiv., 10**).—In 2 Cor. v., 10, we read "the judgment-seat of Christ." This is explained by the statement in Rom. ii., 16, that God will judge the secrets of men through Jesus Christ, and in the speech of Paul, in Acts xvii., 31, that God will judge the world by the man whom He has ordained. Here, as he is about to quote from Isaiah xlv., 23, he refers only to the supreme Judge, without reference to His agent.

Am persuaded in the Lord Jesus (**xiv., 14**), that is, as being in communion with Christ, or, as we might say, I am convinced as a Christian.

Happy is he that judgeth not himself in that which he approveth (**xiv., 22**).—This must refer to the danger of doing that which is not clearly sanctioned by conscience. The man of strong faith is happy if his conscience is perfectly satisfied with the freedom of his conduct.

Is condemned (**xiv., 23**), literally, "has been condemned," that is, by his conduct; as we might say, his conduct is reprehensible.

Whatsoever is not of faith is sin (**xiv., 23**).—This means that whatever a man does against his conviction of what is right is sin, although the act, considered in the abstract, may be perfectly innocent. From the use of "faith" in this chapter we learn that it implies a deep and living persuasion ; that, when sufficiently strong, it lifts one to the spiritual point of view of Christ himself, in which merely outward and ceremonial distinctions disappear ; that it may be adequate to produce a genuine Christian life, and yet not strong enough to raise one above all unnecessary scruples.

Bear the infirmities (**xv., 1**).—In connection with the example of Christ compare Matt. viii., 17.

Christ pleased not himself (**xv., 3**).—This appeal to the example of Christ, without reference to any particular event, implies some knowledge of his life on the part of the readers. We can hardly doubt that his life and teaching formed part of the regular instruction in the churches. The quotation is from Ps. lxix., 9.

According to Christ Jesus (**xv., 5**); as we might say, agreeably to our Christian profession. But Paul's phrase is more expressive.

Glorify the God and Father of our Lord Jesus Christ (**xv., 6**).—As Christ's object was to bring men to God, as God was the supreme object of Christian faith, so to glorify God was the chief end of Christian conduct. Where that end is steadily pursued, unity is the result. Our quarrels spring from our seeking a variety of lower ends, and from a secret love of our own glory.

Minister of the circumcision (**xv., 8**).—This is no concession to judaising Christianity, but states the historical fact that Christ lived and taught among the Jews.

Promises, mercy (**xv., 8, 9**). There is no opposition between these, as though the Jews had a claim upon God, while the Gentiles were wholly dependent on His compassion; for the promise was itself an act of grace, and, like grace, stands in antithesis to the law (see Rom. iv., 13 *sqq.*; Gal. iii., 16 *sqq.*), and, on the other hand, the Gentiles were included in the promise (Rom. iv., 17; Gal. iii., 8, 14, 22, 29). The difference, therefore, is historical: the promises were made *to* the fathers of Israel, but *for* the world; and therefore, although the fulfilment of the promise was for all alike, yet the recognition of God's mercy on the part of the Gentiles was something new.

As it is written (**xv., 9**).—The quotations are from Psalm xviii., 49; Deut. xxxii., 43; Psalm cxvii., 1; and Isaiah xi., 10.

The God of hope (**xv., 13**), suggested by the closing word of the last quotation. Hope, which looks to the future, is twin sister of faith, which reposes in the present. Joy and peace wait upon them; and they live in the power of the Holy Spirit of God. With this beautiful benediction the hortatory portion of the Epistle comes to a close.

Having completed the main subject of the Epistle, Paul now adds a section explaining why he has ventured to admonish the Roman Christians, and referring to his past life and his future plans (xv., 14-33).

Filled with all knowledge (**xv., 14**).—It is well to note such hyperbolical phrases, as they show what an insecure basis for dogma is furnished by oriental style. The apology here made refers, I believe, only to the advice just tendered about the strong and weak. It amounts to this: I am sure you do not need my admonition, and that you have yourselves sufficient knowledge to guide you; but as the Apostle of the Gentiles I have ventured to remind you of the principles you profess. The words are an example of delicate courtesy.

A minister, ministering (**xv., 16**).—The noun denotes properly one who fulfils a public office. The participle comes from a different root, and relates to one who discharges a sacred function.

The offering up of the Gentiles (**xv., 16**).—Observe the sacrificial figure.

I have therefore my glory (**xv., 17**).—There may be here some reminiscence of the way in which Paul had been compelled to defend his apostolic authority both in Galatia and in Corinth. But a reference to his labours is part of the title which he pleads to advise Gentiles, and at the same time is his excuse for not having visited Rome at an earlier date. The view that he is excusing himself for intending to visit Rome seems quite contrary to the clear sense of the passage.

Signs and wonders (**xv., 19**), words which are used of miracles. Only miracles of healing, such as frequently accompany depth of religious impression, are ascribed to Paul. He refers to gifts of healing as existing in the

Church (1 Cor. xii., 28), but gives us no particulars about himself.

From Jerusalem, and round about even unto Illyricum (**xv., 19**).—He is referring, not to the initial point of his ministry, but to its extent, and therefore properly selects Jerusalem, where we know from Gal. ii., 2, that he preached his Gospel. We have no record of a visit to Illyricum; but the account in Acts is sometimes very fragmentary, and it has been suggested that there is room for a visit in Acts xx., 1, 2.

Fully preached the Gospel of Christ (**xv., 19**).—Another hyperbole, meaning that no other promising fields were open to him.

That I might not build on another man's foundation (**xv., 20**).—This had been his ambition in the east, and would naturally continue to be so in the west. Nevertheless he was anxious to preach in Rome (i., 11, 15). The natural inference is, not that the words are spurious, but that the church in Rome was not founded by any particular man, but grew up gradually from the influx of Christians into Rome, through the constant communication between the provinces and the capital.

As it is written (**xv., 21**).—The quotation is from Isaiah lii., 15.

A certain contribution for the poor (**xv., 26**).—This is referred to also in 1 Cor. xvi., 1-4; and 2 Cor. viii., ix.

That I may be delivered (**xv., 31**).—It is evident that Paul was aware of the great danger which he would encounter in visiting Jerusalem, and was doubtful about the reception which he had to expect even from "the saints." We may suppose that he was desirous of doing all he could to secure the good-will of the mother Church, and by the interchange of friendly offices prevent a final separation between Judaic and Gentile Christianity.

Together with you find rest (**xv., 32**).—It is evident throughout this passage what complete sympathy Paul expected to find in Rome. There he looked for a haven of rest and peace after his stormy controversies, and before he set his face towards an unknown and distant land.

In a few kindly lines Phœbe is now commended to the hospitality of the Christians in Rome (xvi., 1, 2).

She was a servant or deaconess of the church at Cenchreæ, the eastern port of Corinth, on the Saronic Gulf. She had been a "succourer," or rather patroness, of many, receiving them into her house, and caring for them. Among those who had experienced her kindness was Paul himself. She was probably the bearer of the letter.

This commendation is followed by a great number of salutations (xvi., 3-16).

This list is without example in the rest of Paul's Epistles. The reason probably is that in writing to churches where he knew all the members it would have been invidious to select particular names; whereas in Rome his knowledge was so limited that he was able to send a greeting to all whom he knew either personally or by reputation. Aquila (*vv.* 3, 4) was a Jew of Pontus, who had settled in Rome, from which together with his wife Prisca (or, in the diminutive form, Priscilla) he was driven by the decree of Claudius. They repaired to Corinth, where they became attached to Paul (Acts xviii., 2). With him they proceeded to Ephesus, where he left them (*ib.*, 19; 1 Cor. xvi., 19). We do not know when they "laid down their own necks" for Paul; but it may have been during the riot at Ephesus, and the danger to which they were exposed may have furnished the reason which induced them to return for a time to Rome. Subsequently we find them once more at Ephesus (2 Tim. iv., 19). There is no record of the imprisonment of Andronicus and Junias along with Paul—one more evidence of the fragmentary character of the narrative in Acts. They were "of note among the Apostles," a term used in a wide sense, of those who were sent out as missionaries. The primitive apostolic band is described by Paul as "the twelve" (1 Cor. xv., 5). Those of the household of Aristobulus and of Narcissus (*vv.* 10, 11) were probably slaves in the establishments of wealthy men. It is probable that a large number of the Christians in Rome belonged to the class of slaves or of freedmen.

All the churches of Christ salute you (**xvi., 16**).—Paul ventures to send this unique salutation, knowing what a deep interest was felt by all the churches in the establishment of a Christian community in the metropolis of the empire.

A paragraph is now very unexpectedly inserted, warning the Romans against false teachers (xvi., 17-20).

Paul must have had some reason for dreading the influence of such men, and have thought it well to put his readers on their guard; and as the warning is quite unconnected with the general subject of the Epistle, there was no good place for its insertion before. It is generally assumed that the men referred to were Jewish Christians, simply because Paul's antagonists generally belonged to that class; but there is nothing in the passage itself to suggest this. The plausible and eloquent talk, the love of good feeding, and the implied assumption of wisdom, point rather to Greek adventurers, who, when they had failed elsewhere, sought to impose on the simplicity of the Christians.

The benediction (**xvi., 20**), according to usage, marks the close of the Epistle, so that the remaining verses must be regarded as a postscript.

Greetings from various friends follow (xvi., 21-23). Four of the names, Lucius, Tertius, Gaius, and Quartus, are Latin. Tertius wrote the Epistle, either taking it down from dictation or making a fair copy from the Apostle's less elegant manuscript. He inserts the salutation for himself, and so uses the first person. Gaius, in whose house Paul seems to have been a guest, was probably the disciple of that name whom Paul had baptised (1 Cor. i., 14).

In the ordinary text a benediction is once more inserted (**xvi., 24**). It is omitted by the Revisers in accordance with the best authorities.

The Epistle closes with a long and involved doxology (xvi., 25-27). The genuineness of this is doubted by many able scholars, chiefly on account of the varying way in which it is treated by the manuscripts, some of the best inserting it at the end of chapter xiv., a few giving it in both places, and a few omitting it altogether. The style also shows affinities with that of the later Epistles. The subject is too technical for discussion here, and the reader who desires further information must seek it in larger commentaries. Its presence or absence does not affect our interpretation of the Epistle, and therefore a decision of the question is of subordinate importance.

The revelation of the mystery (**xvi., 25**); that is, the hidden purpose of God, including the calling of the Gentiles (see Eph. iii., 4 *sqq.*), which had been made known in the writings of the Prophets, and now had been made historically manifest in the person and mission of Christ.

To whom (**xvi., 27**).—The insertion of the relative breaks the construction; but it is too well attested for us to omit it. The antecedent is " the only wise God."

The doxology, whether it be from the Apostle's own hand or not, is well suited to the subject of the Epistle, and, though it is not sanctioned by Paul's usual practice, forms, with its concentrated thought and lofty sentiment, a worthy close of this great spiritual treatise.

EPISTLE TO THE PHILIPPIANS.

INTRODUCTION.

THE church at Philippi was, so far as we know, the first Christian church in Europe, certainly the first founded by Paul. In the course of his second missionary journey the Apostle, accompanied by Silas and Timotheus, and, according to the general opinion, by Luke,[1] landed at Neapolis in Thrace, and pressed on over the mountain chain into Macedonia, where Philippi was the first city that they reached.[2] The town derived its name from the father of Alexander the Great; but Augustus, owing to the strength of its position, converted it into a Roman colony, and conferred upon it the *Jus Italicum*, so that at the time of Paul's visit it was under the immediate government of Roman magistrates. We may infer that the Jews were a very small element in the population, for we hear nothing of a synagogue, but only of a place of prayer outside the city, and of an address, not to a mixed congregation, but to the women who assembled there. The only conversion that is mentioned in connection with this Jewish oratory is that of Lydia, who was not a Jewess, but a proselytess from Thyatira. Further, we are told nothing of opposition on the part of Jews, and the severe treatment

---

[1] Acts xv., 40; xvi., 3, 11; xvii., 14, 15.
[2] Acts xvi., 12, where πρώτη probably refers to position, not to distinction, Thessalonica being the capital. See Lightfoot's note, *Philip.*, p. 49.

of Paul and Silas was due entirely to Gentile complaints. We may reasonably conclude that at its foundation the church was exclusively Gentile, and that if, at a later time, it was a mixed society of Gentiles and Jews, the latter certainly did not form an important section of its members.

There is hardly room for doubt that the Epistle to the Philippians was written in Rome. Paul was a prisoner in bonds,[1] and felt uncertain whether the imprisonment might not end with his death.[2] That the loss of liberty was not of very recent date is apparent not only from the wavering between confident hope of release[3] and the resigned anticipation of death,[4] but from the effects which are attributed to his bonds, both among the general public and among the brethren.[5] This state of things points unmistakably to the one long imprisonment, first in Cæsarea and then in Rome. That the lattter was the place where the Epistle was composed is indicated by the allusion to "Cæsar's household,"[6] an expression which comprises the whole of the imperial establishment, including the great retinue of slaves, amongst whom, in all probability, the converts to Christianity were found. The reference to the Prætorium[7] points in the same direction; for though the governor's residence at Cæsarea is described by that term,[8] the language in the Epistle seems to imply something more extensive and important. In Rome the word was used to denote, not a residence, but the body of imperial guards[9]; and as Paul was in the custody of the Prefect of the Prætorian cohorts,[10] he must have had opportunities of exercising his personal influence over a large number of soldiers, to one of whom he was chained day and

---

[1] i., 7, 13, 14, 16.
[2] i., 20–24; ii., 17, 18; iii., 10.
[3] i., 25, 26; ii., 24.
[4] i., 21, 23; ii., 17.
[5] i., 12–18.
[6] iv., 22.
[7] i., 13.
[8] Acts xxiii., 35.
[9] See this established by Lightfoot, *Philippians*, pp. 97 *sqq.*
[10] Acts xxviii., 16.

night. Thus all the circumstances suit Rome as the place of composition.

It is less easy to determine the date. Some would place it as late as possible, so as to leave time for Paul's influence to make itself felt in Rome, and on account of his apparent loneliness, none of his old companions being mentioned except Timothy.[1] Accordingly, on the supposition that Paul perished in the Neronian persecution, the Epistle was written shortly before that event, at the end of 63 or early in 64 A.D., and must be regarded as the last of the Epistles of the imprisonment. Lightfoot, on the contrary, makes it the earliest in the series, on the ground that " in style and tone, as well as in its prominent ideas, it bears a much greater resemblance to the earlier letters than do the Epistles to the Colossians and Ephesians," and that the latter Epistles, especially that to the Ephesians, " exhibit an advanced stage in the development of the Church." The arguments on the other side are not, he thinks, very weighty ; for there was a flourishing Christian community at Rome before Paul's arrival, and this may have included members of Cæsar's household ; and there is actually an allusion to Paul's companions in the expression " the brethren with me salute you," followed as this is by the words " all the saints salute you."[2] Some time undoubtedly must have elapsed to allow messages to pass between Rome and Philippi ; but a very few months at most would have sufficed for this purpose.[3] These reasons may determine our judgment ; but after all the difference of date is not considerable, and does not affect in any way the purport of the Epistle.[4] A changed view of Pauline chronology would oblige us, as in the case of other Epistles, to place the date somewhat earlier.

[1] ii., 19, 20. [2] iv., 21, 22.
[3] See the question discussed in Lightfoot, *Philippians*, pp. 29-45.
[4] The Epistle is of course placed earlier by those who set back the whole chronology of Paul's life.

The brethren at Philippi, having heard of Paul's arrival in Rome, had sent Epaphroditus thither with a present, to relieve his necessities, and to manifest their sympathy with him in his affliction. This "Apostle" of the Church, Paul's "fellow-worker and fellow-soldier," was sick nigh unto death while he was in Rome; and on his recovery Paul thought it well to send him back to Philippi, where his friends had been rendered anxious by the news of his illness. These events furnished the occasion for the letter, which is therefore not adapted to any particular subject or group of subjects, but is an informal outpouring of affection and gratitude, giving a short account of the state of affairs in Rome, and containing such admonitions as seemed likely to be useful. Everything is of course surveyed through the medium of that Gospel to which Paul's life was consecrated, and some of his great thoughts respecting righteousness by faith, and the lowliness and exaltation of Christ, are brought in to give emphasis to his advice, but are not expressed with the clearness and fulness that we could desire. As was natural in the case of one who had to depend on the reports of others for his knowledge of what was going on, whose heart was sick with deferred hope, and the issue of whose trial was becoming more and more uncertain, his feelings fluctuated, and things now appeared more prosperous and again more gloomy, now it seemed that the majority were emboldened to speak the word without fear,[1] and again that all were seeking their own affairs, not the things of Jesus Christ.[2] Joy and sorrow, hope and apprehension, confidence in the success of the Gospel and weeping for those who were enemies of the cross, quiet anticipation of being with Christ and a humble sense that he had not yet attained and was not yet perfect, alternate in the Epistle.[3] But on the whole the

---

[1] i., 14.   [2] ii., 21.
[3] See i., 4, 18; ii., 17; iv., 10; ii., 27; iv., 14; i., 12-18; iii., 18; i., 23; iii., 11-14.

note of joy is dominant. The Apostle had learnt to be "self-sufficing,"[1] not in the proud sense of the fashionable Stoicism, but through the power of one who strengthened him.[2] The Lord was at hand[3]; and in the midst of his trouble he still expected a Saviour from the heavens,[4] and believed that all would be well in the "day of Jesus Christ,"[5]—a trust not destined to be realised in the form in which it presented itself to the Apostle, but doubtless in some grander form, which eye has not seen, nor ear heard.

Notwithstanding the unartificial character of this Epistle, its suitability to the supposed circumstances of Paul and of his readers, and its general agreement with Pauline thought and style, its genuineness does not remain unchallenged. It was denied by Baur, and his attack was followed up by other writers. Replies were not wanting even on the part of those who claim to be members of the critical school, among whom Hilgenfeld may be especially mentioned, and I think the result at the present day is that the genuineness is accepted by the majority of critics, and is rejected only by a few who occupy what may fairly be called an extreme position. In this conclusion we may be content to acquiesce.

[1] iv., 11. [2] iv., 13. [3] iv., 5. [4] iii., 20. [5] i., 6, 10; ii., 16.

PHILIPPIANS.

ANALYSIS.

I. EXPRESSION OF THANKFULNESS AND LOVE TOWARDS THE READERS, AND PRAYER FOR THEM, i., 3-11.

II. PAUL'S CONDITION, AND THE SUCCESS OF THE GOSPEL AT ROME, AND EXPECTATIONS IN REGARD TO THE FUTURE, i., 12-26.

III. EXHORTATIONS, i., 27-ii., 18.
  1. To strive harmoniously for the Gospel, whether Paul should come or not, i., 27-30.
  2. To be of one mind, and not factious, enforced by an appeal to their Christian experience, ii., 1-4.
  3. Further enforced by an appeal to the example of Christ, ii., 5-11.
  4. Consequently, to be obedient and blameless, ii., 12-18.

IV. HE HOPES TO SEND TIMOTHY SHORTLY, AND IS SENDING EPAPHRODITUS AT ONCE, ii., 19-30.

V. A FURTHER SERIES OF EXHORTATIONS, iii., 1-iv., 9.
  1. Warning against Jewish opponents and worldly-minded men, and appeal to Paul's example in embracing the righteousness of faith, iii., 1-iv., 1.
     a. Description of the opponents, and contrast between their principle and that of Christianity, iii., 1-16.
     b. Exhortation to follow Paul in the heavenly life, for many set a bad example, iii., 17-21.
     c. Concluding exhortation to stand fast, iv., 1.
  2. Admonitions to individuals, iv., 2, 3.
  3. Concluding exhortations arising out of the foregoing, iv., 4-9.

VI. THANKS FOR THE GIFT, iv., 10-20.

CONCLUSION, iv., 21-23. Greetings and benediction.

PHILIPPIANS.

COMMENTARY.

The Epistle, as usual, opens with an address and greeting (i., 1, 2).

Paul unites Timothy with himself (see note on 1 Thess. i., 1); but from the third verse he writes in the first person singular, and in ii., 19 speaks of sending Timothy to them; so that there can be no question of joint authorship. "Servants," or rather "slaves," is correlative to the title "Lord" applied to Jesus, and may refer here particularly to the ministry in which Paul and Timothy were engaged. The term "Apostle" is absent, as in 1 Thess. i., 1, which see. For "saints" see Rom. i., 7. For the meaning of the salutation see Gal. i., 3.

Bishops and deacons (i., 1).—It is probable that these are specified because the contribution from the church came through their hands. It is impossible to discuss here the various questions which are suggested by the presence of these words. I can only ask the reader to observe that there is a plurality of bishops, or "superintendents"; that they, along with the deacons or "ministers," are evidently a recognised body of men, though the absence of the article in the Greek seems to show that the body was still rather indefinite; that they are not mentioned in the enumeration of church offices, in 1 Cor. xii., 8-10 and 28, Eph. iv., 11; and lastly, that there is no reference to presbyters.

After the greeting, Paul pours out his feelings of affection for his readers in a thanksgiving, and expression of his confidence and love towards them, and a prayer for their further growth (i., 3-11).

All my remembrance (i., 3): not "every remembrance," as in the Authorised Version. He remembered nothing that was not a fit subject for thanksgiving.

On behalf of you all (i., 4).—The Revisers apparently intend to connect these words with "in every supplication of mine," in which case the meaning is that whenever Paul prayed for the Philippians he did so with joy. The Greek, however, allows us to connect them with the following words; and then the sense is that in all his prayers Paul joyfully included the Philippians. The latter seems on the whole to yield the better sense, and avoids some awkwardness in the expression and an undue emphasis on the "joy."

For your fellowship (i., 5).—We must connect these words with "I thank," which otherwise has no object. The reference is probably to their fellowship with one another, through their common interest in the Gospel; and this inward harmony had been unbroken since the church was founded. In some other churches it had not been so. We should not, however, exclude fellowship with Paul himself, for this is referred to in verse 7.

He (i., 6); that is, God. It is here implied that, whatever human conditions there may be, the initiation and the completion of the higher spiritual life are from God.

The day of Jesus Christ (i., 6) refers to the time of the second coming. It is evident that Paul still regards it as not very far off.

To be thus minded (i., 7), to have the confidence of which he has just spoken. He ought to have it because they are so close to his heart, bound to him in the ties of Christian love; and they are so, because they have fellowship with him in the grace which begins and perfects the good work.

I have you in my heart (i., 7).—The translation in the margin, "ye have me in your heart," seems to me quite inadmissible.

God is my witness (i., 8).—This expression arises simply

from the strength of Paul's feeling, for there is no evidence of any cloud of suspicion between him and members of the church. The case is different in 2 Cor. i., 23. Compare Rom. i., 9.

The tender mercies of Christ (i., 8).—His love for them was more than mere natural affection. Christ's was the great heart from which the heart of Paul derived its life-beats.

Your love (i., 9); not to be confined to their love for one another. Christian love is a permanent and pervasive quality of character, ready, like light, to shine on every object that comes within its sphere. Yet such love is not without discernment. On the contrary, it looks straight into the real nature of its objects, and in proportion to its purity gets nearer to the Divine point of view, and sees things in their true relations.

Approve the things that are excellent (i., 10).—Here, I think, the marginal translation (which is quite admissible) is better. It is suggested by the prayer for "discernment," and the approval of things that are excellent is a very ordinary virtue. The reference is to the fine distinctions of considerate conduct which are visible only to the highest love. The same phrase occurs in Rom. ii., 18, where, however we translate it, it is used with some degree of irony.

Void of offence (i., 10).—The only other place where Paul uses the Greek word is 1 Cor. x., 32, where it is translated, "give no occasion of stumbling." This is probably the meaning here, the avoidance of such occasions being part of the discernment of love.

After this introductory expression of his regard for the Philippians, Paul goes on to speak of his personal affairs, and his expectations for the future (i., 12–26).

I would have you know (i., 12), correcting an opinion which they might naturally have entertained, that his imprisonment must interfere with the progress of the Gospel. It had just the opposite effect.

Manifest in Christ (i., 13) ; that is, it became well known that he was in bonds, not for any crime, but in the cause of Christ.

Prætorian guard (i., 13).—These were a select body of troops, numbering at this time ten thousand, who were stationed at Rome, and formed the imperial guard. As he was in the custody of the Prætorians, and constantly kept chained to one of them, he may have known several of them personally, and his case would become a subject of conversation among the men.

All the rest (i., 13): all others with whom he was brought into contact ; not necessarily all the other inhabitants of Rome.

Confident through my bonds (i., 14).—" In the Lord " may be connected with " being confident " ; but whether we adopt this connection or not, the meaning must be, not that the brethren trusted in his bonds, but that, instead of being discouraged by them, they were emboldened to run all risks for the Gospel, so that in this way too the good work was furthered.

Some indeed (i., 15).—These seem clearly to be an exception to the majority just spoken of. Their motives are envy and strife and a desire to afflict Paul ; and these can hardly be ascribed to the brethren referred to in verse 14. Nevertheless " some also of [or, on account of] good-will " (towards Paul and the Gospel) points back to these brethren, who are here limited to " some " in order to make the clause parallel with the preceding. Who these envious people were is not stated, and it is a pure assumption that they were Judaisers. Paul is apparently satisfied with their preaching, and only objects to its motive. They were most likely fussy and ambitious men, who did not like being overshadowed by the great Apostle.

The one do it of love (i., 16).—This translation makes the passage tautological. I prefer, therefore, the equally admissible rendering, "Those who act from love do it, knowing, etc., but those who act from faction proclaim Christ, not sincerely," imagining that they will afflict me.

Therein I rejoice (i., 18), literally, "in this," that is, in the proclamation of Christ, from whatever motive. As the punctuation of ancient writings is a matter of editorial discretion, I should prefer placing a full stop at the first "rejoice," and a semicolon at the second. Paul, then, taking up the word, turns to the future, "Yea, and I will rejoice; for I know." "*This*" in verse 19 need not then have the same reference as "this" ("therein") in verse 18, which would hardly yield a good sense, but may include all that he has said about his bonds: whatever was happening to him in Rome would turn to his salvation, his participation in the Messianic kingdom.

Supply of the Spirit (i., 19).—This may mean, the supply which the Spirit gives; but then we naturally ask, the supply of what? I think, therefore, it is better to understand the Spirit as that which is supplied, and which Paul hoped to receive in ever-increasing measure. Compare Gal. iii., 5.

Put to shame (i., 20), proved to be an idle dream. The opposite to this was that Christ should be magnified in that very body which was worn with bonds, and might soon, if the trial proved unfavourable, be doomed to death.

To live is Christ (i., 21).—The context shows that "to live" refers, not to the principle of life, but to continuance in life. The condensed expression, therefore, must mean that to continue in life would be a complete devotion of himself to the service of Christ. He could wish nothing better; yet to die would be a personal gain, a release from his bonds, and a closer personal union with Christ.

If this is the fruit of my work (i., 22).—The construction of this verse is uncertain, and the sense rather obscure. The meaning may probably be given thus: It would be a gain to me to die; but if my continuing in life involves fruit springing from my prolonged work, I may well hesitate in expressing a choice. The word rendered "I wot" always signifies, in the New Testament, "I make known." So it may be here, "I make no declaration."

I know that I shall abide (i., 25).—This is simply an expression of trustful assurance; but when Paul wrote the words, he must have thought that his acquittal seemed probable. Whether his expectation was ever realised we do not know. The evidence is uncertain, and opinion is divided.

Your glorying (i., 26), properly, the matter of your glorying, that which gives you occasion to glory. He wishes that this may abound in him through his renewed presence, when he can minister still further to their faith. "*In Christ Jesus*" expresses the spiritual domain within which the abounding must take place.

Paul now proceeds to give some admonitions, which, we must suppose, were suggested by the circumstances of the church (i., 27-ii., 18).

First he exhorts his readers to be worthy of the Gospel, and, whether he came to them or not, to stand fast, and strive harmoniously for the faith (i., 27-30).

Let your manner of life (i., 27); literally, "behave as citizens," a figure borrowed from the Roman citizenship, of which the Philippians, as a Roman colony, would naturally be proud. It is also better suited to the context than the usual "walk," as it suggests a united and organised life, directed by common interests.

In one spirit (i., 27).—The word "spirit" is here obviously used quite in our modern sense to denote the disposition or tone of mind. "Soul" has the same kind of impersonal sense, and is descriptive of the thoughts and feelings. Both are used elsewhere in a personal sense, of the individual seat of the higher affections and perceptions, and of the lower intellectual and sensitive life.

The faith of the Gospel (i., 27).—The Greek words might mean "faith in the Gospel," but here probably signify the faith proclaimed by the Gospel.

The adversaries (i., 28).—There is no occasion to limit these to Jews, even though their attack might be most likely to cause some division in the church. Towards Gentile opponents also it was necessary to present a united front, and divisions among Christians are not, and were not, due solely to the presence of both Jews and Gentiles in the church. Here there is no reference to any doctrinal difference, but only to such divisions as are caused by temper and ambition.

That from God (i., 28).—The gender in the Greek shows that "that" refers, not to "salvation," but to the whole previous clause.

It hath been granted (i., 29).—It was a gift of grace (for this is the meaning of the word) to suffer for Christ. This confirmed and deepened their love.

To suffer in his behalf (i., 29).—The construction is precisely the same as when it is said that Christ died or suffered for (on behalf of) men.

Saw in me (i., 30), when he was at Philippi, where he was scourged and imprisoned. Of his conflict in Rome they knew by hearsay.

He continues the same subject, supporting his plea by an earnest appeal to their Christian experience (ii., 1-4).

Comfort (ii., 1).—The word also means "exhortation," which seems better here: If there is anything in Christ which still exhorts you to be worthy of him.

Consolation (ii., 1): better, "persuasion," "if love has any persuasive power to move you to concord" (Vincent).

Spirit (ii., 1).—In the absence of the article in the Greek I doubt whether the reference is (at least directly) to the Holy Spirit. It rather refers to the "one spirit" of i., 27, the common participation in which would bind them together in brotherly union. It is quite true, however, that this points to the communion of the Holy Spirit.

That ye be (ii., 2).—This is an exhortation, depending on what is implied, though not actually expressed, in the foregoing.

Of the same mind . . . of one mind (ii., 2).—We may perhaps distinguish these by making the former refer to their entertaining the same feelings towards one another, the latter to their all having that unity of sentiment which was involved in the unity of the Gospel and of the Church.

Faction or vainglory (ii., 3).—We must suppose that the church required this exhortation, and undoubtedly the feelings which are condemned might arise between Jewish and Gentile Christians. But differences of principle do not necessarily imply factiousness, and the words contain no evident allusion to any deep-seated division, but only to petty jealousies and conceited claims.

His own things (ii., 4), his own superior advantages. By looking only at oneself, and not at others, one gets an exaggerated idea of one's own importance.

This exhortation is enforced by an appeal to the example of Christ (ii., 5-11).

This passage presents great difficulties, and commentators are by no means agreed as to its interpretation. If we only knew what Paul had already taught the Philippians, our course would be easier; for then we could divine what meaning they would naturally attach to his words. But in the absence of this knowledge, it is almost inevitable for each expositor to assume that his own doctrinal prepossessions were in the minds of the first readers of the Epistle, and therefore furnish the key to the interpretation. In relation to a passage which has been so largely used for dogmatic purposes no one can be absolutely free from bias, and we can only do our best to interpret it from the point of view of pure criticism, bearing in mind that the one function of a commentator is to find out what the Apostle meant. It is impossible, in the present instance, to pursue our task without recourse to the Greek; but for the benefit of those unacquainted with Greek I venture first to suggest the following paraphrase:—Have the humble and self-renouncing mind which you know was in Christ; who, though he was spiritually the image of God, did not think that the being on an equality with God consisted of selfish grasping, but emptied himself of all self-regarding claims and advantages, and assumed the image of a slave, being among us as one that served, and made like the common run of men; and being found in his outward fashion as an ordinary man he humbled himself, and was submissive to the will of God, even to the extreme of dying on the cross. Wherefore also God highly exalted him.

Our first question is, what is meant by "Christ Jesus"? A common, though by no means universal, answer is that the name denotes the eternal Son of God, or at least some heavenly being, in his state prior to the incarnation. The objection to this is the same as that which has been advanced in 2 Cor. viii., 9, that both Christ and Jesus are historical names, and that Paul would naturally have used the term "Son of God," with which he was familiar, if he was referring to a pre-existent condition. The force of this consideration is admitted by several interpreters of unquestioned orthodoxy; and it seems to me decisive, unless the remainder of the passage makes it impossible. So far, however, is this from being the case that in the last verse "Jesus Christ" seems clearly used of the historical person, and it is not likely that it is employed in two different senses within the same passage. We may add that in verse 7 "the form of a slave" is mentioned before "the likeness of men," and this fact suggests that the latter expression does not refer to the incarnation. Some have imagined that the word ὑπάρχων implies pre-existence, and the English Revisers say in the margin that the Greek means "being originally." There is nothing in the usage of the word to justify this notion, and it may be sufficient to refer to the following passages:—Luke viii., 41, ἄρχων τῆς συναγωγῆς ὑπῆρχε; Acts xvii., 29, γένος οὖν ὑπάρχοντες τοῦ θεοῦ; 1 Cor. xi., 7, ἀνὴρ ... εἰκὼν καὶ δόξα θεοῦ ὑπάρχων; and Gal. ii., 14, εἰ σὺ Ἰουδαῖος ὑπάρχων. In none of these instances do the Revisers add a marginal note.

"Being in the form of God" cannot refer to material shape, for this would be quite inconsistent with the spirituality of Paul's conceptions. The word "form" (μορφή) was current among philosophers, and Paul may use it here to some extent in a philosophical sense. In relation to material objects it was the form which was determined by the ideal, the "informing" essence, without which the objects would have been mere indistinguishable lumps of matter. When transferred to immaterial things, it must similarly denote that which expresses their essence, and, as the shape in this case is quite ideal, it must be nearly synonymous with the essence itself. So here the reference must be to some form of manifestation which expressed the essence of God. This, however, does not identify Christ with God, from whom he is most clearly distinguished throughout the passage. If the God-idea (so to speak) dwelt within him, he would be in the form of God. And now the question arises whether this form expresses the metaphysical or the moral and spiritual essence of God. Unfortunately Paul does not use the word except in the present passage; but he occasionally uses cognate words, which I think may determine its meaning here. In this Epistle (iii., 10) we read, συμμορφιζόμενος τῷ θανάτῳ αὐτοῦ, "becoming conformed unto his death." These words are not simply figurative, describing a moral dying to sin. Nevertheless they are charged with ethical meaning; for otherwise the two thieves, and all crucified men, were more conformed to Christ's death than Paul. The fellowship of Christ's sufferings does not mean enduring pain like his, but suffering in his spirit, and in the same cause; and so conformity to his death is confronting death with the same trust and the same love, even though its outward incidents may be quite different. Farther on (iii., 21) are the words "who shall fashion anew [μετασχηματίσει] the body of our humiliation, that it may be conformed [σύμμορφον] to the body of his glory." Here the former expression denotes a change of outward condition, but the latter goes much deeper, and refers to an inward and spiritual change which will make the body an expressive organ of the Divine glory. In Gal. iv., 19, Paul writes, "I am again in travail until Christ be formed [μορφωθῇ] in you." The whole connection points to a spiritual change, the inward growth of the life and spirit of Christ. In Rom. xii., 2, "Be ye transformed [μεταμορφοῦσθε] by the renewing of your mind" obviously indicates a change in the moral aims, and not in the natural substance of the mind; and still more profoundly spiritual is the sense in 2 Cor. iii., 18, "we are transformed [μεταμορφούμεθα] into the same image." And lastly, the consummation of the Christian hope is expressed, in Rom. viii., 29, in these words, "to be conformed [συμμόρφους] to the image of His Son," that is, to have the same all-controlling filial spirit, raising us into the perfect brotherhood of the children of God. This usage seems sufficient to justify us in looking for a spiritual meaning in the present passage. Jesus was in the form of God, not through identity of metaphysical essence, but through participation in the Divine Spirit of Love, giving to his soul, as it were, the Divine impress, and making him supreme among men through the perfection of his communion with God.[1]

The translation and the meaning of the following clause are much disputed. The Authorised Version renders it, "thought it not robbery to be equal with God," suggesting a sense which has been often accepted, that Christ, being in his essential nature God, thought he was not committing robbery in being equal with God. Thus the clause becomes a vapid truism, and forms no antithesis with what follows; and moreover it has no connection with the sentiment of the passage. The English Revisers translate, "counted it not a prize." If this means that Christ did not think being on an equality with God was a thing to be prized and treasured, the sentiment is so immoral that one must hesitate before attributing it to the Apostle. It certainly does not represent the spirit of him who taught his disciples to be perfect as their Father in heaven is perfect. But if, in order to escape from this objection, it be said that the equality here referred to is an equality in grandeur and dignity, the conception is founded on a low anthropomorphism, and is opposed to the central idea of the whole passage, which is to show that the truly Divine does not consist of outward grandeur and dignity.

In any case, whatever is Divine is good, and ought to be prized. It may perhaps have been owing to these difficulties, as well as to a conviction of the proper sense of the word ἁρπαγμός, that the American Revisers have translated, "counted not the being on an equality with God a thing to be grasped." With this rendering the meaning would seem to be that equality with God was something higher than being in the form of God, although one who was in that form might natur-

[1] Ellicott quotes in another connection, in his note on Gal. iii., 28, an instructive sentence from Œcumenius, τῷ ἕνα τύπον καὶ μίαν μορφὴν ἐνδεδύσθαι, τὴν τοῦ Χριστοῦ.

ally aspire to it; and that then Christ, instead of grasping at it, emptied himself, and ultimately received it as a reward for his humility and suffering. This gives a coherent sense; but there are two objections to it. First, "the being on an equality with God" seems, from the structure of the sentence, to be, if not equivalent to at least involved in, "being in the form of God," and to point, therefore, to an equality which Jesus actually possessed. And secondly, in this interpretation the equality can refer only to outward rank and power, which might be the objects of a grasping ambition, and not to spiritual perfection, which does not appeal to the rapacious instincts.

Can we, then, find any other way of understanding the clause, which will better satisfy the requirements of the passage? Ἁρπαγμός, agreeably to its termination, ought to have an active, and not a passive, sense. The Greek interpreters, indeed, give it a passive meaning; and there is sufficient analogy in the usage of other words to justify them in doing so. The word is of such rare occurrence in non-Christian writings that it is impossible to feel certain of its ordinary acceptation; but the two instances which are cited demand the active meaning.[1] Adopting this we may translate, "did not think the being on an equality with God was grasping," seizing everything, the kingdoms of the world and the glory of them, for himself.

For the construction with two substantives, of which one is predicative of the other, we may refer to Philip. iii., 7, 8; Heb. xi., 26; 2 Peter ii., 13, iii., 15; and to the classical instances adduced by Cremer (under ἁρπαγμός) we may add Lysias, *Oratio Funebris*, 13, πατρίδα τὴν ἀρετὴν ἡγησάμενοι. For the sentiment we may compare its opposite in 1 Tim. vi., 5, νομιζόντων πορισμὸν εἶναι τὴν εὐσέβειαν, "thinking that piety was making gain."

In order to understand fully the meaning thus reached, we must notice the words τὸ εἶναι ἴσα Θεῷ, "the being on an equality with God." Ἴσα is adverbial, and can hardly be the same as ἴσος. It denotes, not to be absolutely equal, but to be on an equality in certain respects[2]; and here the equality must be that which is involved in

---

[1] See Cremer, *Biblisch-theologisches Wörterbuch*.

[2] In the LXX. we have, ἐτύρωσας δέ με ἴσα τυρῷ (Job x., 10; see also xi., 12), and πρώτην φωνὴν τὴν ὁμοίαν πᾶσιν ἴσα κλαίων (Wisdom vii., 3). These constructions, however, are not strictly analogous. Theodoret treats the word as equivalent to ἴσος throughout his commentary on the passage, and in other places.

"being in the form of God," that spiritual perfection, as the Father is perfect, which Jesus sets before his disciples as the ideal goal of mankind. It is a question of the highest moment, what does this equality consist of? What is the Divine perfection towards which we are to strive? Is it selfish grasping, as is the way of the great ones, "the divine Julius" and others, who exercise lordship over the nations (see Matt. xx., 25, with the parallels), or self-renouncing and redeeming love? Here we have the thought of Jesus on the subject; and more than the thought, the act, the realisation of the Divine in humanity through absolute self-renunciation. The way to equality with God is the way of the cross, wherein no self-will obstructs the working of the Spirit of God, and it is the life of God which becomes manifest in the life of man.[1]

"But emptied himself, taking the form of a slave," now forms a true and strong antithesis to ἁρπαγμόν. Instead of seizing everything for himself, he kept nothing for himself, but became the slave of mankind. The usual explanation, that he forsook the form of God, and renounced his equality, subverts the whole sentiment of the passage, which finds equality with God in the emptying of self, the form of God in the form of the slave, who dies to redeem his brothers. "Whosoever will be first among you, let him be your slave; as the son of man came, not to be ministered unto, but to minister." Jesus was no less the Lord of his disciples when he washed their feet; and the son of man was glorified, and God was glorified in him, when the traitor went forth to betray him to his doom. The expression, "the form of a slave," is used because Jesus was not literally a slave: he lived out of the inner spirit of service, and his outward life was shaped accordingly. It is also in contrast with "the form of God"; he who was in the form of God came in the form of a slave,—a thing so contrary to the ordinary apprehension of men.

"Being made in the likeness of men" is generally understood of the incarnation; but there are several objections to this. First, it is a very unusual way of expressing the assumption of human nature; and, in fact, it does not express it. Secondly, if understood of the

---

[1] Origen perceived this. He says: "We must venture to affirm that the goodness of Christ appears greater and more Divine, and truly after the image of the Father, when 'he humbled himself' . . . than if he had supposed that the being on an equality with God was ἁρπαγμός" (*Com. in Joan.*, tom. i., 37, p. 72 Lom.).

entrance of Jesus Christ upon the earthly scene, it naturally implies that he assumed the appearance of a man, but was not really human; and we have no reason for imputing such a docetic view to Paul. To say no more, the whole of his argument founded on the resurrection of Christ would be futile. Thirdly, instead of the plural "men" we should expect rather the generic singular. Lastly, this clause would properly precede the one which it actually follows, "taking the form of a slave." This union of ideas suggests another interpretation. The word ἄνθρωπος, though it stands for the genus man, is often used in a derogatory sense, and is thus contrasted with ἀνήρ. Examples are given in the dictionaries, but a few instances may be cited:—ὅτι πολλοὶ μὲν ἄνθρωποι εἶεν, ὀλίγοι δὲ ἄνδρες (Herodot., VII., 210); ὁ τοῦτο ποιῶν οὐκέτ' ἀνήρ ἐστιν, ἀλλὰ σκευοφόρος (Xen., *Cyrop.*, IV., ii., 25); πῶς ἐγὼ ἀλλαντοπώλης ὢν ἀνήρ γενήσομαι; (Aristoph., *Equit.*, 178 *sq.*). Stephanus quotes from Xenophon, ἄνδρες καὶ οὐκ ἔτι ἄνθρωποι μόνον νομιζόμενοι. Ἡ ἄνθρωπος is used of servants, or women of ill-repute (frequently in Lysias, *e.g.*, διὰ πόρνην καὶ δούλην ἄνθρωπον, *De Vuln Præm.*, 3). This depreciating sense is not unknown to Paul. To speak κατὰ ἄνθρωπον (Rom. iii., 5; 1 Cor. ix., 8; Gal. iii., 15) is to speak in a way that might seem beneath his own thought or the dignity of his subject. To "fight with beasts κατὰ ἄνθρωπον" (1 Cor. xv., 32) is to fight like any common man. To "walk κατὰ ἄνθρωπον" (1 Cor. iii., 3) is to fall below the level of one's Christian profession, and yield to vulgar human passion; and this, finally, is expressed by the question, "are ye not men?" (*ib.*, 4), that is, do you not sink back into the common herd? So, in the present passage, the clause before us may mean, as we should say, "being made like one of the crowd." And surely it is a great and significant fact, and one precisely suited to the sentiment which Paul is enforcing, that this man in the form of God was by no outward likeness distinguishable from the mass of men, but moved among them with Divine simplicity, the friend and servant of all.

A similar explanation will apply to the succeeding clause, "being found in fashion as a man." This use of the word "found" is frequent in Paul (see 1 Cor. iv., 2, xv., 15; 2 Cor. v., 3, xi., 12, xii., 20; Gal. ii., 17; Philip. iii., 9). It suggests the idea of an inspection or a looking for: men looked for the world's Redeemer, and found him in the garb of an ordinary, suffering man. Ὡς ἄνθρωπος does not imply that he was not truly human, but only wore the semblance of a man. Cyril of Jerusalem says, ἡμεῖς μὲν ταῦτα, ὡς ἄνθρωποι,

... παραγγέλλομεν (*Procatechesis*, xvii.). Nevertheless the clause as a whole implies that the fashion, the outward appearance, was different from what the common standard of judgment would lead one to expect. This man, alone among men in the fulness of a Divine humanity, was a humble carpenter of Nazareth, by the great ones of the world despised, to the high priest a blasphemer, to the Roman governor an innocent but fanatical fool, whose life was not worth considering. But "he that humbleth himself shall be exalted," and to men of the deepest soul he has become "the power of God, and the wisdom of God." We must not look on the exaltation as some external grandeur conferred upon him as a reward, for this would violate the very lesson which the passage is intended to teach. It is one of the Divine paradoxes of Christianity that humility and obedience and death constitute life and lordship; and for Jesus to have grasped at the earthly trappings of power would have been to cast off "the form of God," and forfeit his spiritual lordship for ever. The "name" which God "gave unto him" seems proven by the context to be "the name of Jesus"; but as this name was not first given to him after his death, the meaning, though not quite accurately expressed, must be that his name was made the greatest among names. Others think the name is "Lord."

Doing anything "in the name of Jesus" signifies, elsewhere, acting under his acknowledged influence and leadership, and I see no reason for departing from the usual meaning here. (See John xiv., 13, 14, xv., 16, xvi., 23, 24, 26; 1 Cor. v., 4, vi., 11; Eph. v., 20; Col. iii., 17; 2 Thess. iii., 6.)

Paul's universe is divided into heaven and earth and the regions under the earth. The persons (not "things") dwelling in these several parts are angels, men, and the souls of the departed. The universe thus conceived is a mere speck in the view of our modern knowledge, and the first and third terms, conceived as the abode of intelligent beings, have utterly vanished. The enormous change in the knowledge of the outward scene may affect our metaphysics, and must completely obliterate the pictorial imagination under which Paul conceived the history and destiny of man; but the great spiritual lessons of the Gospel are not dependent upon time and space. The heavenly courts, with their choirs of worshipping angels, are gone; but Love is still Divine, and he who is lowliest in the service of mankind is still the most lordly; and this confession, which is truly made and felt only under the guidance of the Spirit, is still to the glory of God the Father.

Fidelity to this great example is now enforced in the Apostle's most affectionate manner (ii., 12-18).

So then (ii., **12**), as a consequence of what has just been said: as Christ was obedient and humble, so ought you to be, and never murmur against the will of God.

Not as in my presence only (ii., **12**) belongs to the following exhortation: they were to be even more obedient in his absence than they had been in his presence.

For it is God which worketh in you (ii., **13**).—It is evident that Paul here attributes some power to the human will. The disciples were to work out their own salvation with that reverent fear which men feel when they undertake some great enterprise in which they may possibly fail. But they are encouraged thus to work with self-distrusting zeal by the reflection that they are co-operating with God. The work is His; and the strength of will and hand is derived from Him, though He does not compel men to act, and they may refuse to put forth the energy which it is theirs to give or to withhold. God works in order to fulfil His good pleasure in the salvation of His children. As Christ himself said, it is their Father's good pleasure to give them the Kingdom (Luke xii., 32).

Murmurings and disputings (ii., **14**).—The connection shows that the immediate reference is to murmuring against God, and disputatious reasoning about the requirements of His will.

Children of God without blemish, etc. (ii., **15**).—This is borrowed, though not exactly quoted, from Deut. xxxii., 5.

Lights in the world (ii., **15**).—The comparison is to the heavenly luminaries; so that "the world" here may be used in its physical sense, the ordered universe.

That I may have (ii., 16) implies a motive. The Greek indicates rather the tendency and result of the required conduct.

If I am offered upon the sacrifice and service of your faith (ii., 17).—It is not easy to discover any sense in the idea of making an offering upon a "service" or ministration. Instead of "upon," therefore, we must translate "in addition to." The word translated "offered" means "poured out as a libation." According to the figure, then, the Philippians are represented as ministering priests, who offer their faith as a sacrifice; and Paul says that, if in addition to this his blood is shed as a libation, he will rejoice. Others look upon Paul himself as the priest who offers up the faith of the Philippians, and who, in addition, is ready to shed his blood.

Rejoice with me (ii., 18).—Paul rejoiced with the Philippians in the strength of their faith, and would do so if he had even to die in the cause; so they should rejoice with him that his labour had not been in vain. The ultimate cause of rejoicing is the same in both cases; but by viewing it in its different personal relations we avoid a tautology.

Paul now turns to more personal affairs. He hopes to send Timothy to them soon, and even to visit them himself; and meanwhile he sends Epaphroditus (ii., 19-30).

But (ii., 19).—Although I have spoken of our mutual joy in the triumph of your faith which I anticipate, still I want to be cheered by learning all about your affairs, and therefore I am hoping to send Timothy to you. Others would make the word adversative to the suggested possibility of his death in verse 17, and others to the allusion to his absence in verse 12. "I also" implies the expectation that a visit from Timothy would cheer the Philippians.

Likeminded (ii., 20): either, like me, or, like Timothy, in caring for your interests. Opinions are divided, and there is nothing in the context to decide the question; but I think the reference to Timothy seems the more natural, and, if the reference were to Paul, we should rather expect "likeminded with myself."

They also seek their own (ii., 21).—It is supposed that Paul's usual companions, and especially Luke, were away at this time. Even if this was the case, the saying is rather harsh after the words of i., 14. It may be that Paul had found some of the brethren reluctant to undertake a journey to Macedonia, or to perform some other service which he desired, and that these words only express the momentary disappointment of a man who was imprisoned and ready to die for the Gospel.

Ye know (ii., 22), because Timothy had assisted Paul in founding the church at Philippi.

With me (ii., 22), that is, along with me: they had both served God. The thought of this common service makes Paul change the construction with which he began.

So soon as I shall see (ii., 23).—He wished Timothy to carry news of the trial to Philippi. It is evident that Paul expected a decision soon.

I counted it necessary (ii., 25).—The past tense in letters is often used in relation to the time when the letters were to be read. It is probably so here; for see ii., 29. Paul took advantage of the journey of Epaphroditus to send a letter of thanks by his hands.

Fellow-worker (ii., 25); no doubt at Philippi, in founding and establishing the church.

Sorrow upon sorrow (ii., 27), the sorrow of losing him, in addition to all the trials of imprisonment: others, the sorrow of his death added to the sorrow of his sickness.

Again (ii., 28), according to Paul's general, though not invariable, usage in the order of the words, belongs to "rejoice,"—ye may rejoice again after your anxiety about me.

The work of Christ (ii., **30**) : referring to his journey to Rome with the gift for Paul. To minister to the prisoner of the Lord was a work of Christ.

To supply that which was lacking (ii., **30**), namely, the personal presence of the donors. The pleasure of seeing all his kind friends was the one thing lacking in their gift, and Epaphroditus had risked his life in coming to represent them.

From these personal details Paul passes to a fresh series of exhortations (iii., 1–iv., 9), the main part of which is directed against the false principles of certain opponents (iii., 1–iv., 1).

Finally (iii., **1**).—This translation suggests that Paul intended to close his letter; but the Greek word ("for the rest," "as for what remains") does not imply a speedy end. In iv., 8, it is prefixed to a closing exhortation; but in 1 Thess. iv., 1, and 2 Thess. iii., 1, it serves to introduce a new subject. This seems to be its purpose here, so that we need not regard this clause as the end of the previous subject. To do so makes the transition very abrupt; and the exhortation to "rejoice in the Lord" is fitly prefixed to a warning against the false confidence of dangerous enemies. Compare i., 18, 25, 26, and ii., 17, 18.

To write the same things (iii., **1**).—This can hardly refer to the word "rejoice," even though the note of joy recurs so often in the Epistle; for the succeeding words are inapplicable to this, and point clearly enough to the warning which follows. It is perhaps best to see here an allusion to a lost Epistle, in which the same subject was treated.

Beware of the dogs (iii., **2**).—"Beware of" is hardly a correct translation, the Greek being simply "see" or "observe," or perhaps indicative, "you see"; so that it contains a warning only by implication. The article shows that "the dogs" are a definite class. It is doubtful whether the threefold description points to three classes, Gentiles, judaising Christians, and unconverted Jews, or only to one;

and, if the latter, whether that one consists of Jewish enemies or of Judaisers within the church. Against the latter Paul was quite capable of using strong language; but there is no other indication of the presence of Judaisers in Philippi, and the whole paragraph seems rather to point to men who made no pretence of being followers of Christ. Jews might very well exert a dangerous influence on the church by representing themselves as the orthodox people of God in opposition to an upstart heretic like Paul. They had in their favour all the weight of a venerable antiquity, and an interpretation of the Old Testament which was supported by all their greatest authorities. How easy it must have been to represent Paul as preaching a spurious Judaism.

We are the circumcision (iii., 3).—" We " naturally means Christians as a body, in opposition to Jews. They had the true spiritual circumcision (see Rom. ii., 29), and were the genuine children of Abraham, the man of faith; but the literal Jewish rite is contemptuously described as a mere "concession." So the true "worship," of which the Jews boasted (see Rom. ix., 4), was not the service of the Temple, but worship by the Spirit of God. Compare John iv., 21-24.

I myself might have confidence (iii., 4).—The Greek has no "myself" and no "might." "I" is emphatic in contrast with the Gentile Philippians. Paul does not say that he had no confidence in the flesh, but that, though Christians as such had none, he personally had confidence in the flesh also, that is, as well as in Christ; but such confidence he regarded as of no value. As a fact he had every extraneous advantage of which the strictest Jew could boast.

A Hebrew of Hebrews (iii., 5), that is, sprung from Hebrew parents. This implies more than belonging to the stock of Israel, the theocratic people, for this stock included Hellenistic Jews who could speak Greek only. Paul, though born at Tarsus, was brought up in Jerusalem, and reckons himself as a member of the Hebrew section.

The righteousness which is in the Law (**iii., 6**).—This statement is not inconsistent with Paul's general doctrine. He is speaking from the point of view of his opponents, and says in effect that he had been a strict observer of the Law. He had all the righteousness which the Law could supply, and of which a Pharisee could boast, a scrupulous attention to external requirements. There is no occasion to limit the reference to the ceremonial law; for Paul does not distinguish the moral and the ceremonial law, and morality may be as external as ritual.

Loss for Christ (**iii., 7**).—"For" here, and twice in the following verse, is "on account of," and differs from "on behalf of," denoting rather the *consequence* of his Christian position.

I count (**iii., 8**); that is, I not only have counted, but I continue to count; so that "all things" may refer only to the advantages just enumerated.

My Lord (**iii., 8**), an expression of his personal feeling. He was so filled with a sense of the spiritual lordship of Christ, that his old life under the Law seemed to be quite contemptible in comparison with the new life in him.

Be found in him (**iii., 9**).—It was his desire that, having been lost to the Law, he might, when looked for, be found in Christ. It was still his aspiration to gain him more completely, and be more intimately united with him.

A righteousness of mine own (**iii., 9**).—I am unable to see how the Greek can bear any translation but that which is given in the margin, "not having as my righteousness that which is of the Law." He is not here contrasting man's false or imperfect righteousness with the true righteousness of God, as in Rom. x., 3 (where "their own" is quite differently expressed), but legal with spiritual righteousness. He had had the former; he sought the latter. The latter came "through Christ's faith," "in" being in the Greek simply "of": see the note on Rom. iii., 22. It proceeded from

God ("of" being literally "out of"), and rested upon faith, that being the link with God which drew man up into the fulness of Divine communion, and enabled him to appropriate the Spirit of holiness and love, which is true righteousness.

The power of his resurrection (iii., 10): the power belonging to or inherent in his resurrection, which was a triumph of life over death. Paul wishes to experience the power of the risen and eternal life in his own heart. This would be followed by acquaintance with the fellowship of Christ's sufferings; for this life is opposed to the life of the world, and persecuted by it. So he would be "conformed unto" Christ's "death," not by dying in the same way, but by entering into the spiritual essence of that sacrifice of love.

Attain unto the resurrection from the dead (iii., 11).—The doubt which is here expressed is only the utterance of that humility which springs from aiming at transcendent ideals, and is no stronger than that which we find in 1 Cor. ix., 27. The words seem to imply that the resurrection of men is conditional; but this would be contrary to Paul's teaching elsewhere (see especially Rom. ii., 2 *sqq.*; 2 Cor. v., 10), and it accords with the general tenor of the passage if we understand "the resurrection" here in a special and exalted sense. This may perhaps explain the use of a word for "resurrection" which is found nowhere else in the New Testament.

I press on (iii., 12): rather, "I pursue" the ideal ends already spoken of, "if I may also" overtake and catch that for which I was caught.

One thing I do (iii., 13).—The figure is now drawn from a foot-race, in which the runners strain forward, and have no time to think of anything they have left behind. The best life is found neither in regret for the failings nor in self-satisfaction with the attainments of the past, but in yielding to the attraction of that which is still beyond us.

The prize of the high calling (iii., 14).—This cannot mean that the calling is the prize; for that would imply that Paul had not been already called, and that it was possible for men to win the calling for themselves. The prize, therefore, is that which belongs to the calling. Men are invited to the spiritual race, and God is always calling them upward. For the Roman world of that time, for the Christian disciple always, this call is given and takes shape in "Christ Jesus."

Perfect (iii., 15) must here have rather a different signification from that which it bears in verse 12. There it refers to the complete realisation of his ideal; here to the full apprehension of the ideal itself. We need not limit it to the domain either of morals or of thought; for Christianity, as a form of spiritual life, belongs to both.

Thus minded (iii., 15); have that character of thought and disposition which has been spoken of from verse 7.

Otherwise minded (iii., 15), implying that there may be some point where the spiritual vision is still defective. On any such point further revelation may be expected, with growing experience and insight. Paul does not limit Divine revelation to any chosen band. It was not miraculous and exceptional, but open to every sincere believer.

By that same rule (iii., 16).—"Rule" is properly supplied to complete the sense, and the word is actually found in many manuscripts, though not in the best. "That" has nothing answering to it in the Greek, and it is not easy to see to what it refers. The sense seems to be,—we may not agree upon every point, for some have got farther in the spiritual life than others; but so far as we have attained, let us follow the same rule.

Here the subject started by the warning against "the dogs" comes to a natural close, and the connection does not oblige us to recognise the same men in "the enemies of the cross," of whom he is about to speak. What he has just said reminds him of some within the Church who made a false profession, and did not follow the Christian rule. They are clearly men whose enmity to the cross was not open and

25

avowed, as was that of the Jews; for Paul had repeatedly to warn the Philippians that they really were enemies. Nor can the reference very well be to Judaisers, who, though they were narrow and unscrupulous in their bigotry, were probably men of strict and pure lives; and if it be said that the words " whose god is their belly, and whose glory is in their shame," refer to rules about meats and to circumcision, a bitter irony is introduced, which is not indeed un-Pauline, but is inconsistent with the tone of the passage. I think, therefore, that the allusion must be to members of the Church who had joined it from selfish motives, and with no appreciation of the real character of the new movement, seeming friends who were, in principle, quite opposed to the self-renunciation of the cross. Against such men a frequent warning was necessary, and in contrast with them Paul may without conceit appeal to the example of himself and his companions.

Weeping (iii., 18).—Much is implied by this one word,—his profound regard for all that was signified by the cross, his sorrow for men who could degrade themselves by a sensual and worldly life, his sensitive nature, always easily moved, and now perhaps with weakened nerves and diminished self-command owing to his long imprisonment.

Perdition (iii., 19).—The character of this is not defined, and we may understand it generally of moral ruin, and the loss of blessedness which that involves.

For our citizenship is in heaven (iii., 20).—These men are doomed to perdition, and we must guard against them, because their principles are directly opposed to those of the Christian commonwealth: their thoughts are earthly; those of the Christian must be heavenly.

A Saviour (iii., 20).—This is predicative, and it might be better to translate, " We wait for Christ as a saviour." This epithet is not applied to Christ in the great Epistles of Paul; and in the whole Pauline group it is found only in Eph. v.,

23; 2 Tim. i., 10; Tit. i., 4, ii., 13, iii., 6. He naturally uses it as the sorrows of the world thicken around him, and it seems as though the great deliverance must at last be close at hand.

The body of our humiliation (iii., 21), the body which belongs to our lowly, earthly condition. Paul expected this to be changed into a spiritual body at the time of the second advent (see 1 Cor. xv., 51, 52). The words here used hardly imply his expectation of surviving till that time; for the change was to be effected in the bodies of the dead as well as the living.

To subject all things unto himself (iii., 21).—We scarcely reach the depth of this thought if we understand it merely of a personal ability. It involves the power of the spiritual to subjugate and mould the material; and accordingly those who are unable to accept in the letter Paul's doctrine of the second coming and of the transformed body may still receive it in the spirit.

Wherefore (iv., 1).—This verse forms a conclusion to the foregoing exhortations. With such grand hopes the brethren should stand fast. Paul addresses them in words of the strongest affection. Their kindly remembrance of him brought joy to his heart, and their steadfastness made them, as it were, his victor's wreath in his apostolic contests.

Leaving these general admonitions, Paul now addresses himself to individuals (iv., 2, 3).

We know nothing of Euodias and Syntyche beyond what is here stated. They had helped Paul in the work of the Gospel, probably in founding the church at Philippi, of which we may presume they were now prominent members. Of the source and nature of their differences with one another we are quite ignorant; but we may infer from the style of the exhortation that they were of a personal kind, and showed some want of temper. "In the Lord," in his loving spirit, such differences disappear.

Yoke-fellow (**iv., 3**), probably a proper name, Synzygus, which means a yoke-fellow. Hence the epithet " true " or " genuine," the character answering to the name. The name is not found elsewhere ; but if it is not a proper name, the description seems hardly sufficient to point out any particular person. As Synzygus was to help the women to get over their differences, it is possible that Paul, in playing upon the word, takes it in an unusual sense, " one who yokes together." [1]

Clement also (**iv., 3**).—It seems best to connect these words with " laboured," not with " helped " ; for a reason for helping them is that they had formerly worked cordially with others. It is evident that Clement was a member of the church at Philippi. We cannot identify him with any other known Clement.

The book of life (**iv., 3**), a figure borrowed from a register of citizens. These were all genuine members of the Christian commonwealth.

The exhortation is now once more made general, but is founded on the admonition just given (iv., 4-9).

Joy of a spiritual kind banishes discontent, and with it the inclination to insist on our personal claims. It is closely connected with the " sweet reasonableness " here described as " forbearance." The return of Christ was close at hand, and this solemn thought ought to fill the mind with joy, and dispel all self-seeking and anxiety.

The peace of God (**iv., 7**), the peace which dwells within the bosom of God, a peace deeper than all thought, but of which man participates through the communion of prayer. " In Christ Jesus " denotes, as so constantly with Paul, the spiritual realm within which this takes place. That peculiar quality of life was seen nowhere else. Christ was, as it were,

---

[1] See Lipsius; but the possibility of understanding it so occurred to me independently.

the atmosphere in which the disciples lived and breathed, and found the Divine peace.

Finally (**iv., 8**).—This and the following verse sum up and conclude his exhortations. Here, as everywhere, his great concern is a moral and spiritual behaviour corresponding to the new life of sonship which had been given to the world in Christ.

True (**iv., 8**), referring (if we are to judge from the connection), not to truth of opinion, but to truth of life, the deed corresponding to the pure and healthy thought.

Honourable (**iv., 8**); that is, worthy of honour or veneration.

In me (**iv., 9**).—These words must be connected only with " heard and saw": Paul set an example of the things which he taught and delivered to others.

The God of peace (**iv., 9**).—The thought of verse 7 is resumed, though differently expressed, and indeed carried farther. Not only peace, but God Himself, whose it is, will be with them.

Before closing his letter, Paul returns thanks for the gift (of money) which the Philippians had sent him (iv., 10-20).

The delicate and gracious character of his words has been generally recognised, and it is only through a misinterpretation that one can find them ungracious. We know Paul's independent spirit, and his unwillingness to receive anything that could give an appearance of self-interest to his work. But he was not too proud to accept a gift offered in love. He did not, indeed, need it, and did not wish his friends to tax themselves for him; but he deeply valued their sympathy, and saw in their contribution from their humble means a sacrifice acceptable to God.

Ye have revived your thought (**iv., 10**).—So translated, the words certainly seem to convey some reproach. But they mean literally, " You caused to sprout again your thought for me." The idea apparently is, that long ago they had shown their regard for him in this practical way; they had always been thinking of him, and anxious to send him a gift, but through some want of opportunity were unable to do so; and he was glad for their sakes as well as his own that they were at length able to turn their thought into action.

Not that I speak in respect of want (iv., 11).—Lest the previous words should be misunderstood he adds, in effect, " I do not mean that I was in any want."

Content (iv., 11): properly, "self-sufficing," a Stoical word found only here in the New Testament, though the noun occurs in 2 Cor. ix., 8; 1 Tim. vi., 6.

To be abased (iv., 12), or, to be humbled, that is, in this connection, to have the humiliation attaching to want.

Learned the secret (iv., 12), literally, "been initiated," a figure borrowed from the mysteries.

In him (iv., 13).—Though the reading "Christ" is not supported by the best authorities, we can hardly doubt that the reference is to him, "in Christ" being such a common expression.

Ye did well (iv., 14) is hardly strong enough: rather, ye did a fine, or beautiful, thing. The Philippians did not send Paul what cost them nothing, but in denying themselves for his sake entered into fellowship with his affliction.

Ye yourselves also know (iv., 15): ye, as well as I, can remember that this is not the first time your generosity has been shown. When the Gospel was first preached in their country, some ten years earlier, they alone sent him presents.

In Thessalonica (iv., 16), where, as in Corinth, Paul worked for his own support (1 Thess. ii., 9).

I seek for the fruit (iv., 17); that is, the fruit of spiritual character in themselves, which will grow from their generous deed.

I have all things (iv., 18): I value most the spiritual, not the material, side of a gift; and now I have everything I want, and am quite full, so that you need not tax yourselves any further on my account.

An odour of a sweet smell (**iv., 18**).—Observe how readily the figure of sacrifice is used, though this language carries us back to the time when the gods were supposed to enjoy the savour of victims. When Paul wrote, sacrifices were still an essential part of worship, in the temple at Jerusalem, as well as among heathen nations.

In glory (**iv., 19**).—Connect with "shall fulfil." The expression is probably to be understood adverbially.

The Epistle closes with greetings and a benediction (iv., 21-23).

Salute (**iv., 21**).—The direction is given, we must suppose, to the leaders (perhaps the "bishops and deacons" of i., 1) to whom the letter would be delivered. He names no one, as he wishes "every saint" individually to receive his greeting.

The brethren which are with me (**iv., 21**).—This must refer to Paul's companions in travel, some of whom, therefore, must have been with him, in spite of ii., 20.

They that are of Cæsar's household (**iv., 22**), probably slaves belonging to the imperial establishment. Why they especially sent their salutations we do not know.

Be with your spirit (**iv., 23**).—This reading is the best attested, instead of "with you all." Thus this beautiful and affectionate Epistle closes with almost the same words as the Epistle to the Galatians, which reveals such a different phase of the Apostle's mind.

"A nobly attractive book."

PAUL, THE MAN, THE MISSIONARY, AND THE TEACHER

BY ORELLO CONE, D.D.   Cloth, gilt top, $2.00

CHIEF CONTENTS—PART I. THE MAN: 1. FORMATIVE INFLUENCES; 2. PERSONAL TRAITS; 3. THE CONVERSION. PART II. THE MISSIONARY: 1. THE FIRST YEARS—GALATIA AND THE GALATIAN EPISTLE; 2. PHILIPPI, THESSALONICA, CORINTH; 3. EPHESUS—ROME; 4. THE PAUL OF THE ACTS AND THE PAUL OF THE EPISTLES. PART III. THE TEACHER: 1. THE LAW; 2. "LIFE," "DEATH," AND "SALVATION;" 3. DOCTRINE OF SIN; 4. SALVATION—ATONEMENT; 5. PERSON OF CHRIST; 6. SUPERNATURALISM; 7. FAITH AND JUSTIFICATION; 8. ETHICS; 9. PREDESTINATION; 10. THE CHURCH AND THE SACRAMENTS; 11. ESCHATOLOGY.

"An exposition of Paul as he was."
—DR. THOS. R. SLICER in *The New World*.

"Among the many treatises on Paulinism published of recent years, this book takes a high place. In the present writer's judgment **it surpasses all others written in English in acumen and vigor**. . . . A special merit of the presentation of Paul's ideas **is the fulness and lucidity** with which the subtle and mystical elements of his thought are stated. Dr. Cone's style . . . has a sinewy vigor which makes his book easy reading throughout."
—PROF. E. Y. HINCKS of Andover in *The Church*.

"As **an exhaustive and luminous** account of the life and work of Paul as a missionary to the gentiles and as a teacher, it stands unrivalled. Part III is a masterly exposition of the apostle's thought which leaves nothing to be desired."—*The Aberdeen Journal*.

"Biblical scholarship in America has not produced a more creditable work than this."—*The Christian Register*.

"**A standard work** . . . will for a long time constitute the point of departure for all studies of Paul that are to be taken seriously."
—PROF. H. HOLTZMANN, *University of Strassburg*.

[OVER]

"It is long since so great a conflict of emotions has been stirred within us by any critical production. . . . We have in this book received accounts of the content of Pauline ideas not surpassed for warmth and reverence and plenitude in the writings of Canon Liddon . . . reporting with almost incredible accuracy the height and depth and length and breadth of that spiritual Paulinism which has of late years suffered so many things in the house of its friends."
—President Chas. Cuthbert Hall in *The Expositor*.

"One of the most thorough and suggestive interpretations of the apostle that this generation has produced."
—*The Outlook* (Lond).

"The whole volume is an able one, and has been very carefully thought out."—*The Glasgow Mail*.

"This thoughtful and forcible volume deserves the attention of the scholarly world."—*The Congregationalist*.

"The work is one of great ability and extensive learning, evincing much acumen and exegetical power."
—*The Edinburgh Scotsman*.

"We would say with emphasis that we recognize his ability, his candor, and his frequent insight into the very depths of the subjects he discusses."—*The Spectator* (Lond).

"A solid work of permanent scientific value."
—Dr. O. Pfleiderer, *University of Berlin*.

"He writes from the point of view of an accomplished scholar . . . follows through the Epistles certain distinct lines of thought and doctrine with remarkable vigor and acumen."—Dr. H. Van Dyke in *The Outlook*, New York.

"As a critical study it is thorough, even masterly."
—*The Independent*, (Eng.)

PUBLISHED BY

THE MACMILLAN COMPANY, New York

A. & C. BLACK, London

By W. M. RAMSAY.

THE CHURCH IN THE ROMAN EMPIRE BEFORE A.D. 170.

With Maps and Illustrations, 8vo $3.00

"It is a book of very exceptional value, Prof. Ramsay is a real scholar and of the very best type of scholarship. A thoroughly good book; a product of first-hand and accurate scholarship; in the highest degree suggestive; and not only valuable in its results, but an admirable example of the true method of research."—*The Churchman.*

ST. PAUL THE TRAVELLER AND THE ROMAN CITIZEN.

With Map, 8vo $3.00

"A work which marks an important step in advance in the historical interpretation of St. Paul. . . . It is an immense gain to have the narrative lifted from the mean function of being an artful monument and mirror of a strife internal to Christianity which it seeks by a process, now of creation, now of elimination, to overcome and to conceal, to the high purpose of representing the religion as it began within the Empire and as it actually was to the Empire and the Empire to it. . . . Professor Ramsay has made a solid and valuable contribution to the interpretation of the Apostolic literature and of the Apostolic age—a contribution distinguished no less by ripe scholarship, independent judgment, keen vision, and easy mastery of material, than by freshness of thought, boldness of combination, and striking originality of view."—*The Speaker.*

IMPRESSIONS OF TURKEY DURING TWELVE YEARS' WANDERINGS.

8vo $1.75

"No conception of the real status of Turkey is possible unless something is understood of 'the interlacing and alternation of the separate and unblending races.' . . . Such an understanding is admirably presented in Prof. Ramsay's book, which gives a near and trustworthy insight into actual Turkish conditions."—*N. Y. Times.*

WAS CHRIST BORN AT BETHLEHEM?

A Study in the Credibility of St. Luke. Part I. The Importance of the Problem. Part II. The Solution of the Problem. 8vo, $1.75

"The work is one of which students of biblical criticism will need to take account. It is absolutely candid and straightforward, thorough and discriminating, and courteous to other scholars whose conclusions it sees most reason to condemn. It is a fine piece of work."—*The Congregationalist.*

HISTORICAL COMMENTARY UPON THE EPISTLE TO THE GALATIANS.

8vo $1.75

G. P. PUTNAM'S SONS, NEW YORK AND LONDON.

Recent Publications.

CHRISTIANITY AND ANTI-CHRISTIANITY IN THEIR FINAL CONFLICT. By SAMUEL J. ANDREWS, author of "The Life of Our Lord upon Earth," etc. 8°. $2 00

"This is in many respects a remarkable book. It deals with the important Bible truths, of which little has been heard of late. The same scholarly breadth and thoroughness which characterize the author's 'Life of Christ' are stamped also on this work. . . . The book deserves a thoughtful reading by all Christians."—*The Observer.*

HEROES OF THE REFORMATION.

A series of biographies of the leaders in the Protestant Reformation, men who, while differing in their gifts, were influenced by the same spirit. The series is edited by SAMUEL MACAULEY JACKSON, D.D., LL.D., Professor of Church History, New York University. Each fully illustrated. 12°. $1 50

1.—**MARTIN LUTHER**, The Hero of the Reformation. By HENRY E. JACOBS, D.D., LL.D., Professor of Theology, Evangelical Lutheran Seminary, Philadelphia.

2.—**PHILIP MELANCHTHON**, The Protestant Preceptor of Germany. By JAMES W. RICHARD, Professor of Homiletics, Lutheran Theological Seminary, Gettysburg, Pa.

3.—**DESIDERIUS ERASMUS**, of Rotterdam, the Humanist in the Service of the Reformation. By EPHRAIM EMERTON, Ph.D., Professor of Ecclesiastical History, Harvard University.

4.—**THEODORE BEZA**, the Counsellor of the French Reformation. By HENRY MARTYN BAIRD, Ph.D., Professor of the Greek Language and Literature, New York University; author of "The Huguenots," 6 vols.

For titles of volumes in preparation, write for separate descriptive circular.

THE AMERICAN LECTURES ON THE HISTORY OF RELIGIONS.

Each, 8°, $1 50.

1.—**BUDDHISM: ITS HISTORY AND LITERATURE.** By T. W. RHYS-DAVIDS, LL.D., Ph.D., Chairman of the Pali Text Society; Secretary and Librarian of the Royal Asiatic Society; Professor of Pali and Buddhist Literature at University College, London.

2.—**RELIGIONS OF PRIMITIVE PEOPLES.** By DANIEL G. BRINTON, A.M., M.D., LL.D., D.Sc., Professor of Archæology and Linguistics in the University of Pennsylvania.

3.—**JEWISH RELIGIOUS LIFE AFTER THE EXILE.** By T. K. CHEYNE, of University of Oxford.

4.—**THE RELIGION OF ISRAEL TO THE EXILE.** By KARL BUDDE, of the University of Strasburg, Germany.

G. P. PUTNAM'S SONS, New York and London.

www.ingramcontent.com/pod-product-compliance
Lightning Source LLC
Chambersburg PA
CBHW051246300426
44114CB00011B/913